INTO THE MINDS OF MADMEN

Don DeNevi and John H. Campbell

Foreword by
JOHN E. OTTO
FBI Deputy Director (Ret.)

Preface by
STEPHEN BAND, Ph.D
Unit Chief, Behavioral Science Unit,
FBI Academy

INTO THE MINDS OF MADMEN

How the FBI's BEHAVIORAL SCIENCE UNIT Revolutionized Crime Investigation

Prometheus Books

59 John Glenn Drive
Amherst, New York 14228-2197

Published 2004 by Prometheus Books

Inquiries should be addressed to
Prometheus Books
59 John Glenn Drive
Amherst, New York 14228–2197
VOICE: 716–691–0133, ext. 207
FAX: 716–564–2711
WWW.PROMETHEUSBOOKS.COM

08 07 06 05 04   5 4 3 2 1

Library of Congress Cataloging-in-Publication Data

DeNevi, Don, 1937–
    Into the minds of madmen : how the FBI's Behavioral Science Unit revolutionized crime investigation / Don DeNevi and John H. Campbell.
        p. cm.
    Includes bibliographical entries and index.
    ISBN 1–59102–135–9
    1. United States. Federal Bureau of Investigation. Behavioral Science Unit—History. 2. Criminal profilers—United States. 3. Criminal behavior, Prediction of—United States. 4. Criminal investigation—Psychological aspects. 5. Murder—Investigation—United States—Case studies. I. Campbell, John H. (John Henry) II. Title.

HV6080.D46 2003
363.25'8—dc22

2003016869

Printed in the United States of America on acid-free paper

Dedication

To those men and women who, since the formation of the FBI's Behavioral Science Unit in 1972, maintained positive outlooks on life and their work despite daily involvement with America's most unspeakable, almost indescribable crimes. They believed in something.

And to the children, wives, and husbands of those BSUers who weren't home for birthdays, anniversaries, the 4th of July, New Year celebrations, and the Easter, Thanksgiving, and December holidays because they were bringing beasts to bay.

"Man is a very complicated being, and though he knows a great deal about all sorts of things, he knows very little about himself. This may be the greatest danger of all."

C. G. Jung

"Far more crime occurs in the human soul than in the external world. The soul of the criminal, as manifested in his deeds, often affords an insight into the deepest psychological processes of humanity in general."

C. G. Jung

Contents

CONTENTS

Foreword

John E. Otto
Acting Director of the FBI
and Associate Deputy
Director—Investigations
(Retired)

For the first time in more than thirty years, the Federal Bureau of Investigation, so recently rent by the Ruby Ridge, Waco, and September 11th tragedies, as well as other unfortunate controversies, has opened its doors to the enigmatic inner sanctum of the Behavioral Science Unit. Why?

Because the FBI has found two qualified, scholarly writers to both demystify and demythify the fantasies about criminal profiling perpetuated by popular TV series, novels, and feature length films such as *Manhunter, Silence of the Lambs, Citizen,* and *Hannibal.* In addition, the FBI hopes to fill a void in the public consciousness about the crime-fighting work the BSU has done and is currently doing. Where previous books by retired profilers like John Douglas, Roy Hazelwood, Bob Ressler, and Russ Vorpagel have concentrated primarily on the murders and other crimes each helped solve, Don DeNevi and John Campbell have crafted a definitive record of the BSU entity as a whole, one that is the most respected in all law enforcement. Instead of providing what the market demands, endless success stories befitting hero profilers, the coauthors, as unlikely a pair as you'll ever meet, take a diametric approach, combining the BSU administrative history with its

FOREWORD

training and profiling functions, to show how good men and women climb into the heads of madmen as they go about analyzing crime scenes. Personal recollections and reflections of those who built the BSU, supplemented by material drawn from secretaries and other supportive staff, emphasize the human and social side of the story. Readers come to know the BSUers on a personal level, who they really were, what they achieved, and what their lives and careers were all about.

Though the authors were granted unlimited cooperation and unprecedented access to BSU personnel and crime files, and although *Into the Minds of Madmen* is officially sanctioned, it is far from a bland, bureaucratic puff piece that covers up mistakes and elevates every minor accomplishment into a brilliant triumph. Was the manuscript vetted by the FBI before publication? Of course. But this was only to ensure that information which could compromise ongoing investigations or trials, or might violate rights to privacy, did not become public. To their credit, the authors didn't resort to retelling the same sensational serial-killing stories, such as the accounts of Jeffrey Dahmer, Wayne Williams (except to illustrate John Douglas's role in solving the case), Ted Bundy, the "Zodiac," the "Son of Sam," etc., to chronicle the growth and development of the BSU and the art and science of profiling. Instead, they employed ordinary, everyday, garden-variety types of cases to emphasize how the BSU was inundated annually with requests for help in solving them.

The Federal Bureau of Investigation is indebted for the following fine narrative—indeed, a stirring chronicle that not only documents the courage and heartbreak, resourcefulness and daring of the BSU special agents, but also how the initial waves of pioneers offered their leadership, encouragement, and support for the new ideas which were to grow into policies and programs.

Preface

Stephen Band, Ph.D.
Unit Chief,
Behavioral Science Unit
FBI Academy

They're walking nightmares—these multiple murderers, arsonists, child abductors, homicidal poisoners, serial rapists, sexual killers, bombers, repugnant predators of the weak and helpless, to name just a few—and they've been a part of American history since the beginning. But chasing and apprehending these monsters on a daily basis began only thirty years ago with the FBI's Behavioral Science Unit, later to be made famous by so much fiction.

In the mid-1970s, a new investigative tool was conceived in an obscure, sometimes smelly, basement deep under the halls of the FBI Academy, and it was named the "criminal profile."

Ignored, even snickered at, by many in the Bureau, as well as law enforcement in general (at least until it proved useful), the first wave of BSUers understood how much information was available in and around, as well as upon, the deceased victim. "Study the victim," special agents like Howard Teten and Pat Mullany taught. Creating profiles doesn't involve magic, just meticulous analysis. Soon the BSU was providing assistance to criminal justice professionals in the United States and foreign countries, applying the behavioral sciences to the criminal justice system. As a result of its unique training and research efforts, as well as its successes in analyzing violent crime, police at the federal, state, and local levels turned more and more to the BSU for assistance and guidance in dealing with different, extremely difficult, unusual, and bizarre crimes.

The DeNevi-Campbell book is the first chronicle of its kind describing three decades of amazing work by more than thirty equally amazing BSUers, solving thousands upon thousands of unsolved cases, many of which involved the dreaded serial-type criminal. Their mesmerizing story meshes infamous and not-so-infamous cases with the men and women who devoted their careers to investigating and profiling those who have committed the most heinous of offenses. While encountering every type of criminal, from macabre sexual sadists to the killer of the helpless aged or indefensible young, the BSUers, throughout the life of the unit, have quietly pioneered a profiling method capable of pegging perpetrators who often commit their crimes in different geographical jurisdictions, which complicates the job of identifying, locating and prosecuting them.

Into the Minds of Madmen shatters the nonsense and sets the record straight about what we do as a team. Not only do the authors capture the essence of brilliant, experienced special agents engaging in profound work every day, but also how no one individual profiler ever solved a case all by himself. A team solved it. And what follows is about its members, the joking camaraderie among them, the inevitable burnout of some, the overcynicism of others, the pride of success, and agony of failure. No news story, novel, TV documentary, feature-length film, including the latest profiler movies, has yet been written or produced that tells the true inside story as much as this welcomed account. And that's because Don and John know that, since the serial criminal became the most feared of all America's social enemies, the truth about depravity and unbelievable cruelty is far more astonishing than all the fiction put together.

Author's Preface

Lady Anne: Villain, thou know'st
no law of God nor man:
No beast so fierce but
knows some touch of
pity.

Richard: But I know none, and
therefore am no beast.

It is commonplace for people to label a particularly horrible killer a "beast" or an "animal." It is the way we distance ourselves from such a person, in effect saying, "We have nothing in common with you. You are not even a human being." But no beast engages in lust murder or mass mayhem. No beast rapes and mutilates its old and young. No beast sets fire or engages in kidnapping or fraud. Only humans commit such atrocities, becoming worse than beasts. But because they are human, they are part of us. And if we can understand them, we can also find them. So when local police are stumped and stymied, when they have little hope of tracking down the demons, they turn to the FBI's legendary Behavioral Science Unit. No matter how clever, how systematic or unsystematic the human-killers are in stalking their unfortunate prey, the BSU stalks them, down the paths of their own minds.

But before we start that story, I'd like to say a few words about my coauthor. Rarely in a space such as this does the reader find one author praising the other. Coauthors are supposed to work together, always respectful and tolerant, debating politely when disagreements arise. However, they often become territorial rivals, jealous and paranoid of each other. Familiarity sometimes does breed contempt.

AUTHOR'S PREFACE

Without my coauthor, John Henry Campbell, a deeply respected former unit chief of the Behavioral Science Unit, there would be no book. And because he is a man of heart, coauthorship now has a new definition. Never a journalist, novelist, historian, author, or self-aggrandizing promoter, John is an unassuming, energetic, cheerful man, whom all FBI personnel admire and respect. With a magnetic, boyish enthusiasm, he (like me) has long been attracted by the darkness of the tortured soul—to salvage, when possible; to eradicate, when necessary. And because of his deeply rooted integrity, he would never stand for something he didn't believe in.

In May of 1999, I arrived at the FBI Academy in Quantico, Virginia, at the invitation of Stephen Band, chief of the Behavioral Science Unit, to begin a seven-week operational sabbatical. My assignment? Write the history of the BSU for the people of America. Little did I realize that history would span more than three decades, with innumerable supersleuth profilers working to solve more than twenty thousand unsolved crimes. Three years later, the history, certainly superficial and inadequate, is done. A 600-page history was presented to Stephen Band for use throughout the FBI in January, 2003, as partial fulfillment of the seven-week operational sabbatical assignment. This book is a revised, condensed version for the general population.

On Monday, May 10, 1999, at 8:00 A.M., I descended 160 feet to the third-level basement below the Academy cafeteria and PX, where the Behavioral Science Unit offices are located. Eager to unleash my Pulitzer Prize–worthy prose, I looked forward to perusing hundreds of neatly labeled folders containing thousands of primary and secondary documents, reports, and other historical sources, chronologically filed in cabinets that ranged along the walls of a huge office dotted with conference tables and high-tech retrieval systems. Instead, after an hour of staff introductions and greetings, I was deposited in a twelve-by fifteen-foot office allocated to visiting FBI interns. It was empty save for a desk, chair, telephone, and one coat hanger. I was handed a two-page, photocopied handout—disseminated to visitors and others who write to the Academy for information—entitled, "The Behavioral Science Unit: An Introduction," and told, "Here. Go write a history."

During the weeks that followed, Steve and I clarified the exact nature of the book-to-be and where I might obtain my sources of information. In addition to searching for the names, addresses, and phone numbers of former and retired BSUers, thanks to wonderful staff assistant, Sandi Coupe, I began to gather every magazine, journal article, reference, and report ever published by and about the BSU that the staff and the Academy library had in their possession.

Gradually, the BSUers began to "feel out" the type of person and author I was. Their trust, naturally, was not given freely. I needed time to cultivate it. Obviously, without staff support, there would be no book. Fortunately, as the weeks rolled on, more and more of the staff began to sense how committed I was to portraying the aggregate of professionals at work during the history of the unit rather than focusing on the "profiling genius" of a few. BSUers began to pour out their case summaries, published articles, ideas, concerns, vignettes, and recollections. Though I had known virtually nothing about the unit when I arrived, I began to feel confident enough to be able to discuss even the minutest issues that the BSU faced since its inception in 1972. Although I wished I had known all this when I arrived in May, the process of gathering the primary and secondary sources had been invaluable. Rather than having the core text material handed to me without comment, I had to find it, thus forcing me not only to learn it, but mold it into a narrative. That was the "book" being born as I struggled to gather and interpret the available information.

However, there continued to be mistrust of an outsider . . . a reluctance to fully cooperate and reveal the challenges, struggles, difficult times and also the successes. And so it was that John Campbell was invited to serve as coauthor. It became a matter of: no Campbell, no insider's look at the Behavioral Science Unit. When it was suggested to John that he didn't need me, an outsider, and should write the story himself, John smiled, and to his everlasting credit, declined. When I informed Steve and other Academy friends that John Campbell was to join me, the response was universal: "Don, that's a stroke of genius to include him. He gives the project the stamp of the imprimatur. Suddenly, you and the project are credible."

Who is John Campbell and why is he so critical to the book? Before entering the FBI, John served in the Marine Corps as a captain in Vietnam. Upon his return, he completed a Ph.D. at Michigan State University. Today he is a professor at St. Cloud State University. John's prior FBI assignments, work experiences, accomplishments, special recognitions, professional memberships, research and presentations, and academic achievements are far too numerous to list here. Let it suffice to say that John served as the academic dean of the FBI Academy for almost three years, when he created invaluable curriculum innovations; was assistant special agent in charge of the Omaha FBI Division, where he supervised more than one hundred FBI employees in Iowa and Nebraska; and most importantly, served as unit chief of the Behavioral Science Unit from 1989 to 1992.

The responsibilities of that assignment included behavioral training of agents and law enforcement, research coordination, and the collateral management of the National Center for the Analysis of Violent Crime (NCAVC). Other significant accomplishments in this assignment included the establishment of faculty exchanges, both domestic and international, and implementation of grants and research programs, Ph.D. courses, and national and international symposia. John also served as the executive secretary to the Career Board, working directly for the deputy director of the FBI. He was responsible for the selection and training of all managers of the FBI. In addition to being an investigative special agent in the St. Louis and Detroit divisions, and a field supervisor in the Butte division, where he was responsible for more than thirty special agents and all major investigations in both Montana and Idaho, he was the headquarters supervisor as researcher, profiler, and instructor in the Behavioral Science Unit.

From the "Ivory Tower," as the Academy agents referred to the academic dean's office, to the subterranean cubicles of the BSU, from the field offices of the hot Midwest to FBI headquarters in Washington, D.C., John Campbell, the man with the gentle grin, has been involved with it all.

Perhaps the highest professional compliment paid to my coauthor is one a current BSUer shared with me. He said, "John is the epitome of the FBI 'way,' and yet, he is beyond the consummate Bureau professional. His intellectual agility, his insights and understanding of the BSU's phenomenal hold on the American imagination, and his simple unselfishness make him the perfect partner that someone as unknowledgeable and inexperienced as you needs."

Don DeNevi

About the Authors

Don DeNevi was born in Stockton, California, and educated at the University of Pacific, where he earned both his Bachelor's and master's degrees. At the University of California in Berkeley, he received an Ed.D. in Teacher Education/Higher Education. His teaching career spans more four decades, beginning in the Stockton public schools at the age of twenty-one and continuing in various educational institutions. He recently retired from the criminal justice department at San Francisco State University, where he lectured on organized crime, criminal profiling, extremism, classic crime cinema, and understanding the criminal mind. Within two months of his official retirement he returned to full-time teaching, this time with inmates at San Quentin State Prison. He now supervises all recreation at the prison and he teaches and counsels the condemned on Death Row. In addition to having written thirty-four nonfiction histories and biographies (his latest include *They Came to Destroy America: The FBI at War with Nazi Spies and Saboteurs, Mob Nemesis: How the FBI Crippled Organized Crime, Tennis Past 50*, and *Riddle of the Rock: The Only Successful Escape from Alcatraz*), Don paints watercolors of imaginary San Joaquin and Salinas Valley landscapes. An avid daily tennis player, he is single and lives with his two cats in Menlo Park, California.

John Campbell was born in St. Cloud, Minnesota, and educated at the universities of St. Thomas and Detroit and Michigan State University, where he completed his Ph.D. An executive manager and educator with more than twenty-seven years of diverse investigative, administrative, educational, and managerial experience within the Federal Bureau of Investigation, John has had an extensive background in selection, training, and management of human and technical resources. His major strengths have been team building, planning, and program implementation. He and his wife Marlys have been married for twenty-eight years and have two grown children.

Acknowledgments

Since no archives containing collections of personal memoirs and reminiscences, files on crime cases, manuscript collections or published articles and books about the Behavioral Science Unit exists within the BSU or at FBI headquarters, the National Archives or the Library of Congress, the authors have relied upon the generous help of more than fifty living primary sources—the personalities who founded the unit. All were most eager to assist in documenting, for the first time, the full and true story. They seemed to say, "Because so much remains stored in our minds, largely untouched and soon to be lost forever, let's once and for all set the record straight."

Particularly helpful were the recollections of the "first generation," who founded and developed the unit during the fledgling years of the 1970s. They include Jack Kirsch, John Pfaff, Pat Mullany, and Howard Teten. In addition to providing their many anecdotal and first-hand accounts, each was supportive in reading and rereading the numerous drafts.

Others also assisted in the understanding of the overall sweeping BSU story. Their help was absolutely indispensable in providing guid-

ACKNOWLEDGMENTS

ance at various stages of evolvement, along with critical advice and encouragement. To the following BSUers who, for the most part, are considered "second and third waves," we extend our deepest appreciation: Dick Ault, Swanson Carter, Allan "Smoky" Burgess, John Conway, Tom Conway, Dick Cooper, Roger Depue, Bill Haigmaier, Roy Hazelwood, Dick Harper, Conrad Hassel, Jim Horn, Ken Lanning, Max Noel, Greg McCreary, John Mindermann, Judd Ray, Roland Reboussian, Robert Ressler, Robert Shaefer, Tom Strentz, Bill Tafoya, and Russ Vorpagel.

To the current Academy BSU staff, who contributed to the accuracy of the facts, details, and events, we are also indebted. They include: Stephen R. Band, unit chief; Ed Davis, criminal investigations instructor; Joseph Harpold, community policing instructor; John Jarvis, behavioral research instructor; Anthony J. Pinizzotto, forensic psychologist; Art Westveer, homicide instructor; and the rest of the very talented staff. Then there was the endearing warmth and kindness of Judy Rice, Neil Schiff, Betty Walker, Sandi Coup, Chase Foster, Jim Reese, and Carol Monroe. Their help was desperately needed and very generously given.

A complete list of the books and articles consulted for this narrative is too extensive for these limited pages. However, those that were particularly useful are listed in the bibliography, which is the most current, thoroughly developed ever compiled on the BSU.

Acronyms

AGI	Academy Group, Inc.
AIMS	Arson Information Management System
ASAC	Assistant Special Agent in Charge
BSIRU	Behavioral Science Instructional Research Unit
BSISU (1984)	Behavioral Science Investigative Support Unit
BSU	Behavioral Science Unit
CIRG (April 1994)	Critical Incident Response Group
CPRP	Criminal Personality Research Project
DED	"dissent equals disloyalty," common FBI belief during Hoover years
IRDU	Institutional Research and Development Unit
ISU	Investigative Support Unit
LEAA	Law Enforcement Assistance Administration

ACRONYMS

LEEDS	Law Enforcement Executive Development Seminar
NA	National Academy
NCAVC (1984)	National Center for the Analysis of Violent Crime
NCIC	National Crime Information Center
NEI	National Executive Institute
OJJDP	Office of Juvenile Justice and Delinquency Prevention
PBAU	Profiling and Behavioral Assessment Unit
PCIS	Post–Critical Incident Seminar
RICO (1970)	Racketeering Influenced and Corrupt Organization Law
SAC	Special Agent in Charge
SOG	"Seat of Government," or FBI headquarters in Washington, D.C.
SOARS (1976)	Special Operations and Research Unit
SOAR	Special Operational and Research Unit
U/C	Unit Chief
VICAP (May 1985)	Violent Criminal Apprehension Program
VICLAS	Violent Crime Linkage Analysis System

Introduction

"Does there lurk in the murky mind of murderers and masochists, sex slayers and sadists, a pattern, a picture, a predetermined plan for pillage, passion, and perversion? The answer in most cases is yes. And our job as BSUers is to focus on individuals whose personality traits closely parallel the traits of others who have been convicted of committing crimes similar to those under review."

RUSSEL E. VORPAGEL, IN A LECTURE TO HIS
FBI ACADEMY CLASS, 1982

What local police saw when they entered the modest white home in the southern suburbs of Sacramento, California, at dinner time on the evening of January 23, 1978, was a scene straight from hell. A few minutes earlier, David Wallin, returning home from work as usual, found his twenty-two-year-old wife, Theresa, sprawled out on the kitchen floor, shot through the head and her partially clad body mutilated beyond description. Never had the historic city, dating back to the pre–gold rush days of the late 1840s, witnessed such a grisly slaying.

No sooner had the homicide detectives begun their investigation when they were slammed with another case even more macabre, less than four blocks away in an all-white middle-class community.

After knocking on the partially opened front door of her neighbor's house and receiving no answer, an elderly woman hesitatingly entered. A few moments later, she rushed out to the front porch screaming hysterically for the police. Officers arrived and found three bodies: a woman in her late 20s, shot in the head three times, her body eviscerated as horribly as that of Theresa Wallin; her eight-year-old son and fifty-one-year-old father, both shot in the head execution-style. A toddler, twenty-two months old, was missing. He would be found three months later, beheaded. As in the Wallin murder, there was evidence of cannibalism.

Although homicide inspectors immediately classified the two cases as one because of their bizarre sexual similarities, they were baffled as to the identity of the perpetrator. Were the systematic slayings the work of a single sex maniac or a group involved in ritualistic mutilation murder? Was someone bent on revenge or thrills? Was he or she known to the victims or simply a stranger, possibly an itinerant? Faced with few clues and no answers, the detectives decided to call in the FBI and its fledgling, little-known agency, the Behavioral Science Unit.

It was a stroke of luck for the Sacramento police that Agent Russel Vorpagel was then assigned to the FBI's field office in the state capitol. Russ, who already had extensive experience in solving unsolvable murders, called Robert Ressler, a colleague and friend who, a few years before, had joined the Academy as an instructor. Where local police considered the multiple slayings unique and sensational, Vorpagel and Ressler saw the case as routine. Instinctively and intuitively, each sensed the killer was a neighbor acting alone. Both rejected the detectives' notion that a stranger or an itinerant was involved.

Looking for additional clues, Vorpagel and Ressler spent the next few days visiting and revisiting the murder scenes, asking countless questions, examining and reexamining the little information that was available.

One casual comment by a neighbor stood out. Although it meant nothing to the Sacramento police, the sentence was everything to Russ and Bob: "You know, it's kinda strange, but some dogs and cats have been killed in the neighborhood around the time of the murders."

The next morning, the two agents handed the homicide detectives a sketch of their murderer. The "sketch" was not a drawing or composite of facial features, such as the shape of the head, nose, and ears, or the color of the hair or eyes. Rather, it was a "profile" of the killer, a personality description in less than five paragraphs, eight hundred words long. Based upon the historical patterns of such multiple mutilated slayings, and their own individual experience, logic, and intuition, Vorpagel and Ressler, who never actively pursued or made arrests of suspects in cases of this kind, had drafted what was then described by Larry Monroe, Ressler's chief of the Behavioral Science Unit, as "a source of investigative guidance to local police." That source, or sketch, or profile, read in part:

> Killer is white, male, 27-years old, living within a mile of the area. Has probably been treated in a mental institution and recently released. He is single and unemployed or working at a menial job. He has no friends. Unusual behavior includes being withdrawn and reclusive. Has a high school education or less. He is psychotic, probably schizophrenic. He and his residence are slovenly and unkempt. Evidence of his crimes will be present. He is thin and undernourished. He probably tortures animals. In kidnapping the baby, the killer had stolen a car, suggesting he had walked to the house from his nearby residence.

Now armed with this "investigative guidance" tool, Sacramento police officers began canvassing every residence, including some low-rent apartments, within a mile radius of the murder scenes.

"Do you know anyone fitting this description?" they asked. Within a few hours, one homeowner said, "Yeah. That sure sounds like Richard. He asked me for one of my puppies recently because he said he likes pets." Another neighbor added, "We wondered about him because we never saw the dogs and cats after he took them."

When Richard Trenton Chase's parents were interviewed later that morning, they indicated that their son had recently been released to their custody from a mental institution. After he exhibited strange behavior, including brutally torturing and then killing their family dog, they forced him to leave. Because he was unemployed, the parents paid for the rent on an apartment they found for him six blocks from the murder scenes. Richard's mother brought him food each day, although she was never allowed in the apartment.

Sacramento homicide detectives with back-up support immediately placed the apartment under surveillance. When he left it that afternoon, he was arrested without incident. In addition to finding him thin, emaciated, and unkempt, police discovered human tissue and blood in a kitchen blender, dog leashes and collars on a wall, and a machete and other knives neatly arranged in a cabinet, the only part of the apartment that was orderly. Upon interviewing Chase later that afternoon, police were stunned when the suspect stated that he was twenty-seven years old. Chase told investigators that "he had to do what he did." He believed that "radiation was drying up his blood and destroying his tissues." He claimed he had to replenish his blood and tissue by taking those from a living being.

When informed of Chase's arrest, agents Vorpagel and Ressler were not surprised to learn the suspect matched every aspect of their description. What was pleasant to learn was how accurately their collective intuition pinpointed the killer's age. Within the following year, Vorpagel would be joining Ressler on the twelve-man staff of the recently formalized Behavioral Science Unit while Richard Trenton Chase awaited execution for all five murders on San Quentin Prison's death row. While awaiting his inevitable gassing, he quietly hanged himself with bed sheets in his cell.

*   *   *

The book that follows is the story of the FBI's Behavioral Science Unit, one of several earmarked squads that Director J. Edgar Hoover established during the early 1970s to fight the greatest onslaught of violent crime in U.S. history. Not only was that attack transforming overnight the life and vitality of languid small towns and harried cities, but also overwhelming local police agencies responsible for fighting it. Equally astonished and confused, Hoover and his immediate staff found themselves at the center of increasing and incessant cries for help. Realizing that drones and paper pushers at headquarters couldn't answer the calls, the director assembled the best men and women the field offices could spare—the best of the best—to assume the mantle of national responsibility. New powers would be granted these newly created units in the hope that they would somehow work miracles.

From the frantic recruiting, assembling, planning, and retraining emerged one of several new fountainheads: the Behavioral Science Unit. On May 8, 1972, six days after Mr. Hoover passed away, when the new Academy opened its doors on the U.S. Marine Corps base in Quantico, no one, including the BSU's original founders, Jack Kirsch and John Pfaff, and the leadership brass within the FBI family, envisioned the phenomenal growth and gradual emergence of an even newer elite, an elite among elites, who would not only serve the unit's basic mission of instruction, but also conceive a whole new tactical strategy for homicide inspectors.

Personal reminiscences and reflections of Kirsch and Pfaff, among a host of others, reveal that criminal personality profiling[1] was gradually phased into the BSU curriculum on an informal basis as early as the summer of 1972, when the five faculty members encouraged their students—selected police officers and FBI agents from across the country—to discuss solved and unsolved murder cases with which they were familiar. The instructors, who all had master's degrees in behavioral psychology and backgrounds in either sociology or criminology, insisted that the cases not deal with murders involving robbery, family killings, or murders perpetrated by organized crime. "We need to focus upon the minds of those who commit seemingly motiveless murders," argued Kirsch. As a result of discussions in classes such

INTRODUCTION

as "Crime Scene Analysis," the instructors would note that, in similar crimes of the past, the offenders were a great deal alike. Thus, in subsequent classes when students presented unsolved crimes similar to ones previously discussed, the instructors provided spontaneous verbal profiles for all those assembled. Meanwhile, the students would utilize the information upon returning to their police departments or agencies. Generally, they would report back that the use of faculty-generated profiles saved countless investigative man-hours by properly focusing the investigation. In many instances, the profiles were credited with being directly responsible for solving the crimes.

In the mid-1970s, as other police departments and investigative agencies realized the potential of BSU assistance, the number of cases received for profiling by the instructors increased dramatically. Since the faculty's primary role was teaching, the unsolved files could only be analyzed on a time-available basis. Because the volume of requests grew to such unanticipated proportions, William H. Webster, who had been sworn in as FBI director in February of 1978, formalized the criminal profiling adjunct so that submitted cases could be assigned to specific individuals such as Russ Vorpagel and Bob Ressler for profiling. By 1980, the BSU staff had grown to twelve. In addition, fifty-five special agents were selected from various offices within the FBI and provided one hundred hours of instruction to prepare them as profile coordinators within their respective geographic regions.

Much has changed since the FBI's first "psych squad" began to informally offer criminal personality profiles based upon aberrant behavior patterns. The work of the Behavioral Sciences Unit today is a far cry from *Silence of the Lambs*, the hit thriller of more than a decade ago, or the more recent *Red Dragon* or *Hannibal*. In *Silence of the Lambs* agent trainee and future BSUer Clarice Starling, played by Jodi Foster, matches wits and quips with human monster "Hannibal the Cannibal" Lecter, and then chases down madman and serial killer, Buffalo Bill, right in his creepy lair. The popular film was shot on location

Introduction

at the Academy, where BSUers were still largely deskbound, hunkered down in a windowless, converted Cold War bomb shelter two floors below the Academy's armory-cafeteria-lounge building. Referred to as "the National Cellar," since it had been excavated and built to serve as a redoubt for Hoover and other high Justice Department officials in the event of nuclear war, the twenty-five offices and conference rooms inspired BSUers to flippantly remark, when asked about their worksite: "We live, play, and work ten times lower than dead folks."

Today, criminal profiling is conducted at the National Center for the Analysis of Violent Crime, an unmarked building located a few miles from the Academy in Aquia, Virginia. There, few people in the world are as adept in entering the minds of society's beasts as the thirty-plus member NCAVC staff. Along with twelve teaching colleagues back in the Academy's subterranean suites, the combined units assist law enforcement officials on an average of a thousand complex cases annually. Rarely cozy who-dunits a la Agatha Christie, the cases involve the most savage, perverse, and bizarre crimes imaginable, ranging from serial killings, sexual assaults, and child abductions to arson, bombings, and diabolical product-tampering plots. After the September 11th attack, the two staffs have taken on the additional responsibility of profiling potential terrorists. "We've seen, and are continuing to see, the worst of the worst," says current BSU chief Steve Band.

In brief, the Behavioral Science Unit was established in the early 1970s as a teaching unit, because American law enforcement agencies needed more than their own intuitive hunches to solve unsolvable crimes, especially multiple or serial murders. Local police simply needed help in determining motives and identities. The National Academy students (meticulously screened top cops, captains, and chiefs of police who attended classes for eleven-week sessions) pleaded with their special agent instructors for fewer abstract lectures and more operational know-how. In response, the instructors gradually shifted from informal discussions around their podiums and desks about who might have done what to whom, to more formal presentations. Hundreds of serial murder, rape, arson, and other violent case histories, as well as interviews and confessions of the criminals, were assembled to illustrate the patterns that would emerge. It wasn't long before the BSU staff was consulting on unsolved cases on a regular basis through the formalized Crime Analysis and Criminal Personality Profiling Program. This in turn led to the Criminal Personality Research Project based upon a $128,000 grant from the National Institute of Justice in 1982, which Bob Ressler coordinated. The goal: to interview thirty-six notorious serial killers and computerize the similarities in their cases.[2]

This was to be the first study conducted on a large number of serial killers. By 1985, Ressler and staff had interviewed personalities ranging from Charles Manson and Richard Speck to David Berkowitz, Sirhan Sirhan, and Arthur Bremer, the man who tried to kill George Wallace. In one instance, BSUers Ressler and John Douglas visited the criminally insane ward at the Mendota Mental Health Institute in Madison, Wisconsin, to interview seventy-seven-year-old Ed Gein, the "Ghoul of Plainfield." His nocturnal excavations in the graveyard of a small Wisconsin town provided Alfred Hitchcock with his inspiration for the movie, *Psycho*.

From the early soothsaying days of the 1970s through the 1980s, the Behavioral Science Unit established an impressive record of furnishing assistance to federal, state, and local law enforcement agencies. Considered a "think tank" for ideas in solving violent crimes, the BSU taught the importance of gathering information about and getting to know the victim in order to understand the criminal. Initial profiling, for example, depended upon the analysis of the interaction between the offender and the victim. Reconstructing the sequence of events before, during, and after the crime was critical in solving it. How a crime was committed became much more revealing than why.

Introduction

Poring over police reports, autopsies, laboratory results, maps, sketches, and photographs of the victims and crime scenes are still more important than visiting the death scene. Such criminal investigative analysis leaves little room to become emotionally slanted in interpreting information, as local police are wont to do when they have a suspect in mind.

Today, the Behavioral Science unit remains one of the instructional components of the FBI's training division at Quantico. Its mission is threefold: (1) to develop and provide relevant programs of training, research, and consultation in the behavioral and social sciences for the law enforcement community that will improve their administrative and operational effectiveness; (2) create bodies of knowledge in specialty areas and conduct applied research on significant behavioral and social science law enforcement issues for use in training, consultation, and operational matters; and (3) provide consultation services to law enforcement upon request.

For its training mission, the unit conducts specialized and applied training for new agents, FBI in-services, and symposia, as well as for the National Academy Program, international police officers, field police schools, and criminal justice–related organizations and conferences.

In its research component, BSUers focus upon developing new and innovative investigative approaches and techniques for the solution of violent crime by studying the violent offender and his or her behavior and motivation. Some of the research is conducted in partnership with outside researchers and through interagency agreements with the Justice Department.

For consultation, the unit coordinates with and supports other Bureau units, such as the National Center for the Analysis of Violent Crime and of the Critical Incident Response Group, which provides operational assistance to the FBI field offices and law enforcement agencies.

This book tells the story of the unit chronologically, highlighting

INTRODUCTION

a select number of cases and introducing many of the profilers who came on board over the past thirty years. Since some of these profilers specialized in solving certain types of crime, examples of those crimes are used to introduce the profilers, but also introduce the reader to the stresses of their work. One important chapter shows various crises within the FBI and how BSUers faced them while counseling fellow agents. Although somewhat case-focused, taking on a "Hardy Boys' Detective Manual" element, the book is more of an evolution and how that evolution spawned certain outstanding crime solving personalities and their unparalleled work.

NOTES

1. The term profiling was popular and used loosely until it lost standing in the early 1990s, when it became confused with drug profiling. When BSUers talked about profiling, they were talking about a process far more complex than the kind of checklists state police use to zero in on suspicious cars and drivers passing through their jurisdictions. BSUers needed a name that encompassed more than that, and eventually settled on the currently preferred term, "criminal investigative analysis."

2. One such case deals with a man previously convicted of abducting children from shopping malls and then murdering them. The BSU was particularly interested in how he persuaded his victims to come away with him. The answer: he would wrap his arm in a bandage and sling, then get children to help him carry a load of packages to his car, which would be located in a deserted area of a parking lot. "When we went to New York to talk to the 'Son of Sam,' David Berkowitz," says Robert Ressler, "he told us that on the nights when he couldn't find a victim to kill he would go back to the scene of an old murder to relive the crime and to fantasize about it. Now, that's a heck of a piece of information to store somewhere to see whether other offenders do the same."

Mindset
of a Murderer

"In the 1970s, whether you called, wrote, or simply walked up to us before or after class with a killing you couldn't solve, any one of us dozen or so in the BSU, anytime or anyplace, the corridors, lavatories or library, would gladly offer our subjective opinions on the mindset of the murderer to help you catch him. As impromptu as it was, we weren't afraid to shoot from the hip and we usually hit our targets. We did this thousands of times."

JACK KIRSCH, FORMER BEHAVIORAL SCIENCE CHIEF, IN A 1999 INTERVIEW.

"His instant advice was incalculable. Really, in just a few minutes and in just a few words Agent Reese wrote a textbook case for us in saving a number of police officer's lives."

DEPUTY CHIEF OF POLICE CHARLES E. HINMAN, MORNING OF AUGUST 11, 1979.

Who can say how often a casual remark, an observation, a spontaneous hunch, a bit of advice, or a serious discussion by a BSUer contributed to the capture of a murderer? One thing is certain, however. The creative intuitiveness coupled with experience in crime scene analyses were equally important, if not more so, than a slew of minor clues found around the murder victim.

Take, for example, what happened on a very hot and humid evening in early August of 1979, when Special Agent James Reese was in Hampton, Virginia, to present a three-day refresher conference on the potential of criminal profiling for local police. Reese, who had joined the FBI eight years before and transferred to the Academy in 1978 as an instructor in the Behavioral Science Unit, had served as a platoon leader in the Mekong Delta in Vietnam, logging more than fifty combat heliborn assaults and earning the United States Bronze Star and the Vietnamese Distinguished Service Cross. Currently, while working on a number of profiling cases, including handling investigative leads, incidents reports, and transcripts of interviews, Reese was also breaking new ground in the areas of law enforcement stress and burnout, hypnosis use, and psychological services for FBI personnel.

By chance that morning, police chief George C. Austin and his deputy, Charles E. Hinman, both from Newport News, a suburb of Newport, Virginia, attended Reese's opening address, "A Psychological Assessment of Organized and Disorganized Murderers."

For the special agent, the three-day conference was going to serve, in part, as a vacation, since it was the first time that the FBI had allowed him to be accompanied by his wife, Sandy, and their two-and-a-half-year-old daughter, Jamie. After teaching all day and retiring for the night the telephone rang just before midnight. It was deputy chief Hinman of the Newport police department. "Jimmie, I hate to bother you so late, but many of us heard you speak this morning and we need your help urgently. Can you come right down to the lobby? We're waiting for you." Apparently, a suspected murderer armed with a high-powered rifle was holed up in a wooded area not more than a few miles from the hotel. A police officer and his dog had been sent into the woods to flush him out. But the suspect confronted them at gunpoint, ordering them out of the woods.

Within minutes of the call, Reese was sitting in the lobby around a table with Hinman, Austin, two detectives, a district attorney, and several heavily armed members of the Newport SWAT team. For several minutes, chief-of-police Austin laid out the information they had.

"This is all I've got," Austin began. "A Mrs. Rhonda Allen Matthews, a white, twenty-eight-year-old, pregnant head housekeeper for the Colonial Courts Motel in Newport News, was found dead in a motel bedroom near a small forest with her hands handcuffed behind her back. She had been shot three times, execution-style at almost point-blank range, in the abdomen with what was certainly a high-powered rifle, which the killer fled with. We believe the murderer is Reginald Kilpatrick, a twenty-five-year-old, unemployed black who had been living in the motel room without the manager knowing about it. Interestingly, the door to the motel room where she was found was heavily barricaded from the inside. The suspect escaped through a rear bathroom window and fled into the woods behind the hotel."

"Was there any evidence of robbery, sexual assault, or other motive?" interrupted Reese.

"Not that we can determine at this point, but the murderer left a diary and a Marine Corps seabag full of clothes in the motel room. Because you had been teaching about homicides and people who keep diaries and souvenirs of their victims, we decided to get you out of bed. Our question to you is whether we should go in after the guy? We have forty police officers and five police dogs stationed with shotguns and revolvers around the perimeter. We're lucky the one officer and his dog got away. Will you come to the scene and do a profile or assessment of the subject? We want to bring in a helicopter to light the woods up."

"Let me read the diary on the way over," Reese responded. "It might provide some psycholinguistic clues. Meanwhile, simply close all roads around the area and seal him off. No helicopter or lights."

After reading the diary on the drive over to the motel and studying the crime scene, Reese decided it was not a good idea to go into woods that night, adding that Kilpatrick would undoubtedly fire at the helicopter and its crew, or, for that matter, anyone else flashing lights. "A search-and-destroy mission will create havoc and you don't need havoc so close to town." Furthermore, the subject was probable an ex-Marine recently released from a mental institution. "While not qualified to diagnose, and in the BSU we are not allowed to label people, I believe him to be paranoid schizophrenic based upon his behavior in the motel room and his writings found in the diary, which are full of racial terms like 'gook,' 'chink,' 'yellow bastard,' 'Charlie,' etc. Vietnam vets don't usually use terms like that, but he is a discharged Marine and when you capture him, you'll find he has dug four or five foxholes out there in the trees, plus he has plenty of ammunition for his rifle, and is in full Marine Corps gear." Reese concluded by insisting upon calling to him throughout the night with bullhorns in order to coax him into surrendering. "He won't, but at least you'll keep him awake until morning, when he'll be easier to capture or, if necessary, shoot. Remember, legally and morally, you have to try to talk him out. Now, excuse me. I'm going to call John Douglas, a colleague and friend of mine in the BSU for a second opinion."

Austin and Hinman listened intently, nodding in agreement.

When awakened around 2:00 A.M. that morning in his southern Virginia home, Special Agent John Douglas, who along with fellow BSUer Robert Ressler had been interviewing many of the nation's most infamous serial killers, was supportive. Senior to Reese in the BSU by six months, and his traveling-lecture companion when assigned by the unit chief to teach two- and three-day symposia to law enforcement agencies across the country, Douglas advised, "This guy would have killed anyone who entered that room. I agree that this is a murder of opportunity, not one of lust or sexual in nature. The diary tells us it's the whole world against him and therefore he needs to kill. He needs to protect himself. This is a functional psychotic who's not capable of clear thinking. He's transient, paranoid, opportunistic, and disorganized. I think you're right when you say he won't give himself up and will probably come out shooting." Douglas, who earned a master's degree in educational psychology from the University of Wisconsin and had already profiled such killers as Richard Speck, Charlie Manson, Sirhan Sirhan, David "Son of Sam" Berkowitz,

Albert "Boston Strangler" DeSalvo, and Arthur Bremer, was one of the most respected criminal profilers in the Behavioral Science Unit, and Reese sought his opinion more than anyone else's.

"Do you agree with me that he handcuffed her after she was killed?"

"Yes," answered Douglas. "Post-mortem."

"That he shot her in a panicked surprise when she entered unknowingly? That his paranoid or ideation told him to kill?"

"Yes."

At approximately 5:45 A.M., the Newport SWAT team entered the woods with Newport News police. They approached within fifty feet of the suspect, who stood up and fired on them. Kilpatrick was immediately hit five times and died after thirty days. The police discovered that his high-powered rifle was, in fact, a Marine carbine. Kilpatrick had dug six foxholes, had 351 rounds of ammunition for his carbine, and was dressed in full Marine Corps gear: helmet, flack jacket, web belt, canteen, and assorted battle knives. Furthermore, the subject's father was a high-ranking officer in the Corps.

Later that morning, when Reese resumed his lecturing during the second day of the refresher conference, Austin and Hinman dropped by to inform the assembled group of the night's events. They were astonished that the special agent's advice for the stakeout and capture had proven so successful, and wondered if Reese would explain to the class his reasoning behind the advice.

Reese laughed, "Why not? It's all part of a day's or, for that matter, a night's work. Just remember that the key to every crime, which is really a unique puzzle, is found in the common traits in both criminals and crime scenes. You can't package paranoia, rage, hate, fear, or abnormal sexual drives. If you look close enough you can find them at a crime scene. It's very important at the beginning to determine whether a murder is planned or unplanned, rational or irrational. Shooting Mrs. Matthews once could be considered a small rage compared to the need to shoot her three times. Three times suggests an exaggerated rage or fear. If it's fear, then you have a paranoid doing the killing."

A hand went up in the audience and a young police officer asked, "Sir, what I don't understand is exactly how you heard the few facts available, studied the crime scene, read the diary, then arrived at the logical conclusions you did. Will you explain how you arrived at the belief the suspect wouldn't give himself up and would come out shooting?"

Reese smiled and answered, "Sure, just look for the clues, then combine your experience and what academic knowledge you have to intuit, to guess, to follow a hunch."

Reese then went on to outline the six main behaviors that led him to his conclusions in less than two hours' time. The first thing he looked for was a motive. There didn't appear to be one. With no motive, there couldn't be a plan. So the murderer killed as a result of an irrational thought. Irrational thoughts suggest disorganization in behavior. The second important fact was the heavily barricaded motel-room door, locked from within. That told Reese that the suspect was paranoid and fearful about the world being out to get him, and that he became further disorganized and irrational. This was demonstrated by the fact that he fled through a bathroom window without closing it behind him. He was in such a state of confusion that he left all his personal possessions behind in his sea bag, including his diary and discharge papers with his name and identification tags.

Third, when the unfortunate Mrs. Matthews entered the motel room unexpectedly, the subject was surprised; he panicked and impulsively decided to erase the threat. In an irrational, paranoid mode of overkill he shot her not once, but three times—not because he was angry, but because he was irrationally fearful. That overwhelming fear manifested itself in yet another behavior. Although the police had to await the medical examiner's autopsy report, Reese was "willing to bet a dollar to a donut" that Kilpatrick handcuffed the woman after he murdered her. Handcuffing the victim post mortem was yet another indication of his extreme paranoia. He didn't want her to get up, tell, or come after him. Again, the action was the result of irrational, disorganized thinking with paranoid schizophrenic tendencies.

The killer's personal hygiene was another characteristic suggesting a psychotic. The motel room's toilet hadn't been flushed, the bed was filthy and unmade, the few clothing items in the sea bag were damp and dirty, to say nothing of the overall food-stained condition of the carpeting and the room's foul odor. Apparently the motel staff had not checked the condition of the room for weeks.

Finally, there were the entries in the diary Reese discussed with Douglas, hinting that Kilpatrick was extremely fearful of certain groups. The racial slurs meant a deep-rooted, perhaps unconscious hatred for all races other than black, and since he might perceive police departments in Virginia as being predominantly white, he would attack rather than give up.

"Gentlemen, remember that we never use the word 'always' when it comes to profiling. In fact, at present, there is not one single textbook to guide us. So I had to rely on simple evidence, previous experience dealing with organized and disorganized murder cases, a touch of psycholinguistics, good old-fashioned intuition, and finally, what I've learned from officers like yourselves."

Reese praised the Newport SWAT team and the Newport News police for their well-trained professionalism. "Everybody was comfortable with what was going down that night, although no one was allowed to smoke, talk, or move. Their detailed and predictable approach to the operation alleviated much of the anxiety that can gnaw at the nerves in a standoff with an armed suspect. No, my part was routine. Theirs was the textbook case."

No one can say how many SWAT team members or officer lives were saved that steamy hot night of August 10, 1979.

INTO THE MINDS OF MADMEN

*   *   *

Compared to the tracking and apprehending of the more sensational serial and lust killers of the 1970s and 1980s, like Theodore R. Bundy, John Lindley Frazier, John Gacy, and Wayne Williams, among a host of others, the innocuous Kilpatrick case has long since faded into obscurity, a tragedy remembered today only by the Matthews family. No team of BSUers—"mind hunters," as they soon would be nicknamed by the popular magazines and movies—sat around a conference room table poring over photos of the victim and analyzing the murderer's diary, then predicting haphazardly, haltingly, and possibly partially successfully Kilpatrick's behavior. In fact, had Hinman telephoned the BSU chief that night no one would have been on duty. If he had called the next morning, he would have been politely rebuffed: "Sorry, but the FBI agrees to provide profiles in only a narrow selection of crime, primarily multiple rape or child molestation and motiveless murders in which the nature of the killings points to a major psychological abnormality in the perpetrator. Your case does not fit our criteria, unfortunately."

By chance and as luck would have it, Jim Reese was in a position to exemplify the original and true Behavioral Science Unit mission: when called upon, offer advice, even if it's instantaneous and inconclusive. Whether you're with a team or all by yourself, help law enforcement the best way you can. The first wave of BSU founders were strong teaching personalities with plenty of investigative experiences to augment their theories. The second wave, much like the first in character qualities, added a third dimension: develop criminal personality profiles when requested, always verbal and nothing in writing, since the written word could come back to haunt you, your chief, and ultimately the Bureau. Like his dozen or so colleagues back at Quantico, Reese was ready to serve with his qualities of old-fashioned common sense, a creative intuitiveness, the ability to quickly isolate emotions while analyzing a murder scene and its victim, and

40

arriving at logical conclusions in reconstructing the killing, utilizing the perpetrator's reasoning processes.

* * *

On the Monday morning following the Kilpatrick case, Reese descended to the Academy's sublevels and his basement office in the Behavioral Science Unit to resume his daily work, along with special agents Larry Monroe, the reluctant unit chief, Jack Pfaff, the former unit chief, Roy Hazelwood, Tom O'Malley, Dick Ault, Bob Boyd, Roger Depue, Roger Davis, John Mindermann, Dick Harper, Swanson Carter, Roger Davis, Bob Ressler, and John Douglas. And the work that awaited him and the others was not to perfect a formula, easy-to-apply technique, or five-step method to psych out the most heinous of criminals, but to attempt solving the unsolved cases stacked neatly on their respective desks or the conference room table. The BSUers, like the rest of the nation, were experiencing one of the most disturbing phenomena in American history: murders where police found bodies but no motives. In 1966, there were 644 such deaths in the United States, or 6 percent. By 1979, the numbers soared to 4,118, or 70 percent. In 1960, one American homicide in ten went unsolved; by 1979, more than one killing in four was unsolved. While there were 3,500 murderers in prison, including some 1,260 on death row, criminologists believed there were as many, or more, still walking the streets uncaught. Many, if not most, would undoubtedly murder again. And among that group were possibly more than thirty who were repeat or serial killers. In fact, Department of Justice officials felt that murders where the perpetrators escaped justice were nearing 40 percent.

"So," recalls Reese, "there we were, hunkered down in our offices far below the Firearms Unit, struggling to outsmart the bastards. And, boy, did we need each other. We had this image of [being] armor[ed], that the work of poring over photographs of absolutely anguishing, terrifying killings didn't bother us. Most of the time we couldn't even eat our lunches or sleep at night. You try dealing with photos of decapitated children, for example. We needed to have each other; we needed to support each other; we each needed second opinions. Fortunately, our work was a kind of glue which held us together. The horrible work bonded us in a way no other work could."

A month after the Kilpatrick case, Reese received a letter of commendation from Director Webster that the entire BSU staff could share. In it, he wrote, "The timeliness with which your presentation of a retraining session in behavioral science for National Academy graduates coincided with a local fugitive situation allowed you to give a practical demonstration of the techniques under discussion. Your success in this and similar matters is proof of your unique ability to use theoretical principles to aid in the resolution of actual cases. I am truly grateful for your consistently diligent efforts."

Less than five days after reveling in the commendation from Webster, Reese was called upon one afternoon by the Executive Director of the FBI to report to the command center at headquarters in Washington, D.C., "to assist in appraising a profile" of a hijacking subject holding fifty-five hostages on a commercial airliner on the Seattle-Tacoma International Airport tarmac. The hijacker's demands were $100,000 in cash, a parachute, and a jet. Along with two other BSUers, Reese worked throughout the night by phone with the police department SWAT team, the Port Authority, the FBI SWAT team, local and state police, and the FBI negotiator. The crisis ended around 3 A.M. with the hijacker settling for a "rental car and a cheeseburger." As the young man deplaned for the car he demanded, members of the FBI SWAT team hidden under the plane grabbed him and the briefcase. As Reese and the other profilers at headquarters had predicted, the hijacker had no bomb. The three BSUers drove home to sleeping families. The hijacker went to jail, only to be released at a later date and killed in the commission of another commercial airline hijacking.

Then, in November of that same year, Reese was dispatched by Unit Chief Monroe to Jacksonville, Florida, to teach an advanced criminology school. While there, he asked to interview Arthur Frederick Goode, to better understand the mindset of the homosexual serial killer. Incarcerated at Raeford State Prison and awaiting execution, Goode had been convicted for abducting young boys, ten to thirteen years old, forcing them to engage in various sexual behaviors, and then murdering them. Reese and Special Agent Tony Rider interviewed Goode for some six hours. During that time he admitted he later enjoyed writing disgustingly descriptive letters to their parents, describing what he did to their children. "We were talking to him to try and learn more about who commit these types of crimes," Reese recalls, "and, of course, I didn't expect to see him show any remorse. But what I saw certainly surprised me: an extremely cold, calculated response to even the most sensitive questions regarding his killings. Upon leaving his death row cell area, Goode reinforced what we in the BSU already knew about psychopathic behavior. In an effort to assert his ego and recapture control at the last minute, he asked me with a grin, 'Do you have little boys at home?' In the seven or eight years I had spent in the FBI up to that point, the hardest thing I had to do was to turn my back and do nothing except leave."

One final incident in Reese's life, which all BSUers have faced and all too frequently, still occurs among BSU profilers: a year or so after interviewing Goode, Reese was profiling a case in which all of the children in a family were slaughtered. Each was shot in the face with a shotgun while asleep in their bedrooms. In an effort to come up with a profile, he and several other BSUers had to spend an inordinate number of hours staring at the photos of the sad scenes and the "faceless" children. "A few nights later," recalls Reese, "I walked into my daughter's room in order to tuck her into bed. She was lying under the sheets with her back to me, almost sleep. I couldn't leave the room. I had to walk around and around her bed to make sure she was all right. I couldn't leave her. I simply couldn't leave. There were tears in my eyes. In law enforcement, this is referred to as 'vicarious victimization.'"

*   *   *

Taken by themselves, the Kilpatrick murder and Seattle-Tacoma hijacking profiles didn't amount to much—even Reese admits that—certainly not significant enough to record for classroom posterity back in the Academy classroom. Like all FBI special agents, and especially those assigned to the Behavioral Science Unit, Reese's training and experience prepared him to tackle any challenge successfully, no matter how easy or difficult.

The incidents at Raeford State Prison with Arthur Frederick Goode and his own daughter Jamie's bedroom are more revealing of the man and his character. Symbolic of how every BSUer coped in his own way and time with the aftermath of tangled emotions, fears, and anxieties generated by the daily profiling, Jim says, "What I advised on those occasions was nothing more or less than what any one of my colleagues would have imparted. Recommendations, guidance, warnings, advice—that was what we were being paid to give. Somebody had to give it. Not one of us ran from it, or hesitated, or complained about it. And not one of us regretted giving it because it was usually good, very good. Do I still see bloodied children lying in bed without faces? Yes I do, just as my partners down there in that basement can't forget those images in their cases that have gone beyond the pale."

The Predecessors

2

"One must do as the animals do, who erase every footprint in front of their lair. . . ."

MONTAIGNE

lthough the origins of criminal profiling are uncertain, Dr. Thomas Bond, during the Whitechapel, or "Jack the Ripper," murders in London in 1888, is often credited with having developed the first primitive profile. But this was alternately attributed to Dr. George Bagster Phillips, the city's divisional police surgeon. Bond, a private physician who personally examined the wounds of two of the victims, Mary Kelly and Alice McKenzie, and studied the medical notes relating to four earlier victims, made the comment that the killer "must be a man of great coolness and daring." In addition, he commented upon the murderer's expertise and the probability that the Ripper had killed at least five other victims.

In 1987, a set of Bond's long-lost medical notes, written for Scotland Yard on November 10, 1888 (after the postmortems), revealed that he definitely believed all six women had been murdered by the same man. He wrote:

> The killer obviously shows a great deal of expertise, both anatomical knowledge and surgical skill, in the mutilations. The injuries to the throats had been perpetrated by someone who knew the position of vessels, at any rate where to cut with reference to causing speedy deaths. He is right-handed. He has a mature technique severing the throat all round down to the spinal column. I see in each murder evidence of similar design to the former Whitechapel murders, viz.

INTO THE MINDS OF MADMEN

> Sudden onslaught on each of the prostrate women, the throat skill-
> fully and resolutely cut with subsequent mutilations, each mutilation
> indicating sexual thoughts and a desire to mutilate the abdomen and
> sexual organs. I am of the opinion that the murder of each was per-
> formed by the same person who committed the former series of
> Whitechapel murders.[1]

Meanwhile, his friend and colleague, George Phillips, one of the world's initial forensic pathologists at the time, believed that you could infer a particular criminal's personality by examining his behavior with the victim. He recognized that the postmortem removal of some of Annie Chapman's organs and other mutilations (one of the Whitechapel victims) could only have been done by someone with medical knowledge. The clean, precise incisions certainly suggested professional skill and experience. Hence, Phillips, consulting with Dr. Wynne E. Baxter, London's coroner, engaged in wound pattern analysis, arguing "any mutilation which takes place after the murder suggests the character of the man who does it." The two, along with Bond, offered law enforcement the first formal indication that under-standing the murderer's behavior leads to perceiving his personality traits. To this day, the essence of profiling is knowing what happened to the victim through his or her specific injuries, or lack thereof, com-bined with other forensic material to understand the personality of the offender.

Worth noting, by the way, is Robert K. Ressler's unique perspec-tive on the psychology of a person who would commit the heinous Whitechapel killings. Bob contributed much to the early development of criminal profiling while a member of the Behavioral Science Unit.

> I visited the sites of the Ripper murders with John Grieve, director
> of intelligence for New Scotland Yard, and learned a lot about the
> murders. We walked the steps of Jack the Ripper: some of the resi-
> dences were still there. . . . Based on this tour, I became convinced

that the police had looked for the wrong sort of suspects. . . . The type of victims, the haunts they frequented, and the circumstances of the murders all made it much more likely that the perpetrator was of the same social class as the prostitute victims; if the killer was noticeably upper class, his presence in the area would have been remembered and remarked upon by the locals.

It also seemed clear to me that the Ripper had been a "disorganized" killer, a man who was mentally deranged and becoming more so with each victim. The escalation of violence, the dismemberment, and the general disorder of the crime scenes were evidence of this. . . . It is likely that he might well have gone off the deep end entirely, been so crazed that he could no longer even commit crimes, and have landed either in a suicide's grave or in an institution for the insane. . . . Suicide or confinement until death would explain why he was never apprehended.

Jack the Ripper's murders, though they did not include coitus, were nonetheless sexual, because the murder weapon was a knife, and the thrusting of the knife into the body was a substitute for thrusting the penis. . . . Serial murderers, in general, do not use guns, which kill people from a distance; serial murderers want the personal satisfaction of causing death right there at hand.

Sexual satisfaction for Jack the Ripper . . . derived from seeing the victim's blood spill. In Jack's case, there were even more overt signs that the crimes were sexual, since he cut out the uteruses of many of his victims. . . . Because the satisfaction from such crimes is sexual, there is always the likelihood that the perpetrator will strike again, since the sex drive continues even after the deed is done.[2]

Some argue that the real origin of criminal profiling began with Cesare Lombroso, an Italian physician who was born in 1835 and died in 1909. He believed the criminal was a throwback to a more uncivilized time. According to Lombroso, the true criminal was a distinct anthropological type, which he referred to as "atavistic." His book, *L'Uomo delinquente*, published in 1876 but never translated into English, was expanded over the course of five editions to a three-volume work. The only book in English on Lombroso's work that carried a similar title was *Lombroso's Criminal Man*. This book was authored by his daughter, Gina Ferrero, and published by Putnam's Sons in 1911. Lombroso wrote the introduction to the book.

With the expansion of *L'Uomo delinquente* between 1876 and 1897, Lombroso changed his stance somewhat, due to the criticism received by the first edition. Finally, in 1899, he wrote *Crime: Its Causes and Remedies*, in which he added the potential impact of socioeconomic factors. In the expanded version, he included intelligence-related characteristics among his classification theories, referring, for example, to feeblemindedness (a moral imbecile) rather than IQ levels. The extent of his "personality typing," as many writers have since called it, was to state that criminals had no moral sense and were vain and cruel.

Lombroso was never known for including geography or intelligence as part of his method of classification, as some have claimed, although he had shown some interest in geographic studies. Some years before, as an army physician in Italy, Lombroso had conducted anthropometric measurements on some two thousand soldiers in connection with his attempts to learn more about the incidence of "cretinism" and pellagra, a disease caused by a deficiency of niacin and protein in the diet. In this, he was trying to determine if soldiers from different regions of the country had physical differences, and if these differences correlated with the disorders. Lombroso never really explored geography as it related to criminal behavior. The first theorist who recognized the relationship between crime rates and geographic regions was Adolphe Quetelet (1796–1874), a Belgian statistician.

As late as the 1950s the Positive School of criminological thought, based on an extension of Lombroso's logic, argued that some people are born to be criminals. "They have no free will and therefore the emphasis should not be on guilt or innocence, but on dangerousness," the theory went. Criminals should be treated according to their needs and the needs of society. They shouldn't be punished when they commit a crime; but there should be no attempt at education and rehabilitation. Rather, the focus should be on their maintenance, as well as the security of the public. Taken to its extreme, this approach included individuals adjudged born criminals, but who had not yet committed a crime.

Such beliefs were used by much of Europe well into the 1930s and modified as needed by the Nazis before and during World War II. Today, the same concepts form the foundations for many radical and extremist groups espousing the various theories of human eugenics. Moreover, the criminal laws of several nations still include statutes derived from this form of thought. For instance, those beliefs provide the underlying foundations for the reluctance of many penal systems to emphasize rehabilitation.

Most typology theories are complicated and several are still around and active. If you're a criminal profiler, these beliefs and their originators have to be known and understood. Take Dr. Ernest Kretschmer, a German psychiatrist, for example. Kretschmer typed criminals according to four main body types, following the original typologies of functional disorders developed by Emil Kraepelin (1856–1926). In England, Charles Goring compared three thousand foreign prisoners to British Royal Engineers, looking for Lombroso's characteristics. He found only differences in stature and body weight.

The anthropologist Ernest A. Hooten reattempted this research, comparing thirteen thousand prisoners to seventeen thousand non-criminals, and found similar results to those of Lombroso. William Sheldon of Columbia University categorized delinquents by endomorphic, ectomorphic, and mesomorphic body types and their corresponding temperaments in the late 1940s and early 1950s. There are several others, including Sheldon and Eleanor Glueck, as well as the most recent, Richard Herrnstein and Charles Murray, who wrote the book *The Bell Curve.*

INTO THE MINDS OF MADMEN

For a few moments, consider the September 22, 1907, Sunday Magazine section of the *New York Herald*, in which an article appeared entitled, "The War of Science on Scientific Crime: Chemistry, Physics, Anthropology, Philology, Optics, Mathematics, etc., All Used in New York Detective Bureau's Great Fight Against Society's Brainy Outlaws."

> Out of the old Central Office, as the Detective Bureau of New York is familiarly known, there is growing a new organization which, animated by a purely modern spirit, discards much of the tradition so tenaciously held to in the past and seeks to adopt methods that effectively will meet the complex and scientific aspects of the crimes of today. In fact, today, being carefully worked to a realization in the New York's ideal Detective Bureau, are men who not only know to the last letter the natural history of criminals, but also men versed in languages, chemistry, toxicology, mathematics, electric science, microscopy, psychology, anthropology, enthropometry, and other branches which comprehend modem man and his criminal activities.

Unacknowledged and unappreciated to this day is the fact that the NYPD's fledgling Detective Bureau, although one of the most corrupt in American law enforcement at the time, not only demonstrated significant expertise in crime scene analysis, but also endeavored to grasp the type of person whose criminal mind, with all its potentially bizarre behaviors, was most likely to commit the crime. Some in law enforcement, as well as in the BSU, are reluctant to say the above article illustrates that the New York Detective Bureau was using advanced procedures and techniques as early as 1907. According to Jim Reese, who has written extensively on police psychological services, the earliest involvement of behavioral scientists in the law enforcement field appeared to be in 1916, during the selection of police candidates. Behavioral scientists from universities were employed part-time to conduct psychological testing.

50

The Predecessors

It seems that the early days of the New York Police Department and its Detective Bureau were problematic. The patrol division and the detective division were separate entities and often in conflict with one another. Both were run by ward bosses, and many of the detectives were former criminals themselves. This was done deliberately in the belief that "it takes a thief to catch a thief." This was also the method used by the French. The Sûreté contained many former criminals. In fact, one, Eugene Vidocq, was so good that he became chief of the Sûreté for a time.

All of this was less than twenty years after Dr. Sigmund Freud discovered the unconscious; one year before the birth of the Bureau of Investigation, a new federal investigative force; twenty-seven years prior to the reorganization of that force into a more comprehensive Federal Bureau of Investigation (whose goal was to become the premier law enforcement agency of the government, and the major service to assist local law enforcement agencies across America); and a full sixty-five years before J. Edgar Hoover encouraged FBI special agent Jack Kirsch, among others, to prepare and introduce a broad range of new instructional classes at the FBI Academy in Quantico, Virginia, that would improve the Bureau's new thrust into forensic science.

From biblical times there have been attempts to employ both deductive and inductive reasoning to determine potential and actual criminal personalities. More recently, in such literary works as Shakespeare's *Julius Caesar* and Edgar Allan Poe's "The Murders in the Rue Morgue," crude attempts to categorize abnormal behaviors by means of physical attributes appeared in print. Certainly, Sir Arthur Conan Doyle's Sherlock Holmes, Agatha Christie's Hercule Poirot, Bull Dog Drummond, the Thin Man, Mr. Wong and Charlie Chan, Ellery Queen and Mickey Spillane, to say nothing of Miss Jane Marple and Sgt. Joe Friday, as well as all the other superdetectives of this century, believed that evidence always spoke its own language of patterns and sequences to reveal the offender.

INTO THE MINDS OF MADMEN

And, to his everlasting credit, so did J. Edgar Hoover. In fact, it can be argued that his appointment as director of the Bureau of Investigation in 1924 set the stage for cautious, reasoned change in what was soon to be known as the Federal Bureau of Investigation. Thanks to Prohibition, crime, corruption, and violence became facts of life in American cities in the 1920s, and Hoover was the first to establish an operational means to tackle this new kind of gritty urban reality.

Say what you will about the man, it was his personal vision that initiated an evolutionary process calculated to ensure that the organization was attuned to the challenges that were certain to confront the modern nation in the years ahead. On November 24, 1932, with a borrowed microscope and a few pieces of scientific equipment, the Bureau's first technical laboratory opened for business. Hoover's goal: be ready and able to help both federal and local investigations by examining and analyzing blood, hair, firearms, paint, handwriting, typewriters, and other evidence. The cornerstone for federal scientific investigations was laid. Needless to say, this was an enormous boost to American law enforcement.

During its first year of operation, the laboratory conducted fewer than a thousand examinations. Most were handwriting analyses from extortion cases; the rest were studies of firearm specimens. In the decades that followed, it was obvious that more specialized techniques would be needed to analyze more difficult physical evidence ranging from machine guns to tool marks, saliva to sperm stains. For Hoover and Congress, effective law enforcement meant cooperation among various police agencies. Once and for all, politics had to be removed from police work. And most important, sound policing could be achieved by sharing the Bureau's own training facilities. Hence, in July of 1935, twenty-three carefully chosen police officers met as the first class of what is known today as the FBI National Academy. Sessions were held at the Department of Justice building in Washington, D.C., until 1972, when they were relocated to the newly completed training complex on the western portion of the U.S. Marine Base in Quantico.

The Predecessors

Meanwhile, in response to such unchallenged bank-robbing and cop-killing gangsters as Charles "Pretty Boy" Floyd, Alfred Bates, George "Machine Gun" Kelly, John Dillinger, "Baby Face" Nelson, Clyde Barrow and Bonnie Parker, "Ma" Barker, and Alvin "Old Creepy" Karpis, Congress passed a series of anticrime laws in May of 1934 which expanded the Bureau's jurisdiction over interstate crimes committed by these killers. Hoover was delighted, because the new laws, at long last, provided his men with a broad range of enforcement powers and protection, including the death penalty for anyone murdering a federal agent.

Then, with Hitler about to overrun Europe and the Japanese expanding aggressively into Asia, coupled with disturbing memories of German espionage and sabotage during World War I, President Franklin Delano Roosevelt, on September 6, 1939, formally authorized Hoover to investigate all matters relating to threats against America's safety and security.

One drama after another soon began to unfold: espionage and counterespionage, the relocation and internment of Japanese, Italian, and German Americans; the violation of neutrality laws; U-boats entering U.S. waters to land German spies and saboteurs. Although busy with all this, the FBI continued its efforts against crime, the prime targets being opportunists attempting to capitalize on the shortage of domestic goods that resulted from the effort to win the war. For example, a black-market operation was smashed in Pennsylvania that involved the diversion of nylon, essential in the manufacture of parachutes, from military use to the production of hosiery. In another example, evidence was also gathered that led to the conviction of a manufacturer of military explosive devices, who had cut down on the charges in grenades and incendiary bombs to squeeze a few more cents out for himself.

With the Bureau constantly tracking, surveilling, and arresting, a coded order arrived in a New York spy house from the Abwehr, German military intelligence in Hamburg: "Under no circumstance attract the attention of the FBI." During all World War II, thanks in part to Bureau vigilance, no enemy agent had the opportunity to commit a single successful act of sabotage crippling the United States, nor was *any* known act of enemy-directed sabotage successfully committed.

One of the earliest known psychological assessments, formally commissioned to produce a profile for predictive purposes, involved, of all people, Adolf Hitler. During the early months of 1943, General William "Wild Bill" Donovan, founder and director of the recently organized and little-known Office of Strategic Services (OSS), and a man of brilliance, imagination, and bravery, suggested to Dr. Henry Murray, former director of the Harvard Psychological Clinic in Cambridge, Massachusetts, and then chief of the OSS's psychological assessment staff, that a "psycho-historian" be employed to develop a psychological profile on the Third Reich's evil genius and his apocalyptic inclinations. That is, what conclusions could a psychological investigator draw from Hitler that might prove useful to the OSS? Could psychoanalytic insight somehow be applied to modern, mechanized warfare?

Murray, whose team of psychologists tested and selected the toughest and most psychologically sound volunteers for covert operations overseas, turned immediately to his old friend, Dr. Walter C. Langer—a New York neo-Freudian who was not only a private psychoanalyst but also a member of the Progressive Education Association's Commission on Human Relations—to conduct a "long-range diagnosis" for allied war planners, including Hitler's most plausible moves as Nazi Germany crumbled around him.

Classified "top secret," the 135-page report prepared by Langer, who employed Freud's principles to disinter the dictator's psyche and degeneration, presented a number of predictions of uncanny accuracy. In addition, the analysis provided new personality insights unobserved by historians relying upon general observations and traditional research methods.

Three major sources were tapped: exhaustive interviews with

those who had known Hitler personally, such as Nazi Party founder Otto Strasser and Princess von Hohenlohe; 1,100 pages of biographical information, including speeches and other minor writings, compiled by three analytically trained assistants; and the careful dissection and analysis of Hitler's book, *Mein Kampf*. Via such indirect assessments, Langer was able to inquire into the dictator's troubled family background, his sexual pathologies, death fears, Messiah complex, vegetarianism, and other characteristics. Then, drawing on his clinical knowledge of psychiatric patients with similar traits, he was able to foretell Hitler's increasing isolation, his frequent rages, and thus the general deterioration of his mental condition.

Langer not only outlined Der Führer's various manias (wolves, severed heads, pornography), phobias (horses, germs, moonlight, syphilis), and numerous contradictions, but also catalogued Hitler's strengths, including will-power, self-discipline, courage, tirelessness, ability to manipulate crowds (which he considered feminine in nature), as well as rhetorical power. As he pieced together an incredible jigsaw puzzle, he concluded that the "Führer personality" was a grossly exaggerated and distorted conception of masculinity that showed all the earmarks of a "reaction formation created unconsciously as a cover-up for deep lying tendencies that he despises."

"Hitler," Langer wrote, "is not a single personality, but two that inhabit the same body. The one is very soft and sentimental and indecisive. The other is hard, cruel and decisive. The first weeps at the death of a canary; the second cries that there will be no peace in the land until a body hangs from every lamppost!"[3] And, of course, this duality led precisely to the horrible excesses that occurred in Nazi Germany's twilight.

Available to only a handful of American and British officials during the war, and tucked away gathering dust in the National Archives until 1972, the analysis emerged as the first masterpiece of personality probing and profiling. Combining investigative boldness and imagination, Langer surmised that Hitler was a common neurotic psychopath with schizophrenic tendencies. He was not insane, but certainly emotionally ill, lacking normal inhibitions against antisocial behavior. A desperately unhappy man, the dictator was plagued with anxieties, doubts, fears, guilt, and loneliness. He was spending his whole life, including waging war, in an unsuccessful attempt to compensate for feelings of helplessness and inferiority. Hitler's career, in short, was clinically an elaborate, defensive, psychosexual acting out of deep dreads and self-loathings.

And because the Nazi press portrayed Der Führer as a man of steel who would never lose his nerve no matter what the provocation, Langer focused upon his immortality and images of death. "As Germany suffers successive defeats, Hitler will become more and more neurotic," he warned the OSS. "Each defeat will shake his confidence and limit his opportunities for proving his own greatness to himself. He will probably try to compensate for his vulnerability by stressing his brutality and ruthlessness."[4]

Williams College historian Robert G. L. Waite wrote the afterword of Langer's book, *The Mind of Adolf Hitler: The Secret Wartime Report*, which was published immediately after the report was declassified. Waite said, "Since Hitler could not vanquish the Allies, he manufactured ruthless 'victories' over the Jews in the gas ovens. At the same time, he vowed to destroy Germany itself. 'Not a German stock of wheat is to feed the enemy; not a German hand to offer him help. He is to find nothing but death, annihilation and hatred.'"[5]

Waite went on to praise Langer's use of psychoanalytic principles to study a dictator's psyche. Certainly, the study included conflicting and mistaken information and misinterpretations galore, with little historical context in which to view them, but Dr. Langer's basic prediction that Hitler's most plausible move would be to commit suicide while Berlin burned around him came true.

William L. Langer wrote about his brother in the foreword to *The Mind of Adolf Hitler*.

The Predecessors

This psychological study of Hitler was a pioneer effort to apply modern psychological findings, not to a distant historical figure, but to one who was very much alive and busily engaged in making history. As far as I know, this was the first systematic attempt to deal with a pressing political problem in this way. The final product may have some shortcomings, of which my brother is only too keenly aware. Nevertheless, his effort set the pattern for later investigations of this type. While it is and always has been impossible to psychoanalyze personalities with whom direct and frequent contact is out of the question, it has been demonstrated that a good deal can be done to study their character and make their actions more meaningful by gathering all pertinent data and subjecting them to the dispassionate evaluation of qualified persons who have clinical experience to draw from. . . . Why, after all, should not the psychological aspects of human personalities and problems be taken into account just as religious, economic, or geographic factors have long since been considered?[6]

As for himself, Langer rightfully wondered, years later, how history would have been changed if the results of his personality profile had been made public during the war itself, thereby encouraging the German Resistance Movement to attempt additional assassination efforts after the unsuccessful July 20, 1944, bomb plot.

Incidentally, Carl G. Jung had his own appraisal of Adolph Hitler. He wrote in 1946:

After the catastrophe, complete lack of insight into one's own character, auto-erotic self-admiration and self-extenuation, denigration and terrorization of one's fellow men (how contemptuously Hitler spoke of his own people!), projection of the shadow, lying, falsification of reality, determination to impress by fair means or foul, bluffing and doublecrossing—all these were united in the man who was diagnosed clinically as an hysteric, and whom a strange fate chose to be the political, moral, and religious spokesman of Germany for twelve years. Is this pure chance?

INTO THE MINDS OF MADMEN

A more accurate diagnosis of Hitler's condition would be *pseudologia phantastica*, that form of hysteria which is characterized by a peculiar talent for believing one's own lies. For a short spell, such people usually meet with astounding success, and for that reason are socially dangerous. Nothing has such a convincing effect as a lie one invents and believes oneself, or an evil deed or intention whose righteousness one regards as self-evident. At any rate they carry far more conviction than the good man and the good deed, or even than the wicked man and his purely wicked deed. Hitler's theatrical, obviously hysterical gestures struck all foreigners (with a few amazing exceptions) as purely ridiculous. When I saw him with my own eyes, he suggested a psychic scarecrow (with a broomstick for an outstretched arm) rather than a human being. It is also difficult to understand how his ranting speeches, delivered in shrill, grating, woman-ish tones, could have made such an impression. But the German people would never have been taken in and carried away so completely if this figure had not been a reflected image of the collective German hysteria. It is not without serious misgivings that one ventures to pin the label of "psychopathic inferiority" on to a whole nation, and yet, heaven knows, it is the only explanation which could in any way account for the effect this scarecrow had on the masses. A sorry lack of education, conceit that bordered on madness, a very mediocre intelligence combined with the hysteric's cunning and the power fantasies of an adolescent were written all over this demagogue's face. His gesticulations were all put on, devised by an hysterical mind intent only on making an impression. He behaved in public like a man living in his own biography, in this case as the sombre, daemonic "man of iron" of popular fiction, the ideal of an infantile public whose knowledge of the world is derived from the deified heroes of trashy films. These personal observations led me to conclude at the time (1937) that, when the final catastrophe came, it would be far greater and bloodier than I had previously supposed. For this theatrical hysteric and transparent imposter was not strutting about on a small stage, but was riding the armored divisions of the

Wehrmacht, with all the weight of German heavy industry behind him. Encountering only slight and in any case ineffective opposition from within, the nation of eighty millions crowded into the circus to witness its own destruction.[7]

Meanwhile, out in the Pacific, our effort to profile Japanese military leaders for predictive purposes was equally impressive. Sadly, not many know the incredible story of Captain Ellis M. Zacharias's determination and success at profiling those who held the fate of the Far East in their hands. Only in 1946, less than a year after Japan's final acceptance of Allied terms for peace, did the full record come to light, when G. P. Putnam's Sons published *Secret Missions: The Story of an American Intelligence Officer*.

The 433-page hardcover was an extraordinary memoir of Zacharias's twenty-five-year war of wits, nerves, and words against the Japanese secret service, culminating in a master stroke of psychological warfare, which some have argued broke the Japanese will to resist (long before the atom bombing of Hiroshima and Nagasaki). Unfortunately, at first, the story interested few. With no blood or guts and little overt heroism, the book didn't sell and was removed almost immediately from bookstore shelves. Later, *Secret Missions* became a best-seller. Zacharias rendered invaluable service to the field of psychology in general, and personality profiling in particular. On page 22, he wrote, "To know what the others think, and how their actions are stimulated by their thinking processes; to know what they have and what they intend to do with their forces; to know our opponents and partners in the international chess game lends immediate strength to ourselves and should save us from unpleasant surprise."

In some ways, Zacharias, who retired as a rear admiral, was more of a profiler than Dr. Walter Langer. Langer never met or knew Adolf Hitler. Instead, he employed indirect assessment techniques. Zacharias, on the other hand, had succeeded as a naval intelligence officer in the 1920s, gaining the confidence of Admirals Yamamoto, Nomura, Suzuki, and Yonai, as well as other Japanese militarists, while stationed in Tokyo. The firsthand insights he gained about the warlords' thoughts and plans for world domination were unrivaled in Allied military annals. Using direct assessment strategies as well as indirect ones, he successfully predicted, for example, each of the militarists' behaviors between February 1944 and August 1945, including who was likely to surrender rather than seek a "wasteful and unsanctified death by suicide," and who might wage war to the bitter end.

In his final chapter, Zacharias and his staff, much like the BSU's threat-assessment team today, blueprinted the measures that America had to take to remain informed of any aggression that might be plotted again, and "how to guard our security against the machinations of foreign agents in the Atomic Age."

Unfortunately, *Secret Missions* is long out of print, housed in unused basements and attics of public libraries, or in storage in major university libraries. This is sad, because anyone interested in the roots of criminal profiling will appreciate the unique perspectives and achievements of Captain Zacharias, perhaps America's first true profiler.

*   *   *

While Langer and Zacharias were at work creating profiles of how dictators, generals, admirals, and other military leaders would behave in the final months of inevitable defeat, an unassuming, mild-mannered man began terrorizing the city of New York by setting off small bombs in public places. It was not until 1957, more than fourteen years and thirty-seven bombs later, that a Waterbury, Connecticut, man was caught, not by the NYPD or Waterbury cops, but by Dr. James A. Brussel, a knowledgeable Greenwich Village clinical psychiatrist and criminologist, whose approach to profiling was primarily diagnostic. For example, "No one acts without motivation," wrote the famed criminal psychiatrist. "The motivations behind the acts of madmen possess their own logic. The psychotic murderer does not act wholly irrationally. There is a method to his madness. There is a logic, a rationale, hidden behind what he does and how he does it, however wildly bizarre and completely without reason it appears to be."[8]

Brussel profiled the Mad Bomber as a paranoiac. Unlike a paranoid schizophrenic, he argued, a paranoiac is able to plan, talk, and act in an organized manner. He does not suffer hallucinations—rather, he suffers from delusions, or false beliefs. The primary delusion of a paranoiac is usually that someone is out to get him. Once one understands the paranoiac's delusions, therefore, what he does can be understood logically.

Like Langer and Zacharias, Dr. James A. Brussel is another of the unsung heroes in the history of criminal profiling. He said he could diagnose an unknown offender's mental disorders from behaviors detected at the crime scene. "Facts can be worked back," he once commented, "to deduce the type of person that would commit the crime." In part, Brussel would infer the personality of an unknown perpetrator by comparing his criminal behavior to his own experiences with the behaviors of clients in his psychotherapeutic practice and patients in the clinic who shared similar disorders. He also insisted, believe it or not, that certain forms of mental illness could be linked to specific physical builds, a theory not unlike those of Lombroso and his followers, or that of Kretschmer. As a result, the perpetrator's physical characteristics were included in the profiles he developed during the 1950s and 1960s of unsolved murder cases.[9]

In addition to having an impeccable reputation in New York police circles, Brussel was assistant commissioner of the N.Y. State Department of Mental Hygiene. The author of half a dozen psychology books, ranging from the mystery novel, *Just Murder, Darling*, to *The Layman's Guide to Psychiatry*, he served as a neuropsychiatrist during World War II and the Korean conflict. Later, he engaged in counterespionage activities in Mexico for the FBI and CIA. Brussel was destined to accurately profile New York's Mad Bomber in 1956, although his profile of the Boston Strangler in 1964 led police astray.

Beginning in 1940 and continuing through the next decade and a half, a mysterious and potentially dangerous man had been detonating small, garage-made bombs on Manhattan windowsills and under theatre and subway seats. Initially, the city paid scant attention to the detonations, since no one was injured and there was little damage to property. But over the years, the bombs increased in size and force, and New Yorkers grew increasingly terrified.

More than thirty-five bombs were fashioned during the Mad Bomber's strange career. When some failed to explode, crime lab technicians photographed them. Many looked like large penises. Occasionally, the perpetrator wrote to the police, newspaper editors, civic leaders, utility presidents, and metropolitan and state officials. The unusual bombs and letters were all the police had. So little was known about the bomber that virtually anyone in the city, including nuns and priests, could be picked at random as the suspect. While pressure mounted to catch the Mad Bomber, the police grew increasingly frustrated.

In his smoothly written autobiography, *Casebook of a Crime Psychiatrist*, Brussel recounts how his personal friend, Captain John Cronin, chief of the NYPD's Bureau of Missing Persons, asked if Inspector Howard E. Finney, the director of the N.Y. Police Departments Crime Laboratory, and a man with a master's degree in forensic psychiatry, could meet with him in his office on the seventeenth floor of the State building at 270 Broadway, across from city hall.

When they met a few days later, Finney came right to the point: "Our case is one of straw-grasping. We're stumped. Here's a bundle of letters and photographs. Solve it."

"I don't know what you expect me to do," replied Brussel. "If experts haven't cracked this case, what can a psychiatrist know about it?"

The Predecessors

"Give it a whirl, doctor," smiled Finney. "Sometimes the difference between failure and success is a new thought."[10]

Brussel, of course, accepted the challenge. After all, he had repeatedly aided the police by appearing as an expert witness in numerous murder trials, demonstrating to juries how intuition, coupled with logic and deduction, could solve a crime. Cases that the tabloids called the "Christmas Eve Killer," the "Wylie Murder," the "Sunday Bomber," and the Coppolino killing were but a few he helped solve.

Within days, Brussel provided Inspector Finney with an image of the Mad Bomber. A summary of it appeared in the *New York Times* on Christmas day, 1956:

> Single man, between 40 and 50 years old, introvert. Unsociable but not antisocial. Skilled mechanic. Cunning, neat with tools. Egotistical of mechanical skill. Contemptuous of other people. Resentful of criticism of his work, but probably conceals resentment. Moral. Honest. Not interested in women. High school graduate. Expert in civil or military ordnance. Religious. Might flare up violently at work when criticized. Possible motive: discharge or reprimand. Feels superior to critics. Resentment keeps growing. Present or former Consolidated Edison worker. Probably case of progressive paranoia.

"This news story didn't contain all my predictions," said Brussel, "but it crystallized the major ones. The profile told enough to embarrass me severely if I turned out to be grossly wrong."

What the *Times* chose to ignore was that the profile indicated the Mad Bomber was undoubtedly paranoid, sexually abnormal, hated his father, was obsessively loved by his mother, and probably still lived with her or a maiden sister somewhere in New Hampshire, Connecticut, or Maine. He would be of average build, middle-aged, foreign-born, and Roman Catholic. And when the police finally caught him, he would be wearing a buttoned, double-breasted suit.

Brussel then took the unusual step of personally writing to the Mad Bomber via a public letter that was published on the front page of the New York *Journal American*. A week or so later, the Mad Bomber replied, citing his smoldering anger and absolute hatred for a utility company that had wronged him and others in the past. A search of Consolidated Edison records quickly led Finney and the police to George Metesky, a fifty-three-year-old, unmarried, former Con Ed worker living with his two unmarried sisters in Waterbury, Connecticut. When arrested, he was in his robe. For the ride to police headquarters, he changed into a double-breasted suit, just as Brussel predicted.

In his *Casebook*, Brussel describes how crimes of bombings and arson are usually those of obsessive-compulsive, paranoid personalities. Their neuroses generally peak around the age of forty-five or fifty. In eastern and southeastern Europe, bombs and daggers are the choices of weapons for protest purposes. The grammar in the Mad Bomber's letters alone pointed to central or Eastern Europe. And since more of the people in these regions are Roman Catholic, and since the largest population of these first- and second-generation Europeans lived in Westchester County and southern Connecticut, it wasn't difficult to profile these characteristics.

> Unconsciously, Metesky fashioned his bombs like penises because of unresolved psychosexual issues when he was a little boy. The W's in his letters always have rounded bottoms, suggesting women's breasts. M and the other letters, neatly printed in block form, have no sexual connotations. Being part of a nationality that cherished strong family ties, he most likely would have had to live with his parents or sisters. That part wasn't difficult to figure out. Nor was the fact that he was meticulous and feminine, possibly homosexual, and always wearing the neatest, primmest, and most protective male attire possible: the buttoned double-breasted suit.[11]

The Predecessors

When he was finally arrested on a cold, dreary night in late January of 1957, Metesky was the model of unfailing politeness, constantly smiling and eager to oblige. He insisted he be allowed to wear his favorite blue, pinstriped, double-breasted suit on the way to police headquarters. Proudly, he showed the arresting officers his workshop in the corrugated-iron garage behind the house. The floor was swept; the bench was clean; the tools were all hanging in their racks. The place was so immaculate you could have eaten dinner there. Brussel couldn't have been more correct in his assessment.

There was one final prediction about the Mad Bomber: he would never respond to psychiatric treatment; psychoanalysis would wash off him like water off a duck's back; and, when finally institutionalized, he would turn into a satisfied person who would attend church services regularly and be helpful to the hospital administration in whatever work was assigned. BSU profilers say that such behavior is characteristic of all serial bombers, from Metesky to the Unabomber.

In later interviews with Brussel, Metesky insisted that his bombs could never hurt anyone. Ridiculous! He simply wanted to call the world's attention to the "dastardly deeds" committed by Consolidated Edison. The last question Brussel asked Matesky was, "Is it possible, George, that during all that time you were planting bombs you could have been mentally ill?" Smiling, he answered, "It could have been, it could have been. But it wasn't." Then, he bowed graciously and left the interview room. He was allowed to wear his double-breasted blue suit instead of hospital garb, and remained smiling for the remainder of his sentence at Matteawan State Hospital, a civil corrective institution for mentally ill criminals. When he was eventually released, he died in peace at home.

At the time of its publication, *Casebook of a Crime Psychiatrist* was reviewed negatively. One book reviewer wrote, "This is mildly sensational and trivial stuff, written in the breathless style of a crime reporter with an extraordinary ego." Maybe so. But such a criticism does not alter the fact that *Casebook* was the first crude manual in criminal profiling for police use. And, what adds further importance to the text is Brussel's admission that criminal profiling was prone to human error, and that he himself had often screwed up. The most famous instance was in the case of the "Boston Strangler."

Between June of 1962 and January of 1964, thirteen sexual strangulation murders were committed in the city of Boston. Although police believed they were related, they were unsuccessful in developing viable suspects. On April 10, 1964, Dr. Brussel was ushered into a spartan, third-floor room in an old brownstone house that belonged to Boston University. Some fifteen men were present, the most distinguished being John S. Bottomly, the assistant attorney general of Massachusetts, who had been assigned by the governor the full-time task of catching the serial killer.

Since traditional investigative efforts had proved of little value, and since no leads had turned up, Bottomly called a meeting with a group of physicians and psychiatrists, including an anthropologist and a gynecologist—henceforth known as the Medical-Psychiatric Committee, the nation's first profiling committee—to establish a "psychiatric profile."

"I hope you can do your Mad Bomber trick for us here, Dr. Brussel," Bottomly said with a grin.

Again, Brussel wondered out loud how he and the other group participants hoped to succeed where murder detectives had thus far failed. Bottomly then described the sex-related deaths of the victims: seven elderly women followed by six younger women. Could this mean there was more than one killer?

Certainly, responded the profiling committee, believing that the psychosexual behavior differed between the two victim groups. For example, they believed the older victims were being strangled by a man who was raised by a smothering, domineering, seductive mother. The younger group was murdered by a homosexual male acquaintance.

The Predecessors

Since each had been choked and decorated with colorful ribbons or scarves, everyone, from police unit chiefs to cops on the beat, from publishers to peanut vendors, psychology students to psychiatrists, had a theory about who was committing the sexual stranglings.

In *Casebook of a Crime Psychiatrist*, Brussel describes how he "puzzled his way around the truth, bumping into it, tripping over it, but never quite seeing it." He was looking for a pattern, as was everybody else, or some common denominator among the victims or the circumstances that could lead to a deduction of who the Boston Strangler was.

> I didn't know. Like everyone else, I was troubled by the odd combination of similarities and differences in the two groups of victims. I didn't know whether the similarities were more important than the differences, or, vice versa; didn't know where to focus my attention. All through that three-week period, while waiting for the next meeting of the committee, I puzzled over the question. Looking back on the affair now, I groan at my own blindness. The single most important truth about the crimes was staring me in the face all the time. It was a truth so simple, so obvious, that everybody had disregarded it. It was the one psychological handle by which the case could be grabbed, hauled from the realm of speculation, and held down on a table for scientific examination.[12]

This simple truth, of course, was that all the victims were women.

Meanwhile, the newly formed Medical-Psychiatric Committee insisted that the deaths indicated there were two murderers, not one, basing their opinion solely on the fact that the first group of murders involved only elderly women, while the second group consisted of young women. In addition, insisted the committee, the psychosexual activity in both sets of killings differed. Privately, Brussel smiled and politely disagreed. Then, after the strangulations mysteriously stopped for a year, the committee disbanded.

INTO THE MINDS OF MADMEN

Meanwhile, Brussel tried to convince Bottomly that the killings were the work of the same person. He speculated that the murderer was of southern European descent, since garroting is one of the most popular methods of killing in that region of the world. He added,

"The Boston Strangler is unconsciously strangling his mother each time he placed his hands around a woman's throat, acting out some unresolved Oedipal conflicts. In fact, I bet that the older female victims in one way or another resembled the murderer's mother in height, weight, skin complexion, or hair coloring. Each of the victims may even have had a voice that reminded the strangler of his mother."

"What about the five younger women?" asked Bottomly.

"If you'll notice," responded the psychiatrist, "there is a gap in between the murders of the seven elderly women and six younger women. This is because what happened to the killer was, in two words, instant maturity. He had suddenly grown, psychosexually, from infancy to puberty to manhood. He had to commit these murders to achieve this growth. Thus, part of the man's struggle was with his lack of potency since most of the victims had been molested with objects in their vaginas. There is no or little evidence of intercourse or ejaculation. Yes, in Mary Sullivan's case, the killer ejaculated on the carpet next to her body. But, I believe that in some horrible, unexplainable way, the strangler has 'cured' himself."[13]

Brussel saw the Boston Strangler as a paranoid schizophrenic who was muscularly well proportioned. And since the paranoid reaction doesn't usually reach its peak before the prime of life, the killer was probably in his late twenties or early thirties. Because he could enter these women's apartments easily, he was probably good-looking, ingratiating, and wearing work clothes that suggested he was a maintenance man. "He's neatly-shaven and his fingernails are clean. His hair is always combed; probably having a mane of hair the average girl would envy. He is certainly unmarried and a loner."

Although Inspector Bottomly was friendly and courteous, it was obvious he was skeptical. Brussel was still one of the very few who believed in a single Boston Strangler.

Then, in November of 1964, a man identified as Albert DeSalvo came to the attention of homicide inspectors for a bizarre series of "Green Man" sexual activities in and around apartment houses. A police sergeant telephoned him at home, asking if he'd mind dropping by headquarters the next day to answer some questions. DeSalvo answered by blurting out, "Thank God! I've been stopped!" Police, at long last, had their Boston Strangler; he subsequently confessed to his psychiatrist. Furthermore, he "fit" much of the profile that Dr. Brussel provided Bottomly. The police closed the case without filing charges, and he was never tried for the killings. It turned out, however, that some of the Strangler's characteristics didn't match what Brussel had projected. For example, he did not have an unqualified hatred for his mother. She had not been domineering, although Albert knew her to be indifferent to him. She was out of the house most nights, beat him when she returned, and spawned the emotional trauma of maternal rejection.

In addition, the Strangler was not homosexual, as Brussel believed. Police spent thousands of hours investigating Boston's homosexual communities, all to no avail. DeSalvo had been heterosexually active since his early teens, and his wife told police that Albert demanded sex five or six times a day. In addition, he had been honorably discharged from the military and had worked steadily in construction for ten years.

Brussel's ability to interpret murderous behaviors and then translate psychiatric insights from those behaviors into investigative realities was certainly, and continues to be, an approved and effective tactic. But he had, and still has, his critics. For example, Jon Zonderman writes,

Brussel's profiling work, like that done for police for many years by most other consulting psychiatrists and psychologists, was done from a perspective of psychiatric diagnosis and treatment. The subjects of profiles often were described in clinical psychiatric terms, such as borderline personality or paranoid schizophrenic. The problem with this format is that it does not translate very well from the clinician to the investigator; the concept of a psychopathic monster is very different from the idea of a criminal whose behaviors, while clearly deviant, often are ordered and rational within his own context. The shifting of focus in profiling, from describing a condition of mental illness to describing a set of behavioral characteristics, allowed profiling to become far more helpful to investigators.[14]

In 1973, Albert DeSalvo was sentenced to life in prison at the maximum-security Bridgewater State Hospital for the Green Man sexual crimes. A fellow inmate stabbed him to death in his cell.

While law enforcement eyes were focused upon the Boston Strangler, a number of events, including some provocative research studies, were unfolding that would assist in the growth and development of criminal profiling. One of the least known, but most important, began in 1958, when a ten-year veteran of the Los Angeles homicide division, Pierce Brooks, used the public library and its newspaper collections to search for analogous MOs during an ongoing homicide investigation. This was the primitive forerunner of the Violent Criminal Apprehension Program (VICAP), which was spawned twenty-seven years later. Today, VICAP is considered by intimates, as well as critics, as "the farthest FBI planet out there" because of its unusual approaches to capturing criminals.

Another important milestone during these early years was the publication in 1960 of S. Palmer's *A Study of Murder* (New York: Thomas Crowell). This book presented, for the first time, results of a three-year study of some fifty-one murderers who were all serving life sentences in New England. According to Palmer's analysis, a typical killer was between the ages of twenty-two and twenty-four when he killed. Typically, a gun was employed during a heated confrontation. Invariably, the murderer was from a low socioeconomic class and had little education. Occupation skills were nonexistent. The mother was essentially a highly depressed woman who had been the victim of spousal abuse for years. The killer experienced neglect, abuse, deprivation, and, especially, "psychological frustration" throughout his childhood. This study, the first of its kind, in addition to Pierce's library research efforts, became the foundation for the future profiling of serial murderers.

In the years that followed, similar studies echoed Palmer's conclusions. Whether from doctoral dissertations, master's theses, or formal governmental studies, the results were the same: America's serial killers in the 1970s were white, in their mid-twenties, most likely knew their victims, and either jealousy or monetary gain was the most probable motivation behind the murders.

In the David "Son of Sam" Berkowitz case which unfolded in New York City during a thirteen-month period between 1976 and 1977, an unusual "criminal profile" was provided the investigators. With a "madman" on the loose firing a .44-caliber revolver at young couples as they sat in their parked cars at various borough locations, the NYPD invited Dr. Murray S. Miron, a psychology professor at Syracuse University, to submit a "psycholinguistic" analysis of the cryptic messages "Sam" was sending local tabloids, claiming he was acting under instructions communicated to him by a neighbor's dog.

Psycholinguistic analysis is today a sophisticated method of examining a murderer's spoken or written communications for clues to the origins, background, and psychology of the speaker or writer. Every sentence, phrase, syllable, word, pause, and comma is automatically scanned by computer for what it can reveal about the person who has communicated the message. When a letter is received, such as the one sent by "Sam," the psycholinguistic expert enters it into a computer by means of a terminal keyboard. The computer then scans the message and assigns each word to a set of categories that research has identified as important in the characterization of a threat. This computer also tabulates occurrences of punctuation, speech hesitancies, misspellings, and sentence structures. The expert also has at his disposal a "threat dictionary" composed of 350 categories with more than a quarter of a million words.

Today, the computer available to the BSU psycholinguistic staff stores over 15 million words gathered from analyses of ordinary spoken and written English. Any unusual usages or word occurrences are flagged by the computer for closer analysis.[15] By weighing the vocabulary usages of an author or speakers against the usage employed by the average speaker, the BSU profiler can derive a set of "signature" words that are unique to that person and which can be expected to match across differing communications.

The psycholinguistic profile of "Son of Sam" stunned all concerned in terms of how close it came to the "fit" of the suspect. Despite the fact that several eyewitnesses believed the shooter was in his mid-thirties (Berkowitz had a receding hairline), the profile correctly placed the killer's age between twenty and twenty-five. In fact, Miron's profile of Berkowitz included the information that the murderer was of average height, but overweight (he was both); that his mother was either dead or separated from the family (Berkowitz had been adopted and his adopted mother died when he was fourteen); that his father was ill or aged (he was retired); and that Berkowitz would continue to attack young, attractive women until caught. And, when finally caught, he would surrender meekly to the authorities, as he eventually did.

THE EVOLUTION OF THE FBI

When disclosures of duplicity by the Soviet Union surfaced after the end of hostilities, including theft of atomic secrets and other intelligence data by communist agents, the FBI laboratory was already at work deciphering KGB-generated messages. Before long, agents had identified and arrested numerous Russian spies, including Klaus Fuchs, Julius and Ethel Rosenberg, Lt. Col. Reino Hayhanen, and Rudolf Abel.

During the 1950s, the nation experienced a 70 percent rise in serious crimes. A decade later, the offenses jumped 148 percent. President John F. Kennedy's assassination, as well as that of civil rights leader Dr. Martin Luther King Jr., among some of the other infamous tragedies in our history, were assigned to the FBI for handling. When Brink's Inc. was robbed on January 17, 1950, in Boston, and when Jack Gilbert Graham's bomb exploded in his mother's luggage aboard a passenger plane over Colorado, killing forty-four innocent people (for her insurance monies), the FBI was there. When three young civil rights workers disappeared in Mississippi on June 21, 1964, the Bureau, then the lead investigative agency charged with the responsibility of enforcing the country's civil rights laws, went to work. Soon eight men, including a deputy sheriff and the Imperial Wizard of the White Knights of the Ku Klux Klan of Mississippi, were arrested, convicted, and sentenced to imprisonment.

By 1961, Hoover had received expanded jurisdiction over organized crime and two of its major sources of illicit revenue, gambling and loan-sharking. Soon additional statutes were signed into law, including sports bribery, extortionated credit transactions, hoodlum infiltration of legitimate businesses, bribery of local officials in gambling matters, interstate transportation of wagering paraphernalia, and numerous "white-collar crimes," including large-scale embezzlements, investment swindles, and fraudulent bankruptcies, among others.

By 1972, and in keeping with Hoover's investigative priorities that had been evolving since his appointment as director in 1924, the Bureau's objectives, methods, and strategies were constantly undergoing analysis and realignment. The director's insistence of a "quality over quantity" approach assured that the FBI gave priority attention to the forensic laboratory (including fingerprint identification), training, and information dissemination services, so that they could assist other criminal justice agencies in fulfilling their responsibilities to the citizens they served. One area of assistance involved the burgeoning crime of serial murder.

THE PHENOMENON OF SERIAL MURDER

Thus far, no one has been able to pinpoint America's first serial murderer (someone who kills ten or more victims) or document with accuracy the serial killing of the 1700s and 1800s.[16] Certainly those centuries, including the early 1900s, provided an abundance of accessible victims with little likelihood of apprehension. Most of the perpetrators probably died of natural causes, taking the number of their victims to the grave with them.

By 1900, however, the phenomenon of the serial murder was well known to law enforcement in America. Whether in the year 2003 or 1903, male serial killers have not discriminated in terms of who they murdered: other men, women, the elderly, the young, prostitutes, transients, hitchhikers, patients, etc. According to Philip Jenkins, a professor in the administration of justice program at Pennsylvania State University and the foremost authority on extreme serial murder cases (ten or more victims) in the United States during the twentieth century, law enforcement realized a serial killer was on the loose every twenty months or so.

By the late 1970s, local police were informing their presses that such a murderer was at work in their communities on an average of every four months or so. This doesn't imply there were more such killers in the nation in the late 1970s than in 1903. As Jenkins points out, "the U.S. population was considerable smaller in the earlier period. America had 76 million people in 1900. By 1920, there were 106 million. In 1940, we were up to 132 million." Thus, in the first third of the century, the nation had only between one-third and one-half of its present population and, according to Jenkins, "the rate of serial homicide was consequently higher than it might appear."[17]

Furthermore, adds Jenkins, if the United States is compared to the world's other nations between 1900 and 1940, we are at the top of the multiple homicide list. As far as is known, most countries, especially those of Europe, rarely, if ever, experienced a serial killer. Germany, because of serial murderers Peter Kurten and Fritz Haarmann, is the exception. The United Kingdon, too, knew a few, especially Frederick Field in the 1930s. Today, England can boast it has the second most prolific serial killer known to man: Dr. Harold Shipman. Where transients Henry Lee Lucas and Ottis Toole may have murdered more than three hundred over a decade or so, Shipman, as a trustworthy and attentive physician, quietly murdered 215 patients over twenty-three years. Today, he is serving fifteen life sentences without a chance for parole.

By 1915, as Jenkins's research shows, Chicago was the number one American city to be linked synonymously with multiple homicide—not in terms of the actual number of serial killers at large in that sprawling metropolis, but because of the number of victims. In the early 1890s, dozens, if not hundreds, of murders of women were committed by H. H. Holmes, especially during the popular, well-attended Chicago World's Fair of 1893–1894.

Then, during the following two decades, Johann Hoch may have strangled dozens of married women. To this day, an additional twenty to twenty-five sex-related slayings are unsolved, which may or may not have been perpetrated by Hoch. Mass poisonings by Herman Billik and the killings of Belle Guinness, who left graves in the backyards of her various Chicago residences, account for an additional fifteen to twenty victims. "Like California in the 1970s, Chicago had become unfortunately associated with serial murder. The reputation was supplanted in the 1920s by the notoriety of the even worse depredations of Prohibition gangsterism," Jenkins concludes.

According to U.S. Justice Department figures on the history of serial murderers in the U.S., the years 1795–1850 may have produced five known individuals; 1851–1900, twenty; 1901–1925, thirteen; 1926–1950, twenty; 1951–1975, sixty-six; and 1976–1993 produced 331. These last 331 serial killers murdered 1,964 victims, in addition to being suspected of killing 1,285 other victims. If we combine all the known and suspected murders by serial killers over the whole twentieth century, we have a total of almost 4,500, averaging approximately fifty a year.[18]

Thus, we see that following World War II and the beginning of the nation's baby boom, an increase in serial murder began that gained momentum during the late 1960s and early 1970s. Obviously, this new phenomenon began to both concern and interest Americans. While the mass media announced every tragic death, the public grew more and more fascinated, as reflected by the number of novels and feature-length motion pictures dealing with the topic. Serial killing became the storyline of more U.S. films between 1978 and 1983 than in the entire history of motion pictures dating back to 1910. Although law enforcement agencies at all levels were certainly focused upon apprehending multiple murderers, there had, to this point, not been a serious or systematic effort to discuss, plan, and offer any insight or understanding of the serial crime, whether it was murder, rape, fire-setting, etc.

The new phenomenon, however, was eagerly embraced by the men of the Behavioral Science Unit.

Notes

1. Philip Sugden, *The Complete History of Jack the Ripper* (New York: Carrold Graf), 1994.

2. Robert K. Ressler, *I Have Lived in the Monster: Inside the Minds of the World's Most Notorious Serial Killers* (New York: St. Martin's Paperbacks, 1997).

3. Walter C. Langer, *The Mind of Adolph Hitler: The Secret Wartime Report* (New York: Basic Books, 1972).

4. Ibid.

5. Robert G. I. Waite, afterword to *The Mind of Adolph Hitler*, by Walter C. Langer.

6. William L. Langer, foreword to *The Mind of Adolph Hitler*, by Walter C. Langer.

7. Carl Jung, *The Collected Works of C. G. Jung*, ed. Sir Herbert Read, Michael Fordham, and Gerhard Adler, vol. 10 (London: Routledge and Kegan Paul, 1966), paragraphs 400–443.

8. James A. Brussel, *Casebook of a Crime Psychiatrist* (New York: Geis Associates/Grove Press, 1968).

9. Brussel's world-famous contemporary, William H. Sheldon, then of Columbia University, was a major proponent of this type of categorization. This was pretty much the thinking in the 1950s. Considering the publication of *The Bell Curve* in the 1970s, this shouldn't be so hard to believe. Don Gibbons of San Francisco State University was also a proponent of this theory in 1950–1970. See his *Changing the Law Breaker*, published in 1965.

10. Brussel, *Casebook*.

11. Ibid.

12. Ibid.

13. Ibid.

14. Jon Zonderman, *Beyond the Crime Lab: The New Science of Investigation* (New York: Wiley and Sons, 1990).

15. Howard Teten and Pat Mullany had been doing this by hand before Miron became involved. In fact, Mullany had been directing Miron's investigative efforts for several years before this.

16. See Philip Jenkins, "Serial Murder in the United States, 1900–1940: A Historical Perspective,"*Journal of Criminal Justice* 17 (1989): 377–92; and his "A Murder Wave? Trends in America, Serial Homicide, 1940–1990," *Criminal Justice Review* 17, no. 1, (spring 1992): 1–19.

17. Jenkins, "Serial Murder."

18. Philip Jenkins, *Using Murder: The Social Construction of Serial Homicide* (New York: Aidine de Gruyter, 1944), pp. 29–47.

3 Supersleuths or Crazy Caballeros?

"In the beginning the eleven of us behaved as a bunch of crazy caballeros on the backs of cops running round and round in a two-ring circus . . ."

AN ANONYMOUS BSUER

"Those early years? I remember this: each of us was called upon day and night to absorb and perform, absorb and perform. Absorb the disappointments and discouragements and doubts of our law enforcement students who were nonetheless insisting upon us to accomplish what everyone else knew was damn near impossible..."

BSU CHIEF JACK KIRSCH

As early as 1969, a brand new FBI unit was formally being planned that would soon earn a reputation for both teaching and furnishing assistance to federal, state, and local law enforcement agencies, especially in analyzing unsolved violent serial crimes, including murder.[1]

By everyone's account, the true father of the newly christened BSU was Jack Kirsch, who would serve officially as its chief for eight months. Because the unit was his brainchild, Jack was responsible for selecting and negotiating the intra-Bureau transfers of its personnel. Jack was well qualified for such an undertaking. He had served as a special agent for nineteen years and had been engaged in police education and training for some fifteen years. He had taught officers at all levels, from raw recruits to the highest echelon of Bureau managers. Previously, Jack had been assigned as the police training coordinator for the FBI in the Chicago and Pittsburgh field divisions. In each, he was responsible for surveying the training needs of municipal, county, and state law enforcement agencies, preparing curriculum for subsequent presentation to members of these agencies, scheduling instructors to handle the topical matters, auditing and critiquing such presentations, as well as offering instruction in those areas encompassing his own expertise in firearms, defensive tactics, roadblocks, riot control, etc. In short, Jack had the unique qualifications of a background in both police education and police training, which was one of the reasons Director Hoover had selected him to head the first BSU team.

Intrinsic to his unique qualifications was the fact that Kirsch was well acquainted with the nature of police instructors, their problems, and limitations. He had operated both as an instructor and as a supervisor of instructors. He says, "Because I noticed over the years that certain individuals seemed to possess some basic ability to instruct police officers and 'to cause learning' in their respective topical areas, while others with the same general qualifications and backgrounds could not, I chose for my Master of Arts degree topic the subject 'The Successful Police Educator: A Profile.'"[2]

*   *   *

In February of 1966, Jack Kirsch, a crew-cut, good-natured, and easy-going guy, alive with enough energy and spirit to organize an entire United Nations, let alone a future faculty of twelve, received a phone call from Inspector Rufus R. Beaver at Bureau headquarters. Jack, assigned to the Pittsburgh division office as the police training coordinator, and currently working criminal cases, was advised that a new training facility was under development in northern Virginia, and that two "old-line police instructors" were to be transferred back to Bureau headquarters in order to assist in the further planning and staffing of the multi-million-dollar institution.[3] He had been selected as one of the two "old line police instructors."

Supersleuths or Crazy Caballeros?

Kirsch was unsure how he felt when he heard the news. The two "old-line instructors" would be enrolled in a graduate school within the greater Washington, D.C., area in order to attend advanced courses in the Behavioral Sciences. To Jack's delight, the other selectee was Special Agent Eugene "Crick" Crickenberger, a man he had known for years since the two attended a mob and riot control in-service. At the National Academy, then housed at headquarters in Washington, D.C., Crick, a patient, pleasant man, counseled while Jack taught.

In May of 1966, Jack was summoned to Hoover's office in the old Justice Building at Pennsylvania Avenue and Ninth Street in downtown Washington, D.C. As he took the elevator up to the fifth floor where the director had a corner office, Jack felt no trepidation. He had met and been in the presence of both Hoover and his associate director, Clyde Anderson Tolson, on other occasions.[4] Sam Noisette, the black special agent who was Hoover's doorman, had been an acquaintance since the fall of 1950.

Unlike some ex-agents, Jack never once engaged in any innuendoes, rumors, half-truths, gossips, or old bureau tales. He felt, "The two were of the finest people I was privileged to know. They were straight arrows in every respect, and a lot of people didn't know how well off they were until the old man and Mr. T were gone."

Some have said that an atmosphere of anxiety, even fear, permeated the Bureau's halls and offices. An ex-agent, Joe Schott, wrote that there were subordinates to the Chief and Mr. T who believed that if you earned a master's degree, especially in sociology, psychology, or economics, you might be considered "subversive." "Nonsense," laughed Jack when he heard such talk.

After greeting a smiling Miss Gandy, Hoover's secretary, Jack was ushered into the director's spacious office. "In my meeting with Mr. Hoover," Jack recalls, "I was assured that I had his full backing for the behavioral science project. That was a very personal and private moment for me, one that I will cherish to the day I die." Of course, Jack's appreciation and acknowledgement of "the Old Man" was echoed by virtually all the early BSUers who worked for and understood Hoover.

Early in 1967, Director Hoover ordered the Planning and Research Unit (PRU) to develop a police management training program for local, county, and state law enforcement. At this time, the law enforcement community, with federal funding through the Law Enforcement Assistance Administration (LEAA), was doing a very credible job so far as basic recruit training was concerned. Hoover was receiving calls from police chiefs throughout the country attesting to this training emphasis on the lower levels, but protesting that not enough was being done for command level personnel and chiefs. There was literally no place other than the National Academy where chiefs and/or their command personnel could turn for assistance in supervisory and executive-type training.

In order to implement Mr. Hoover's directive, the PRU selected several experienced field agents for transfer to the training division. Because Jack and Crick were already in place and had the necessary behavioral science backgrounds, they were asked to help in this instructor-development process. With regard to the actual materials to be taught, they realized that all parts of the psychodynamics of human behavior—human relations, leadership styles, motivational principles, human interaction, small group processes, self actualization, selective and group perceptions, etc.—would have to be structured and related to law enforcement problems and solutions. The main goal of the course was to enable police supervisors and managers to succeed in current and future leadership roles through enhanced behavioral skills. Knowing that organizational effectiveness is heavily based on sociological and psychological principles, participants were urged to become more effective in their human interaction concerns. A direct by-product of this learning activity was to increase productivity by directing the efforts of others.

This forty-hour police management program immediately became a cornerstone of the curriculum for the new academy. Until the new installation opened, two-man teams of management trainers constantly travelled throughout the United States, preaching and perfecting this new management philosophy. "Bud" Teten, one of the original members of the BSU, was part of this early management training effort. Because Crick was heavily involved in the training of these two-man teams, as well as structuring the content of the materials being taught, he was assigned as a management trainer in July of 1968. In addition to conducting the research for and writing his master's thesis, taking his comprehensive exams, teaching and counseling National Academy students, and other duties, he traveled as a member of a two-man management team until the new academy opened in May 1972. With few exceptions, the two-man management teams became the nucleus of the Management Science Unit (MSU). The MSU continues to this day to train police supervisors and managers, using behavioral science concepts applicable to modern police organizations, principles identified and translated to the everyday work environment and universally accepted because of their practicality.

As an aside, they realized shortly after the academy opened that they were offering advanced management training to everyone except their own managers. Today, supervisory and executive training is an integral part of the responsibilities of the MSU and the career development of FBI personnel. For several years after he retired, because the demand for this type of training remained, Crick continued to travel as a private consultant and trainer throughout the United States From 1987 to 1997 he was under contract to the International Criminal Investigative Assistance Program (ICITAP), administered by the U.S. departments of State and Justice to conduct similar training throughout Central and South America.

Known as the Training and Inspection division before training broke off as a separate division, its small-group sessions, along with those of the new agent and FBI National Academy classes, were conducted in a training wing of the FBI headquarters, the old fourth-floor passageways of the Justice Department building in downtown Washington, D.C. The Planning and Research Unit conducted the screening process for the training division, along with Jack and Crick. Little did anyone realize, including Kirsch and Crickenberger, that they were really grooming the BSUers of the future.

The screening committee's ultimate selection criterion was a thorough knowledge of the police subculture, plus an ability to teach. They were interested in a candidate's interpersonal behavior, decision-making processes, and formal organizational skills. As they questioned and listened, they quietly noted the individual's optimism, self-confidence, morality, leadership potential, social interaction, values, perseverance, etc.

Most of those selected were already police training instructors with considerable training experience. Others were former high school or college instructors. In each case, cognitive abilities and teaching skills were carefully evaluated in both the interview and later during attendance at one or more of the in-service training sessions. After the selections had been determined, and the agents agreed to transfer, those without master's degrees and teaching credentials were sent to colleges and universities near their homes to obtain them.

Once the agent obtained the required degree or credential, prior to the Academy's opening, he was transferred to Headquarters where, in most cases, he was assigned to the training division.

Although filled with mixed emotions about the new assignment, Jack knew he had no choice. It was a fait accompli: he was headed back to Bureau headquarters for the third time in fifteen years. He was happy in Pittsburgh, his field office of preference, having been recently transferred there from Chicago, where he had been the police training coordinator. Both he and his wife were from Erie, Pennsylvania, only a hundred or so miles from their families and friends. Now, having to go back to college at the age of forty wouldn't be easy.

Meanwhile, Crick, a native Virginian, had been assigned to the

Seattle field office. He worked in a number of resident agencies covered by Seattle, for example, Yakima, Port Angeles, and Vancouver. Little did the two realize, in July of 1966, when they were reunited in Beaver's office at headquarters for their final instructions, that they would become best friends, living next door to each other in northern Virginia for the next thirty-one years. "Sociology friends used to call us a basic small group, a dyad," smiles Kirsch.

At SOG, or "seat of government," the affectionate euphemism for FBI headquarters, Jack and Crick received their reassignments to the training division's Planning and Research Unit (PRU), the "shop" directly responsible for staffing the new academy. Unit Chief, Inspector Chris Moran, was a crusty, caustic veteran of the Bureau. Kirsch recalls, "Old Chris Moran was an earthy guy you just couldn't help loving. He really knew his way around the bureaucracy. His number one man was Dr. Bill Mooney, who later became the assistant director of the training division at Quantico. To show you how critical they were to us with regard to the decision-making process, all the administrative work was handled by the 'M&Ms' [Moran and Mooney]. When a memo was written by Crick or myself, and later Pfaff, Brewster, or Holland, or any of the other agents assigned to PRU, it went through Mooney and Moran to Deputy Assistant Director Tom Jenkins, and then to our assistant director, Joe Casper. If it cleared Casper's office, it could be routed to any of the other divisions that might have an interest in the contents. After all the concerned parties signed off, the memo went to Tolson's office, and eventually in to the Old Man himself. Hoover read an inordinate amount of mail, often taking it home with him. I know for a fact that he personally approved Crick and I as forerunners of the BSU."

In as much as Jack and Crick were Hoover's initial guinea pigs for the Academy's experimental behavioral science program, it's interesting to see how amazingly similar the two were. During World War II, both enlisted in the U.S. Army Air Corps (the "brown shoe air-force") at the age of seventeen; both enrolled in a liberal arts college under the G. I. Bill; Crick majored in psychology while Jack majored in journalism with an English minor (there was no sociology major at his college in 1946); both married their childhood sweethearts while in college; and both entered the Bureau upon graduation in 1950.

Although both were from the East Coast (Jack from Pennsylvania and Crick from Virginia), both started their FBI careers as agents on the West Coast (Crick in San Francisco and Seattle; Jack in Los Angeles and San Francisco). Both had almost daily contact with law enforcement since both worked criminal cases in the field (stolen cars, checks, interstate theft, selective service violations, deserters, bank robberies, unlawful flight fugitives, etc.).

Before the opening of the Academy, both were active in police training, Crick as a counselor for the new agent session at the Bureau and Jack as a firearms instructor and lecturer. In 1966, when both were transferred back to headquarters, each had over fifteen years of service in the FBI. Both were with their original spouses and each had three children. For over thirty-one years, the two lived next door to each other in northern Virginia. Both have recently celebrated their golden wedding anniversaries, and they are best friends today.

"But most important of all," says Jack, "both of us were old-line police instructors. We taught techniques and mechanics of arrest, stopping cars and transporting prisoners, handcuffing, collection and preservation of evidence, crime scene searches, report writing, and a host of other general law enforcement topics to the everyday working officer. In addition, we were authorized to teach mob and riot control techniques, having attended a specialized, two-week school to prepare us for this task. The Bureau was aware that we had been totally accepted by and into the law enforcement community and Mr. Hoover was counting on this as the lynchpin of our Behavioral Science endeavors."

The third "old-line police instructor" to be reassigned to PRU was special agent Dick Kohler, a well-known, vociferously loyal Special Agent, who was already attending graduate school at Catholic University and was slated to be the audio-visual expert at the new institution. Says Jack, "Dick was a former police officer and a terrific instructor. Crick and I considered ourselves lucky to have him assigned with us. Thus, the Behavioral Science Unit owes its very existence to PRU (the Planning and Research Unit) and three very dedicated and totally committed FBI agents trying to make Mr. Hoover's dream come true."

The challenge for Kirsch and Crickenberger was to find a graduate school that would admit them. After all, both men were already in their forties. In addition, these were trying times for both America and the Federal Bureau of Investigation. Dominating the newspaper headlines were civil rights marches, with their often resultant violence, black militant posturing, anti-Vietnam war protests, strident student sit-ins, sleepovers and shut downs of university administrative offices, bombings and burning of churches in the South, lure-in ambushes and killings of police officers, and cries of "Freedom now!" None of these events endeared the FBI to academe. To some officials in higher education, FBI agents were little more than pariahs; to others, they were plain nuisances. In Jack's and Crick's cases, the two had been absent from the university too long. After all, their transcripts were more than sixteen years old.

The two found the perfect university for the social sciences courses and degrees they needed, nearby George Washington University. In addition, they had the perfect "hook." The chairman of the sociology department, Dr. Robert Brown, happened to be the brother-in-law of a friend and fellow FBI agent, Bob Hurley. Brown risked his reputation by inviting the two aging agents to academically challenge the twenty-year-old "kids" for a semester. In September of 1966, Jack and Crick began their trial runs. Sitting in the first rows of each of their classes, taking careful notes, spending hours preparing for tests, and meticulously researching and writing their term papers, the two stunned everyone by receiving straight As, to the chagrin of fellow agents and classmates.

What made going back to college an even greater challenge was the fact that Jack and Crick had numerous other responsibilities besides earning degrees. They were scheduled to lecture before new agent classes, in-service groups, and the incoming National Academy classes, prepare bulletins and materials for the Bureau's Field Police Instructor Corps, in addition to handling a host of other duties that the SOG chiefs believed were in the best interest of the Bureau's training division. Jack recalls:

> But we were on our way, and as far as what we taught the new agents, in-service classes and the like, we would send up appropriate memoranda after approval by the M&Ms, but I doubt if there was a handful of personnel who understood, or even cared, what we taught. We were the old pros of the police training profession and they relied upon us to do the right thing. And we did. Every unit, every section, every division head had their own nut to crack, and recruited appropriately trained and/or educated people to do the job. We decided what the course content would be, what the syllabus would contain, what text books would be bought, what outside reading materials would be selected, and, in many instances, who the students would be. We even structured our materials as if we were the students. Street time told us what was really needed out in the real world and we did our best to provide it. We pioneered teaching values and police-community relations thirty years ago. Today it is one of the foremost topics on all law enforcement and most political agendas.
>
> Meanwhile, Bill Mooney, willful, steadfast, and meticulous, initiated the search for academic validation and conducted most of the contact work with various areas of Academe. As they did this, the M&Ms periodically reviewed our materials. But neither of them had the in-depth know-how to impose. Besides, we were part of the PRU

and we were just doing our assigned responsibilities. They trusted our judgment and we did not let them down. I used the same management philosophy when selecting our original crew and when we opened at Quantico. Pick the very best people you can find, assign the mission, and then get out of the way. I had one advantage however. I had some idea of what had to be done. But, I didn't impose. And no one ever let us down . . . especially when we took our show on the road in an attempt to hone our presentations and flesh out programs of instruction for future years at the Academy.

In those early, often halcyon days, new agent training at Quantico consisted of lectures on federal laws under FBI jurisdiction, FBI rules and regulations, firearm training, and practical problems related to crime scene investigations and arrests. New agents and old, as well as their trainer-instructors, slept on narrow beds, four to eight in a barracks room, and ate their meals in a small dining room. The cuisine was certainly nutritious and adequate, but nothing to leave home for. Since the academy was located in a dense forest, miles from Interstate 95, and since few cars were available to go anywhere, the after-work hours were somewhat empty.

In his memoirs, *No Left Turn*, Joseph L. Schott describes new agent training in the late sixties and early seventies:

> Evenings were dull, dull, dull. We could loll on the beds in the dormitory rooms upstairs or slump in the chairs of the drab lounge on the ground floor, reading such scintillating periodicals as *Readers Digest* and *American Legion Magazine*. We could go to the movies on the Marine base or to downtown Quantico and drink beer. We had to sign out on a register when we left the building in the evening and sign in again when we returned before the 11 P.M. curfew.
>
> Bang, bang, bang on the firearms training range all day—pistols, shotguns, rifles, and submachine guns. The practical problems simulating crime investigations consisted of lifting fingerprints,

making plaster casts of tire tracks, photography, and so forth, and simulated arrest situations. The nucleus of the academic curriculum was the Big Manual, the Bible of the FBI. It was called the Big Manual to differentiate it from the Handbook. There were really two big Manuals: the Manual of Instructions and the Manual of Rules and Regulations. The Manual of Instructions contained a listing of all the violations of federal law, as well as all the other investigative matters under the jurisdiction of the FBI. It cited pertinent parts of the law for each, listed the elements of the crimes in one-two-three order, and outlined suggested procedures to follow in investigating each. If an agent screwed up a case in some way and a supervisor or inspector found out that one of the suggested procedures had not been followed, the agent could get into trouble for committing a "substantive" error.

The Manual of Rules and Regulations was the Old Testament of the Bureau, laying down rules of personal conduct that were as punitive and unforgiving as the ancient laws of the Hebrews. The manual contained the revealed word of the Director and catalogued most of the mortal "subs" (substantive errors) that could be committed by an FBI agent. . . . The Big Manual was in a constant state of revision and enlargement. Most of the thickness of the Manual of Instructions was caused by the passage of new laws for the FBI to enforce. Most of the thickness of the Manual of Rules and Regulations could be attributed to the corpses of those careers killed for breaking the Director's rules or committing acts that the Director condemned.[6]

Russ Vorpagel, who joined the BSU in 1978 as a profiler, recalls, "I knew Kirsch and most of the others who formed the first BSU wave, or group, as early as 1964. After that, the concept started snowballing. The President asked Hoover to teach more local police training. Hoover said, 'Sure, we'll do all the training you want. But we don't have the manpower.' So the president asked Congress for 450 new FBI positions, strictly for men (there were no women in the Bureau at that time) to do police training. So, it wasn't long before local law enforcement began sending its officers to police training in both the old Marine Corps chow halls at Quantico. But less than one hundred cops were brought in twice a year. And it wasn't long before that jumped to 250 men and women four times a year, a real increase. And who did the first teaching? Crick and Cherry. We called Jack 'Cherry' because Kirsch means 'Cherry' in German."

By the time Vorpagel met "Cherry," Kirsch and Crickenberger, among others, were heavily involved with teaching at the National Academy. This, of course was not the behavioral science unit, which would not be formed for another seven years. "Those two fellas," says Russ, "more than anyone else started the sophisticated retraining of local police."

In 1964, the National Academy at the FBI facility in Quantico consisted of six prefabricated plywood dormitories, three small classrooms, the use of the Marine chow hall, and its basement with small-arms gun range. Women, of course, were banned from the National Academy. Russ recalls, "The SAC [Special Agent in Charge] in charge of the Academy would not allow women to teach. In fact, he almost had a heart attack when women were dispatched from headquarters to teach the staff how to make overhead transparencies, cut-outs for the overheads, etc."

Two of Vorpagel's favorite stories from these early years at the National Academy in Quantico deal with SAC "Shakey Shirt" Sloan. In the first episode, Russ recalls that as soon as the supervisor had left for a Friday night party, he, Teten, and a few other agents, certain Sloan would not return that night, began playing hearts for money, a card game that FBI rules prohibited. Well past the 11:00 P.M. curfew, and with a bottle of brandy in the middle of the table, Sloan walked in from a pouring rain. Dripping wet, and having had a few too many drinks himself, he looked around the room and screamed, "Lights are supposed to be out! What are you doing in here? What's going on? Where's Wright?"

For a moment, the group froze. Then, soaking wet, Wright walked in. Immediately spotting Sloan, he said disgustedly, "I've been looking for the log in order to sign in."

"Yeah, then what's the brandy doing on the table?"

Russ responded without hesitation, "Well, we're rehearsing a skit on what goes on in drinking and gambling houses and houses of ill repute and prostitution. We're going to be teaching how people get ripped off when they drink too much. So, we're simply setting up a skit on what we're going to be teaching."

Sloan peered at the table and the men for a moment, then mumbled, "Aw, bullshit," and stomped out. Russ, who was not one of Sloan's favorites, says that the SAC was not happy that evening.

On another occasion in 1964, Russ drove his red Renault to the Academy from Baltimore. Of course, having a private car on Academy ground was forbidden, but Vorpagel still had his military papers and ID with him, so he was able to easily obtain a Marine permit. But unfortunately for Russ, Sloan, at the time, wanted to buy a new Renault. As soon as he spotted it in the parking lot, he wanted to know who owned it so he could find out if the owner liked the car.

Russ says, "After he checked around and learned that the registration belonged to me, he went ape-shit, screaming and yelling about insurance. I yelled back, 'I have insurance!' He yelled back, 'You've got to get that car out of here by the weekend. And next weekend, when you go home after you get the car outta here, you go by bus!' If you don't already know it, some of the SACs were unreal, unreasonable, and just plain crazy. Many of them in the beginning didn't like police training. But, all in all, in spite of the Sloans, we had a good time. We were able to overcome."

Russ adds, "So our small circle was really the precursor to the BSU. Oh, we certainly had our annoyances. For example, Teten and I roomed together and naturally sent our shirts out to the cleaners together. In those days the shirts would come back all mixed up; we were always trying to figure out whose underwear belonged to whom. His name was in the collars of my shirts; my name was in his shirts. But we could live with all that. There were greater issues to deal with, like how a lot of FBI people felt that all cops were untrustworthy, and Teten and I and the others had to fight that prejudice."

Meanwhile, although the Behavioral Science Unit did not exist during the late 1960s, Jack and Crick were beginning to visualize an interdisciplinary curriculum that would address current issues. Then, as now, students—intelligent, skeptical, pragmatic, and certainly outspoken—asked, "How are your lectures going to help us on the job?" Of course, Jack and Crick, anticipating such a question, also wondered about the relevance of presentations and how they might adapt sociology to everyday law enforcement problems.

Naturally, many of the National Academy's police officers, and FBI agents and cadets attending the classes, equated Jack and Crick, the new behavioral science majors, with social workers. While the two educated their students regarding the socialization process—how humans learn, their physical and social needs, the various structures of their value systems, the social stratification in the United States, the nature of juvenile delinquency, etc.—it was soon apparent that something more than an elementary course in sociology was needed if a meaningful curriculum in behavioral science was to become viable. Jack recalls:

Crick had majored in psychology at the University of Virginia and he began to structure his educational endeavors more into that area. We were proving to ourselves and to the skeptics both inside and outside of the Bureau that we could do it. We concentrated on human values and how they were attained. Police community relations was factored into the mix with the addition of another 'old-line instructor,' Special Agent John Pfaff, into the unit. 'Old Slick' was an accomplished general police instructor who was completing a graduate degree in political science at American University in the district. The year was 1968 and Washington, D.C., was burning down.

INTO THE MINDS OF MADMEN

A large part of Jack's and Crick's instruction to the National Academy students was delivered in the main classroom of the FBI annex at Ninth and Pennsylvania Avenues in downtown D.C.[7] The classroom was an architectural antique of blackened gray stone, as dank and gloomy as Macbeth's castle. The building was vast, with high ceilings that the Bureau had converted into a beehive of cubbyholes and classrooms by building partitions and lowering ceilings with plywood. During those early years, the National Academy normally consisted of a hundred students in addition to whoever audited or simply sat in from headquarters. Students sat six or seven across, row upon row, "about as far as you could see." The classrooms were damp, sultry places in summer, and damp, chilly places in winter. Most annoying was the constant whir of electric motors, heaters, and fans all year long.

To handle such a large number in the lecture hall, and at the same time provide a give-and-take situation, required more than one instructor—hence the creation of the team-teaching concept, two instructors in one classroom, another FBI first. One instructor was in front of the class while the other remained in the rear, ready to take over his part of the presentation. Often, both lectured in front of the class. Not only did the new teaching technique keep the students awake during the sweltering humid days of summer, but it allowed the instructors to engage in meaningful dialog with relatively small groups. Howard Teten recalls:

> Prior to 1972, each National Academy consisted of one hundred students and there were two sessions per year. They sat in a long, narrow room on the fourth floor of the old Justice Building in Washington, D.C., with window air conditioners running right beside them. I forget how many seats it was across, but there were only about six or eight. The length of the room made it hard to hear if your name was in the last part of the alphabet. Students had to be

94

passed a microphone to ask questions. I assure you, the new Academy classrooms were a *great* improvement for both the student and the instructor.

Jack Kirsch, Eugene "Crick" Crickenberger, Dick Kohler, and John Pfaff were slowly coming of age in an increasingly complex Bureau maze, least of which was a fledgling "behavioral science" unit that brought, at best, a faint and amused smile of doubtful recognition to the FBI veterans. Focusing upon the future of their brand new unit, Jack and Crick looked forward to the opportunity of hiring men with equally shrewd, creative brains.

The four "old-line police instructors" were still learning, voraciously, at break-neck speed, and yet in a sense humbly. As they began searching for staff to "pigeonhole" for appearances before the National Academy from the hundreds of possible special agent candidates at work in the field, Jack, Crick, Dick, and John impressed everyone with their peculiar listening qualities. They sat slumped down behind their modest desks, guiding the interviews and the endless questions, never dominating or controlling, turning their intent, restless eyes on one man after another as if trying, as each spoke, to seize what was valuable from each of their personalities to absorb it into the program. They were searching for strong, aggressive, independent men like themselves. "Even the M&Ms had made staff selections," says Jack, "and good ones at that!" Anyone who appeared diplomatic or submissive was politely dismissed.

"Take, for example, Pat Mullany," says Jack with an impish grin. "It was obvious from the get-go that this psychologist of note, and a former Christian Brother [a Catholic half-priest usually assigned to teach a Catholic school] to boot, was a winner. He was recruited to give lectures before the NA and was enrolled in a number of classes in New York to update his expertise. And, there was Howard 'Bud' Teten, a special agent in Memphis who had worked the King assassination, who became the Bureau's foremost criminologist. This pair wrote the first book on profiling. We now had the nucleus of our instructional team in place."

In 1970, not only was the PRU assigned to staff the Behavioral Sciences Unit, but Jack and the entire unit were busy selecting additional personnel for both the Management and Educational Units. By then, Jack and Crick had completed their course work at George Washington University and were finalizing their master's theses. For his study to ascertain the profile of a successful police educator, Jack chose the Job Analysis and Interest Measurement (JAIM) as his social-psychological instrument. So did Crick, whose research centered on the Police Community Relations Officer.

A year later, with their master's degrees completed, the time had come for the two to take their show to police departments across America. While Crickenberger assisted the Management Unit, Kirsch and Pfaff worked on a values/police/community relations concept; Mullany and Teten refined their profiling concepts. Dick Kohler was working on staffing and audiovisual, and not of the nascent BSU. It was beginning to look as though the basic curriculum for the new Behavioral Science Unit, set to open the following year, would encompass the latest information from the fields of sociology, psychology, criminology, and political science. The team, in short, was conceiving a practical, sixty-hour course for everyday police officers.

With the recently constructed, brand-new Academy set to become operational in May 1972, it was imperative that the four-man team of Kirsch, Pfaff, Mullany, and Teten, which at times was not formally designated as anything, determine how many instructors it would require to teach 1,200 students a year, rather than the 200 who were currently completing their instruction in the headquarters annex. In addition, Jack had to negotiate the accreditation of the Academy's new curriculum with a major university. Granting academic credit to those successfully completing the programs was paramount, and, to this day, still is.

Supersleuths or Crazy Caballeros?

Obviously, nearby University of Virginia was the team's logical choice. It had prestige and was readily accessible. Jack was selected to contact the chairperson of the psychology department. A meeting was arranged between the two, but after a lengthy discussion, Jack returned to the Academy without a commitment. The psychology department faculty had voted no. Jack remembers, "Our Academy people in the other disciplines had better luck with the university. Management, education, legal, and the forensic sciences had all scored victories. Behavioral science was once again the odd man out in academia."

The team's second choice was the sociology-anthropology department at the University of Virginia in Charlottesville. With a few reservations and qualifications, Jack was welcomed with open arms and Professor Eddie Erickson was assigned as the chief liaison officer. "Eddie was an anthropologist with a first-class mind," says Kirsch, "and he promised to teach me the principles of his profession if I would acquaint him with mine. He had no law enforcement background and I laughed that we were even, since I couldn't spell anthropology. We became fast friends, and to this day the BSU gives the Eddie Erickson Award to the top behavioral science student in each class. Eddie died young, but his enthusiasm and guidance were indispensable to us. Without him, we would still be looking for a place to hang our academic hat. In fact, Eddie had such an effect on me personally that after I graduated from GWU, I enrolled in the anthropology department at Catholic University and learned how to spell the word!"

With a university now guaranteeing BSU accreditation, Jack and his staff were ready to select the final instructors to supplement the original team. With Crick firmly in the clasp of Kirsch's police management team, Pfaff, Kohler, and Teten launched a series of interviews. They decided the unit needed a minimum of ten instructors, plus Jack, who fully intended to share in the teaching duties. "With our team teaching concept approved at the highest level," recalls Jack, "we thus put the first BSU squad together. We called ourselves 'The Winners,' and the appendage was no misnomer. Each man was a winner in his own right. Ten of the eleven were armed forces veterans. We all had graduate degrees. Most of us were general police instructors who had 'been on the boards.'"

With admiration and deep affection, Kirsch listed the initial BSU team in the following manner:

1. Unit Chief: Me;
2. My #1 Man: John "Old Slick" Pfaff;
3. Criminologist Howard "Bud" Teten: USMC veteran, former police officer, our first profiler, subsequent unit chief of Institutional Research at the Academy;
4. Psychologist Pat Mullany: Bud's partner in the profiling business, retired as a special agent in charge of a major field office; Pat was the first FBI agent to ever officially negotiate with a subject holding hostages, and created many of the original concepts involved with negotiations; later, he would serve as the president of the Society of Former Special Agents of the FBI, Inc.;
5. Criminologist Con Hassel: USMC Purple Heart veteran, LLB, master's degree, prime mover in creation of the hostage negotiations concept; during his eight years as Chief of Special Operations and Research Unit, he was responsible for all crisis management training, including hostage negotiations and all the operational tactical training for the FBI Hostage Rescue Team, as well as certain elite U.S. and foreign military units;
6. Psychologist Tom Strentz: Con's partner in hostage scheme; also USMC; Ph.D.; broadened the "Stockholm Syndrome," a hostage negotiation theory and technique;
7. Dick Harper: identifies himself as the "liberal sociologist"; a great instructor who, after his tour at the Academy, was given a squad in the field;
8. Larry Monroe: USMC, a jack-of-all-trades who took over the BSU after Pfaff retired, was section chief at the Academy when

he retired in 1994; he developed and taught a course "Urban Police Problems";

9. Bill Peters: an old line instructor, truly bilingual; taught sociology, some psych, eventually assigned as a Legat in South America;

10. Jim Siano: basketball star at Seton Hall in New Jersey, taught police community relations and a host of other subjects; after a tour on the inspection start, became a field office supervisor;

11. Al Whittaker: U.S. Naval Academy graduate, after a short stay with BSU was transferred to the New Agent's Training Unit, later became a SAC.

These new arrivals taught a range of community relations, sociology, and crisis intervention courses. Howard Teten and three others taught the applied criminology course which he had developed while part of the "Flying Management Training Squad." Four taught the course, employing team-teaching techniques. Teten and Mullany made up one team, while Hassel, Strentz, and I made up the other. Although the opportunity to meet command-level law enforcement personnel from different departments all across the nation was interesting, the assignment wreaked havoc on the home lives of the agents.

On May 10, 1972, the Academy, after much preparation, finally opened its doors. Jack and his men offered a sixty-hour survey course approved by UVA. For the, first time in law enforcement, sociology, psychology, criminology, and political science (police community relations) were integrated into a parlance that all NA students could understand.

Soon the Academy was in the forefront of law enforcement education, with police veterans from across America arriving with a wealth of street smarts and experience and a basic, high-school education. Each who attended roomed with another, with a complete set of behavioral science texts placed in their rooms. Reading assignments introduced students to a new vocabulary, while Jack's staff was available to counsel or assist in any way possible. Whenever someone with a college degree attended the NA, Kirsch arranged for that person to earn additional graduate units.

Erickson and the Charlottesville faculty were as good as their word. The BSU prospered, and, after the initial "shakedown" course was taught, the staff was prepared for anything. They taught anyone and everyone, no matter at what level of education or locale: in-service classes, local police schools, and state law enforcement academies. Repeatedly, they took their show on the road and taught wherever requested, including colleges and universities. They held symposia on a variety of subjects, always with Eddie Erickson standing by, if needed.

And who was the consistent, unyielding strength behind the fledgling, sometimes unorganized BSU staff in those early days? "Why, the secretaries, of course!" acknowledged Jack Kirsch recently.

After the "Winners" had been finally assembled, and before we really became operational as a teaching force at the Academy, everyone knew that an eleven-man squad could not operate long without an experienced secretary. We lucked out when we found Kathy V. Bryan, who had formerly been the secretary of a general criminal squad in our Washington field office. I nicknamed her "Kate the Great" because she too was a "Winner." Not only was Kate a superb stenographer, she was an administrative assistant long before there was such a position in our future. She screened all my incoming calls, fended off undesirables, proofread all outgoing materials, set up a tickler system to insure all assignments were met, organized and managed the files so pertinent data was easily retrieved, kept my calendar so that I showed up where I was supposed to be when I was supposed to be there, and in general was our girl Friday. She was bright, vivacious, and the mother of two little girls. Kate made it a pleasure to come to work. I wanted to take her with me when I was reassigned, but to do so would have left the squad unglued and "Old Slick" speechless. I am sure she kept the BSU in line until Judy Rice took over. And God bless Judy Rice, too. We really lucked out when we got those fine, great, classy ladies as our secretaries back-to-back.

In return, Judy Rice says, "You could search the world over and you would not find a better, more wonderful human being than Jack Kirsch. Jack was highly respected and he had power, but you never knew it. He was one of the kindest, most decent people the FBI was honored to have employed. I never heard anyone say anything derogatory about Jack. Everyone loved him. It was a sad day for the Academy when he retired. He was, and is, pure gold."

Then Jack was promoted to Branch chief, and was in charge of a number of units: "Our assistant director, Tom Jenkins, called me to his office early in January of 1973. He told me I was being reassigned from the BSU to the Academy administration, and that in all probability, Jack Pfaff would take over the squad. I remained in daily contact with most of my original crew during the next five years until I retired, as well as to this day. The old bromide still rings true. New friends are silver, but old friends are gold."

Jack remained at the Academy until he retired. Russ Vorpagel recalls how Kirsch was so enthusiastic about his teaching of police techniques that on one occasion he almost lost his life.

Cherry, in those early years at the Academy, was teaching some very Mickey-Mouse course such as "Crime Scene Analysis," or "How to Investigate a Homicide." He took us into a field next to the firing range, and said, "Now, go look for a body. When you find it, begin a crime scene analysis by searching and collecting evidence." He had hidden an old mannequin under some old sod. One of the agents spotted the "body," and with our search over, the evidence collected, and the scene investigated, Cherry said, "Now we're going to search for some fugitives." He walked us over to the mock village that had been built on the FBI grounds and ordered, "O.K., now you guys get into that building where the 'fugitives' are hiding. These guys are deserters and you're to bring them out." Well, there were five cops in our group with all kinds of experiences doing just this. We had a better idea of how to handle the deserters than he did. But we said nothing and went ahead to get into the mock building. As we went in through the front, Jack went around the back, pounded on the back door, couldn't break in, so dove right through the plate glass window. Now, the window wasn't high enough and with Jack's height and weight going through the plate glass, the crash took his scalp off from the top of his head all the way to the back. The dive actually tore his scalp right off. You can imagine the blood, to say nothing of all the shock and surprise of us cops and agents. Cherry was in an ugly shape. But, being the good guy that he was, and still is, he recovered nicely. And, it was the Old Man himself who later gave Jack special permission to wear a crewcut. No other FBI agent had been given that special permission.

Russ adds, "As well intentioned as Cherry and Crick were teaching us police supposedly new police training methods, they weren't teaching us much we didn't already know. But, we shared what we knew and the instructors were decent enough that we all got along fine."

One of the first murders that Teten and Mullany teamed for dealt with the unsolved disappearance of seven-year-old Susan Jaeger during the early morning hours of June 24, 1973. While on a camping trip with her family in Montana's Headwaters State Park, Susan was snatched from her tent before dawn as her parents slept nearby. Apparently the abductor had been studying the family with binoculars from a nearby hill. Peter Dunbar, an agent in the FBI's Bozeman, Montana, office, and later the U.S. Attorney for Montana, was confronted with an abduction without any leads and called Howard Teten. Dunbar had attended Teten's lectures at the Academy and now needed his assistance.

Bob Ressler (a newly arrived instructor at the Academy), Teten, and Mullany—affectionately known to some BSUers as "the triple threat"—analyzed Dunbar's memos, reports, photos of the kidnapping scene, and various police depositions and diagrams. They concluded that the "unsub" (a police term for an "unknown subject") most likely to be involved had stumbled upon the family outing during his habitual night prowl and impulsively cut through the victims' tent and grabbed the little girl.

From their growing experiences in such matters, and their accumulated knowledge, the three BSUers concluded the kidnapper was a young Caucasian male, a loner who was born in Bozeman and did not live far from the campsite, and who more than likely murdered the seven-year-old. Pat Mullany recalls, "We felt the killer was a subtle combination of simple schizophrenia and a psychopath, murdering for the sheer purpose of exploring body parts. We warned Pete Dunbar, who had a daughter the same age and took this case very personally, that this killer would be saving body parts as souvenirs."

Armed with this rather crude profile, Dunbar and Bozeman police narrowed the area's suspects down to a twenty-two-year-old Vietnam veteran, David Meirhofer, after a neighbor telephoned police to complain that he showed unusual interest in his children. By coincidence, Dunbar had gone to school with Meierhofer's mother and he knew David personally. Dunbar was stunned. "How could a former Boy Scout, three-year Marine veteran, a nice looking, well-groomed, gentle, courteous, exceptionally intelligent, and well-educated building contractor be guilty of such a kidnapping and so grisly a killing?" he asked Teten.

Although an informant had fingered Meirhofer as a possibility, no physical evidence linked him to Susan Jaeger's disappearance. Then in late January 1974, bone fragments were found among the ashes in several burning barrels located at a farm Meirhofer frequented. On the theory that the bone fragments might be human, they were submitted to a physical anthropologist at the Smithsonian Institution. He was able to piece together a skull and, by repositioning the teeth, identify the skull as that of a local nineteen-year-old woman who had been missing for some time. The woman, it turned out, had rejected the suspect's advances and had disappeared shortly thereafter.

Suddenly Meirhofer was back in the spotlight. Surprisingly, his attorney, Douglas Dassinger, demanded that David be given a polygraph as well as "truth serum." He passed both. Dunbar, who had set up a command post at the abduction site, concluded that the triple threat Teten-Mullany-Ressler team, and the informant, were dead wrong. On July 25, a month later, Pete officially ended the ground search for Suzy. "Somehow he had prepared himself to pass," recalls Mullany.

Back at the Academy, the three were nonetheless convinced that Meierhofer, who they insisted was a subtle psychopath, had coldly murdered both females regardless of whether he passed the "truth" tests. "It just was so obvious to us that he was the kidnapper and killer," recalls Teten. "We simply had to keep going in order to convince the authorities out there." Mullany adds, "We felt the little girl was dead. And we predicted that because the kidnapper would covet the victim for himself, he would call the family."

Then, on the first anniversary of Susan's abduction, a man telephoned the Jaeger home in Farmington, Michigan, claiming he was the kidnapper and was keeping their daughter alive. "I bought her a birthday present," he said. To prove he was the abductor, he identified correctly Suzy's birth defects, including her "humpy fingernails." Susan's mother, Marietta, who received the call, turned on a tape recorder that Teten and the Bozeman police had advised her to keep next to the telephone.

Initially, Meirhofer sounded arrogant, even taunting. "But," recalls Mrs. Jaeger, "my reaction was not what he anticipated. I told him that I truly, honestly forgave him, and that leaving Montana for home in

Supersleuths or Crazy Caballeros?

Farmington was the most difficult thing I had to do, since it felt like breaking continuity with both the situation and Suzy. My concern and compassion for him somehow took him aback. He let his guard down and just broke down and cried." According to an FBI voice analysis, the caller was Meirhofer. But in Montana at the time, a voice analysis was insufficient to obtain a probable-cause search warrant.

Mullany, Ressler, and Teten offered a bizarre suggestion: allow Mrs. Jaeger to fly to Bozeman and meet Meirhofer. Pat argued, "After listening to the tape, I was absolutely convinced that he could be dominated by a strong woman. All our evidence was circumstantial. We were at a critical point."

The meeting was arranged to occur in Dassinger's office. Marietta pleaded with David to tell her about Susan. Meirhofer showed no emotion and said little. It was obvious he had been warned by his attorney not to say much, lest he incriminate himself. Pat commented after the encounter, "He'll call again. He wants to rid himself of guilt. Next time he calls, he'll tell the family that Suzy is dead. None of us wanted to let go. Marietta was our only link to David."

Within three days of Marietta's return to Michigan, she received a collect telephone call from Salt Lake City. A "Mr. Travis" explained that he, and not the "man up in Bozeman," had kidnapped Susan. Before he could explain further, Mrs. Jaeger responded, "Well, hello, David. What a surprise to hear from you." Meirhofer wept a few moments, incriminated himself, then hung up.

On the strength of Mrs. Jaeger's sworn affidavit of that phone call, Dunbar attained a search warrant. In David Meirhofer's residence, the FBI and local police found Susan's body parts and the fingers of Meirhofer's former girlfriend. Dassinger urged the killer to tell the truth. When confronted, David, with no show of emotion, calmly confessed to the killings, including those of two small boys who had disappeared a few years before. In Susan's case, he said he dragged her one hundred yards back to his pickup, where he strangled her.

INTO THE MINDS OF MADMEN

Within a few days of his incarceration, David Meirhofer hung himself with a makeshift rope made of towels from his cell. Before he committed suicide, Marietta told him once again that she forgave him.

The general public was unaware of the role played by the Behavioral Science Unit in assisting law enforcement to solve the unsolvable until a newspaper article appeared on the front page of the Friday, February 15, 1980, issue of the *Chicago American*. Entitled "They Study the Strangest of Slayings—Little Known FBI Unit Profiles Bizarre Killers," the exclusive was authored by Patricia Leeds after interviewing Bob Ressler and Russ Vorpagel with the full approval of the Bureau's public relations department and Roger Depue, newly appointed chief of the BSU. It was time, Bureau authorities felt, not only to share the success of the unit with the American people, but also to alert America and the world to what was available to law enforcement.

For the first time, the general public learned a few details about the BSU. As Leeds described it, the program had three main divisions: 1) crime scene analysis; 2) profiles of unknown suspects; and 3) analysis of threatening letters. "Ours is a clearinghouse for bizarre, seemingly motiveless murders," Ressler explained. "Our department does not deal with murders involving robbery, family homicides, or organized crime."

NOTES

1. Although the Behavioral Science Unit was officially established in May of 1972 when the Bureau opened the doors of the new Academy at Quantico, it had been "unofficially" conceived some six years before. Few know, or care to appreciate, that—contrary to popular opinion—the BSU was not the inspiration of J. Edgar Hoover.

2. Jack would submit a thesis to Dr. Richard Stephens, professor of

sociology at George Washington University some nineteen years after receiving his Bachelor of Arts from Gannon College in 1950. The 152-page thesis developed new and significant insight into that segment of the FBI population which occupied the police educator's role. The profiles Jack established appeared to Stephens, as well as officials at Headquarters, to be valid and capable of providing meaningful knowledge when utilized with an adequate sample. In short, Kirsch argued that the individual brings certain qualities with him when he enters the Bureau or some other occupation or profession, and is changed in some degree during the organization's ensuing socialization process. He then proceeded to define the occupational role of the successful police educator in the FBI.

3. The old FBI Academy was also at Quantico with the rest of the Marine Corps buildings and dormitories. The old Academy was too small to handle the number of new agents going through in the 1950s and 1960s, so students and agents were only sent there for firearms (they were bussed out to the present ranges) or for in-services.

4. Tolson was five years younger than Hoover and joined the Bureau in 1928, four years after his friend and mentor. He was a relatively handsome man, well dressed usually in a dark suit, white shirt, and the usual subdued necktie. His black hair was turning a becoming gray at the temples. Everyone in the Bureau knew him to be the Director's closest friend and confidant—among other things. A few special agents feared him because of his reputation for being a hatchet man for "Eddie."

5. Joseph L. Schott, *No Left Turn* (New York: Praeger, 1975).

6. Ibid. In 1949, there were 120 different classifications of investigations. By 1971, there were 180.

7. The Washington Field Office (WFO), which handled investigations within the District of Columbia, was housed in the Old Post Office (OPO) building at Twelfth Street and Pennsylvania Avenue.

4

Pioneering Criminal Profiling

When the BSU called its first class to order on Monday morning at 7:30 A.M. on May 3, 1972, the agents who reported to work along with Kirsch were John Pfaff, Jim Siano, Howard Teten, Pat Mullany, Conrad Hassel, Tom Strentz, Dick Harper, Larry Monroe, Bill Peters, and Al Whittaker. Initially, they occupied offices on the ground floor of the main classroom building. Then, in 1973, as the team grew and needed additional space, the unit moved to the basement of the Academy Library, where "offices" were created with partitions. One BSUer even transformed the broom closet into his office. Another move, into the Forensic Research Center, occurred in 1982, and only in 1983 did the entire team move to the windowless, Cold War bomb shelter consisting of some forty rooms in the subbasement, 160 feet below the lounge/dining hall, where the BSU remains today.

During the past thirty years, many assisted in pioneering the growth and development of the Behavioral Science Unit. But, by virtually all accounts, whether from colleagues or secretaries, serial killers or FBI directors, no one was more able or played a more pivotal role in its leadership than Howard "Bud" Teten, the "godfather" of criminal profiling.

Tall, broad-shouldered, brown haired, and spectacled, Teten was a handsome man with strong, chiseled features that displayed a smiling, good-natured, almost meditative expression. Although his unassuming simplicity, natural dignity, and quiet fatherly confidence inspired admiration and a new standard of openness from the start, Howard was a no-nonsense criminologist and instructor. Those getting to know the man soon realized that his reassuringly self-possessed demeanor belied the underlying firmness and force of his will and determination. In defining his own personality, Howard says:

> Old-time friends have referred to me as "a friendly dragon" because they say I conceal my real opinions and feelings and then suddenly react when my ability to tolerate something runs out. Perhaps this is true. One old-time agent at Quantico, Ed Tulley, unit chief of the education unit, often referred to me as "the friendly vulture" because he felt my friendliness concealed an underlying remote watchfulness. While he was noted for his sardonic wit and sarcastic remarks, his comments were only half in jest. According to him, even though I was always friendly, my years of profiling had made me unfeeling, and I often seemed to view others as specimens whose personalities and motives were to be examined.
>
> I realize that these are not particularly attractive descriptions of me, but they are in many ways accurate. The years of profiling have taken their toll. I know that I am afflicted with what Freud would call "isolation of affect" and it somehow holds me apart. I have few friends and there are even fewer people that I really trust. Knowing what humans are really capable of doing to each other makes you aware that civility is a luxury which can be discarded at will. This knowledge robs you of your feelings and makes you far more wary of your fellow man. In some ways, I suppose, I was like Teddy Roosevelt: I believed in walking softly but carrying a big stick.

The idea of trying to identify, via a specific profile, the perpetrator of a homicide, rape, or other horrible crime, was born during the years Howard Teten was assigned to the San Leandro, California, police department as identification officer. Now graduated with a degree in criminology, Howard nevertheless continued his study of forensic medicine and abnormal psychology. Because of his deep love for reading material from the different academic disciplines, he chose a broad range of books describing deviance and criminal behavior by theorists in a number of fields. These included Morel, Quetelet, Simmel, Charcot, Durkheim, Adler, Lombroso, Skinner, Freud, Gross, Aliport, and Sheldon, as well as histories of famous practitioners, both real and imaginary. Sherlock Holmes, for instance, was a favorite. Howard says, "studying the theories of different disciplines seems to be frowned upon in most academic settings, but I think studying human behavior from the viewpoint of several different disciplines added greatly to my understanding and background."

With such a combination of reading and experiences, Howard slowly began to realize that it was possible to establish a relationship between a victim, the characteristics of the crime scene, and the perpetrator's personality. He was the first person to introduce law enforcement to the part psychological disorders might play, and made some fairly accurate determinations of the type of disorder involved by studying the crime scene. However, there was little opportunity to employ this newly discovered relationship, especially when it came to an unsolved murder, because San Leandro had so few murders. And, if the city experienced one, it was usually solved within the first forty-eight hours.

In 1962, Howard joined the FBI. He was assigned to various offices during the next seven years and gained an M.A. in sociology, but there were few opportunities to formalize the theories underlying his profiling concepts. It wasn't until he was transferred to Washington, D.C., and the training division that he had the opportunity to develop a course emphasizing his profiling techniques. Says Teten about the thinking behind the techniques:

> In the method of profiling I developed, the crime(s) were the primary source of all information concerning the personality traits and

lll

mental status of the perpetrator. The findings from the crime scene and the backgrounds of the victims dictated the manner in which any interviews [of suspects] were to be conducted. Later, when training other instructors, I tried to emphasize this as much as possible, but none of the other guys had ever been a crime scene technician. This is one of the areas where the original approach was changed as more and more profilers applied their own areas of expertise. Remember that an FBI agent really doesn't do many crime scenes, particularly those involving homicides and rapes. These are almost always local crimes and, as such, are handled by local police crime scene specialists. Bob Ressler started the analyses of the crime scenes left by known serial killers in preparation for their postconviction interviews. This was a unique technique and it proved to be extremely valuable. By having experienced agents do this, the information obtained added immeasurably to our understanding of how crime scene characteristics were related to the personality traits and mental status of the perpetrator. This added knowledge more than made up for a profiler's lack of experience in investigating crime scenes.

In retrospect, the knowledge gained from these interviews also greatly reduced the difficulties originally associated with training effective profilers. During the period between 1973 and 1975, I had "conned" library researcher Judy McWilliams into working almost full-time doing research for me, but the research was limited to scouring the literature for references to relationships between personalities, disorders, and crimes. While this added considerable knowledge to the approach, it was slow going and not really of great help training additional profilers.

After his transfer to headquarters and his assignment to the training division's "Flying Management Training Squad" for almost a year, Teten asked his unit chief, Tom Brownfield, for an opportunity to present a lecture entitled "Applied Criminology" that he had developed. Brownfield offered four hours during the next NA session, provided Teten could make it fly in a field school.

Teten discussed the presentation with the FBI police training coor-
dinator for the New York City area. After describing the course, the
coordinator found the detectives and crime scene specialists in Suffolk
County, New York, to be particularly interested in the new approach.
A school was set up and shortly thereafter Teten delivered the first
Applied Criminology course.

A month or so later, Howard delivered his Applied Criminology to
the National Academy in two two-hour sessions. Although the lectures
were well received, it was obvious they needed more work and polish.
"Moreover," says Howard, "I think it bothered the students to have the
same instructor teach police management and then turn around and
teach a rather unusual approach to crime scene investigation. They
were interested though. There were plenty of questions."

Teten recalls, "Some believe that the development of the profiling
procedure evolved out of a lecture. Well, yes, I suppose to some extent
it did, but I had developed the procedure prior to developing the
course. I actually wrote the course while on the management squad,
and knew it would work if it were applied correctly. However, since I
had been assigned to an instructional position, the only way I could
see to bring the procedure to the attention of the police was to develop
a course which showcased the technique."

Tom O'Malley, then the resident FBI agent in Amarillo, Texas, and
later a member of the BSU at Quantico, learned about the course a few
weeks later. After consulting with the police agencies in the region, he
asked Howard to deliver the lecture to the area detectives and crime
scene specialists. There was a caveat, however. Howard needed to
expand the course to several days. O'Malley had talked to a graduate
of the last NA session about the course and the officer had said that
Teten needed more time to fully explain the procedure.

Deeply pleased with all the sudden recognition, Teten enlarged the
course to four-hour sessions over four days. The additional hours
allowed him time to elaborate upon his technique as well as time for

questions and responses. With the course now a virtual success, Howard invited the Amarillo police to reopen their unsolved murder cases as part of the course. Almost immediately, Teten and the Amarillo officers were able to construct a profile in one case and identify a possible suspect, who confessed after being interviewed.

Naturally, word of this success spread. Unit chief Tom Brownfield, who was amazed over the Amarillo arrest, had been skeptical about Teten's technique and his course from the beginning. To his credit, he allowed Howard to add the course permanently to the National Academy's fall and spring schedules. Since Teten expanded the course's eight hours to thirty, he needed assistance. His initial choice, already being groomed by Kirsch and the selection team, was agent Pat Mullany, then assigned to the New York office. Not only did Pat have an advanced degree in psychology, but he was a teacher. Most important of all, he was willing. Says Teten,

> I can't stress enough the importance of Pat Mullany to the success of the profiling concept. You see, the course I originally built contained most of the basic theories found in any standard criminology course. There were discussions on the positive school and the classical school, demonology, phrenology, and the various other biologically based approaches, a summary of the theories making up the social model, and finally, an overview of the psychological theories. During the first segments of the course, I explained the evolution of the different theories and the implications associated with each in terms of responsibility and punishment. These included everything from brain disorders to environment and from the born criminal to learned behavior. I felt that this background information was necessary to prepare the students for the profiling procedure which I brought out at the end of the psychological model. This is where my first partner, Pat, came in.
>
> At the time, my knowledge of abnormal psychology was limited. Pat was a full-blown psychologist and was able to provide the

kind of depth and orientation I lacked. Even though I had checked each of the disorders and their characteristics with two separate psychiatrists for accuracy while writing the course, it didn't really take off until Pat added his considerable expertise (as well as his great skill as a lecturer). It can truthfully be said that, while I wrote the course, he made it a success.

The next request for Howard's applied criminology course was from the West Point Military Academy for its Regional Police Training Seminar. Since West Point was in the New York divisional area, it was not difficult to have Pat join him in a presentation. "We hit it off right away," says Teten.

In order to keep both of us on topic, we devised a method where we both stood in front of the class at the same time. I would talk about the crime, what was found at the crime scene, and how these findings might be interpreted. Pat would then chime in with a description of a particular mental disorder which matched the interpretation and the features typical to such a person. These features would include such things as age, occupation, social life, etc. It worked well, and we called it our version of team teaching. Later on, we were occasionally referred to as "Mutt and Jeff," or more commonly, "Frick and Frack." I never did know what that meant, but they never threw us out, so it must have been good.

The next Applied Criminology course that was offered was for the Coronado, California, police department. The chief had sat in on Teten's presentation at the NA and wanted his detectives and crime scene people to hear it. Again, the course was well received. To Howard, however, the real victory was getting the SAC in New York to allow Pat to fly to California to participate. Since the New York office would have to pay Pat's travel costs, the FBI approval of the request was iffy at best.

INTO THE MINDS OF MADMEN

When the Academy opened its doors in 1972, Howard and Pat, as well as a number of other agents, were brought in to staff the Behavioral Science Unit. After several NA sessions, word was out that some of the BSUers were profiling offenders of certain types of crimes. The cases they used were old with few leads, dead in the water. However, the profiles developed by Teten and Mullany had resulted in the identification of some offenders, while promising leads for others. Soon the two BSUers were receiving telephone calls from homicide detectives from all over the nation, while those assigned to attend the National Academy were bringing their own unsolved cases with them for analysis. Thus, throughout these initial years, Teten and Mullany profiled hundreds of cases, many over the telephone. As odd as it may seem, these first BSUers tried to keep their profiling efforts informal, seldom writing and sending letters containing the profiles—certainly not letters on FBI letterhead.

Teten, Mullany, and the staff believed it was important to maintain an aura of anonymity. Becoming too well known, they believed, was counterproductive. Under Mr. Hoover, as old timers know, maintaining anonymity was a strict but unwritten rule. And that thinking remained for a number of years after his death.

The decision to maintain agent anonymity was sound. It transferred any success and fame associated with a high-visibility arrest and conviction from a single agent to all agents. This provided every FBI agent with more prestige. And the greater the prestige, the more cooperation during an investigation. Such prestige resulted in fewer problems during the arrests, and reduced any potential retaliative action against an individual agent. Profiling would not reach any level of official Bureau approval for five or six more years when Roger Depue, Robert Ressler, and John Douglas developed the first protocol for preparing a profile and the response that was to be sent to inquiring police departments. As the number of profiling requests increased, the BSU slowly began to specialize. Says Teten,

It soon became apparent that the different types of crimes were so complicated it would be necessary to specialize. While most of the guys became fairly proficient at homicides in general, many soon began to branch out into specific types of homicides or other types of crimes. Others became interested in applying the principles of profiling to other areas.

Later, when Dick Ault arrived, he became highly skilled in profiling espionage agents and defectors of various types. Tony Rider focused on profiling arsonists. Pat Mullany became very adept at profiling extortionists and kidnappers based on their messages and notes. Con Hassel and Tom Strentz placed their emphasis on an in-depth analysis of hostage takers and hostage situations. In fact, their continued work in this area eventually resulted in the formation of the Special Operations and Research Unit (SOARU). Jim Reese and John Mindermann switched over to stress and stress management.

As time passed, many of the agents found it possible to expand their areas of specialization. In addition to homicides and their original specialty areas, they conducted additional research into even more esoteric areas. For instance, I took on homicides by poisoning, hostage situations, kidnappers, and cult crimes. Mullany expanded more deeply into psycholinguistics and profiling the hostage takers. Hazelwood changed his concentration to rapes and sex crimes. Lanning, coming along somewhat later, went into child abuse and cult crimes. Harper and several others concentrated on conflict management (domestic disturbances and abuse). Meanwhile, Ressler and Douglas handled all the incoming general cases.

After reading Brussel's book, *Casebook of a Crime Psychiatrist*, in 1972, Teten had wanted to meet Brussel. Later the following year, during one of his hostage negotiation workshop excursions to New York, he called for an appointment. Needless to say, Howard was excited as he took the elevator to the seventeenth floor of the State Building in lower Manhattan to meet the aging Freudian psychiatrist, who was still practicing in his old office. Says Howard,

He was a wonderful old gentleman and certainly experienced in his brand of profiling. He had prepared profiles on the Mad Bomber of New York, the Boston Strangler, for the Wylie Murders, and a for number of other high-visibility cases. During that first meeting with him, I was so impressed I asked if he would teach me his technique. I said that I would be happy to pay whatever he charged. His reply was that neither I nor the FBI could afford his charges, and since it was against his policy to offer reduced rates, he would have to donate his time. I saw him several more times during that next year and learned a great deal, but I disagreed with some of the assumptions contained in his approach. Even so, several of his profiles were successfully used to capture offenders, the Mad Bomber, George Matesky, being one of the more notable. Whatever our differences, and they were purely philosophical in nature, he was certainly one of the finest, most caring gentleman I have ever come across.

Soon to be added to the original group were some other men who would contribute heavily in developing the concept of profiling and hostage negotiations: Roger Depue, Frank Ochberg, Bertram Brown, Captain Francis (Frank) Boltz, Assistant Commissioner Peter Walton, and David C. Veness of the New Scotland Yard.

Each would play a prominent role in the growth and development of the unit. For example, Roger Depue established the fellowship program between law enforcement personnel outside the Bureau and the BSU, as well as monitored the international data gathered on serial murderers, serial rapists, serial child molesters, etc. To this day, that list is still being added to and is in wide circulation. By all accounts, Roger was the model for the unit chief in *Silence of the Lambs*.

Frank Ochberg was a psychiatrist and the assistant director of the National Institute of Mental Health, whom Conrad Hassel brought in to assist in teaching NA students. He developed concepts and strategies for solving actual cases for the Bureau and other law enforcement agencies. Bertram S. Brown was also heavily involved in the inception of the Unit and made many unique contributions to it.

Frank Boltz, a captain in the New York City Police Department and later commander of the NYPD Hostage Negotiations Unit, invited Teten and Mullany to lecture before the first hostage negotiations school in 1972 or 1973. He also served as a lecturer and consultant during the formation of the Bureau Hostage Negotiation Training program and helped both the BSU and SOARU programs by providing a continuing source of profile data from various hostage negotiation courses.

Peter Walton helped Conrad Hassel set up the Bureau's Hostage Negotiation Training Program and provided input based on his experiences with New Scotland Yard. David Veness, the number two man at New Scotland Yard, was trained at the Academy and established a faculty exchange program between the FBI Academy and the New Scotland Yard's International Police Manager's Training School at Bramshill.

Working in two-agent teams, the initial BSUers conducted one- to two-week, forty-hour training courses (referred to as road or field schools) on a variety of subjects. These were available to all larger police agencies and regional police training schools throughout the nation, or for that matter, just about anywhere else the limited FBI budget would allow. When not teaching an NA session or a new agents training class, their schedule was two weeks out and two weeks in.

Recently, Connie Hassel commented about Frank Boltz and Dr. Harvey Schlossberg, a NYPD officer psychologist: "They were the first people to train negotiators for the NYPD before the FBI even got started. We sent our people through their school and stole everything they had. Frank was the first leader of the NYPD hostage negotiation team. We changed some of his methods and don't always agree tactically, but his help and unselfish friendship were invaluable. He still is unselfish in his assistance."

Soon, topics such as "child molesters" would emerge, like Applied Criminology had, as simple, two-hour blocks of instruction. When someone truly became interested in it, as Ken Lanning did, he would develop it into a forty- or even an eighty-hour course, by conducting a bibliographic search of the subject, consulting police and other agencies about it, and then teaching it. Eventually, the early BSUers would see more cases of a particular crime than any other law enforcement agency, since they were more in contact with law enforcement people all over the nation.

Meanwhile, along with their teaching responsibilities within the National Academy, all were expected to continue offering workshops in the field when requested. And, of course, as profiling requests increased in the mid- and late-1970s, the agents were expected to squeeze those in as well.

When, in January of 1973, Jack Kirsch, who had been appointed BSU chief eight months before, was reassigned at the Academy, John Pfaff, the senior agent of the group, was promoted to BSU chief. Al Whittaker transferred to new agents training, while Pat Mullany and Jimmy Siano, getting restless with Academy teaching, applied for the Inspection Squad.

During those years at the Bureau, a one-year assignment to the Inspection Squad was a must if an agent hoped to be promoted to assistant special agent in charge (ASAC) or special agent in charge (SAC). Years later, Pat ended up as ASAC in the Los Angeles office while Jimmy became a field supervisor in the Dallas office.

In February of 1975, Richard L. Ault Jr. transferred to the BSU after a year or so as special agent in Kansas City, and almost five years in Cleveland. He had been interviewed and hired by Jack Pfaff, a kindly, soft-spoken, mercurial unit chief who looked upon his job as making sure everyone had lots of teaching assignments. Like the other members of the BSU, Ault's mission was to teach police in the National Academy, at field schools throughout the United States, and just about anywhere else the budget would allow. He was one of the first fifty negotiators who taught the course, "Hostage Negotiations." In addition, Dick offered "Crises Intervention," a course which literally taught police how to break up domestic terrorist situations without getting killed. Says Dick, "In fact, I taught all topics except the sociology stuff, such as the 'Social-Psychological Aspects of Community Behavior,' and remained pretty much a generalist my whole time at the Academy. I was also involved in teaching 'Applied Criminology,' all the profiling techniques, but counseled and supervised by Teten and Mullany. This was a red-hot new topic. It was still more or less untested. We were spreading the gospel of hostage negotiations rather than just SWAT applications."

Ault's BSU "avocation" began when he assisted agents from the Washington field office who were looking for additional help in doing their "indirect assessments in espionage and foreign counterintelligence (FCI) cases." Dick remembers, "While the profiling (later called 'crime scene assessment') was fun, different, even Sherlock Holmes-ish, the real fun was in being able to play mind games with the competition [foreign intelligence]."

To Ault, indirect assessment was, and still is, closer to what "practical" behavioral science is really all about compared to profiling. Indirect assessment is little more than employing behavioral information about a known person to attempt to determine what "makes him or her tick," and combining that information and its interpretation to predict the problems the investigator faces. Profiling, on the other hand, starts with the behavior (like a crime scene) and tries to extrapolate the personality capable of that behavior.

Today, Dick is still on contract to the FBI for services in the area of foreign counterintelligence and domestic and international terrorism. Then, as today, his work is classified. This isn't surprising, since Dick was the only person in the FBI at the time who did these things regularly. "It was easy for me to build a more-or-less full-time service out of the Bureau. Since I had that exclusivity, the FBI asked me to continue the work after I retired. It was rather flattering," he says, "because the Bureau traditionally tends to 'throw away' its talent after they retire."

In spite of the classification for what he was working on, Ault has an article on the concepts of indirect assessment approved by the Bureau for publication in Roy Hazelwood's book, *Practical Aspects of Rape Investigations* (2d ed.). Dick conceived the term "indirect assessment," because it was obvious that one could not go directly to a suspect and test him or her for personality characteristics. However, a great deal of important information about the behaviors of suspects could be gathered in various circumstances.

It was this indirect assessment that overlapped the term "psychological autopsy," causing a great deal of confusion among law enforcement. Dick emphasized that indirect assessment had all the elements of a psychological autopsy but was much, much more. He used it successfully on real people to make predictions about their behavior, as well as shape interviews and assist in the recruitment of foreign spies to work for the United States. Ault knew the techniques were valid because they had worked for him for years in foreign counterintelligence and terrorism.

Meanwhile, when Dick Ault arrived in 1975, there were eleven members assigned to the BSU. During the course of the next few years, there were a number of men and women who drifted through the unit but didn't remain. When Ault arrived, those already busy at work were Howard Teten, Pat Mullany, Roger Depue, Larry Monroe, Tom O'Malley, Con Hassel, Tom Strentz, Bob Ressler, John Mindermann (developing the Stress Management Police course) and Dick Harper.

During the next two years, they were joined by Jim Reese, Bob Fitzpatrick, Roy Hazelwood, and Bob Boyd, a retired Metro D.C. homicide detective. Bob, who soon thereafter died of cancer, was revered because he brought to the BSU an extensive murder investigative experience that no BSUer had. After all, BSUers were investigators, but not necessarily of homicide. Bob was followed by Winston Norman, homicide detective, and eventually by Art Westveer, from

Baltimore's homicide division. John Douglas was not on the scene yet. When he arrived in 1979, the BSUers were pretty well entrenched.

Of course, there were several who had been profiling all along, because they were teaching "Applied Criminology." These included Teten, Mullany, Ressler, Hazelwood, Ault, and Reese, who didn't seem to like it very much. Says Ault about his early years,

> Dr. Langer's profile of Adolph Hitler was one of the first things I remember reading when I came into the BSU. It was the essence of indirect assessment [as opposed to profiling], and the sort of work I really enjoyed doing, and in fact got to do as an "avocation" [as opposed to a formal program in the BSU] when I would assist SAs in the espionage arena. I was the only person who did it regularly; even though I worked criminal and organized crime cases in the field, I loved foreign counterintelligence cases and the attempts to outpsych the opposition. Bear in mind that profiling was looking at one aspect of behavior (the crime scene of an unknown perpetrator) and trying to guess what sort of person would do such a thing. Indirect assessment was looking at as much of the behavior of a known person as possible and trying to predict how they would behave in certain circumstances. Although the profilers did some of that, it seemed more by rote than by exercise of psychology or behavioral science. Remember, Douglas had very little behavioral science background, and Ressler was a criminology major in school. Indirect assessment was more akin to an application of psychology principles than profiling.

As the BSU evolved, the staff began to realize there were three "legs" to the BSU tripod: teaching, research, and consultation. Without any one of the legs, the Behavioral Science Unit could not function effectively. It was easy for the staff to gain consultation experience because the police the BSUers taught would bring in all their "old dog" unsolved cases (now called "cold" cases) and ask for help.

The BSU staff also handled several other "programs" as they developed: in 1977, for example, the forensic use of hypnosis in cases; in the early 1980s, trying to develop some sort of computerized program to track unsolved murders to see if they could be linked to perpetrators; working to develop an efficient stress-management program with the newly arrived John Mindermann, Jim Reese, Bob Schaefer, and John Campbell; and trying to introduce an effective psychological services program for the FBI. For this latter program, the Behavioral Science Unit hired Dr. David Soskis as sort of a "free-range" psychiatrist for the Bureau. But Soskis was soon overwhelmed by the number of agent responses. That problem, along with internal politics, brought about the demise of the effort after a few years.

In the late seventies and early eighties, with Bob Ressler, Roy Hazelwood, Tony Rider, and Dick Ault in the BSU fold, a third group transferred into the unit. Among them were James Reese, John Douglas, Tom O'Malley, Bron Mogenis, Swanson Carter, Bob Fitzpatrick, Ken Lanning, Roger Davis, and Bob Boyd. Conrad Hassel was promoted chief of the Special Operations and Research Unit. Joining him in SOARS was Tom Strentz.

Many agents didn't work in the unit very long due to the student rating system and the fact that all agent instructors came to the Academy on a trial basis. Many agents either were not good enough as instructors and were transferred or couldn't handle the stress and asked out.

In 1977, Teten suffered the loss of his voice from repeated lecturing. This added to Jim Reese's teaching load, since he had been paired with Teten when he came into the unit. Reese was also in training at the same time, so he was expected to teach, observe, listen, and learn while Howard whispered the criminology part of the applied criminology course, then lecture on the psychological part from his own background and the material prepared for him. Howard's deep whisper would often, and without warning, go out completely. When that happened, he would simply sit in the rear of the room and nod "yes" or "no" while Jim lectured using Howard's notes, slides, and overheads.

Then, a month or so later, Howard ruptured a disk which required an immediate operation. While recovering from the surgery, and with his voice slowly returning to normal, he spent most of his bed time developing profiles. "Fortunately, a number of the profiles led to cases being solved, and the higher-ups were so impressed they decided I should have a Ph.D.," he smiles. "It sounded like a good idea at the time, so I applied to the University of Maryland and was accepted in the psychology department. I attended classes on a part-time basis for two or three years."

In the years that followed, Teten did little other than attend classes and develop profiles. Then in 1980, he was promoted to unit chief of the recently formed Institutional Research and Development Unit. Recalls Teten,

> Even in those days, the BSU was somewhat divided. There were the criminology-psychology instructors . . . , the sociology management group, and the police/community relations . . . group. While we knew each other and saw each other every day, we were not really teaching the same things. Further, the Academy operated a student rating system and we were always in competition with the other instructors for high ratings. This caused some anxiety, since receiving several low ratings in a row could result in your replacement. As a result, some of the instructors were not as social as they might otherwise have been.

For Howard, the new assignment was a challenge because the Institutional Research and Development Unit was on its last legs and in danger of being disbanded. But Teten and his team were soon able to prove the value of the unit. And, with the addition of staff, the IRDU was slowly resurrected and expanded. Its activities soon involved all the research in the Bureau not associated with the laboratories. Included were such assignments as conducting psychological testing on all new agents, conducting job-task analysis for the special agent position, developing agent preselection criteria, overseeing the development of selection tests, conducting a nationwide police training needs assessment, and developing programs to protect agents assigned to high-risk duties.

In fact, between 1982 and 1986, the IRDU had at least twenty research projects underway at all times. One was a much-needed cost/benefit analysis of criminal profiling. The research unit also assisted in field investigations. On one occasion, it provided a unique method of proving corruption by developing statistical procedures for determining how often a situation would occur by chance. On another occasion, the Teten's IRDU designed a sampling technique to prove that a particular crime had occurred. Says Teten about himself,

> During this time, the early 1980s, I developed some sort of an odd-ball reputation. Every time the field would get some weird case, such as those claiming demonic involvement or an attack by aliens, etc., I was asked to investigate. Back in 1972, I had requested that a sampling of the letters received by the Bureau or Mr. Hoover from individuals with possible mental problems be forwarded to me. My intent was to change the names, remove any possible identifying information, and use them for instructional purposes in the applied criminology course. Well, as the years passed, many of my former students also sent in letters for my use. My name apparently got around as someone interested in the more unusual types of cases. You wouldn't believe the requests. At one point, my immediate supervisor told me that he didn't really want to know what I was doing. He only asked that I advise him if I was going out of town. I was required to leave a telephone number where I could be reached and give him some idea when I would be back.

During these critical developmental years of the Institutional Research Unit, Safeguard was born. Although not really a part of the BSU, its importance to the Bureau was, according to many, almost unparalleled in FBI history.

In 1972, shortly after the death of J. Edgar Hoover, the FBI started placing agents undercover as a method of gathering evidence. Hoover had been opposed to the concept from its inception, believing firmly that since agents were not criminals, they would not be able to act like criminals. Says Teten,

> There is more than a grain of truth to this—many agents are unable to work undercover for this very reason. After several years, it became apparent that we were losing too many undercover agents. By this I mean that an unusual number of undercover agents were leaving the Bureau. Others were getting themselves into serious trouble by committing crimes or otherwise behaving in a manner which greatly limited their credibility in court. Still others were becoming unaccountably rebellious and unproductive after participating in a successful undercover project.

In 1978, Teten was approached by an agent in the Undercover Management Unit. He knew Howard personally, as well as his longtime interest in undercover work. "Can you help us figure out why we're losing so many agents?" he asked.

Of course, this challenged Teten unlike any problem that he had worked on thus far. During the next year or year and a half, he traveled to some twenty field offices and interviewed every undercover agent he could find. Howard already knew stress was the culprit and his goal was to identify the most common sources of stress associated with undercover work.

Using a reverse-profiling technique, Teten tested some four hundred agents who had worked undercover and remained in undercover status for a month or more. Upon his return to the Academy, he developed an informal performance rating system to determine how their supervisors and peers rated them as undercover agents. The data provided him with the primary psychological characteristics of those agents who were most effective as well as those stressors which were the most troublesome. Says Teten,

> The results of this study were quite revealing; however, the stressors identified were so corrosive that they overshadowed the effects associated with differences in personality. So I conducted another study. Using a much larger sample of experienced undercover agents from the FBI and several other agencies, it was possible to identify the particular types of personalities most vulnerable to the stressors found in undercover operations.
>
> With these data, I was able to develop a protocol, referred to as the Safeguard System, to protect the undercover agent from the psychological dangers of undercover work. Essentially, the protocol involves a preselection interview, a selection procedure, periodic monitoring while the agent is in an undercover status, a debriefing at the conclusion of the project, and a follow-up interview some six months after the end of the assignment.

In essence, the Teten procedure was rather straightforward, requiring that the undercover coordinator be carefully trained in conducting the interviews. Training the undercover coordinators were several mental health professionals, in addition to Teten, if his assistance was needed. Howard adds, "It took some time to convince everyone to follow the protocol. But by using the procedure, we were able to significantly reduce the number of agents lost as a result of undercover assignments."

It was Bob Ressler who saw Russ Vorpagel's teaching potential. Ressler convinced Larry Monroe, who was unit chief in 1979, to bring Russ into the BSU. But since Vorpagel had retired from the Bureau and returned to military service, he was at sea aboard a navy destroyer when he finally received Monroe's telegram. Russ returned the call at the number Monroe indicated, but it was 3:00 A.M. in Manassas, Virginia, where Larry and his wife lived. Carol, awoken out of too deep a sleep, answered and thought the call was a wrong number or a drunk. She hung up. The next morning, Larry said to his wife, "Oh, no! I've been waiting for that call for a week!"

When Vorpagel arrived at the Academy, he was placed in fairly cramped quarters with the other BSUers. "John Mindermann had an office all to himself. Russ Vorpagel was in the office with Tony Rider. Jimmy Reese and Dick Ault shared an office. Ressler was there, and so was Hazelwood and Bob Boyd. Hassel and Strentz were assigned to SOARS. We had quite a nice little family. It was cozy and comfortable and we put in long hours. Since I could do homicide profiles, I had no problems working within the group, or filled in . . . as guest lecturer whenever someone went on the road."

Russ recalls that by 1982 there were five profilers working full-time: Russ, Ken Lanning, John Douglas, Bob Ressler, and Roy Hazelwood. "Ault was off doing his statistics, John Mindermann and Jim Reese, their police stress classes. For us five profilers, work was challenging and creative. Yes, it depressed Ken. Yes, we often felt sick to our stomachs. But we had a job to do. We were to offer support to law enforcement that couldn't do the job. After us, there was no one. If we didn't help solve the case, who would? That's why every now and then we enjoyed a little foolishness to release the pressure, tension, and workload of profiling murderers."

In 1982, the profilers didn't teach on Wednesday mornings. At that time, the Behavioral Science Unit was located on the first floor of the Foreign Science Research building. The staff had large, airy rooms in relatively new areas and were mildly pleased with their quarters.

There was one particular case that Russ will never forget: "This murder in Logan, Tennessee, was one of the most difficult I had ever worked on. And since Wednesday morning was the time to convene and look over the case facts, we assembled at 8:30 A.M. as usual. Photographs of a murdered young woman were laid out on the conference room table. 'Look at how the body is mutilated,' I commented. . . .

'Everything has been done excessively!' Someone commented, 'It's obvious it was done by a simple schizoid.' Someone else said after a moment, 'Yes, but a simple schizoid doesn't drive a car.'" (A simple Schizoid can't drive because he can't pass the test to get a license.)

The murder was grisly.

"The young woman was found twenty miles from where she had been babysitting. She had been thrown or displayed in a dump, flat on her stomach. Her legs had been spread out, looking like a frog swimming in water. She's naked and some of her private parts are displayed as if the killer is trying to disgrace her as well as shock the public," summarized Russ. "Not only has her head been scalped and breast sliced off, but also she's been sexually assaulted. So, guys, what do you think?"

"Hey, this one is easy," piped up Douglas. "Two people killed her!"

For a moment there was a stunned silence. Russ looked at Ressler, who in turn looked over at Hazelwood. Douglas smiled.

"Why, of course!" laughed Vorpagel. "There are too many signatures here, too much hate."

Russ telephoned the homicide lieutenant in Logan and informed him of the BSU decision that the killer was local, a man who had one or more accomplices. The lieutenant smiled, "You guys in the BSU are something else. In fact, if you turn out to be correct, I'll kiss all your asses in Macy's front window, plus give you an hour to gather a crowd."

Russ rushed the profiles, one of a schizoid personality, the other of an antisocial, to Logan. Still, the lieutenant wouldn't believe the BSU profiles. But when he finally got around to reinvestigating the murder with the assistance of the profiles, he found enough evidence to arrest three suspects, a former boyfriend of the young woman, a girlfriend of his, and a "flaky" friend of the former boyfriend. It wasn't long before the three confessed to killing her for various reasons. "That lieutenant never kept his promise about Macy's," says Russ. "But he was most appreciative of our efforts. And of course, John Douglas was the one who saw the crime scene clearly where the rest of us did not. He did a great job on this case. This case had been a real mess, and it was the first one where we began to realize that Wednesday mornings were more than just fun and games. These cases were not simple and as easy as we thought."

In those early years, there was a feeling among the BSU profilers that they would not profile until local police had followed all their leads to their logical conclusions. Once the few leads had been adequately exhausted, and the murder remained unsolved, the case would be accepted by the BSU. "But this was stupid," Russ comments, "because we'd get these cases after two or three years. The stacks of reports were getting to be five feet high. Even the Royal Canadian police were coming down, saying, 'We know this case is eleven years old, but would you please take a look at it?' Well, of course we did. And for our cases, and theirs, we had to go over every word, since there were usually witness and suspect interviews. We read because a phrase or a word here or there might turn the case. Larry Monroe and later Roger Depue argued with headquarters that we were succeeding and that the Bureau would simply support us with more staff and funds. The Bureau answered, 'O.K., you're right. We'll send you out by plane to look at the body and scene if the case is really, really important.' And, I believe that this is how we finally got the BSU going. As far as I'm concerned, the true BSU didn't really begin until 1978."

According to Vorpagel, the BSU staff were employing "proactive techniques." For example, "Jimmy Wright and Roy Hazelwood went to San Antonio with a profile of the killer of one of our FBI secretaries. They advertised in the newspapers that arrests were imminent and that the killer had probably killed before. He had staged the scene a little bit and he lost his cool because no such crime had been in that area before and he probably told someone about it. Now, the killer, seeing the story in the paper, starts to think the guy he told will feel his life is in danger and will talk. And the guy who was told probably figures in order to save his own life from the guy who told him he better come in and let the Phoenix Police know about it."

"Well guess what? The next morning the guy who was told showed up and blew the whistle on the killer. Jim and Roy were back at the Academy before the end of the week."

One of the toughest, grossest cases Russ worked on, which the BSU profilers didn't solve, dealt with a killing by a gang of bikers of one of their own. It was an unsolved murder that the staff practically gave up on.

A young woman and her male companion came into police head-quarters and expressed fear that her boyfriend had been killed at a nearby farm frequented by a gang of bikers. The police dispatched a squad car and two detectives to the farmhouse where the boyfriend had last been seen. It was immediately obvious to the detectives that the farm was a den of biker-thieves. It wasn't long before they spotted a headless, mutilated body. The feet, hands, and penis had been cut off. In addition, there were multiple wounds all over the corpse, which had been dead a few weeks. "What a mess!" says Russ. "After the police hauled the remains out, they were thoroughly baffled by the grossness of the mutilations and killing. They sent the photographs and other crime scene reports to us and we, too, were completely baffled."

Meanwhile, the detectives discovered some film in the house, along with a large collection of guns and stolen property. "They took their sweet time developing that film, feeling it was of little or no value. Back at the academy, we agreed there was just no way we could figure out a profile for such a horrible slaughter. The guy's feet had even been spiked by a big butcher knife. There was no evidence this had been a ritualistic murder or sacrifice."

Then the police lab unit finally processed the strip of negatives. "I was at my desk when the telephone rang. It was one of the lieutenants who had been investigating the case. 'You won't believe what we have,' he laughed! Well, what he had was the entire visual record of the murder. The girlfriend and her male companion, as well as a few other bikers, had decided to take pictures as they executed their poor friend.

"Pictures showed the guy with his feet being spiked, the fellow sucking his thumb, trying to suck his penis, picking his nose, among other things. All the participants, including the victim, had been high on an assortment of drugs and they didn't know what they were doing. They even forgot they had taken the pictures. So the girl and her companion, who had committed the murder as well as photographed it, were sincere in reporting to the police that the victim was missing. That's what hard drugs will do to you. They were so stoned and so bombed out for a week or more that they simply couldn't recall the killing. And when they were shown the photos, they were horrified, then started blaming each other. The lesson we learned here, and never forget, is that a murder by someone on drugs is often so irrational, so bizarre, that it simply can't be profiled."

Russ Vorpagel's overall assessment of his years and profiling efforts in the Behavioral Science Unit is positive and packed with fondness. He says, "We did a lot of good work and solved a lot of cases. God, how busy we were! We all taught at least fifteen hours a week. Besides that, we were supposed to write, write, write. Furthermore, we had to be all over the country putting on schools for local law enforcement. Then, if someone on the staff was away, like Reese or Ressler, I would fill in for them, or if I were away, someone would fill in for me.

"Yeah, those were important years, filled with fun and sadness, too. There were things no one talked about. Yet, it wasn't all those gory, horrible, awful pictures we looked at, either. We could look at them, be relaxed about our analysis, make comments about them, and even laugh now and then. Some police officers in class resented our humor or jokes we'd sometimes tell. You don't know how often I was written up. Suicide was especially sensitive. I'd talk about suicide at length, associating it with deep mental illness, or make a comment, and one year I had three women cops complain to the dean of the Academy that I was a callous man. And, of course, I'd have cops actually pass out from the photos.

"I'd flash it on the screen. Sure, it was very horrible. But we got through it primarily because we didn't look at it like life. In a way, we regarded each murder as an abstract challenge.

"But I really loved the guys. Pfaff, Monroe, and Depue were never profilers. They were educators, although Roger [Depue] was a former cop. I felt a special kinship with Ault, Depue, and Hassel because, like me, they too were in the Marine Corps. Where Hassel got one Purple Heart, I got two. Ressler and Hazelwood had also been in the military for ten or fifteen years and had extensive investigative and police training and experience. Those two guys really knew what they were doing. So did John Mindermann, who had been a cop before joining the BSU. And as for me, I didn't miss a trick. That's why I'm considered a legend. I did get away with—No!—I performed a lot of feats that most other BSUers or agents in the 'Big B' couldn't have. For example, whenever I put on schools, I knew how to get the most out of my 'per diem,' including hopping along with others to get mileage. I had some nice trips, had an impeccable reputation, and stayed on until I retired at the age of fifty-five. All in all, I'd say I had a good tour."

It was during these years that Vorpagel gained his reputation as the nonpareil of comedians within the FBI. The following are but a fraction of the humorous incidents his colleagues recall.

In the first session of a police-community relations course he was about to teach, Russ entered the classroom, walked up to the blackboard and wrote his name, "Professor Dorabout," then turned to the assembly of sixty police and snarled, "I thought I was about to teach cops who I respect. I came all the way down here to work with law enforcement men and women dedicated to upholding justice. But now as I look around me I see different. I've taught pigs before, even piglets. But this is the first time I've had to teach old brute sows!"

"Of course," Russ recalls, "They wanted to kill me. And after trying to keep a straight face for ten minutes, I had to leave the room. I came back, started laughing, and explained 'You see how trigger words can throw people off? As sworn police officers one of your first lessons is to measure your words with the public.' Well, after a moment's reflection, they started laughing while throwing paper balls at me."

On another occasion, Russ placed a blank cartridge in a starter gun. Then, while disassembling the pistol he put it to his head and pulled the trigger. At the huge bang, the police officer in the front seat of the class passed out.

In the police ethics class he taught, Vorpagel dressed up as a priest: clerical collar, gray coat, and all. In that session, the students had to address him as Reverend Vorpagel. Every now and then he would walk into class dressed as an Indian.

Later, because he was a bomb tech, he was one of the few at the Academy who had been assigned a car; of course, his ever present SAC hated him for it. So one day Russ dropped a large, steel ball-bearing in the gas tank, which of course could be heard rolling back and forth in the tank as he drove. When the SAC had to be driven to headquarters for a meeting, he asked Russ what the banging was and where it was coming from. With a serious face, Russ responded, "Oh, that's an unexploded grenade one of the students who hates me dropped into the tank."

In class, Russ was not above faking being stabbed or having his own throat cut, with artificial blood dripping all over the lecture hall floor, in order to teach certain cutting methods. "O.K.," he'd say to his class, "somebody loan me a knife so I can demonstrate murder wounds." Of course, another student or two would pass out watching the "blood" he had carefully concealed in the palm of his hand flow all over.

On one occasion, Vorpagel, while demonstrating how easy it was to make nitroglycerin, deliberately dropped the capsule and made a dash for the exit. That sent the class of sixty to the floor.

Intermingled with such light moments were some of the most gruesome murder photos in American crime history. "Part of my job was to toughen these police officers, to harden them, to set the stage for future toughness. I would encourage them to get reassigned to something easier in their police forces, such as the burglary or vice details, if they couldn't deal with the color photos I was putting up on the screen. Naturally, a number of my students complained about my teaching, the humor, the seriousness. And, just as naturally, I got a lot of write ups from my SAC," Russ recalls.

As far as Vorpagel's sense of humor with the clerical staff was concerned, the young secretaries, always gullible, always stung, loved it. One morning, Susan Efimenco, the BSU clerk said, "Oh, I see you're going to headquarters this morning." "Yeah," answered Russ, "I have to attend an autopsy." "Well," she smiled, "Will you bring me back a present from one of the nearby stores?" "Sure," smiled Russ, his mind already at work. When he got to headquarters, Vorpagel went into a jewelry store, asked for a small box with some tissue in it, and went back to the autopsy.

He took an olive from the cafeteria at lunch, and, when he returned to Quantico that afternoon, handed Susan her "present." "Well," recalls Russ, "You can imagine what happened when I presented her with the jewelry box and she opened it. She screamed, dropped the box, and with the olive rolling across the floor, I said, 'Yeah, that's one of eyeballs from that rotten bastard we autopsied this morning.' Susan almost fainted.

"On another occasion, Kathy Meadows, the young but outstanding

BSU secretary, had the hiccups. Since I had the office next to hers, I shouted through the wall, 'Quit hiccupping, It's bothering me!' Well, the poor thing kept hiccupping, so I put a blank cartridge in my starter pistol, walked into the office, and fired a blank shot into the floor and she screamed. Her hiccupping stopped, and I went back to my office and resumed my work. Roger Depue, the unit chief at the time, thought my action was a little in excess."

But, Russ insists, there had to be some levity, some humor, and some lightness because of the very tragic work they did, day in and day out. As an example of that work: "Jimmy Reese, who was teaching police stress at the time, came into my office and saw the color photo of a dead little blonde daughter with maggots covering his entire face. Jimmy, who had a blonde boy about the same age as this one, slammed it down. 'I can't take this work anymore,' he said quietly. He turned away, walked into Chief Depue's office and said, 'I never want to do another profile again. You have to reassign me to something else.' And Jimmy went on to become one of the top instructors at the National Academy on police stress.

"Jimmy was one of the nicest, gentlest men you could ever meet. Never said a negative word about anyone. In fact, in a lot of ways, he was really very innocent. I remember once he asked a female cop in his class, 'What would you say about the kind of woman who would proposition me in a bar? Pretend for a moment I'm alone at a bar and she walks over and starts to hustle me. What kind of woman is that?' The female cop looked at Jimmy and said, 'She'd have to be pretty hard up.' Reese was so naive that he once locked his keys in the car and got very upset and frustrated. 'Oh, I have to go to Washington and get another set of keys. Look at what I've done.' I laughed, grabbed a coat hanger, went down to the car and within seconds had it open. He was amazed! He had never opened a car door, or seen it done, with a coat hanger."

5

The
Nine

"Was there ever a Golden Age in the BSU? I don't know. Maybe during a time between 1975 and 1985, when The Nine were in search of killing enigmas to destroy. You see, the true story of the BSU is about three or four different aggregates of very strong and unusual personalities coming together at the right time in the same place to work miracles. No one individual was or is today the BSU. It was a group, a chemistry at work, something very special that can't really be defined in words or history."

A CURRENT BSUER ON THE TEACHING STAFF AT THE ACADEMY

We asked, during a recent interviw, "You mean, then, the Nine were able to combine body, mind, and spirit to solve the most difficult of crimes?" The answer was an unequivocal, "Yes." As one anonymous BSUer laughed recently, "Take a quart of synergy, sprinkle in a pint of synchronicity,[1] and a touch or two of insanity, and you wind up with a bowl of psychosynchronic-synergism. That was us!" The difficult work of a number of contributors results in a whole greater than the sum of its parts. Such was the synergy in the Behavioral Science Unit during the late 1970s and early 1980s.

As invited observers of innumerable crime scenes and active participants in hundreds upon hundreds of paper and photo autopsies, the so-called Nine—Conrad Hassel, Larry Monroe, Roger Depue, Howard Teten, Pat Mullany, Roy Hazelwood, Dick Ault, Robert Ressler, and John Douglas—often felt like kidnap victims desperately struggling to learn where they were from the few and small chinks of light they perceived through their blindfolds. Both within the Academy and outside with law enforcement agencies, they taught, consulted, interviewed, researched, and profiled to assist in stemming the ever increasing tides of serial murder, rape, hostage taking, arson, espionage, and counterespionage. Not only were they helping make America a fraction safer, but also were offering a model of what crime detection might be. Because of their achievements, half a century from now, criminologists, as well as all law enforcement personnel, will have much better definitions for the types of criminals they are expected to delineate.

This chapter identifies those enduring icons who, in their own way, nurtured, contributed, dedicated themselves, and made incomparable contributions to the growth and development of the Behavioral Science Unit. Today, all are still alive, still active, and on call for law enforcement. Each, still a formidable character, continues to carve out a life and a legacy.

Conrad Hassel

Take for example, Conrad Hassel. Long recognized as one of this nation's top specialists in hostage negotiations, Conrad, a compelling man with an impish grin, now in his middle sixties, was involved in the very beginning of the formation of the unit.

"Connie," as he is still affectionately referred to by his retired BSU colleagues, served as a "grunt rifleman" and later as a squad leader in the "B" Company Fire Team, First Battalion, First Marine Division, Fifth Marines, Fleet Marine Force during the Korean War. After that conflict, during which he received a Purple Heart in addition to the Korean Service Medal with two campaign stars, Hassel attended the University of Portland (Oregon), then returned to the Holy Cross School, where he graduated with a B.A. in English literature and philosophy. From there, he headed east, where, in 1961, he earned a Juris Doctorate (J.D. degree) from Duquesne University School of Law in Pittsburgh, Pennsylvania. It was at this time that he was recruited into the FBI.

From the very beginning, Conrad meant, in one way or another, to create, influence, administer, and propel the agency he had decided to devote his career to. Almost immediately he was assigned to Mississippi and Alabama. From 1964 to 1967, Hassel investigated hate crimes, including the murders of the three civil rights workers, Goodman, Schwerner, and Chaney, as well as the murder of Mrs. Viola Liuzzo and other murders committed by the Ku Klux Klan.

In late 1964, Connie was transferred from the Mississippi FBI field office to the Los Angeles field office, then on to the resident agency at Long Beach. The Long Beach transfer was his eighth in the Bureau, including brief resident agencies in Boston and Springfield, Massachusetts.

Meanwhile, Hassel learned that a new FBI Academy was being planned for Quantico, Virginia, and decided he would try for an instructional position. Friends at Bureau headquarters advised him that his chances would increase if he had a master's degree in addition to his B.A. and J.D. So, during evenings and on weekends, he attended Cal State University at Long Beach, where he earned his Master of Science degree with an emphasis in criminal psychology and sociology.

While working for his M.S., Hassel continued investigating former Soviet and Soviet-bloc espionage operations—as he had done while serving in counterintelligence in Boston—and targeting organized crime matters and thefts from interstate and foreign shipments on the docks in Long Beach, San Pedro, and Terminal Island.

Conrad eagerly awaited the call from Quantico, but no transfer was offered. That is, until an incident occurred during the summer of 1972, when a decision he made captured headlines across America.

On the late afternoon of Friday, July 12, Conrad was the only special agent working in the FBI field office when the telephone rang. It was a call from the Long Beach Coast Guard Station, notifying the FBI that a forty-foot ketch had been stolen by seven "longhaired hippie types" and was in the Catalina Channel heading for the open Pacific. Hassel commented that it sounded like a job for the LAPD's harbor division, since the boat had been stolen from its berth at Fleitz Landing in Los Angeles Harbor. Conrad hung up without further discussion or thought. The caller telephoned again a few minutes later and informed Hassel what the LAPD had said: since the million-dollar ketch was now outside the three-mile limit, it was under federal jurisdiction and in Hassel's hands.

Cursing beneath his breath, Conrad called the Assistant U.S. Attorney and inquired if indeed the FBI had jurisdiction of the problem. The Assistant U.S. Attorney wasn't sure, but authorized Hassel to take action. Conrad and his partner, Jim Freeman, were immediately flown by helicopter out to the eighty-foot Coast Guard cutter *Cape Hatteras* and lowered by a rope ladder onto the cutter's deck. Both agents were still wearing their suits, white shirts, ties, and street shoes. "Needless to say," Conrad recalls, "we certainly felt we were out of place on board the craft dressed like junior bankers." But he confidently grabbed the loud hailer and walked out on the bow of the cutter and demanded that the malefactors immediately "douse sails" and "heave to" so they could board. No response.

"Jim and I were at a loss as to what to do next, as the captain of the cutter, who had informed us that the yacht was a ketch named *Resolute* previously owned by Spencer Tracy, was on the radio with his headquarters in San Diego. The local Coast Guard commander in San Diego ordered the crew of the cutter to fire a few rounds from the .50-caliber machine gun mounted across the bow of the cutter, which was done," Conrad remembers.

Meanwhile, the Los Angeles press somehow got wind of the story and dispatched their own boat loaded with TV cameras. In addition, someone on board the cutter was giving the *Los Angeles Examiner* and *LA Times* a blow-by-blow description. Hassel's own SAC, "not one of your understanding bosses in the Bureau," knew absolutely nothing about the action until he watched it on the evening news. Says Conrad, "To put it mildly, he was not amused, since he was getting inquiries from Washington headquarters and was unable to answer any of them, since only me and Jim knew what was going on."

Nothing in his FBI training had prepared Hassel for a sea chase reminiscent of Prohibition days. After much soul searching and discussion, and with the ketch headed farther out into the Pacific, the two decided to seize the *Resolute*. They organized several members of the crew with their own M-1 rifles, then threw grappling hooks aboard, and went over the side to board the vessel.

Fortunately, once on board the *Resolute*, they met with no resistance from five men, federal fugitives, and two fifteen-year-old sisters, all of whom were arrested on charges of grand theft. But all the men were unable to transfer to the cutter because the ocean had become increasingly rough. There was little choice but to be towed back more than twenty miles to the Coast Guard station, arriving there early the next morning as a small army of reporters and cameramen, who had set up klieg lights, awaited them in the dark.

The incident, which was now known nationwide and even ended up on the front page in various foreign countries, got Conrad his coveted position at the FBI Academy. Although certain "semi-notorious senior officials back at FBI headquarters" were angry with him, Jack Kirsch, who headed the Inspection and Training Division, decided Hassel was exactly the kind of man he needed and "through a series of machinations, I ended up as an instructor at the Academy assigned to the BS unit," laughs Conrad. "I was surprised about that assignment, notwithstanding the M.S. in crime. After all, I had a B.A. in English literature plus a law degree and saw myself more as a poet and/or a lawyer. But as soon as I arrived, I was told by some wag that I was selected for the BSU because I had a serious psychological problem which was technically named Terminal Wise-Ass Syndrome."

When Hassel arrived from Long Beach in August of 1972, Tom Strentz, Pat Mullany, Jack Pfaff, and Howard Teten were already in place. In fact, Kirsch asked Tom if he thought he could work with Hassel as a team of two. Strentz said, "Of course." To this day, Strentz never allows Conrad to forget his choice, since Hassel wound up serving as Tom's boss in the Special Operations and Research Unit.

"Soon cops started bringing in, and then mailing in, unsolved murders," Hassel recalls, "and we were spending all our time reviewing the cases and trying to help solve them, and provide leads on where to locate and how to interview the suspects. The Bureau at first paid little attention to the work of the unit. But soon it came knocking on our door for assistance in areas it couldn't handle and we were very helpful. Not only this, but profiling became a science *cum* art. Of course, the real leaders and innovators in profiling and hostage negotiation were Bud Teten and Pat Mullany. Our unit was even starting to get a reputation in Europe, since we were beginning to solve cases for various foreign law enforcement agencies. In fact, later, one of our newcomers, Roger Depue, solved a serial murder case in Switzerland."

In the middle and late 1970s, the Behavioral Science Unit grew many subunits to carry out all the tasks given to them. This meant the units kept adding programs and staff as required. In fact, the Bureau, as well as various police agencies, made so many requests during the mid-1970s regarding hostage issues that it was apparent a course on hostage negotiations was necessary. By 1974, approval was granted for Teten and Mullany to team-teach the first ever such course at the Academy.

In 1975, Mullany was called to Indiana to negotiate with a bank robber who had wired a 12-gauge shotgun around a bank manager's neck. Pat conducted a face-to-face negotiation and successfully resolved the dangerous situation when he secured the release of the hostage and the surrender of the subject. However, he found himself in trouble with the Bureau for assuming the responsibility to offer the gunman immunity from prosecution if he freed his hostage. No one will ever know how many lives Pat saved during that incident. And to this day, he has never received the credit he deserved for that effort. After that he would say, concerning requests for his expertise by local authorities, "Sorry, don't do McDonald's."

After the Munich Olympic disaster occurred, the Bureau became concerned about terrorism, especially against the United States. Once again, Jack Kirsch got into the act, this time by writing a $250,000 grant proposal to study terrorism and all its domestic facets. The new unit was known as the Special Operations and Research Unit (SOARU); Hassel was named unit chief and soon Tom Strentz, as well as various other tactical experts, joined him. It included both behavioral and tactical experts.

Conrad started teaching hostage negotiations, crisis management, and terrorist history, among other courses at the Academy. Soon he branched out by teaching local police departments and the military about the techniques and strategies of hostage negotiations. Much of this was done by phone from the FBI's Crisis Center at headquarters. During Hassel's tenure as unit chief between 1976 and 1984, SOARU was involved in most of the aircraft hijacking cases, as well as other hostage or terrorist cases that took place in the United States during those years. Roger Depue and various BSUers were dispatched to European police agencies to assist on actual cases. In London, this led to an eventual exchange with Scotland Yard and other police staff, faculties, and students between the training academies of the United Kingdom and the FBI Academy. The first faculty exchange almost resulted in disaster.

Roger Depue recalls that it was during the summer of 1976 that the first faculty exchange program at the FBI Academy began with an exchange of faculty members between the prestigious Bramshill Police Staff College in Bramshill, England, and the Behavioral Science Unit. The BSU sent John Mindermann to England and Bramshill sent Peter

Watson to America. Larry Monroe was responsible for making sure Peter had a meaningful experience during his tour of duty in the States. One of the activities Larry thought Peter might enjoy was seeing a Civil War battle reenactment at Bull Run Park in Manassas, Virginia.

Larry hyped the reenactment until Peter was excited to see it, but due to heavy traffic, they missed it. As they sat in the spring heat amid the deadlocked traffic they could hear the muskets firing and a barrage of cannon fire. Larry was humiliated, distressed, and very angry. That evening, Roger Depue told Larry that he was going to West Virginia to open up his cottage for the summer and maybe Peter would like to accompany him. It might not be very exciting, but at least Peter would get to put his feet into a different state of the union.

Peter said he would be "delighted" to go with Roger to West Virginia. On the following morning, Peter was collected from the FBI Academy and Roger, his wife Sharon, and Peter headed west. It had occurred to Roger that it was spring and the Shenandoah River would probably be filled with the mountain run-off and might present an interesting canoe ride. He packed a dry change of clothes for himself and Peter, who was about the same size. Once at the cottage, Roger offered Peter a cold beer and they commiserated about their past experiences in the military and law enforcement. As they walked around the cottage checking to see that it was unmolested during the long winter, they spotted the canoe, tipped on its side against the building. Roger asked, "Peter, you wouldn't be interested in trying that thing out on the river, would you?" Peter grinned and said, "I'd be delighted." And he took a long pull on his Budweiser.

As they lifted the Grumman nineteen-foot canoe off of the top of the car, Roger observed that the river was high and the water was running swiftly, despite the wideness of the river at that point. Peter climbed aboard and seated himself in the narrow bow with his paddle across his knees. Roger placed the remaining beers into the bottom of the canoe, then pushed off from the shore and carefully sat in the rear.

The Nine

The river easily took the slender craft out into middle where the current moved more quickly. "Are you ready for another beer, Peter?" Roger asked. Peter responded, "Right, mate." Things were going well.

As the canoe rounded a bend of the river and became more narrow and rocky, the current picked up considerably. Roger began to wish he had had one less beer as he realized that successful navigation through the remaining portion of the trip would take some skill. Around the next bend he could see the water rushing through the rocks, sending sprays of white foam into the air. Suddenly he became aware that he had failed to put life preservers in the boat, an omission he had never made before. As the water buffeted them through the narrow passages between rocks, he imagined the headlines "FBI Agent Takes British Police Official to His Watery Death."

The canoe take-out point was only about a mile ahead, but that mile was the wildest portion of the ride. The huge rocks made control extremely difficult. The canoe had to pass under a bridge, then through jutting rocks until an opening appeared that led to the elevated riverbank. When the opening appeared, they would have to paddle for all they were worth to make the diagonal shot to the bank. Along the riverbank, the roots of large trees protruded into the water, which could be grasped to keep the canoe from continuing down the river. In all seriousness, Roger told Peter to listen up. "Peter," he shouted, "When we go under the bridge I will steer us towards large rocks on the right; there will be an opening and we will have one chance to shoot through it. Understand?" Peter, seemingly oblivious to the danger he was in, responded with a hearty, "Righto, mate."

As they rounded the last bend in the river, they could see the water smashing into the pilings of the bridge, sending foaming spray into the air. Roger said, "Peter, when I tell you to dig, you paddle hard on the left side of the canoe." In a moment they were under the bridge and into the wild water of the large rocks. The sides of the aluminum canoe smacked the rocks as it moved swiftly between them. Then, there was the opening, with a clear view of the tree roots along the riverbank. "Dig!" Depue screamed. "Dig!" The two men paddled with all their strength and the canoe made a sharp move toward the bank. Finally, the front of the canoe rammed into the tangle of roots along the bank and Peter reached forward to grab handfuls of roots. He then secured the canoe to a large, thick root. They crawled out of the canoe, onto the heavy roots, and eventually onto the bank. Finally, they dragged the battered aluminum boat out of the churning water. They almost collapsed on the muddy bank. There were two full Budweiser beers remaining in the bottom of the boat. They turned the canoe over and sat on it while they drank the beers and waited for Roger's wife to arrive with the car.

Roger looked with considerable admiration at his partner. He said, "I have to tell you that I wasn't sure we would make it. If we missed our cue, we could have gone down the river to the dam and maybe over it." Peter held up his can of beer and touched it to Roger's. He winked and said, "One must have faith in one's mate, mustn't one?"

In addition to programs like the exchange with Bramshill, the SOAR's unit would help train America's highly elite military units and exchange military students and instructors from elite units in England, Germany, and Israel, with whom the unit ran joint training exercises. The SOAR's unit, under Hassel's leadership, also ran a series of international terrorist symposia at the FBI Academy, which were organized by Joe Conley, another unsung hero who used to run the terrorist squad in New York. He made contacts worldwide with police and intelligence agencies because of his particular expertise in hostage negotiations. He also traveled throughout Europe and the Far East presenting professional papers and lectures, testifying before Congress, and lecturing to delegations from the United Nations. The SOAR's unit was heavily involved at this time with the security for the Lake Placid and Los Angeles Olympics.

"It was my intent that the SOAR's unit would be the Bureau's resource for counterterrorism, and it was in that spirit that the initial hostage rescue team was selected by the SOAR's unit and received some of its training from our staff," says Hassel. "The idea of such a resource was borrowed and duplicated within Scotland Yard, with the exception that they used their military as a reserve team."

Today, Conrad feels credit for the SOAR's unit growth and development must also be given to Captain Francis Boltz of the New York Police Department; Dr. Frank Ochberg, former assistant director of the National Institute of Mental Health and Assistant Surgeon of the U.S.; Deputy Director Peter Walton, New Scotland Yard; and Assistant Commissioner David Vaness, New Scotland Yard. "Without the help of these people," says Hassel, "neither the BSU nor the SOAR's unit would have been so successful."

In terms of what made the staff unique, and what seemed to "click" between the men of the Behavioral Science Unit, and eventually the SOAR's unit people, was, according to Connie, "the fact that we all came from very humble beginnings, and had to work awfully hard for whatever we achieved, such as our education and degrees. We were all exposed to similar experiences both in the military and the FBI, mainly the Marine Corps, and we all got shot at and sometimes hit. I guess you might call it the same kind of bond that exists among Marines in combat. At least that's the way it seemed at the beginning."

Hassel felt the greatest success of the BSU was to get it "institutionalized," not only in the Bureau but also internationally. The second largest success, in his thinking, was to bring the fields of psychology, psychiatry, and mental health together and with law enforcement in general. "For years these disciplines had been natural enemies. Now, a degree of respect among them had been achieved, which has been very beneficial to all."

Conrad continues, "My biggest personal disappointment was the failure of the Bureau to establish the SOAR's unit as the primary Bureau instrument and focal point—including expertise in crisis management, behavioral science, and the tactical and technical expertise required in a terrorist incident—as it was while I was chief. I think this effort would have saved much grief in some of our recent efforts against terrorists. It should also maintain close liaison with the Center for Disease Control (CDC) in Atlanta and the Nuclear Search Teams."

After serving in the Bureau for more than twenty-three years, Conrad Hassel retired in the spring of 1984. Since then he has been practicing law in northern Virginia, where he specializes in criminal defense, domestic relations, wills, and estates. He was appointed Guardian ad Litem by the Virginia Supreme Court, a position that requires him to protect the rights of children and incapacitated citizens. He also was appointed Commissioner in Chancery where he sits as Circuit Court Judge to try certain domestic relations cases. Conrad is also an affiliate professor with George Mason University in Fairfax, Virginia.

Incidentally, the very first article to emanate from the Behavioral Science Unit and appear in a professional journal was written by Conrad and entitled, "The Hostage Situation: Exploring the Motivation and the Cause." Published in the September, 1975, issue of the *Police Chief*, less than three years after the BSU was formally organized, the 3,000-word article focused primarily on viewing the kidnap-hostage situation by examining the subject's motivation. Conrad explored the rational political motive, the motivation of escape, the prison hostage situation, the mentally deranged, the nature of the sociopathic personality, the victim, and the need for a coordinated response. Wrote Hassel,

> The hallmark of any police reaction in a kidnap/hostage situation must be blending of tactical response and behavioral know-how. This requires the development of team tactics using blocking and containment forces. It requires expertise in weapons use, deployment, and instant communications; and it requires the use of behavioral experts coordinated by coolheaded and professional leadership. This is a challenge that is being met by many police departments.
>
> Admittedly, much of that knowledge which would enable police or anyone to predict human motivation and response is not known.

However, detailed analysis of each new hostage situation by professionals in law enforcement and behavioral science increases the ability of the police to refine their response while adding to that body of knowledge which will save lives.

Almost no one in the history of the Behavioral Science Unit has received more distinction or higher recognition than Connie Hassel. Recently, we asked if he would share with readers his successes. After considerable pressure and persuasion by us, friends, and colleagues, Connie related the following incidents:

"With regard to discussing further interesting or amusing incidents, I assure you that many such incidents do exist, but just about every one of them would be an admission of the violation of some Bureau regulation, and as a lawyer, I think discretion is the better part of valor.

"I can say that on one occasion, on one of the many aircraft hijacked from Miami to Cuba, Tom Strentz was given permission by the Cuban government to travel to Cuba and negotiate the incident. The hijacker was a bank robber, and Tom was at the end of the runway in Miami in an aircraft, ready to take off, when the hijackers surrendered. I'm sure the decision to allow Strentz to go was made close to the top of the Cuban government; probably Castro himself was involved, since this was the first and last time such permission was ever granted. It would have been a great opportunity to establish ties with the Cubans.

"On another occasion, some federal prisoners who were in the basement holding cells of the Federal District Court House in Washington, D.C., took over the basement and Howard Teten and I started negotiating by phone. Somehow a local disk jockey got on the phone with the hostage takers. We had just about convinced the prisoners to surrender, but the disk jockey talked them into demanding a plane for Cuba. This represented one of the many times the media were less than helpful. It took us several more hours to end the situation.

"On one occasion, in the late seventies, the Philippine embassy was taken over by an individual who somehow got into the ambassador's office, held a gun to the ambassador's head, and demanded to speak to Marcos. Howard Teten and I were advisors on the scene, and the agent in charge asked me if he should allow the call to go through. I told him no since, knowing a little about Marcos, I was afraid that they would merely end up screaming at each other and raise the tension, further endangering the ambassador. About that time, Mrs. Marcos flew into Washington with an entourage and wanted to enter the embassy and talk to the hostage taker. Again I was asked whether she should be allowed in. Once again I said no, since I felt that Mrs. Marcos was not trained in negotiation and she might be injured. Fortunately, our negotiation was eventually successful and the ambassador was released.

"I might mention that in addition to my law practice, I was not out of the Bureau for a week when I was recruited by . . . [the CIA]. Because I had made presentations in that country before, in 1993 I was personally requested by the interior minister of an African country to help resolve an aircraft hijack. I was flown to that country and ended up negotiating for five days with the hostage takers, two males and a female, one of whom was a former paratroop officer armed with hand grenades. I was unable to talk them out of hijacking the aircraft; they wanted to fly to Rome and demanded one million dollars. I got them to accept transportation to a neighboring country and no money and release all hostages except the pilot and copilot. I thought that was a pretty good deal, but the minister of the interior refused to let the aircraft take off. I and one companion returned to the plane the following morning. During the night, the government had placed commandos under the aircraft by stealth. Since the aircraft was small, a jet commuter, the rear hatch was only waist high. It was my job to give the hijackers one more chance to surrender and, if they refused, to give the signal for the commandos to assault. I got all the hijackers standing in the rear hatch; they were unaware of the commandos. I could look down and see the commandos, and up at the hijackers. I was unable to talk the hijackers into surrendering and gave the signal and stepped aside. Two of the hijackers were killed immediately, and two of the passengers were wounded, though both recovered.

"I was personally commended by the president of the country, and awarded the Intelligence Star, the second highest-award for valor given by the . . . [CIA]. The medal was presented at Langley, Virginia before about two hundred invited guests chosen by me and representing family, friends, and of course, many present and former FBI agents. The medal was presented by James Woolsey, the director of the agency. I was advised that there had been some four hundred of these medals awarded since 1949 . . . and about two hundred of those were posthumous. I was also advised that I was the only former FBI agent who had been awarded one."

HOWARD "BUD" TETEN

Imposing and formidable, the professionalism of the legendary Howard Teten as well as his universally acclaimed, breakthrough criminal-profiling theories, are, by everyone's account, a hallmark in the annals of the Federal Bureau of Investigation. On the personal level, even his few critics, who mumble he's too "airy" and "an intellectual adventurer," acknowledge that his brilliance and readiness to assist have inspired affection, even awe, not only among his colleagues, but among law enforcement across the nation.

This vibrant man, called "the Gentle Titan" by teaching colleagues, is a compelling mix of intellect, accessibility, and simple, basic kindness. His distinguished, thirty-year career is peppered by honors, distinctions, and services that are unparalleled to this day.

Howard began his law enforcement career almost by accident.

Recently discharged from the U.S. Marine Corps and newly married, Howard entered Santa Ana College under the G.I. Bill for Korean War veterans. While in school, he relaxed on weekends by target shooting at a local pistol range. Due to his shooting proficiency, he soon came to the attention of local sheriff's office personnel, who also used the range. Within months, Howard was offered a job as a paid reserve and it was only a short time before he was trained and handling patrol assignments throughout the county.

Howard soon began to develop a particular interest in the intricacies of crime scene analysis and the collection of evidence. This interest resulted in many discussions with Jack Cadman, then chief of the county crime lab. Eventually, the interest turned to fascination and Teten decided to pursue a career in this field. Armed with the promise of a position in the crime laboratory upon completion of a criminalistics degree, Howard graduated from Santa Ana College and entered the School of Criminology at the University of California, Berkeley.

At Berkeley, Teten came under the tutelage of the noted forensic psychiatrist, Douglas Kelly. While not losing his interest in crime scene investigations, he became enthralled with the workings of the deviant mind. Moreover, Dr. Kelly advised him that he didn't have the type of personality necessary for the often lonely, repetitive work required in a crime laboratory. O.W. Wilson, the director of the school and a famous police chief in his own right, agreed. As a result, Teten ultimately switched his focus from criminalistics to a dual approach emphasizing police management and the psychological aspects of crime.

During this same time, his growing family made it necessary to supplement his G.I. Bill and he joined the San Leandro Police Department. After recruit training at a regional police training academy nearby, he was assigned to the midnight shift, an assignment that, while it allowed him to continue his schooling, offered precious little time for family and sleep. In 1960, when he graduated from the university, he was promoted to a position within the identification division. There, his duties included the processing of prisoners after their arrest and conducting crime scene investigations.

Two years later, in 1962, Howard joined the FBI. Here again, fate had intervened. Teten had contacted the Secret Service in San Francisco regarding a position. However, when he went to their office, he found they did not accept applicants who were over six foot four inches in height. While exceptions were occasionally made, he knew that, at six foot six inches, it was unlikely in his case. While in the federal building in San Francisco, he decided to visit the FBI office. Five hours later, he received a letter ordering him to report for FBI training in Washington, D.C. Though accepting the position meant a slight loss in pay, he was on his way.

After completing new agents training, Howard was assigned to the Oklahoma City field office. He arrived in July of 1962 with a pregnant wife and in 100-degree heat. They rented the first house they found with an air conditioning unit. He stayed in Oklahoma City only two short months before being transferred to a resident agency in Muskogee, Oklahoma. His work there was varied and exciting. And, with only two other agents in Muskogee, he was pretty much on his own. This was fine, except that occasionally his police and FBI training would conflict and place him in awkward positions. On one occasion, after leaving a jail with a signed confession from an incarcerated subject, he realized he had not advised him of his rights. Advising a suspect of his rights was not then a requirement for local police agencies, but it was necessary within the federal system. With some trepidation, he returned to the jail and was finally able to obtain a usable confession after an apology and a detailed explanation.

His second office of assignment was Cincinnati, then eighteen months later, Memphis, where he stayed until 1969. On arrival in Memphis, he was made the primary firearms instructor and police training coordinator for the division. These duties were, of course, in addition to his regular investigative assignments and required that he spend considerable time going from town to town throughout central and western Tennessee. In 1967, he attended an in-service school for general police instructors at the old FBI Academy in Quantico. Shortly after his return to Memphis, he was contacted by the special agent in charge of the office and asked if he would like to obtain a master's degree at the local university in preparation for becoming an instructor at the new FBI Academy being constructed at Quantico. Teten said yes, and in 1969, armed with an M.A. in sociology from Memphis State University and four children, he and his long-suffering wife undertook the move to headquarters.

Now with the rank of supervisory special agent and assigned to the training division, Teten spent the next few years teaching police management road schools. These were thirty-six- to forty-hour schools and seminars conducted for police executives at larger police departments and police academies throughout the United States. Each member of the four two-agent teams taught four hours a day while on assignment. The schedule was two weeks out and two weeks in each month. While in town, the agents upgraded their lesson plans and visual aids and lectured before the NA and various in-services. It was a killing pace, and all were delighted when the "flying management squad" was disbanded in the spring of 1972 and they were transferred to the new FBI Academy. Seven of the agents were placed in the Management Science Unit. Teten however, as a result of his newly developed course, Applied Criminology, was assigned to the Behavioral Sciences Unit.

With the opening of the new FBI Academy, Howard was teamed with Pat Mullany. During the next few years, the two of them refined and expanded the theoretical foundations of the psychological profiling procedures contained in the Applied Criminology course. Their lecture style was to use real crimes whenever possible and NA students were encouraged to bring their unsolved cases to the classroom. Within weeks, NA students were reporting that "old dog" cases were being solved. Soon cases were arriving at their desks by mail and by telephone. Within months, significant portions of their time were taken up with the analysis of unsolved murders, rapes, abductions, kidnappings, and extortions. Even so, this was a time when the nation was being overwhelmed by hostage takers, both in the air and on the ground. Teten and Mullany, working together, applied the basics of profiling to the hostage taker and developed the essence of a new technique—hostage negotiations. This, like psychological profiling before it, eventually developed into a major instructional area.

In 1978, after a back operation and the development of a chronic voice problem, Teten was selected to attend graduate school at the University of Maryland. Temporarily relieved of his teaching responsibilities, Howard focused primarily on specialized forms of profiling, forensic hypnosis, and alternative research methodologies. In 1979, he was awarded a Ph.D. in criminal justice. In 1980, he was promoted to unit chief and placed in charge of the Institutional Research and Development Unit (IRDU).

During this same time, the FBI undercover program was experiencing serious problems. After the completion of an undercover assignment a disproportionate number of agents were leaving the Bureau, committing crimes, or becoming disciplinary problems. Teten, known for his interest in undercover work, was asked to find the answer to the problem. After almost two years of research, interviews, and psychological testing, Teten was able to both identify the sources of the problem and offer a solution. Since it protected the psychological health of undercover agents, Howard called it the Safeguard program (see chapter 4). It involved a series of psychological tests and interviews and required the use of agents specially trained to evaluate personnel before, during, and after an undercover assignment. While there was some reluctance to accept the program, it was finally implemented. Its effectiveness was immediately apparent. The Safeguard program, like that of psychological profiling and hostage negotiation, is still utilized in the FBI.

As the reputation of the personnel working at IRDU began to grow, the unit became involved in a broad range of research endeavors. A nationwide police training needs assessment was conducted, and the job of the special agent was quantified with a job-task analysis—a project so large that at the time the only computer capable of analyzing the data was at an Air Force base in Texas. There were other types of research as well. Over the years, Teten had acquired a reputation for his willingness to tackle just about any type of problem and had used the writings of psychotics as teaching tools. For many in the Bureau, this meant that any exotic, offbeat problem was forwarded to IRDU. Crimes appearing to have cult or "other world" dimensions appeared on his desk frequently, including killings associated with demonic symbols or talismans, cattle mutilations, and entrails laid out in the shape of signs near a crime scene. Between 1982 and 1985, the IRDU had approximately twenty research/investigative projects going at any one time.

In January 1986, Howard Teten retired from the FBI. Shortly thereafter, he started his own consulting corporation. The next twelve years saw him employed on a wide range of jobs. Under the auspices of the U.S. government, he provided advice and assistance to authorities in some twenty-eight nations. In addition, working with another company, he conducted police management studies and risk assessments in over twenty cities and counties in the United States. Now retired again but still busy, Howard continues to prepare profiles when they are requested, examine the facts in alleged cult crimes, and make occasional presentations dealing with the psychological health of undercover agents.

PAT MULLANY

Jack Kirsch contacted Pat early in 1971 and asked if he was interested in being reassigned to the Academy when it opened the following year.

Pat, of course, was delighted to go academic, and suddenly Jack was a powerful new force in his career.

Previously, Mullany had served as a relief supervisor in Los Angeles. Then, according to Pat, "The carrot was waved to go to New York and attend Columbia University with the objective of getting a doctorate." This was to be accomplished before the opening of the new Academy facility, less than sixteen months away! "I was to get ready to join the new faculty. . . . I changed my office of preference from Los Angeles to New York and within less than three months I had a transfer in hand."

That spring, Pat left Los Angeles, where it was eighty-six degrees, and arrived in New York City, where it was a freezing three degrees. Not only was he in shock, but no one had prepared for his arrival, no admission papers had been filled out for Columbia, and he also found sixty-one cases to investigate! Mullany's first assignment was to serve as the FBI's liaison with NYPD for the West Eleventh Street townhouse bombing. "It was a classical example of the left hand not knowing what the right was doing. Columbia University never became a reality and my Ph.D. became a distant dream. Manhattan College was the reality. There, I enrolled in four classes on weekends where I later received my master's degree."

Needless to say, Pat was slightly unnerved at what had occurred. But being in New York at that time gave Kirsch the opportunity to transfer him to the new Academy. And, when he was in the Justice Building in downtown Washington, D.C., he offered what he felt was a new addition to the traditional Academy curriculum: abnormal psychology. "My preparation to teach before them," recalls Mullany, "was Kirsch sending me cryptic notes from Walter McLaughlin, whom I never met. I guess my approach was to teach the police that there are people in society who act abnormal and they have very little control over themselves, and, yes, there are another grouping of individuals who behave with animal responses and do not care."

Fortunately for Pat, and in spite of having been a religious brother, he had worked with delinquents and knew how to handle cops. For example, he knew enough to know that they had a better grasp on behavior than most psychiatrists, although they rarely knew the American Psychological Association's *Diagnostic and Statistical Manual* (DSM) classifications and their origins. "In a nutshell, I survived and enrolled in and passed Constitutional Law, required by the Academy. My abnormal psychology course was the most refreshing of all."

"Going to Washington, D.C.," recalls Mullany, "gave me the opportunity to meet with a man that I have the highest regard for as a professional and friend, Howard Teten. It was Howard that came up with the idea to merge his criminology with my psychology. It was a brilliant concept and it was the original kernel that grew into what is now commonly referred to as the BSU. Howard was far more of a detail person than I, and while I counted buses bringing in protestors at D.C. civil rights demonstrations, he started the formulation of what became the textbook in applied criminology. He is to be totally credited with authorship of that document and I will take credit for much input."

There existed an interesting relationship between Teten and Mullany for the next six years. Howard leaned toward research and studies while Pat turned more operational. Teten focused his intelligence, intuition, and imagination on crime scene photographs, especially if the crime was unsolved. The two men spent hours in those early years taking their course out to the police departments across the country. "We went to homicide institutes to teach," says Teten, "and we got invited to New York City to participate in Frank Boltz's first two hostage classes."

Mullany adds, "Let me make a brash statement. The concepts developed were planted by us, Teten/Mullany, for everything that developed years later into programs and centers for violent crime. Let me lay them out one after the other and in order:

The Nine

1. Psychological profiling
2. Hostage negotiations
3. Hypnosis as an investigative tool
4. Psycholinguistics
5. Profiling/psychological testing of undercover agents
6. Trauma counseling
7. Threat assessment
8. Assessment of intelligence targets
9. Victimology—'The Stockholm Syndrome.'

Conceived by Teten/Mullaney, each of the nine areas of study was handed down to the new members as they entered the unit. Some of the earliest and greatest contributors were, of course, Conrad Hassel, Tom Strentz, and Roger Depue. "While I make an across-the-board statement, giving the Teten/Mullany team credit for the origination of these concepts," says Pat, "the individuals who followed grew the concept."

An example is that after Teten and Mullany returned from the NYPD hostage class, they immediately called the BSU together and announced that this was where they had to go. Howard and Pat taught the first hostage negotiation classes at the Academy and on the road. "The others grabbed on and added to what was being taught. Psychological profiling was being done out of a shoebox until I made Howard tell me what he was doing," recalls Pat. "Complex cases were discussed and we reached out to the unit members for ideas. We knew people killed the way they lived. Now, we had to apply it to crime scenes." There were many local cases reviewed, many with successful recommendations. The very first case this was applied to within FBI jurisdiction was Susan Jaeger's kidnapping in Bozeman, Montana (see chapter 3).

As early as 1972, the Behavioral Science Unit was beginning to permutate. Jack Kirsch, John Pfaff, Dick Harper, Roger Depue, Larry

Monroe, Tom O'Malley, Jim Siano, Alan Whittaker, and even Bill Peters were the true sociologists of the unit. Hence, they were edging towards a mastery of everyday urban police issues. They looked upon "society" as the potential beast. But Teten and Mullany were always preoccupied, even driven, to the potential individual beast. "It is true that we were all one unit," says Mullany, "but we were as different as black and white."

Reflecting upon the BSU in mid-1970s, Pat continues, "We brought in a third generation of behavioral science members in approximately 1974 and 1975. Like Hassel and Strentz, Bob Ressler and Dick Ault were two who contributed. Then Bob Fitzpatrick arrived in the unit, although he did not last long. Fitzy could cover a class and lectured well, but he tired quickly and left for headquarters. Ressler and Ault were different. Bob was bright and daring, never afraid to try something new. He took psychological profiling a step further, interviewing the mass murderers and serial killers, and suggesting a database be established. With no approval and on his own, he ventured into a unique and serious area of study. Meanwhile, Ault stayed more structured and did a great job in the trenches.

"What was common to us all was a leadership that was for the most part academically inadequate. Many of the assistant directors we had were regarded for their fieldwork but had no sense what it was to be part of a university. Fortunately, for the most part they stayed out of the way and we were able to develop programs that would live for decades. Great expectations surrounded one assistant director. But he turned out to be the worst for the academy. He put demands on the faculty that were for his own interests. Individuals who came into the BSU with a zealous spirit of upward achievement did not last too long."

In those early formative years, politics within the academy were apparently subtle. There was division within the faculty: those who were outspoken for excellence, and those who quietly sat back, not exposing themselves to criticism. For the most part, the outspoken were also the "workers" and "innovators." These were the people who really drove the ideas that would last. "Unfortunately, in an organization like the FBI," says Pat, "there is some truth that if you stay away from an operational division and remain too long in the training division, you can lose touch with the real work of the FBI."

In Pat's case, he felt he was standing on the bridge between two forces. But unlike many at the Academy, he had the opportunity to engage in a variety of operational cases. Mullany had a strong personal relationship with Dick Gallagher, who was the assistant director of the criminal division. Out of that relationship, and trust, Pat and Dick had referred to them, by other BSUers, Dr. Murray Miron from the Syracuse University. Pat personally handled Miron during his early work with the FBI. His initial entry into the BSU was during the Patty Hearst case, when he analyzed the tapes and predicted she would become a member of the Symbionese Liberation Army.

Says Pat, "Although Dr. Miron did some very good initial work, I feel, looking back today, that I helped create a monster. My faith and confidence in Murray Miron diminished as the years went by. He used the same hackneyed material to obtain several contracts with other federal agencies. He was a personal embarrassment. For me personally, the ultimate betrayal was when he authored a book on hostage negotiations using several cases I was personally assigned and without ever telling me he was writing a book or asking for my input. There were numerous inaccuracies in his writings. But the killer was when he referred to me in his book; he misspelled my last name, this word expert. The last case where I had exposure to Miron was on a nuclear extortion matter in North Carolina. His analysis was so horrid, I had major problems in convincing the criminal division not to listen to him."

Shortly after Patty Hearst was captured and was put on trial, Mullany enjoyed the privilege of appearing for the prosecution in San Francisco on what happens, psychologically, to a person in captivity.

INTO THE MINDS OF MADMEN

In 1975, the Detroit division had a horrendous case where over fifty patients became victims of someone injecting them with Pavulon, causing respiratory arrests. Pat consulted with Dr. Herbert Speigel during the course of interviewing victims using hypnosis. Speigel, a renowned New York psychiatrist who pioneered the early research and investigations on what happens to victims in captivity, was a major resource during those early years.

As a direct result of teaching many of the hostage classes in the earliest years, Mullany became the FBI's lead negotiator. He was used in numerous national cases and received a great deal of recognition for it. 1977 was a bumper year for hostage negotiations: Tony Kiritsis in Indianapolis; Corey Moore in Cleveland; and the Hanafi Muslims in Washington, D.C., where 137 people were held hostage, all occurred within a three-month period. Pat worked on these cases day and night until they were successfully negotiated. The pressure on Pat was incredible, mostly stemming from the politics surrounding the cases and the Bureau's transition from a closed organization to a more open one.

Again, Pat had to face the question: were he and the other BSUers instructors or were they operational? The heated debates continued. "I believe as the years went by they have developed a reasonable approach, realizing that there was expertise that had to be used in real live Bureau cases and that we should not keep this expertise on a shelf when it was needed," Pat says.

It was during this time that Mullany received one of the "worst ass-chewings" of his thirty-two-year career in the FBI. It came from Jack McDermott, the associate director, after Pat successfully assisted in the Hanafi Muslim case. The issue? An interview with Mullany appeared in the *Washington Post* concerning the FBI and hostage negotiations. Did McDermott realize that Homer Boynton, assistant director of public affairs, had arranged the exclusive for the purpose of getting the Bureau good, and long overdue, exposure? Obviously not. For some unknown reason Pat hadn't gotten around to telling them.

In the years that followed, Pat became a permanent member of every command center when there was a hostage taking or hijacking. "Never did I realize, until told by Director Webster, that this role helped me in the general Washington area when I was being promoted to the ASAC position. Looking back, I cannot cite exactly when the training division was first drawn in to supporting the criminal division in ongoing cases. I do not recall anyone that did it to the extent that I was called upon."

Then, in 1978, the Teten/Mullany team started to break up. Pat was appointed to the State Department committee to combat terrorism, while continuing to lecture on the psychology of the terrorist. "I testified before Congress, in conjunction with the terrorism section of the criminal division while I was in the training division. There was a great tug on me from headquarters and quite frankly, there were times I wondered who I worked for."

After Pat was assigned to headquarters on the inspection staff, where he served for seven months, he was appointed unit chief in the terrorism section. There, he completed many of the supervisory duties of that program. Even while on the inspection staff, Pat was able to share his expertise with the New Orleans division on a particularly gruesome serial murderer, which ended in an arrest and conviction.

While unit chief in the terrorism section, Pat lectured worldwide on terrorism matters with emphasis on behavioral science. He was honored to be asked to the State Department to assist in the Iranian Crisis, which lasted 444 days. He was present for every major hijacking or hostage case occurring in the United States. Mullany testified in the area of victimology before the U.S. Supreme Court when it dealt with the case involving the Innocent Victims of Wounded Knee. Pat was pleased that, although he sat at headquarters somewhat checkmated by his former colleagues back at the Academy, he was being called upon to do many things including initiating in the training division.

Pat smiles as he concludes, "When I read or look at the news on television and hear mention of a police department's hostage negotiation team being called out, I feel very proud. When Teten/Mullany started back in the early seventies, there was no such thing. When I see the TV shows, such as *Profiler*, etc., I get a kick and realize that big money is being made of a concept that Teten/Mullany made fly."

LARRY MONROE

Lost in the shadows of the Behavioral Science Unit, whose reputation in profiling, hostage negotiations, etc., was gradually growing nationally, was Larry Monroe, affectionately known as "The Chief" to his staff. A handsome man with strong, well-formed features and a gentle, smiling, good nature, he was also a pioneering administrator with pluck and political skills, and a home-loving husband and father of three daughters.

He received his baptism by fire at the Academy thanks to the managerial leadership of his two predecessors, Jack Kirsch and John Pfaff, and learned the art of teaching from colleagues like Howard Teten, Pat Mullany, Roy Hazelwood, Bob Ressler, and Con Hassel. By March of 1978, Monroe was primed for the most challenging responsibility of his career.

Kirsch had predicted at the conclusion of his tenure as unit chief that the strain of BSU leadership ruled out men of ordinary intelligence, physique, and discretion. Future chiefs would have to be picked from among a very small class of the best, most wise, disciplined, prudent, and even athletic agents the FBI, and hence the BSU, had to offer.

By all accounts, Larry was all this and more. Chin tilted high, a reassuring, quiet, and self-possessed look about him announced he was always accessible and never tired of answering questions or impugning the motives of his opponents at headquarters.

Born in the Bronx in 1941 and a devout Catholic, Larry graduated from Holy Cross College in Worcester, Massachusetts, in 1963, where he received a Bachelor of Science degree in political science. After a short stint as a Marine Corps officer, Larry attended City University of New York's Graduate School of Police Administration. In November of 1964, he entered the FBI and served in the Jacksonville, Jackson, and New York City field divisions.

While on duty fulltime, Larry attended Long Island University in the evenings and on weekends. In 1974, he was awarded a master's degree in criminal justice. In addition, he graduated from the First National Executive Institute. Earlier in 1972, however, he was assigned as an instructor in the Behavioral Science Unit. Then, upon completion of a seven-month tour with the Planning and Inspection division, Larry, on March 13, 1978, was appointed unit chief of the BSU.

During Larry's tenure in the training division during the early 1970s, he specialized in urban police problems with specific emphasis on research and instruction in the areas of police/community relations and affirmative action, and urban politics. In 1973 and 1974, he directed the Bureau symposia on police/community relations and designed and supervised the training division's command-level, two-week specialized seminar in urban police problems.

Monroe was also involved in all aspects of the training division's priority training programs, including being a member of the executive staff of the FBI National Executive Institute (NEI), Law Enforcement Executive Development Seminar (LEEDS), as well as serving on the new agents and National Academy curriculum committee. His lecture-ships, memberships, and awards for service in the betterment of police/community relations are too numerous to mention here.

As unit chief of the Behavioral Science Unit, Larry both initiated and supervised numerous advanced research projects such as the Criminal Personality Research Program, which included psychological criminal analysis, psycholinguistics, hypnosis, and informant development and occupational stress and personal issues.

Other highlights of Monroe's FBI career include his 1990 appointment as academic dean of the Academy, a position he held until his retirement in 1994. But as chief academic official, Larry created the Bureau's Human Resource Development Plan, including coordinating liaison with all major national and international law enforcement organizations. He was the Academy's principal coordinator with the academic community and directed the FBI's affiliation with the University of Virginia, for which he had also served as adjunct professor since arrival at the Academy in 1972. Beginning in 1994, Monroe was employed by USATREX International as an independent contractor with the office of Antiterrorism Assistance, U.S. Department of State.

Of all his contributions during his thirty years of service, the one that he was proudest of was the arrest of Angela Davis, one of the FBI's "Ten Most Wanted Fugitives," on October 15, 1970. Wanted for unlawful flight to avoid prosecution for murder and kidnapping, Davis was captured at a midtown New York City hotel by Monroe and two other agents. She was charged in connection with the attempt by San Quentin convicts to escape while in the Marin County Superior Court in San Rafael, California, on August 7, 1970. During the escape attempt, three inmates, James McClain, William Christmas, and Jonathon Jackson, were killed. Jackson, age seventeen, who entered the courtroom carrying a gun Davis allegedly smuggled in for him, took Superior Court Judge Harold J. Haley hostage by taping two shotguns to his head. In the ensuing shootout that occurred on the street below the courtrooms of the Frank Lloyd Wright–designed Civic Center, Haley was killed and Assistant District Attorney Gary Thomas was seriously wounded. Angela Davis, who currently teaches courses in philosophy at the University of California at Santa Cruz, was twenty-six years old at the time. Larry traced a trail of phone calls from Angela Davis to David Poindexter, a wealthy Chicago resident, after the former Black Panther fled northern California following the failed escape attempt and subsequent shootout.

The Nine

"Miss Davis," Monroe began, "planned to flee to Cuba. In fact, she even went so far as to buy a textbook in elementary Spanish. If not, she certainly was headed for Canada. My agents learned through phone company records that a call had been placed three days after the Marin shootout to a Chicago apartment from the home of Franklin Alexander in Los Angeles. Alexander was a longtime friend of Miss Davis and a cochairman of her defense committee. Her car was found abandoned near his home. The Chicago apartment was rented to a "David Day," who was really Poindexter.

Then, Larry recalled, on August 14, 1970, a call was made from the Poindexter apartment to a phone booth near Alexander's home. After Monroe and his team linked Davis to Poindexter, they traced the pair to Florida through information gleaned from Poindexter's mother. Although they missed the couple there, on October 9 they searched a Miami apartment in which they had been staying, and Larry not only found the Spanish textbook, but a roll of film containing some fifty photos of Davis taken by Poindexter. He also found a notebook in which the fugitive said she "was not guilty and that she was being forced in exile." Larry sent copies of the photos to agents in New York, showing several hairstyles. But it was his team of agents checking some thirteen motel parking lots and garages that led to the arrest of Angela Davis. In one motel, an agent found the Toyota purchased for Poindexter by his mother in Florida.

Monroe chuckled as he described the circumstance of Davis's arrest in a hallway of the Howard Johnson Motor Lodge in New York City, where she was grabbed by his men and a wig "snatched" from her head. "Miss Davis's attorney, Howard Moor Jr., called our arrest a 'lucky guess' and the result of a 'dragnet approach,' but we were sure the woman we arrested was Miss Davis. And she was arrested because of good, old-fashioned legwork and intelligent investigative work by our team."

On Tuesday, October 20, 1998, Lawrence "Larry" John Monroe passed away at the age of fifty-eight. A long and meritorious career in federal law enforcement service was over. He is survived by his wife of thirty-two years, Carol, three daughters and their husbands, four sisters, and one brother. Also surviving Larry are four grandchildren and numerous nieces and nephews.

ROGER DEPUE

"It is his elixir, the core of his life," a former colleague and current business partner commented recently about Roger's love of the Behavioral Science Unit. "While other Bureau unit chiefs were considered termagants, Depue had, and still has, an unassuming simplicity of manner, a special tranquility, even a reassuringly quiet, meditative look about him that does not bespeak his force or firmness, and his genius for organization."

Tall, broad-shouldered, and always nicely dressed, Roger is a handsome, good-natured man who inspires confidence and admiration. Under his leadership, cherished lifelong friendships were forged. And as the BSU was often mocked, even martyred and marketed, the "great campaigner" kept the unit alive, functioning, and on course.

Born in Detroit and raised in Roseville, Michigan, Roger is the middle son of a police inspector and grew up in a family of five boys. After serving a tour of duty in the Marine Corps, he was married and raised three children. In Michigan, he served as a police officer and eventually became the chief of police in the city of Clare at the age of twenty-seven. He also was employed as the Clare County Juvenile Officer, where his duties included working with neglected, abused, and delinquent children.

After receiving his B.S. in psychology from Central Michigan University, he entered the FBI in 1968. As a special agent, he was assigned to the New Orleans and the Washington, D.C., field offices, receiving specialized training in a number of areas, including qualification as a police instructor and a firearms expert, and he was selected to be a member of the first FBI SWAT team, "Spider One." His investigative experience included civil rights, organized crime, fugitive, kidnapping, and extortion cases, and he investigated such cases as Watergate and the Freeway Phantom.

After receiving his M.S. in society and law in the administration of justice from American University in Washington, D.C., Depue was promoted to supervisor in the Behavioral Science Unit. Roger conducted training, directed research on the aberrant behavior of individuals and groups, and provided operational support during ongoing cases. In addition, he supervised the BSU's crime analysis, criminal profiling of violent offenders, community analysis, and group profiling.

In 1980, Depue was promoted to chief of the Behavioral Science Unit (after Larry Monroe's promotion to dean of the Academy) and in 1984 he became the first administrator of the FBI National Center for the Analysis of Violent Crime. Two years later, in 1986, Roger received a Ph.D. in counseling and development from American University and established psychological services programs to assist law enforcement officers experiencing job-related stress and trauma. He retired from the FBI in 1989 and immediately founded the Academy Group, Inc. (AGI), a forensic behavioral-sciences consulting firm specializing in the analysis of violent behavior for law firms and planning strategies for dealing with violence in the workplace. In addition, he has consulted with numerous companies and worked with over fifty "Fortune 500" companies resolving a wide variety of workplace problems.

On a more personal note, two years after the death of his wife in 1993, Roger entered a seminary where he did advanced study in philosophy counseling inmates at the Connecticut Maximum Security Prison. In January of 1999, he rejoined AGI, where he works as a consultant to business once again in the area of problem resolution in the workplace. He is also currently a consultant to the FBI and lectures regularly at the FBI Academy on a variety of behavioral science topics.

In short, Depue has held various administrative positions in numerous professional organizations, professorships at major universities, and has received many prestigious honors and awards. He has provided briefings to top U.S. government officials, including White House staff. Roger has testified before both houses of the U.S. Congress, attended and lectured at White House conferences, and has made presentations to top-level corporate executives. He is married to Joyce Ridick, a clinical psychologist, and currently resides in rural Virginia.

RUSSELL VORPAGEL

The respect and admiration criminal profilers of the Behavioral Science Unit have for Russ, since he joined the staff in 1979, are visceral feelings that derive from views of him as an implacable, quintessential colleague of exceptional character who exudes genuine warmth and empathy.

Certainly, there were those who were prone to judge his work ethics, sense of humor, and overall behavior in the Bureau as bizarre, according to the nostrums themselves. But Russ's quick mind, easy spontaneity, punctured from time to time with sulphurous blasts at those he found contemptible, endeared him to virtually all, from President Richard Nixon and FBI Director J. Edgar Hoover to the Academy custodians.

To show how much Russ exemplified the BSU spirit and imagination, consider a few of the following comments from colleagues at his retirement party on July 30, 1982, after twenty-two years of FBI service.

Larry Monroe: It was my initial intention in bidding you a fond adieu to enumerate the countless humorous and often hilarious situations in which you inevitably found yourself during your distinguished career in the FBI. . . . You are one of the few agents that managed to combine both a theatrical and investigative career as you posed on numerous occasions as a priest, male chauvinist libertarian, police officer, and God knows what.

Roger Depue: FBI Agent, attorney, criminologist, chess tournament champion, scholar, demolitions expert—the list goes on and on. You are a very complex and talented man, Russ. You possess the ability to build little ideas into masterful works of art, and at the same time, explode formidable structures into smithereens. As a manager of behavioral scientists, one would think that I would be somewhat immune to surprise and at times, outright shock. Not true! You have constantly amazed me with your uncanny ability to do the unexpected. I have finally figured out that you are predictably unpredictable.

Dick Ault: Your leadership, in a field fraught with forensic fact-finding firsts, is still undisputed.

Tony Rider: Though we worked together only a short period, I gained immeasurable knowledge from your experiences and insight. My only regret is that I did not have more time to explore your aberrant nature and distorted sense of reality. I think in time, I could have helped you.

Secretary Susan Efimenco, who, among all the BSUers, perhaps knew him best: I have learned a great deal from you during the years we have worked together (and some of those things I definitely could have gone on forever without knowing!) Your ever vociferous, ostentatious, redundant, pedantic, affable, gregarious, electric, and lovable personality makes you by far the most memorable character I have ever had the privilege to know.

From such comments, obviously, a psychological profile begins to emerge. Was Russ really a comedic renegade? Or a renegade angel who sometimes ran afoul of the Bureau's apparatus? Certainly he was no drone, dangerously trapped in the melancholy predicament of facing endless, frightening murder. As one of his former colleagues commented recently, "It would be easier to cast God for a Hollywood movie than to cast Russ and his genially deadpan style." Born in Milwaukee, Russ enlisted in the Navy in 1944 and served as a medical corpsman, spending this time in the war in Japan. Upon his discharge in the spring of 1946, Russ, in his own words, "screwed off." He recalls, "Under the G.I. Bill, I entered premed classes, got Cs and Ds. I dropped out and went to work at Nash Motor Company as an inspector. I quit, took a job building saddles, got engaged, went back to school, got married, took police oral exams, scored in the top 10 percent, joined the Milwaukee police force, and then the Korean War began. I was drafted, and went back as a corpsman. I was sent to the front line in Korea and attached to a Marine rifle company. I performed amputations on fingers and toes and plugged sucking chest wounds. I was hit by a mortar and my buddies threw me into the back of a truck filled with the dead, thinking that I, too, was gone. I recovered and was sent back to the front line, where, within a few days, I was hit again. This time they decided to send me home. I saw so many men suffering; I was horrified. Horrified at the chaos racked on the bodies of men. Horrified because the tiny amount of training of corpsman wasn't enough. I vowed that, should I survive, I would learn everything I could about any job I was in so that I would never have these feelings of incompetence and inadequacy, and the loss of self-worth that comes from them. It was then that I developed a deep hunger for psychology."

Back in Milwaukee, Russ returned to his police duties and enrolled in a college evening program where he worked for his B.A. Meanwhile, he was promoted to the vice division, and later to crimes of violence. Going to school during the day, he worked the 7:00 P.M. to 3:00 A.M. shifts. Observing how successful he was, the dean of the college asked Russ if he intended "to be a lawyer or a cop."

In 1960, Russ joined the ranks of the FBI and was placed in the training of local police officers investigating unusual and bizarre crimes. In those early years, he served as a special agent in New York, Detroit, Sacramento, and other assignments. As a member of the Behavioral Science Unit in 1979, Russ, of course, was a natural to assist the others in putting the psychological profiling team on the map. Featured on CBS's *60 Minutes*, he trained FBI personnel around the world and has taught courses in law enforcement to local and federal officers in thirty states and more than a dozen foreign countries. Eventually, Russ obtained his law degree from Marquette University.

Today, Russ is a consultant and expert witness in criminal cases for his students in law enforcement and prosecutors. He has authored *Profiles in Crime*; his second volume is due shortly. Proudly, Russ says, "My wife Nancy and I have been married for half a century. We have resided in Granite Bay, California, since 1967. We have two sons and a daughter, nine or ten grandchildren, and another nine or ten great-grandchildren." Not bad for a legend of legends.

ROBERT "ROY" HAZELWOOD

Journeying into the labyrinth of sexual aberration, even for a psychologically healthy man long recognized as its leading specialist, is difficult, demanding, and draining. Yet for almost thirty years, Roy Hazelwood has faced the horrors of homicides, generally of women, with their grisly severed heads and limbs, stuffed vaginas, wellsprings of blood, and otherwise unspeakable slaughter. Few have had the strength to enter such a domain.

A pleasant, unprepossessing man with a razor-sharp mind and an encyclopedic memory, Hazelwood, who spent twenty-two years in the FBI, sixteen of them in the Behavioral Science Unit, delivers a different tale of criminal knowledge and expertise. In the miasma of murder, although buoyed by a wide and brilliant array of BSU talent and accomplishment, Roy is without peer.

Before joining the FBI, Hazelwood served eleven years in the U.S. Army's Military Police Corps, attaining the rank of major at the time of his discharge. During those years, he not only received his Bachelor of Science degree from Sam Houston State College in Huntsville, Texas, in 1960, but also spent a one-year fellowship in forensic medicine at the Armed Forces Institute of Pathology in Washington, D.C., in 1969. Later, in 1980, he earned a Master of Science degree from NOVA University in Fort Lauderdale, Florida. Between 1972 and 1976, Roy gained criminal investigative experience in the Norfolk, Virginia, and Albany, New York, FBI offices. In 1976, he became a supervisory special agent in the Management Aptitude Program at the FBI Academy, transferring as an SSA a year later to the BSU's National Center for the Analysis of Violent Crime.

During the following seven years, Roy, now an experienced profiler, became one of the world's leading experts on the mind and behavior of the sexual criminal, from sexual sadist to sexual rapist, from autoerotic killings to staged suicides.

In 1994, Roy retired from the FBI's BSU and joined the Academy Group, Inc., the consortium of twelve retired BSUers now engaged in private forensic work for the government, industry, and criminal justice. During the past six years, Hazelwood has served as a consultant to law enforcement agencies throughout the United States, Canada, Europe, the Caribbean, and Puerto Rico, providing case consultations on rape, murder, child molestation, equivocal deaths, and autoerotic fatalities. In addition, he has testified as an expert witness in local, county, state, and federal courts. He was summoned before a presidential committee and committees of both the U.S. Senate and House of Representatives.

Roy has personally interviewed incarcerated sexual offenders responsible for over eight hundred rapes; addressed more than two hundred thousand professionals; offered specialized training in violent crime to more than twenty highly selective symposia and associated conferences. Memberships in professional organizations and TV and radio appearances are too numerous to mention.

In addition to authoring thirty journal articles, he has written or coauthored four books: *Autoerotic Fatalities* (1983) with Park E. Dietz and Ann Burgess; *Practical Aspects of Rape Investigation* (1987 and 1995) with Burgess; *Deviant and Criminal Sexuality* (1993) with Ken Lanning; and, with Stephen Michaud, *The Evil that Men Do* (1999). He has also contributed five book chapters and participated in numerous research projects.

Today Roy and his wife, Peggy, live in southern Virginia.

RICHARD L. AULT

Of all the legitimate, unsung heroes of the Behavioral Science Unit's early years, Dick Ault, a man who never wrote a book about his experiences, sought publicity, or tooted his own horn, stands out heads and shoulders above most of the others. Among the many reasons is the extraordinary expertise he gained during his twenty-four years in the FBI, nineteen of which were on assignment in the BSU. There he conducted thousands of profiles of violent crimes and thousands of behavioral assessments of criminals for law enforcement and the intelligence community.

After four years of service in the U.S. Marine Corps, Dick returned to Montgomery, Alabama, in 1965 to enroll in Huntingdon College, where he majored in psychology. After receiving a Bachelor of Science and master's degrees from the University of Alabama, he joined the FBI in 1969 and was assigned as a special agent to field offices in Kansas City and Cleveland. He retired from the Bureau in 1994 to help establish The Academy Group with Roger Depue.

During his tenure in the Behavioral Science Unit at the Academy, he served as a supervisory special agent and deputy unit chief of the NCAVC. His teaching focus was on the psychology of violent offenders, behavioral traits and tendencies, interviewing and interrogation techniques, product tampering, suicide, criminal sexuality, equivocal death, betrayal of trust (espionage), and the psychology of spies. Needless to say, Ault has engaged in innumerable research projects on violent offenders and has repeatedly testified before congressional committees.

Today, Dick is executive vice president of The Academy Group, Inc., and still serves as a consultant to the FBI on espionage issues. His expertise includes the assessment of people who threaten violence. He currently conducts analysis of threatening communications, such as letters and tapes that are sent to company officials, to determine the seriousness of the threats and to profile the authors. He also consults in premises liability cases, conducting analyses of the behavior of criminals to provide insight into their personality, motivation, and modi operandi. For example, Dick's purpose might be to evaluate whether existing security techniques might have truly deterred the offender, or whether any other security measures would have worked.

Dick also testifies as an expert witness in federal and state courts in criminal and civil matters, and in areas such as crime scene analysis, interrogation and interview techniques, forensic hypnosis, wrongful death, homicide, and other issues.

Dick describes his work in the FBI:

> In addition to the fact that I was a "generalist" in the BSU, my full-time "avocation" and the work I loved most stemmed from the fact that I was the only agent in the FBI's BSU who worked "full time" for the FBI Intelligence Division (also known as Division Five). I was their tame shrink, whose job was to assist field agents (or head-quarters when requested) who were working intelligence, espionage, foreign counterintelligence, and/or domestic and international terrorism (it wasn't as much a fad as it is now). I provided that assistance in the form of "direct" and "indirect" personality assessments

of folks who were of concern to the FBI. If the Bureau needed a direct assessment of an asset (an informant), I'd conduct it. If they needed an indirect assessment of a potential asset (foreign intelligence officers, or whoever the Bureau agents thought they needed to recruit) to see what his or her weaknesses were, I'd do that. If they needed an indirect assessment of a traitor or other spy to see what methodology would best work to gain a confession or succeed in an interview, I'd do it. It was more challenging than crime scene analysis (or criminal investigative analysis), because it dealt with "mind games," and was closest to clinical work that I cared to do. I was the only one who did this regularly for the FBI from 1975 to about 1994 (and beyond, but there were others who did it too after 1994). There was no formal program established by the FBI for it. My skill was advertised by word of mouth. Must have been pretty successful, though, because I did a whole lot of cases each year. Also got to conduct research into the psychology of treason, espionage, hackers, and terrorism by being allowed to conduct numerous structured interviews and tests on a number of these people.

Robert K. Ressler

Try to imagine for a moment a basement Behavioral Science Unit wonderland with strong personalities, conflict, humor, incidents, endless meetings and murders in the mid-1970s. Imagine Chief John Pfaff ingeniously outmaneuvering the unit's isolationists and critics at both SOG and within the Academy, and fruitlessly fighting for additional funds. And, standing smack in the middle of this relatively new niche, imagine a forensic specialist on the verge of achieving every personal career ambition an FBI special agent and BSUer could aspire to.

Those who know him best say Robert Ressler is blessed with a positively herculean constitution. In spite of his terrific work ethic and pace, to say nothing of the endless and unimaginable photographs and descriptions of murder that cross his desk, Robert is in excellent mental health and physical condition. The quality most responsible for his prodigious achievements over the span of his career and retirement is an unflagging zest for challenging, creative work. Only history remains to determine his exact rung on the profiling ladder.

Born in 1937 in Chicago, Bob received his Bachelor of Science degree from Michigan State University in 1962, and his Master of Science degree from the same university in 1968. Before entering the FBI in early 1970, he served ten years with the U.S. Army as a military police and criminal investigation officer, and retired from the USAR in 1992 with thirty-five years of both active and reserves service and the rank of colonel.

Upon entering the Bureau, Ressler served in Chicago, New Orleans, and Cleveland, working interstate thefts, forgeries and securities frauds, prostitution, pornography, and organized crime matters. In 1974, he was selected as a counselor for the 96th Session of the FBI National Academy, followed a few months later by appointment as a special agent supervisor and assignment to the Behavioral Science Unit as a criminologist and instructor.

For the next sixteen years, Bob routinely taught and researched criminology, abnormal criminal psychology, hostage negotiation, threat assessment, criminal personality, profiling, crime scene assessment, and criminal investigative analysis. In addition to introducing many of the programs that led to the formation of the FBI's National Center for the Analysis of Violent Crime, Ressler conceptualized and initiated the Violent Criminal Apprehension Program (VICAP) and served as its first program manager between 1984 and 1988. He was one of several BSUers who conceived and developed the Bureau's criminal personality profiling program.

Ressler's past and present professional and academic affiliations, professional organization memberships, grants and research projects, specialized training taught, courtroom consultations, media and entertainment consultations, media appearances, academic honors and awards, to say nothing of publications, quite literally number over a thousand.

Suffice to say that Robert originated and directed the FBI's first research program of violent offenders, interviewing and collecting data on thirty-six serial and sexual killers, which resulted in two textbooks, *Sexual Homicide: Patterns and Motives* (1988) and the *Crime Classification Manual* (1992). He also coauthored his memoirs *Whoever Fights Monsters* (1992), *Justice is Served* (1994), and *I Have Lived in the Monster* (1997). His book and real life experiences have served as inspiration for books written by Mary Higgins Clark, among other authors, as well as for the books and films, *Red Dragon*, *Silence of the Lambs*, *Copycat*, and Chris Carter's TV series, *The X-Files* and *Millennium*. He has also served as a consultant to the TV series *Profiler*.

Ressler retired from the FBI with twenty years of service on August 31, 1990. Today he is an active criminologist in private practice and the director of Forensic Behavioral Services International, a professional organization dedicated to training, lecturing, consultation, and expert witness services. To this day, he focuses on violent criminal offenders, particularly in the area of serial and sexual homicide.

Russ Vorpagel recalls an incident involving Ressler that Bob would just as soon forget. "Bob was a pretty straight-arrow type of guy, a real down-to-earth, honorable guy. On one occasion, while visiting and lecturing at one of my police schools, the local police department threw a party after classes in a nearby bar at one of the larger hotels. So Bob was at the bar relaxing and having a few drinks. A young lady was seated there too, and she struck up a conversation because she had attended one of his lectures earlier in the day. Being the gentlemen that he was, he bought her a drink or two. She began talking rather loosely and Bob became quite embarrassed. So he casually excused himself to go to the men's room. When he came out, instead of returning to the bar, he headed straight to his car. But the lady was standing next to the car waiting for him! And was she pissed! She called Ressler a white honky, said he didn't want to have anything to do with women, and pulled a gun on him! Of course, poor old Bob was a little shook up. Luckily, there were three or four cops standing around nearby who came over to calm the woman down.

"Although she wasn't a full cop, the woman was a police dispatcher at the local sheriff's office. She had recently gone through a divorce and was now running around. She believed she had made a conquest of a true FBI profiler and wanted to go home with him. Because she thought Ressler had dumped her, she was furious. Of course, we don't know if she would have actually shot Bob, but I always used to tease him about the incident. So, the next time you see Ressler, tell him Robin was asking for him. You'll see him blush."

John Douglas

Most of America knows John Douglas from reading his bestseller, *Mind Hunter: Inside the FBI's Elite Serial Crime Unit* (1995), in which he describes how he "entered the minds of some of the country's most notorious serial killers" and founded the FBI's Investigative Support Unit. His two books that followed, *Journey Into Darkness: Follow the FBI's Premier Investigative Profiler as He Penetrates the Minds and Motives of the Most Terrifying Serial Killers* (1997) and *Obsession: The FBI's Legendary Profiler Probes the Psyches of Killers, Rapists, and Stalkers and Their Victims and Tells How to Fight Back* (1998) cemented a legacy in the popular culture as the world's premier profiler.

A native of Hempstead, Long Island, John's ambition was to be a veterinarian. While in high school, he spent his summers shoveling cow manure for the Cornell Extension Service in Ithaca, New York. When Cornell University rejected his application for admission as a freshman, he enrolled at Montana State University. "When I bombed out of there, I went home to Long Island for awhile, then decided to join the Air Force." Stationed in New Mexico, he began taking night and weekend classes at Eastern New Mexico University. While working out in the university gym, he met an FBI agent who urged him to become a special agent.

"I knew nothing about the FBI or anything that it did. Heck, I didn't even know how to spell FBI."

In 1970, during his first week as a cadet at the FBI Academy, Douglas fell in love with the work. After serving five years as a field agent, primarily in Milwaukee, Douglas returned to the Academy in 1975 to take a course in hostage negotiations taught by the Behavioral Science Unit's Howard Teten, Pat Mullany, Dick Ault, and Robert Ressler. During that five-week course, Douglas's name "got around the BSU and Mullany, Ault, and Ressler recommended me to Jack Pfaff, the unit chief then. Before I left, Pfaff called me down to his basement office for an interview. He told me the instructors had been impressed with me and told me to consider coming back to Quantico as a counselor for the FBI National Academy program. I was flattered by the offer and said I'd very much like to do that."

As a counselor, Douglas was responsible for a section of students consisting of fifty senior, seasoned law enforcement officers. By the time the tough, eleven-week course was concluding, both the BSU and the education unit offered him positions. John chose to join Pfaff's group: "The work seemed more interesting."

During the infamous Jaeger-Meirhofer case (see chapter 3), Teten and Mullany validated their belief in behavioral analysis as an investigative tool, and encouraged Douglas and Ressler to take the new craft to the next step of becoming an avowed FBI discipline. The next year, 1977, Ressler and Douglas began the Bureau's first serious research survey of the criminal mind—an interview survey in the nation's penitentiaries of more than fifty notorious killers, including Sirhan Sirhan, Charles Manson, Richard Speck, David Berkowitz,

John Gacy, Edwin Kemper, etc. Later, Douglas became a supervisory special agent and served as program manager of the Bureau's Criminal Profiling and Consultation Program, which included crime analysis. He supervised a staff of enforcement agencies throughout the world. At the time he was also an adjunct faculty member of the University of Virginia, the University of Houston Law Center, and National College of District Attorneys, as well as a senior research fellow at the University of Pennsylvania. Prior to retiring in 1995, he headed the FBI's Investigative Support Unit (BSISU) for five years.

Numerous retired BSUers today say that John was a sincere, hard-working special agent who almost instinctively gravitated to profiling serial killers, "lock-stepping" Ressler all the way. What Douglas brought to the unit was courage and hard work. He fostered and developed the ideas of his predecessors and achieved a great deal of personal attention through *Silence of the Lambs*. A conflict developed between Douglas and Ressler and was most unfortunate. My personal feeling is that Douglas was threatened by Ressler and reacted accordingly. Credit was going in large part to Bob for all the research conducted in the early days on the more bizarre killers in the United States.

Said another BSUer, "Later, after years of working side by side, they developed some sort of rivalry none of us could fathom. They both enjoyed the limelight, the publicity—Douglas probably more than Ressler. But Ressler loved it, too; don't get me wrong. And each began to resent the other. Soon they realized how famous they were becoming, how much money they could make in book-writing. Remember, now, that headquarters would not allow you to write books until you retired. So the two raced each other to retire. Although Ressler was older and was the first to publish the inner secrets of profiling, Douglas soon caught up. Each has written five or six books, all well received, especially in Japan where the people really love this sort of thing. And to show you the split between the two, each were present to interview Edwin Kemper, the Santa Cruz, California, serial killer of fifteen or twenty women. So a photograph was taken of the two on each side of Kemper as he sat in the middle. Both Douglas and Ressler received copies of that photo and both included it in their respective books. But in Douglas's book Ressler is omitted, showing Kemper being interviewed by Douglas. In Ressler's book, the same photo is shown but with Douglas omitted, as if only Ressler was interviewing Kemper. Both were present at the same time to interview the monster, but each cut the other out! I suspect the current staff has respect for each and for what each has contributed."

Most retired and current BSUers feel that Douglas's greatest profiling achievement was that of Wayne Williams. On Jan. 13, 1981, Douglas traipsed through the secluded, wooded sites where five of Atlanta's missing and murdered children had been found, so he could formulate a profile of the killer.

Victims Alfred Evans, Edward Hope Smith, Milton Harvey, Christopher Richardson, and Earl Lee Terrell were all found in wooded areas of south Atlanta. Douglas advised police to use the profile he developed as a "guide" in evaluating suspects as they emerged in the investigation. When Williams became a suspect, not everything in the profile matched, but there were marked similarities. Following are excerpts from that report (in italics) and data on Williams culled from investigative files:

Your offender is familiar with the crime scene areas because he is, or has resided in this area. In addition, his present or past occupation caused him to drive through these areas on different occasions. The sites of the deceased are not random or "chance" disposal areas. He realizes that these areas are remote and not frequently traveled by others.

According to task force files, while doing freelance work for WAGA-TV in 1978, Williams shot one assignment at Redwine Road and another at Interstate 285 and Washington Road, near Redwine Road. The bodies of Richardson and Terrell were found on Redwine, and Harvey's body was found nearby.

INTO THE MINDS OF MADMEN

That same year, Williams shot videotape at Boat Rock and Campbellton roads, not far from Suber Road, where the body of victim Jeffrey Mathis was found. Williams also had an assignment on Niskey Lake Road, where the bodies of Smith and Evans, the first two victims, were found in July 1979. Even when he knew he was under surveillance by police, Williams repeatedly drove to Niskey Lake Road to pick up one of his protégés, a member of the Gemini band.

A frequent tactic (to abduct "street smart" kids without being seen) is offenders' impersonating the law enforcement official who shows concern for the victim's safety, places him into his personal vehicle, and promises to take the victim home. He may, conversely, admonish the victim for walking the streets late at night and threaten to arrest the victim.

A neighbor who said he had known the Williamses for more than twenty years told FBI agents that neighborhood kids thought Williams was a policeman because he drove "detective-looking" cars, carried a badge, and gave orders to the kids. "Many of them thought he started acting crazy two to three years ago . . . he would approach kids in official-looking vehicles, telling them to get off the street or he would lock them up." Another neighbor told investigators that about two years earlier Williams had threatened to "arrest" him, showing him some sort of badge.

Williams was arrested by East Point police in 1976 on a charge of impersonating a police officer. When a detective-type car of Williams's was repossessed on December 31, 1979—five months after the string of slayings began—officials found a police siren; blue, red, and amber emergency lights; a police scanner; a CB unit; and headlights equipped with flashers.

In all probability, your offender is black. Generally, offenders of this type are fixated on same-race victims.

Williams is black. All the victims he is accused of killing were black. Several acquaintances testified at the trial that Williams had a deep disdain for lower-class blacks, whom he called derogatory names.

The Nine

Your offender has, in all probability, a prior criminal history for aggressive and/or assaultive behavior. . . . He will always carry a weapon of some sort on his person and has threatened to use it on others in the past.

Williams's only prior criminal record was for impersonating an officer, unauthorized use of emergency equipment, and filing a false stolen-auto report to police. At the time of his arrest on the first two charges, he had a 12-gauge shotgun in his four-door Plymouth.

Employees of Southern Ambulance Services, which Williams sometimes visited, testified that Williams liked to "scuffle" with them, and one employee said that he sometimes sprayed him with Mace.

His favorite colors are black, dark blue, and brown. This can be observed particularly in the clothing he selects to wear and the color of the auto he drives.

Williams's wardrobe favored drab browns. According to task force files and trial testimony, he drove numerous cars, both rented and owned, between 1979 and 1981. Their colors were faded white, burgundy, light blue, silver gray, brown, yellowish-brown, white, and blue.

This offender, in all probability, is single. He has always had difficulty relating to members of the opposite sex. As a youth, he was sexually abused. . . . The odds are high that he has spent time in juvenile detention homes, as well as other forms of incarceration.

Williams was single, and acquaintances told investigators that Williams was rarely seen with women and had no apparent girlfriend. A woman who worked for Williams in his struggling music business testified at his trial that she had had sex with him, but he had insisted to investigators during earlier interviews that she had not. However, investigators uncovered no evidence that Williams had been sexually abused, nor did he ever spend time in juvenile detention.

Information about Williams's sexual identity was mixed. Several acquaintances said they thought he acted "sissy," had a high voice, and displayed homosexual tendencies. None of the youngsters who worked

with him, however, said he had approached them sexually. Two prosecution witnesses testified about Williams's alleged homosexuality. One
youngster said Williams fondled him. A man said he saw Williams
walking down the street holding hands with victim Nathaniel Cater
shortly before Cater disappeared. Williams denied both accounts.

*Your offender will generally fall between the ages of twenty-five
and twenty-nine.*

Williams was twenty-eight when he was arrested.

On May 22, 1981, the free-lance photographer and self-described
talent scout was stopped for questioning by a stakeout team on a
bridge over the Chattahoochee River. Two days later, Cater's body
was discovered downstream, and Williams became a serious suspect.

Douglas's involvement with Williams did not end there. As the
FBI's expert on serial murderers, Douglas sat in on Williams's nine-
week trial to help Fulton County prosecutors plan their cross-exami-
nation of Williams and other defense witnesses, using a second profile
he had prepared for them. He concluded that Williams "is very much
like other serial killers researched and interviewed in the past by FBI's
Behavioral Sciences Unit."

"Wayne Williams, in all probability, thought he would really be
enjoying this trial," Douglas wrote as the prosecution wound down its
case. "The personal attention he would be getting is something he has
never legitimately obtained. He has made feeble attempts to attain
fame by being a disc jockey, ambulance attendant, talent scout, and
police officer. All these positions represent power—particularly power
over others. Wayne Williams, like many serial killers, never can
imagine himself being convicted of his crimes. Serial killers think they
are too intelligent to get caught."

Douglas's psychological profile of Williams has never been
released, but a copy was obtained by the *Atlanta Journal-Constitution*.
From files on the case opened to the public by DeKalb County police,
the newspapers also secured the first profile Douglas prepared before

Williams emerged as a suspect. The two documents provide an intimate look at the role psychological profiling played in the investigation and prosecution of the Atlanta slaying cases. They were based on characteristics found to be common among the more than twenty-five serial and mass murderers interviewed. Serial killers, the psychologists determined, generally have average to above-average intelligence and are articulate. They closely follow media coverage of the cases, change homicidal methods to suit their needs, have frequent changes in employment or are self-employed, and often are the only son in a family. The report also said that serial killers of children, in particular, often were pampered and overprotected in their youth and may fixate on either boys or girls.

"It all fit," said Joseph Drolet, an assistant district attorney in Fulton County who helped prosecute Williams. "It confirmed many of our thoughts in regard to the case." Drolet became even more impressed with Douglas's profiling a few days before Williams took the stand, when the defendant claimed he was ill and was taken to Grady Memorial Hospital. Douglas had predicted that Williams, upon seeing his own counsel losing ground, might try to "feebly attempt" suicide to gain sympathy or feign a mental breakdown. Doctors who examined Williams could find nothing wrong with him.

For the courtroom profile, Douglas used data on the victims, crime scenes, and evidence on the case as well as investigators' findings about Williams. "The Atlanta child killings commenced when stress in the life of Wayne Williams became unbearable," Douglas wrote. "He was living alone with parents old enough to be his grandparents, and he probably resented this. His parents, both college-educated and retired schoolteachers, were achievers. Between age twenty-one and twenty-three, while fairly bright and articulate, Williams found himself falling to one failure after another, even going so far as causing his own parents to forfeit their savings by securing a loan for their son's personal business" and later causing their bankruptcy.

"Wayne Williams is an angry young man seeking power, who wears a mask to cover his personal inadequacies. The Atlanta serial murder case was his first success, and this furnished a sense of power to him. Wayne Williams orchestrated this case at will. He challenged authorities, intimidated them, and played out his own script. He got almost every police jurisdiction involved in this case, and then created scenarios where all police jurisdictions would become involved."

Assessing the trial testimony before Williams took the stand, Douglas observed that Williams had been "trapped in lies" and that witnesses had testified they had homosexual experiences with him. "Williams probably does not consider himself a homosexual; however, killer John Gacy of Illinois did not either. [Gacy sexually assaulted and killed thirty-three boys and young men.] . . . As the prosecution closes its case, he, for the first time, is concerned."

Before Williams took the stand, Douglas provided an outline for cross-examining him. He recommended that prosecutors keep Williams on the stand as long as possible, focus on his failures in life and the inconsistencies in his earlier statements, and concentrate on his alleged homosexuality. Except for the homosexual angle, prosecutors followed the outline. And, they said, it worked. The second day he was on the stand, Williams became argumentative and lashed out at prosecutor Jack Mallard, calling him a "fool." At one point, when Mallard asked Williams if he had been coached for his testimony, Williams responded forcefully "No. You want the real Wayne Williams? You got him right here."

Williams, twenty-nine, was convicted in February 1982 of murdering Nathaniel Cater and Jimmy Ray Payne, whose deaths were among thirty slayings of blacks investigated by a police task force between 1979 and 1981. Police later alleged Williams was responsible for most of the other slayings and closed those cases. Williams, now serving two life sentences, is appealing his convictions.

In spite of the amazing successes in profiling since Teten et al.

began the process on an informal basis in 1972 to 1973, and the growing understanding of the serial criminal's mind, no one knew how best to cope with multiple crimes committed in different cities, counties, or states. Men like Henry Lee Lucas and Ottis Toole had combined to murder 350-plus unfortunate victims in twenty-two states, strengthening the BSU call for a state-of-the-art, streamlined National Center for the Analysis of Violent crime that, among other goals, would collect and collate all available information on unsolved crimes across the nation. The new databank, complete insofar as possible crimes, would be named the Violent Criminal Apprehension Program (VICAP).

NOTE

1. Defining sychronicity as early as the 1920s, Carl Gustave Jung wrote, "A synchronic event is the coincidence between an inner image or hunch breaking into one's mind (or group of minds) and the occurrence of an outer event(s) conveying the same meaning at approximately the same time. That is, undeniable inner psychological symbols, or thoughts, coincide regularly with equally undeniable outer events. Such events can only take place if the individual has a strong emotional participation with the event. Synchronistic events rest on the simultaneous occurrence of two different psychic states."

Aerial view of the FBI Academy. (Photo courtesy of the Photographic Unit of the FBI Academy.)

Cesare Lombroso. (© Bettmann/CORBIS)

James A. Brussel. (© Bettmann/CORBIS)

Captain Ellis M. Zacharias as he appeared before the Senate.
(© Bettmann/ CORBIS)

George Metesky, the alleged "Mad Bomber." (© Bettmann/CORBIS)

Dick Ault   John Campbell   John Douglas

William Hagmaier   Roy Hazelwood

(Photos courtesy of the Photographic Unit of the FBI Academy.)

Kenneth V. Lanning

Larry Monroe

Jim Reese

Robert Ressler

William Tafoya

A crime scene analysis session.

John Douglas conducting a briefing on a case reflecting
a hostage situation.

(Photos courtesy of the Photographic Unit of the FBI Academy.)

Art Westveer teaching a death investigation case.

Sharon Smith in a National Academy class.

Unit chiefs of the BSU. Left to right: Jack Kirsch, Jack Pfaff, Larry Monroe, Richard McCarty, Roger Depue, and John Campbell. (Photo courtesy of John Campbell.)

Past meets present. Jack Kirsch, first BSU chief (left), sits with current chief, Stephen R. Band, Ph.D., at the "famous" Globe and Laurel Restaurant, near the FBI academy outside Quantico. (Photo courtesy of Stephen Band.)

"Sir, we don't have spit."

The inspector stared at him incredulously. "Excuse me, Monsieur Poirot, you claim you know who killed three people. And why? All you mean is that you have a hunch, right?"

Poirot smiled. "Inspector, I know. I really know. And I see you are still skeptic. But first let me say this: To be sure means that when the right solution is reached, everything falls into place. You see that in no other way could things have happened."

AGATHA CHRISTIE, *THE CLOCKS*

Helen was an ordinary-looking white female in her mid-twenties who led a reclusive life. And because she was only 4' ll," weighed less than ninety pounds, and suffered from kyphoscoliosis (a slight curvature of the spine), the young woman was extremely self-conscious. Living with her mom and dad in a Philadelphia apartment building, part of a racially mixed, twenty-three-building public-housing project, Helen was employed as a teacher's aide for handicapped children in a nearby day care center. Tragically, she would suffer a horrible death at the hands of what was then termed "a lust murderer."

At 8:10 A.M. on the morning of Tuesday, April 12, 1976, Helen, on her way to work in the childcare center, chose to walk down the stairs rather than take the elevator from her fourth-floor apartment. Between the fourth and third floors she encountered someone who had a reason to be there. Either he resided in the apartment house complex or was an employee of some sort. Because Helen neither fought, ran, nor screamed, she didn't perceive the individual as a danger. Either the man was dressed in the nonthreatening uniform of a janitor, postman, or housing cop, or the young woman knew or recognized him.

In any event, Helen's nude body was discovered by her aunt and niece a little more than seven hours later on the roof of her apartment building. In addition to having been strangled with the strap cut from her purse, and pummeled about the head and face, the nipples of her breasts had been severed after death and placed on her stomach. Written in felt pen on the inside of her thigh was "you can't stop me." On her chest was scrawled "fuck you." Her good-luck piece, a small gold pendant in the form of the Jewish Chai sign, was missing and presumed removed as a souvenir by the killer. Helen's panties had been pulled up and over her head. Her nylons had been removed and tied loosely around her wrists and ankles near a railing. The pierced earrings she had been wearing were placed symmetrically on both sides of her head. An old, discarded red umbrella and felt pen had been shoved into Helen's vagina, and a comb from her purse placed in her pubic hair. Her jaw and face had been so badly beaten that all her molars were loosened. She suffered multiple, facial bone fractures caused by blunt force. Helen's death was caused by asphyxia. Postmortem bite marks were found on her thighs, as well as numerous contusions, hemorrhages, and lacerations over the entire body. The murderer defecated near the young woman's body and covered the victim's dress and underwear with his feces.

When Philadelphia police responded to a radio call of a homicide and saw the mutilated corpse, they immediately notified the detective bureau, which in turn called the forensic crime scene unit, the medical examiner's office, and the county district attorney's office. Within twenty-four hours, a task force of some thirty detectives and supervisors were at work on the case. Meanwhile, the local media was relentless in sensationalizing the heinous murder.

In the weeks and months that followed, the intensive investigation involved more than two thousand possible suspects. Record checks of known sex offenders proved fruitless. Handwriting samples were taken to compare with the printing on the body. City and county jails, prisons, and mental hospitals throughout the state were checked for recent arrests or admittance of people who might have violent sexual histories. All to no avail.

With no suspects, and after more than six months without new information or leads, Philadelphia's assistant chief of police, who had attended the National Academy classes at the FBI Academy the year before, placed a telephone call to John Pfaff, the Behavioral Science Unit chief. He knew that, upon request, special agents with accumulated investigative experience were available to deduce certain criminal characteristics that could prove useful in identifying perpetrators. "We have no motive for the murder and not one suspect. Even our street informants and potential tipsters aren't responding to our $1,000 cash payment for information. Sir, we don't have spit." The assistant chief asked if someone on Pfaff's staff would prepare a psychological suspect profile from the information available.

"Of course," responded the unit chief. "Normally, we don't take sex-related murder cases. And although we're very select in the unsolved cases we do take on an informal basis, this one is similar in nature to a murder we helped solve last year in Columbia, South Carolina. In that killing, the nude, mutilated body of a twenty-five-year-old mother of two was found with her two breasts removed, her reproduction system ripped out, and numerous cuts and stab wounds. There was even evidence the murderer had engaged in anthropophagi, that is, the consuming of her flesh and blood. Our staff considered the case to be that of a 'lustful' type. In analyzing your victim and both the crime and death scenes, we'll determine if the murder was the more common sadistic homicide or the uncommon lustful. We'll differentiate in detail between the two in our evaluation." Pfaff then listed the inputs that would be needed by his BSUers to generate a profile of the murderer.

The following morning, a Philadelphia police officer was dispatched by patrol car to the FBI Academy. Arriving in Quantico late that afternoon, he presented Pfaff with six large envelopes containing numerous photos of both the death and crime scenes, photos of the physical evidence, the preliminary police and autopsy reports, details about who Helen was, and a report on various forensic information available at that point. By the time the BSU offices were locked down for the evening, Roger Depue, Bob Ressler, and John Douglas were perusing the inputs.

And by the time Pfaff arrived for work at 8:15 A.M. the next morning, the three were in the conference room reconstructing the crime to determine if the murder was organized or disorganized, sadistic or lustful. By noontime, after considerable and often heated discussion and debate, during which other BSUers dropped in to learn of the case and participate in the five stages of the criminal-profile-generating process developed just a few years before, Depue, Ressler, and Douglas were ready to propose to Pfaff a preliminary theory of how the killing occurred and who the murderer might be.

In contrast to the traditional on-site investigation, the off-site criminal-profile-generating process (see fig. 6.1 on page 198) was based upon:

(1) Local police inputs, such as the physical evidence found at the crime scene, the patterns of evidence, if any, Helen's body position, and the weapon(s) used; Helen's background, habits, age, occupation, and when last seen; the forensic data such as cause of death, wounds, sexual acts, autopsy and laboratory reports; photos of the victim and crime and death scenes, including aerial shots; and the preliminary police report, including information on the neighborhood, its socioeconomic status and crime rate, time of the crime, who reported the crime, and police observations.

(2) The decision-process models consisting of homicide type and style, primary intent of the murderer, Helen's risk, the perpe-

trator's risk of being caught, his escalation of the offense, and location of the body factors.

(3) Reconstruction of the killing, its staging and possible motivation; other crime scene dynamics as well as the murder's classification (determined by a manual of categories BSU staff compiled), and whether victim selection, control of the victim, and sequence of the crime were organized or disorganized.

(4) The actual criminal profile, listing physical characteristics, habits, preoffense behavior leading to the crime, postoffense behavior, and demographics.

(5) Once the congruence of the criminal profile has been determined, a written report is provided to the requesting agency and added to its ongoing investigation. The investigative recommendations generated in stage four are applied and suspects matching the profile are evaluated. If identification, apprehension, and a confession result, the goal of the profile effort has been met. If new evidence is generated by another murder, or there is no identification of a suspect, the available information is reexamined and the profile reevaluated for possible revision.

(6) Once a suspect has been apprehended, the agreement between the outcome and the various stages in the profile generating process are examined. If an apprehended suspect admits guilt, the Behavioral Science Unit staff conducts a detailed interview to check the total profiling process for validity.

In creating their psychological profile of Helen's murderer, Depue, Ressler, and Douglas focused on the initial stage of the profile-generating process, the profiling inputs. First, the crime scene evidence determined that everything the perpetrator used at the crime scene belonged to the young woman. Even the comb and the felt-tip pen used to print on her body came from her purse. The killer apparently did not

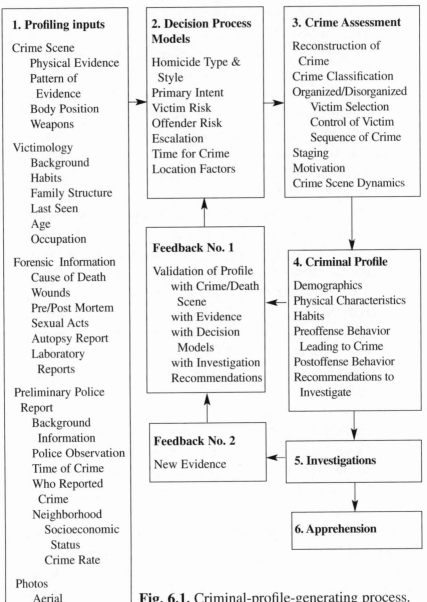

Fig. 6.1. Criminal-profile-generating process.

plan the murder: he had no gun, ropes, or tape for the victim's mouth. He may have accidentally bumped into her that morning in the stairwell as she was descending and he was ascending. The crime scene indicated a spontaneous event, since the offender did not stalk or wait for the young woman. To Depue, Ressler, and Douglas, the crime scene differed from the death scene and the initial abduction was on the stairwell; then Helen was taken to a remote area on the roof.

The BSUers then considered the available forensic information in the medical examiner's report. Of importance was the fact that no semen was found in the vagina, although it was on the stomach and legs of the body. Obviously, the murderer stood directly over the victim and masturbated. There were visible bite marks on the victim's thigh and knees. Furthermore, he cut off Helen's nipples with a knife after she was dead and wrote on the body. Cause of death was strangulation from the strap of her purse. The killer certainly used his fists to render her unconscious, which may have explained why no one heard her scream. The body showed no deep stab wounds, and the knife used to mutilate the victim's breasts was not large, probably a small pocketknife, again suggesting the murderer used a weapon of opportunity. Helen's belts were used to tie her right arm and right leg. Yet he apparently untied them in order to position the body before he left.

In considering the information available for stage two, the decision process, Depue, Ressler, and Douglas were certain the crime's style was that of a single homicide with the murderer's primary intent making it a sexually motivated type of crime. There was a certain degree of planning reflected by the organization and sophistication of the crime scene. The actual idea of murder had probably been in the subject's mind for years. His sexual fantasies may have started through the use and collecting of sadistic pornography depicting torture and violent sexual acts. For the killer, the crime was high risk in that he committed it in broad daylight and there was the distinct possibility that other people who were up early might see him. Furthermore, there was no escalation factor present at the crime scene, to say nothing of the considerable amount of time needed to complete the death. All his activities with the corpse—removing her earrings, cutting off her nipples, masturbating over her—required time and increased his risk of being seen or apprehended. And the location of the killing suggested the killer felt somewhat comfortable in the region. He had been there before and he felt no one would interrupt the slaying.

In assessing the crime, the third stage of the criminal profile generating process, the BSUers insisted the murder was one event and not one of a series of events. It also appeared to be a first-time killing and the perpetrator was not a typical organized offender. There were elements of both disorganization and organization, meaning that the murderer probably fell into a mixed category (see fig. 6.2). Depue, Ressler, and Douglas then reconstructed the crime /death scene to provide an overall picture of Helen's death. What was her reaction? Did she recognize her assailant, fight him off, or try to get away? The subject may have felt he had to kill her to carry out his sexually violent fantasies. He most certainly was known in the housing project and had a reason to be in the stairwell that morning at 8:15—either he lived in one of the apartment houses or he was employed by the complex.

Because Helen probably didn't fight, run, or scream, she didn't at first perceive him as a threat. She either knew him, had seen him before, or felt he was in the stairwell as part of his job as, say, a janitor, postman, or apartment complex security guard. In the sequence of the murder, the BSUers felt the killer first hit her in the face with great force. Second or third blows with his fists rendered the young woman unconscious. He picked her up easily because of her small size, carried her up to the roof landing and spent considerable time in positioning her unconscious body. At that point, he cut the strap from her purse and slowly strangled her until she was dead. He then undressed her and acted out certain fantasies that led to his masturbation. The

Profile Characteristics of Organized and Disorganized Murderers

Organized	*Disorganized*
Good intelligence	Average intelligence
Socially competent	Socially immature
Skilled work preferred	Poor work history
Sexually competent	Sexually incompetent
High birth order status	Minimal birth order status
Father's work stable	Father's work unstable
Inconsistent childhood discipline	Harsh discipline in childhood
Controlled mood during crime	Anxious mood during crime
Use of alcohol with crime	Minimal use of alcohol
Precipitating situational stress	Minimal situational stress
Living with partner	Living alone
Mobility, with car in good condition	Lives/works near crime scene
Follows crime in news media	Minimal interest in news media
May change jobs or leave town	Minimal change in life-style

Crime Scene Differences between Organized and Disorganized Murderers

Organized	Disorganized
Offense planned	Spontaneous offense
Victim a targeted stranger	Victim or location known
Personalizes victim	Depersonalizes victim
Controlled conversation	Minimal conversation
Crime scene reflects overall control	Crime scene random and sloppy
Demands submissive victim	Sudden violence to victim
Restraints used	Minimal use of restraints
Aggressive acts prior to death	Sexual acts after death
Body hidden	Body left in view
Weapon/evidence absent	Evidence/weapon often present
Transports victim or body	Body left at death scene

Fig. 6.2.

murderer was relaxed at the scene, probably knowing that no one would come to the roof and disturb him in the early morning, since he was so familiar with the area and had been there many times in the past. For the BSUers, the crime scene was not staged. Sadistic ritualistic fantasy generated the sexual motivation for murder. Displaying total domination of the victim, the killer further placed Helen in a degrading posture, reflecting a total lack of remorse for the slaying.

Depue, Ressler, and Douglas, however, were baffled by the murderer covering the victim's clothing with his feces. The killing was opportunistic and the crime scene portrayed the intricacies of a long-standing murderous fantasy, but defecation had never been associated with ritual fantasy—at least up to this point. He had to cover the clothing. But why? The presence of the feces at least supported their contention on the length of time taken for the crime, the control he had over Helen, and the knowledge that he would not be interrupted.

For the three BSUers, the positioning of the young woman pointed to an acting out by the murderer of something he had seen before, most likely in a fantasy or sadomasochistic pornographic magazine. Since Helen was probably unconscious, it wasn't necessary to tie her hands. Yet for some unknown reason, he tied her neck and then strangled her. He then placed her earrings in a ritualistic manner and wrote on her body, reflecting some sort of imagery that he repeated over and over in his mind. Helen's Jewish pendant was removed, probably as some type of souvenir that he carried around in his pocket. The BSUers noted that the body was positioned in the form of the victim's missing pendant.

Employing all the information learned during the previous three stages, Depue, Ressler, and Douglas were in virtual agreement about the profile they generated for Helen's murderer. First, the three believed the suspect to be a white male, between twenty-five and thirty-five years of age, or the same general age as his target. As for looks, he was of average appearance and would not look out of context in the housing complex. He would be of average intelligence, although he would have dropped out of high school or college. Neither would he have been in the military, nor would he be employed. His job skills would be blue collar and somewhat skilled. Alcohol or drugs would have had little significance in the murder since the killer struck early in the morning.

Since the suspect would be sexually inexperienced, sexually inadequate, and never married, he would have difficulty maintaining any kind of personal relationships with women. If indeed he dated, it would be with women much younger than himself, since he had an unconscious need to control and dominate all women he came in contact with. He would own a pornography collection. His personality would include sadistic tendencies—the use of the umbrella and felt pen, as well as his masturbation over the corpse, were felt to be clear acts of sexual substitution. They showed controlled aggression, as well as an ongoing rage and hatred of all women.

The assailant's sexual and sadistic acts upon an inanimate body suggested that he was disorganized. Obviously, he was mentally ill, suffering primarily from a depressive disorder. Ambivalence, vacillation, and confusion were his norms. The BSUers speculated that if the murderer carried out such acts on a living human being, someone who was conscious at the time, he would be a different personality type. "The fact that he inflicted acts upon a dead or unconscious person indicates his inability to function with a live or conscious person."

Being a mixture of an organized and disorganized lustful type of killer, the subject was neither remorseful nor subtle. He may have even felt justified in his actions. He left the victim in a provocative, humiliating position, exactly the way he wanted her to be found. Furthermore, he boldly insulted and challenged the police in the two messages he wrote on Helen. In fact, "fuck you" and "you can't stop me" hinted that he would kill again, probably in the same manner.

In concluding their profile, Depue, Ressler, and Reese felt the

203

murderer knew that sooner or later the police would contact him because he either lived or worked in the apartment complex. Somehow, he would inject himself into the investigation by appearing cooperative to the extreme. Yet his goal would be to seek information. And there was even the possibility he might try to contact Helen's family on some pretext or another.

Seven months after John Pfaff, on behalf of the Behavioral Science Unit, submitted the profile generated by Roger Depue, Robert Ressler, and John Douglas, the murderer was caught. During those months, the Philadelphia police reviewed their files of some twenty-two suspects they had interviewed. One man stood out from all the others. His father lived on the same floor and down the hall from Helen's apartment. When police interviewed the father, he disclosed that his son was a patient at a local psychiatric hospital. When administrators at the hospital were questioned, it was learned that the son had been absent without permission on the day and evening prior to the murder.

Police also learned that the man was an unemployed actor who lived alone. His mother had died of a stroke when he was nineteen years old (eleven years before). He had major learning difficulties at both the elementary and secondary levels, resulting in his eventual dropping out of high school. The suspect was white, thirty years old, and had never married. The father was a blue-collar worker and an ex–prize fighter, and the suspect was his only child. At the time of the murder, the man apparently had his arm in a cast. A search of his room revealed a collection of pornography. The suspect had never served in the military, had no girlfriends, and was described as being extremely shy around women. Because he suffered from severe depression, he was receiving psychiatric treatment as part of a hospitalization stay. He had a history of repeated suicidal attempts, mostly by hanging or asphyxiation, both before and after the offense.

The suspect was found guilty and sentenced to serve twenty-five years to life for the mutilation murder. He denied committing the killing and swore he did not know the victim. Police were able to prove that because security was so lax at the mental institution, he was able to come and go as he pleased. The conclusive evidence against him during the trial were his teeth impressions. Three separate forensic dentists, all prominent in the field, conducted independent tests and agreed that the suspect's teeth matched the bite marks found on the victim's body.[1]

Later, Douglas and fellow BSUer Roy Hazelwood added a post-script to this story when they wrote, "While not a common occurrence, the lust murderer frightens and arouses the public as does no other crime. His type of killing involves the death and subsequent mutilating attack of the breasts, rectum, and genital areas of the victim. The crime is typically heterosexual and intraracial in nature and is committed by one of two types of individuals: the disorganized asocial personality, or the organized nonsocial personality."

The organized nonsocial type, according to the two, feels rejection by and hatred for the society in which he lives. His hostile feelings are manifested overtly and the lust murder is the final expression of the hatred he feels. The disorganized asocial type also feels rejection and hatred for his world, but withdraws and internalizes his feelings, living within a world of fantasy until he acts out the fantasy with his victim. The crime is premeditated in the obsessive fantasies experienced by both the asocial and the nonsocial types, yet it is a crime of opportunity, one in which the victim is not usually known to the murderer.

Said Hazelwood at the time, "The use of psychological profiling in a murder such as Helen's may be of assistance in determining the personality type involved. It is a search for clues indicating the probable personality configuration of the responsible individual. It is a useful tool, but must not alter, suspend, or replace prescribed investigative procedures."

Though not on a par with Hannibal Lecter, the serial killer-cannibal from *Silence of the Lambs* and *Hannibal*, nor the likes of Joseph "Shoemaker" Kallinger, Theodore Bundy, and John Wayne Gacy, all operating around the time of Helen's murder, Helen's murderer nonetheless demonstrated the horror of what evil can do.

Like the hundreds of unsolved murder cases that were pouring into the Behavioral Science Unit each year throughout the 1970s, Helen's case was referred by a local police department. From the available evidence and information, Depue, Ressler, and Douglas developed a psychological composite of the killer. Their approach was one of brainstorming, intuition, and educated guesswork. Their profile was the result of years of accumulated investigative experience in the field and familiarity with a large number of cases, some of which were very similar. But up to that point, no formal data bank had been developed against which new cases could systematically be compared. In addition, there was little or no follow-up once an offender had been successfully apprehended and convicted. Consequently, there was very little subsequent input of information which would serve to sharpen and refine the existing body of knowledge.

Serial killing seems to have reached its zenith between 1978 and 1982, matched by claims from law enforcement spokesmen that such murders represented a fifth, or a little less than 25 percent, of all homicides in America. Although there were many more multiple murderers during those five years, a dozen or so captivated the public's imagination: Charlie Manson, Charles Starkweather, Juan Corona, Herbert Mullin, Edwin Kemper, John Wayne Gacy, Ted Bundy, Jeffery Dahmer, Wayne Williams, Ed Gein, Kenneth Bianchi, Angelo Buono, and David Berkowitz. Those personalities alone accounted for more than twenty-eight true crime books and novels and some eight feature length films and thirteen television documentaries. And for years after their convictions, sentencings, and, in some cases, executions, interest in them continued. According to Philip Jenkins, serial killing was the theme of more American films in 1980 and 1981 than in the previous two decades combined.

"Sir, we don't have spit."

Yet neither local and state law enforcement, nor the federal government, offered the public any general explanation of the phenomenon.

But the Behavioral Science Unit showed little reluctance in stepping forward with new views and definitions, such as "serial murder" and "serial crimes," although the actual terms may have originated years earlier. Ressler, more than any other, may have earned the distinction for coining the phrases after his involvement in the David "Son of Sam" Berkowitz case in 1976–1977.

In 1978, to clarify and further define the nature of serial killing, the Behavioral Science Unit embarked upon a series of mini-projects to interview imprisoned lifers, including a number of serial and mass murderers, to not only glean new insights about their killing, thinking, and behavioral patterns, but also aid the unit's ongoing process of profiling those still being hunted. One such effort, dubbed the Criminal Personality Research Project, was funded by the National Institute of Justice in 1982 to interview one hundred imprisoned serial murderers on death row awaiting execution. During the two years that followed, Bob Ressler and John Douglas managed to conduct thirty-six extensive interviews before deciding they had accumulated enough additional information to create new, wide-ranging taxonomies for serial offenders. Hopefully, the research would assist law enforcement with the characteristics of persons at large.

In addition to Ressler and Douglas, comprising the research team were Dr. Nicholas Groth, director of the sex offender program for the Connecticut department of correction, and Dr. Ann Wolbert Burgess, professor and director of nursing research at Boston University School of Nursing. Groth worked extensively with convicted sexual offenders, while Burgess, a clinical specialist in psychiatric mental health nursing, focused upon the victims of sexual assault. The collaboration provided for the first time a multidisciplinary approach to the study of the sex murderer—that is, it combined contributions from the behavioral sciences and law enforcement. By the spring of 1979, the team had established a data schedule for investigative inquiry and offender assessment. Their instrument provided not only guidelines for interviewing subjects such as Helen's murderer, but also a new means, or system, of recording and coding relevant data to permit computer analysis and retrieval. The protocol (which underwent revisions throughout the 1980s) was divided into five sections: (1) physical characteristics of the offender, (2) background development, (3) offense data, (4) victim data, and (5) crime scene data.

After the assessment schedule had been designed, it was administered to three groups of sexual offenders: sex murderers, rapists and child molesters, and sex offenders confined to a mental facility. During the first year of study (the latter part of 1979), twenty-six men who were convicted of a sex-related homicide were interviewed. In the following two years, an additional 125 adult male offenders were interviewed—rapists and child molesters incarcerated across the country in maximum security prisons. By 1982, another one hundred were interviewed, again equally divided between rapists and child molesters. Surprisingly, institution administrators, as well as the offenders themselves, cooperated fully. Although a few of the convicted denied or minimized their culpability, the majority provided new profiles developed by the BSUers.

From the new data, additional offender profiles were developed based upon identifiable behaviors, traits, and characteristics. The new profiles then aided local law enforcement agencies in the investigations of their unsolved cases.

The ability of Hercule Poirot to solve a crime by describing the perpetrator was a skill shared by Roger Depue, Robert Ressler, and John Douglas. Evidence speaks its own language of patterns and sequences that can reveal the offender's behavioral characteristics. Like Poirot in Agatha Christie's *The Clocks*, the profiler says, "I know who he must be." Adds Howard Teten, "and if it's obvious who he is, then it's obvious. Don't try to make more of it than what it is. I mean, it's obvious!"

"Sir, we don't have spit."

NOTE

1. Helen's case example later appeared in an article entitled "Criminal Profiling from Crime Analysis" written by John Douglas, Robert Ressler, Ann Burgess, and Carol Hartman. It appeared in *Behavioral Sciences and the Law* 4, no. 4 (1986): 401–21.

7

Spawning a Nationwide System to Track Serial Killers

"Only those who worked down there in that brightly-lit, sometimes smelly basement know the achievements. No one can possibly know the body count saved by brilliant intuition. Yet, in jealousy or jest, we were known as the 'bull-shit unit.' The BSU has been so thoroughly caricaturized that those who never toiled in that goddam crowded basement bomb shelter can scarcely imagine what the work was all about, how the BSU evolved, changed, evolved some more, then changed yet again. And thanks to tough old Depue, that truly remarkable old priest-turned-multiple-homicide-expert, all the changes somehow fit into a perfect mosaic. The BSU became a truly functional, productive, methodical piece of clockwork."

A CURRENT BSUER

As the number of unsolved homicides, rapes, arsons, extortions, and other violent offenses submitted to what was called the Behavioral Science Unit in the late 1970s and early 1980s increased, the necessity for additional relevant data became obvious. Crime scene information to deduce certain offender characteristics had been pouring in along with requests for help since 1972, when the BSU's services became available to all law enforcement agencies.

Now there was more data available for the BSU staff: information about the offender, his methods of operation, his victim selection, his personality makeup, and his view of himself.

In the spring of 1979, Larry Monroe, as BSU chief, received approval to initiate the Criminal Personality Research Project (CPRP).

At long last, staff could engage in research on violent offenders throughout the country. "Equipped with a protocol that covered most aspects of the offense and many facets of the offender's personality, the special agents conducted extensive interviews of incarcerated violent offenders," recalls Dick Ault.

With CPRP on the books, Monroe set a pilot phase into motion. It was the first project ever, inside or outside the FBI, to analyze the overall crime, paying particular attention to the crime scene.

The study had both quantitative and qualitative approaches to data collection and analysis. Qualitative objectives were to describe the characteristics of murderers, the manner in which they committed their crimes, and crime scenes. The descriptive data obtained would make an important contribution to the documentation of the killer.

Quantitative objectives, of course, were somewhat more complex. First, the CPRP would test, using statistical procedures, whether there were significant behavioral differences at the crime scene between crimes committed by, for example, organized sexual murderers and disorganized sexual murderers. Second, it would identify variables, or specific characteristics, that might be useful in profiling sexual murderers, and which organized and disorganized sexual murderers differ statistically.

To meet these objectives, the goal of the study was to interview and examine one hundred convicted, incarcerated sexual murderers (though only thirty-six were actually interviewed and studied). This was to be the largest compiled sample of available sexual killers interviewed for research purposes. They would not represent a random sample, but would come from geographic areas throughout the nation. Nonetheless, they could be used to indicate characteristics of sexual murderers in general.

For example, all the murderers were male, most were white. Prior to each interview, the killer had exhausted his initial appeal and had consented to participate in the project. All the cases were available for

Fig. 7.1. Sexual Homicide: Motivational Model

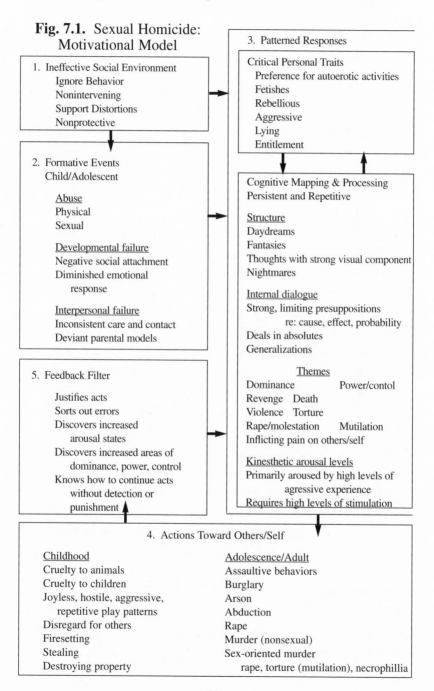

1. Ineffective Social Environment
   Ignore Behavior
   Nonintervening
   Support Distortions
   Nonprotective

2. Formative Events
   Child/Adolescent

   Abuse
   Physical
   Sexual

   Developmental failure
   Negative social attachment
   Diminished emotional
      response

   Interpersonal failure
   Inconsistent care and contact
   Deviant parental models

5. Feedback Filter

   Justifies acts
   Sorts out errors
   Discovers increased
      arousal states
   Discovers increased areas of
      dominance, power, control
   Knows how to continue acts
      without detection or
      punishment

3. Patterned Responses

   Critical Personal Traits
      Preference for autoerotic activities
      Fetishes
      Rebellious
      Aggressive
      Lying
      Entitlement

   Cognitive Mapping & Processing
   Persistent and Repetitive

   Structure
   Daydreams
   Fantasies
   Thoughts with strong visual component
   Nightmares

   Internal dialogue
   Strong, limiting presuppositions
      re: cause, effect, probability
   Deals in absolutes
   Generalizations

   Themes
   Dominance   Power/contol
   Revenge   Death
   Violence   Torture
   Rape/molestation   Mutilation
   Inflicting pain on others/self

   Kinesthetic arousal levels
   Primarily aroused by high levels of
      agressive experience
   Requires high levels of stimulation

4. Actions Toward Others/Self

   Childhood
   Cruelty to animals
   Cruelty to children
   Joyless, hostile, aggressive,
      repetitive play patterns
   Disregard for others
   Firesetting
   Stealing
   Destroying property

   Adolescence/Adult
   Assaultive behaviors
   Burglary
   Arson
   Abduction
   Rape
   Murder (nonsexual)
   Sex-oriented murder
      rape, torture (mutilation), necrophillia

record review. Seven of these men had been convicted of killing one person, while the remainder had been convicted of killing multiple victims. Although some of the murderers had been written about extensively elsewhere, the CPRP was the first to examine them collectively as a subpopulation of murderers and from the law enforcement perspective. Data were collected on a total of 118 victims, primarily women. Nine victims survived and were treated as attempted-murder victims. Several offenders in the study were suspected of additional murders for which they were never brought to trial.

The interviews and data collection for the CPRP, which occurred between 1979 and 1983, were primarily performed by Bob Ressler and John Douglas, both experienced special agents assigned to the Behavioral Science Unit. They incorporated the interviews in conjunction with field schools. Data collection was not the only goal of the interviews. Another goal was establishing credibility with cops by being able to say, "We have interviewed, . . ." One particular example of what actually occurred during the interview phase dealt with one of the most notorious serial killers in California history.

Ressler was interested in Ed Kemper, the infamous Santa Cruz murderer of thirteen young women in California. John Douglas, who was assisting Ressler in the project, left the FBI Academy to join Bob and John Conway of the San Francisco field office for the big interview. Conway had coordinated the interviews in California for Douglas and Ressler. Together they spent three hours interviewing Kemper, who was six feet, nine inches and weighed almost three hundred pounds. All three despised Kemper. Here was a serial killer who was very pleased with what he had done. In addition, he was laughingly descriptive, telling how he often dug up the skull of his mother, whom he had beheaded, and masturbated into it. When the skull's teeth scratched his penis, he became so infuriated that he grabbed a hammer and knocked them out. Then Kemper sadly looked down at the ground and said, "Poor moms, she didn't deserve that."

Kemper slowly and deliberately described how he murdered each of his thirteen victims, virtually all of whom were physically petite and less than twenty years of age. Ressler, Douglas, Kemper, and Conway sat around a heavy table in the Vacaville Medical Facility's warden's office. Instead of answering the two BSUers' questions, Kemper expounded on the minute details of the killings he had committed. Conway, feeling he needed to help retrieve control of the interview from Kemper, slowly raised his right foot until it was positioned against the edge of the table, opposite the serial killer. Then he suddenly pushed with all the strength he had, shoving the heavy table right into Kemper's stomach, and not only knocked all the wind out of him, but surprised Douglas and Ressler, sending them into disarray. Conway growled, "Answer the damn questions."

Kemper was so stunned that he instantly apologized, asking the BSUers to repeat their questions. Ressler and Douglas were extremely annoyed by Conway's tactics and told him so him after the interview.

Later in the interview, Kemper, unable to control himself, lapsed back into his descriptive monologue. At that point, Conway asked him if he ever had sex with a live woman. Although embarrassed, he answered confidently that he had. When Conway said he didn't believe him, and challenged the murderer to name one, Kemper became flustered to the point of anger. Ressler and Douglas watched in amazement.

In a second interview a few months later, Conway cut into the discussion between Ressler and Kemper by saying, "You know, I'm starting to get very tired listening to your bullshit." Kemper glared at Conway for a few moments, then resumed answering the BSUer's questions. But at that point the interview ended abruptly. As the three exited the interview area, one of the doors opened and for a few moments the three were enclosed between two sets of prison doors. Kemper smiled, then leaned down to Conway's eye-level and said ominously, "I'll bet you're scared to death being locked in here with me." Without blinking, Conway coldly responded, "I know what you've done, you sad son-of-a-bitch. But you have no idea what I've done." Before Kemper could digest the words, one of the two doors was open and the three exited, with Kemper continuing to glare at Conway.

Shortly thereafter, Robert Ressler advised Conway that he would never again be involved with him in an interview. Yet on several subsequent occasions, Kemper asked for Conway to participate since he had developed a basic respect for him. Ressler relented. The California State Prison System simply had too many interesting murderers.

Take Sirhan Sirhan, for example. The killer of Robert Kennedy was a short, well-muscled, very intense individual who did not want to be interviewed. When Conway was informed, he asked that he be brought into the interview room anyway. When Sirhan entered the room and saw Conway and Ressler sitting behind the table, he immediately plastered himself against the wall, staring at the two with bulging eyes. He would not respond to any of the approaches the two used to get him away from the wall. Realizing that they were in for a wait, Conway pushed his chair back, put his feet up on the table, and pretended to take great pains in lighting up and smoking a cigarette. Conway asked Ressler how his golf game was, and if he had played any interesting courses lately. Since Bob doesn't play golf, the two engaged in a nonsensical conversation that lasted for a half hour or so. "Looking for the right spot to touch Sirhan," Conway recalls, "I started talking about political prisoners and how and why they won't help themselves. Shortly thereafter, Sirhan asked for a cigarette and came over to the table and sat down. During his rambling conversation, he talked of his hatred of the Kennedys and how a voice had told him to kill Robert because of his support of Israel. Sirhan honestly believed that he had changed the course of world history and most would agree with him."

When Ressler and Conway felt they had obtained all that they could from him, Conway asked Sirhan, since he hated Jews so much, how he could bring himself to have a Jewish lawyer defend him. The interview went downhill from there.

Probably the most unusual of all the interviews to take place was between Ressler, Conway, and the so-called Vampire Killer, Richard Trenton Chase (see the introduction). On death row at San Quentin, Chase appeared every bit the vampire: tall and skinny, with gaunt features and deep-set eyes with dark circles around them. He spoke very slowly, while his long, bony hands and fingers seemed to search for something to do. At one point, while still talking very slowly, he took a half-pint plastic container with some food in it from his cardboard folder and slowly passed it across the table to Conway. Since Conway wasn't hungry, he slowly passed it over to Ressler, who failed to grasp the humor of the situation, since Chase was a cannibal. Ressler asked Chase what was in the cup. The vampire killer explained that it was part of the meal that had been served to him and he wanted the two agents to see what passed for food in state prison. Conway agreed with Chase and said that since Ressler was from Washington, he could probably do something about it. Again Ressler saw nothing funny about Conway's comment and seemed to be strangely affected by both Chase and Conway.

Chase, when asked by Ressler what the circles of blood around the crime scene meant, explained that he used a tin can to scoop the blood out of the corpse's cavity to drink it, then placed the can down, which left the circle stain. Chase concluded the interview by demanding that he be removed from death row because the other inmates were driving him crazy by shouting that he should hurry up and kill himself. Before Ressler had the opportunity to interview him again, Chase hanged himself in his cell.

Mention the Behavioral Science Unit today and Americans immediately flash on the terrifying cinema of *Silence of the Lambs*, *Mindhunter*, *The X-Files*, *Profiler*, *Millennium*, or the gabby buffoonery of the current spate of crime fiction. Yet the area affectionately known by the BSUers as "ten times lower than dead folks"— two stories below the Academy's cafeteria—was "home." For all its perceptible faults, the clean, tidy basement was a place of enormous pride, where professional FBI criminologists arrived each morning to still their inextinguishable hunger for important creative work, meaningful work that meant identifying and assisting in the capture of beasts so fierce that no one else could get close to them.

When less than a decade old, the BSU "home," although functional, was beginning to fray and appear run down. It ran to a pattern of similarly overstuffed, overworked, overtired FBI facilities whose golden days were already past: somewhat shabby for lack of paint and patch-up. Small rooms or cubbyholes, each furnished with an old desk, a lamp whose light bulb was dim, and a miniature rug, were linked by long, narrow hallways with the pervasive smell of old carpets and a basement odor that was impossible to air out.

Copies of class schedules, reports, and assorted journal articles, including mail and packages, lay scattered on battered hall tables near ancient mimeograph machines. Perpetually cleaning drudges with brooms and empty bags plodded up and down, throughout and around. Men often stood around chatting and joking, or patiently listening to each other's rumors, problems, or troubles.

Each piece of hand-me-down furniture, either swiped, borrowed, or begged (use whatever euphemism you wish), clashed with the next no matter where it sat. Although the bathrooms were clean and spotless, the plastered walls were cracking and typically tacky, though the plumbing was not yet faulty.

In a sort of comic surprise, the BSU "boarders" ran to type: saturnine profiler and randy wag; serious intellectual and affable comedian; the thoroughly frank workaholic who knew his job and the garrulous loafer full of shenanigans; the quite homely and perky coquette secretaries. Although there were always good laughs, there was also an intrinsic fear among all—the fear that one day he or she might be transferred out of the unit and assigned back to some lonesome field office. But there was always pride in each other and pride of the group as a whole.

In 1980, when a truly fatherly figure entered the noirish air of sleaze, sexual murder, and every other unimaginable and inhuman killing, to run the rambling twenty-seven-room basement, he could take the ingredients and mold them into something resembling a team ("A leper colony," according to some, "the rejects the FBI needed to hide.")

And this is exactly what Roger Depue did when he assumed the mantle of leadership.

Always well groomed and impeccably dressed in a dark suit, Depue was the majordomo to what he called "the big happy family in our basement home." In early 1984, he had sixteen players on his team, and was eager and hopeful of stretching the number to twenty-five. He genuinely liked his "family," allowing them the run of the "house," triggering their imaginations, and scrounging around to provide whatever anybody needed.

In many ways, the BSU was a resident agency, a large one, considering that it had over a dozen agents assigned to it. Although such a large team had its occasional squabbles, no one became more than normally upset at anyone else. Some at SOG seemed to resent the camaraderie within the BSU. One ASAC referred to the unit disparagingly as "the Club." "But we managed to get along with the bastard without sacrificing our good humor, savoir faire, or aura of FBI charm and dignity," recalls a BSUer.

In return for the tone Depue established in the basement, the team genuinely respected and liked him. Badmouthing, backstabbing, and disloyalty were impossible. His, and theirs, was a warm and realistic command life in the underground bunker, even though law enforcement across the nation had a blowtorch turned their way to solve, solve, solve.

Consider for a moment how the BSU team would sit around the

large table in the conference room where crimes had been analyzed and solved since Jack Kirsch's reign in 1972. When the door of the room was closed, the brainstorming began. Since the room, indeed, the entire basement, was soundproof, anything and everything was allowed, except that whatever was said remained in the room after the meeting was over. Only the finished product emerged.

Each meeting was like a group "free association" exercise in a psychoanalyst's office. The only difference was that these men were all elite FBI investigators, most with advanced degrees in various behavioral sciences. Arguments, ideas, insights, insults, accusations, and solutions flew back and forth. Some "visions" which appeared preposterous at first contained the sparks of successful plans of action.

Take, for example, one steamy hot morning in the basement when the team was talking about a Mafia boss in an organized crime case. Although there were rudimentary air conditioners strategically placed throughout the Academy, and the basement in particular, summer was anathema and the BSUers, like everyone above ground, perspired in Quantico's humidity. "Numerous attempts to make inroads into the crime family had met with frustration because of the don's domination of his pawns," recalls Roger. "Suddenly, in frustration, a tough, street-wise agent offered a solution: 'Why don't we just kill the son of a bitch?' Everyone laughed. Obviously, we couldn't kill him. When the group settled down, an agent across the table responded, 'Maybe we can make him think he's going to die.' Another offered, 'Hey, he's scheduled to have a physical examination in a couple of weeks.' Once again, my team was off in a direction which would eventually con-tribute toward bringing down a Mafia kingpin."

Every now and then, either during the profiling sessions or staff meetings, someone would say something so outrageously obvious, or simply funny, that Larry Monroe felt the comment should be kept for posterity. He fashioned a permanent pin-up board, labeled "The Board—Quote of the Day" and began posting the dumbest quotes to come from BSUers' mouths. Some of the more infamous included, "You're no cop until you've been puked on," "It doesn't mean a thing if you don't pull the string" (borrowed from the army's parachute divisions), "To hell with profiling him. We know who did it. Let's just kill him," "Murderers kill in the way they live," "He tracked it all over me while I was there and before he ran off he threw it at me," "He went through our office like shit through a tin horn," "If you like bull shit, insecurity, and applause, join the BSU." Commented Depue, "You really weren't somebody until you made Larry's 'Board.'"

The board had its positive effects: BSUers were more apt to think before uttering nonsense, and it helped overcome the often depressing grind of facing photos and other evidence of serial murder.

When Roger Depue transferred into the BSU in June of 1974, Howard "Bud" Teten was already somewhat of a legend because of his ability to apply his behavioral science background to unsolved cases of violent crime. Roger admired how Howard, by trying to think like the perpetrator, was able to connect with the thought processes most probably used by the criminal. No one, as far as was known, had proceeded in this manner before. As Howard became more and more proficient at reenacting a murder step by step, tracing the thinking patterns and behaviors of the killer, the more Teten and his colleagues vicariously learned about how most murderers thought. The more successful Howard became at constructing a mental profile of the perpetrator most likely to be responsible for a particular crime, the more successful his colleagues became. Howard was the "father" of the FBI's crime analysis and criminal personality profiling and Roger Depue was the first to honor him for it.

"All of us believed that we, as a team, were responsible for three main thrusts: training, research, and casework. Really, a three-legged stool, if you will. Remove one of the legs and the stool collapses. And none of us wanted that to happen," says Depue. "How often did the phones ring in those overworked years? In the BSU, the phones rang all day long. You suddenly become an 'expert' when law enforcement wants your advice on a problem. . . . We had two sayings in the early eighties: for high performers, 'Promise them heaven, but get that seven,' and as far as self-selection was concerned, we'd say, 'It's not fun to work with stars if you're only a light bulb.'"

The violent crime that had steadily been increasing in America since 1960 showed no signs of abating by 1980. In fact, 1980 became a record year, with almost twenty-four thousand murder victims. Never in American history had there been such unprecedented mayhem in a twelve-month period. Equally alarming were the sky-rocketing rates of other serious violent crimes, such as aggravated assault, forcible rape, and armed robbery. Even stranger-to-stranger, predatory violent crime was steadily climbing, while the number of cases cleared by arrest was diminishing. America's progress toward economic prosperity and a better life was deflated by the downward spiral reflected in crime statistics. Something had to be done, and fast.

In August of 1981, William French Smith, the attorney general of the United States, organized the U.S. Task Force on Violent Crime. His objective was to gather a group of knowledgeable experts in various professions and academic disciplines to analyze violent crime in America. Smith's task force was to recommend steps to curb the rapid increases in violent crime across the nation and to reduce its adverse impact on the quality of life.

Equally significant, the attorney general ordered each U.S. Department of Justice agency to submit an outline of how it could assist a new national effort to reduce the level of violent crime. When the Bureau received its mandate, William H. Webster, then director, began a systematic survey of FBI resources to determine those that would be most appropriate for the national cause. Of course, the Academy's training division was among the first to be called upon for ideas. In fact, after submitting its initial report, the training division was charged with the responsibility of leading the FBI's role in helping combat violent crime in this country. And within the training division, the Behavioral Science Unit became the premier think tank.

Then the following year, in addition to the attorney general's new emphasis on reducing violent crime, in mid-July of 1983, Pennsylvania senator Arlen Specter, chairman of the Subcommittee on Juvenile Justice, for the Committee on the Judiciary, with the strong support of Florida senator Paula Hawkins, began holding hearings on whether to base new legislative and funding decisions on the knowledge and opinions of the nation's leading violent crime "experts." The Ninety-eighth Congress had expressed interest in specific violent crimes such as "missing and murdered children," the "sexual exploitation of children," "unidentified dead bodies," and "serial killers." The goal of the Specter-Hawkins committee was to strengthen the criminal justice system's resources to track and apprehend what seemed to be a new breed of human predator who traveled at leisure and with impunity across the nation, coldly slaying vulnerable women and children for no apparent motive.

At 9:30 A.M. on Monday, July 12, 1983, Supervisory Special Agent Roger L. Depue, Chief, Behavioral Science Unit, testified before the Subcommittee on Juvenile Justice, which consisted of Specter, Hawkins, and fellow senators Jeremiah Denton (Alabama), Charles Mathias (Maryland), Howard Metzenbaum (Ohio), and Edward Kennedy (Massachusetts), on the concept of a tracking system that would collect and disseminate information concerning the patterns of "serial murderers."

It was an unusually hot and humid mid-July morning, and to everyone's dismay, the air conditioning system was barely working. Only a handful of visitors were observing the proceedings.

Senator Specter led off the questioning and Roger Depue answered Senator Specter's questions regarding his own law enforcement background, questions regarding the Behavioral Science Unit to include the functions of training, research, and liaison, questions as to the credentials of the special agents and law enforcement specialists, and the need for Detective Pierce Brooks's VICAP system (see chapter 8).

Roger stated, "I think that it [VICAP] is a suggestion that is long overdue. I am personally aware of the fact that Pierce Brooks has been working on it for a number of years. And then he added, "Last year, in 1982, we received 250 cases for which we completed an analysis and furnished 230 profiles. In 1981, 152 profiles were developed. In 1979, only 43. During 1982, the cases we analyzed consisted of 544 victims of murder, rape, assault, arson, child molestation, and equivocal deaths. Our follow-up study to determine the value of the profiling service last year showed that our technique assisted in the identification and prosecution of offenders responsible for 50 murders and 126 rapes. The year before, in 1981, we contributed to the solutions of 23 homicides and 57 rapes. It's important to keep in mind that these cases were all considered 'unsolvable' when they were referred to the Behavioral Science Unit."

With such testimony, Depue, Brooks, and others were on the verge of convincing Congress that a system to track and analyze serial murders was viable. With some remodeling of the Academy's cafeteria-lounge basement, the addition of a little hard- and software, plus three or four consultants, a National Center for the Analysis of Violent Crime could be easily formed. "Hopefully," concluded Depue, "I can bring Pierce Brooks aboard. And there is a young Ph.D. in engineering who is very bright in the area of data processing, Dave Icove, whom I would like to bring aboard. Dr. Icove developed AIMS, the Arson Information Management System, to effectively combat the arsonist. . . . Then, there's Dr. Murray Miron of Syracuse University, who has developed an excellent, computer-supported, psycholinguistic analysis process for threatening messages. . . . Kenneth Wooden, founder and Director of the National Coalition for Children's Justice, has a plan to use computers to find child victims and the procurers who sexually exploit them. If we had all these fine people and their ideas under one roof, we could work miracles in apprehension."

Spawning a Nationwide System to Track Serial Killers

Since 1982, the Office of Juvenile Justice and Delinquency Prevention (OJJDP) had been discussing the awarding of a grant to a diversified group of individuals made up of criminal justice professionals, academicians, writers, and other interested law enforcement personnel in order to formally establish a pilot VICAP program. Together with the National Institute of Justice, OJJDP funded a conference of interested parties, which was held at the Criminal Justice Center at Sam Houston State University, in Huntsville, Texas, on July 12–14, 1983. This was the same week that Depue and Brooks appeared before the subcommittee in Congress. Representatives from the Office of Juvenile Justice and Delinquency Prevention Program, Department of Justice, and federal, state, and local law enforcement agencies, as well as other interested parties, met to hear and discuss various presentations on violent crime, especially serial murder.

At the conclusion of the two-day meeting, the participants unanimously agreed that a National Center for the Analysis of Violent Crime should be finally established. This agreement, coupled with Depue's forceful testimony before Congress, meant that the NCAVC was in—if not yet formally, then certainly informally. Furthermore, all agreed it would be administered by the FBI's BSU and physically located within the Academy. In short, the nation would have a law-enforcement-oriented, behavioral-science and data-processing resource center to consolidate research, training, and consultant functions for the purpose of providing assistance to federal, state, and local law people who were confronted with "unusual, bizarre, and/or repetitive violent crimes."

It wasn't until eleven months later, on June 21, 1984, when, speaking before the National Sheriffs Association's 44th Annual Conference in Hartford, Connecticut, that President Ronald Reagan formally announced the establishment of the NCAVC. Exercising his political prerogative as an incumbent to announce new programs, Reagan told the assembled two thousand sheriffs and deputy sheriffs that for the first year the new center would be funded with $2.5 million in grants. The FBI, added the president, would absorb the total cost of funding, some $1.5 million, for the second year. The sheriffs responded to Reagan's law-and-order appeal with enthusiasm, interrupting his speech fourteen times.

There were many significant contributors and supporters of the NCAVC, both in the Department of Justice and in other agencies. Without the support of John Walsh, Ann Rule, Doug Moore from Naval Investigative Services, Jim Wooten and Bob Heck from OJJDP (Office of Juvenile Justice and Delinquency Prevention), Lois Haight-Harrington from DOJ, Director James "Chips" Stewart from National Institute of Justice, Al Regnery also from OJJDP, and James O'Connor and James McKenzie of the FBI, the NCAVC would not have come to fruition. Pierre Brooks's police team gave the NCAVC, and particularly VICAP, law enforcement credibility. That team included Brooks, Terry Green from the Oakland police department, Ken Hanflan from the Pacific Northwest, and Jim Howlett from Charlotte.

As it was originally conceived, the NCAVC consisted of four programs—Research and Development, Training, Profiling and Consultation, and VICAP (Violent Criminal Apprehension Program).

In January of 1986, the original Behavioral Science Unit, which governed the NCAVC, was split into two units, each unit responsible for the management of two of the four NCAVC programs. The Behavioral Science Instruction and Research Unit (BSIRU) was to continue the traditional training functions of the first BSU, as well as supervise the research and development and training programs of the NCAVC. The Behavioral Science Investigative Support Unit (BSISU) would administer the profiling and consultation and VICAP programs of the NCAVC. The chief of the BSIRU would be the administrator, while the chief of the BSISU would serve as the deputy administrator.

Depue wrote a year later in the *Law Enforcement Bulletin* (December 1986), "The main idea of NCAVC was to bring together the fragmented efforts from around the country so that they could be consolidated into one national resource center available to the entire police community. In short, it would serve as a clearinghouse for the most baffling and fearful of the unsolved violent crimes. All of us, the U.S. Congress, the Department of Justice, and federal, state, and local criminal justice agencies, are making a difference in America. Now armed with programs like this, we are slowing the downward spiral of violent crime and increasing the risk for the violent offender."

In brief, then, the NCAVC was the new and powerful weapon law enforcement needed in its armory to fight violent crime in America. While BSU research efforts were leading to new insights about violent criminal personality and behavior, NCAVC training programs would disseminate the latest violent crime data and investigative techniques. Back in the basement, more and more cases were being successfully analyzed and criminal profiles formulated with surprising accuracy. BSUers were developing imaginative prosecutive strategies, resulting in faster detections and arrests, and more certain convictions and confinements. The Violent Criminal Apprehension Program (VICAP) was functioning fully in linking unsolved violent crimes to each other throughout the nation and providing assistance in the coordination of complex interagency investigations. VICAP facilitated the use of computer engineering's technological breakthroughs to combat violent crime.

Says Depue, "The concerned efforts of Congress, the Justice Department, and federal, state, and local criminal justice agencies slowed that awful downward spiral of violent crime. . . . Because of the birth of NCAVC, the violent offender was more vulnerable, more at risk."

By 1985 and the establishment of NCAVC, things were finally going the way Depue and his team had hoped they would for so many years. The Behavioral Science Unit had split, or bifurcated (in fingerprint talk), into two BSU subunits: the BSIRU and the BSISU. Roger served as the administrator of the NCAVC and the BSIRU chief, while Alan "Smokey" Burgess became the deputy administrator of the

227

NCAVC and unit chief of the BSISU. Smokey had no previous experience in FBI behavioral sciences, but by all accounts was a thoroughly competent administrator of a highly motivated, creative staff who had the requisite knowledge.

Through Roger and his team's efforts, an applied forensic behavioral science resource for the criminal justice community and public sector had been created. Word spread throughout the country that the NCAVC was a place for investigators, prosecuting attorneys, judges, and corrections officials to go for assistance with perplexing crimes and baffling criminal behaviors. It was a national clearinghouse for the unusual, bizarre, serial, and particularly violent crimes, a place which studied these more rare crimes and behaviors and professed to understand them in order to assist authorities to analyze and explain them, identify perpetrators, locate and apprehend them, successfully prosecute the cases, and convict and incarcerate the offenders.

THE NATIONAL CENTER FOR THE ANALYSIS OF VIOLENT CRIME IS BORN

"The NCAVC's role was to serve as a law enforcement clearinghouse and resource center for the most baffling and fearful of all unresolved violent crimes. Remember, there may be as many as thirty-five multiple slayers still out there. That goes for serial rapists, arsonists, child abductors, etc. There's a growing frequency of all these type crimes, committed not by animalistic, insane-looking, or raving-lunatic-type people, but by the personable and intelligent young men down the street. Since it isn't easy to spot such persons, the NVAVC can help the cop on that street fight back—and win."

ROGER DEPUE, BSU CHIEF, 1986

During the excessively hot and humid summer of 1985, the body of a Baltimore woman in her late twenties was found about 150 yards into a wooded culvert area outside her apartment. Her car was found in the apartment parking lot. Recreating the scene, local police felt the victim was approached after she had parked. It was known she arrived home late. She was found in a stream after being assaulted, drowned, and strangled. Her head had been held underwater while she was strangled. There was no evidence of severe beating of the body. Although some defense wounds were present, there was no mutilation. She was found partially clothed. The only item taken from the victim was a ring of little value. Her shoes, found further down the trail, suggested the location of the sexual assault. Footprints were present around the site. The victim lived in a high-rise with many apartments, parking lots, and cars.

A second victim, a woman in her mid-twenties, was found fully dressed in a wooded area less than a quarter-mile from the location of the first victim. She was not near water. She had been stabbed repeatedly in the chest. Although there was evidence of sexual assault, there was no overkill to the body or mutilation. Again, the victim was arriving home late at night; apparently she parked her car and was abducted before reaching her apartment.

Victim number three was similar in physical appearance, age, and the manner she was killed, to the second victim. There was considerable evidence of sexual assault; underclothing in disarray suggested she was redressed after death. A stocking was missing although her shoes were on.

Several months later, victim number four, a black woman in her early thirties, surfaced in the same general vicinity. She usually worked late and arrived home between 2 and 3 A.M. Her car was also parked where she would have entered the apartment building. Although discovered further away than the other victims, she was still not more than a half-mile from where she lived. There was evidence of sexual assault, and she too had been strangled and drowned. The method and location were similar to the first crime scene and consistent with the work schedule of the victim.

Victim number five, a woman in her mid-twenties, was last seen at a party at 1:30 or 2:30 A.M. She left the party with several people and was later found dead in the same wooded culvert area as the previous victims. She was stabbed several times in the chest and had been partially buried in the culvert. There was evidence of sexual assault.

After five unsolved murders had stacked up and with no leads in sight, local homicide detectives contacted the FBI's National Center for the Analysis of Violent Crime. After studying the responses submitted by Baltimore's investigative team on the standard NCAVC questionnaire, unit chief Roger Depue turned the case over to his profiling and consultation team, who presented the detectives with a personality profile within two days.

Considering all the dynamics and patterns noted in each of the five cases, the profilers concluded that the killer selected only victims who were returning home during the late evening or early morning hours. The assaults generally took place near the victim's homes, as they were walking from their parked cars. The offender was watching the parking areas for single women returning during these times. He took the victims from the apartment complex to wooded areas close by for the assaults. He chose the time and place of assault. Since no scream or resistance was evident, one must assume the assailant carried a weapon and instructed the victims to accompany him to the secluded area. This indicates a persuasive, articulate person who convinced them that no harm would come to them if they did as he instructed. He was manipulative and had a history of antisocial traits and behavior. He was youthful and aggressive, probably a macho type, since he used the same M.O. in each assault. He obviously knew the territory well, both the built-up areas and the surrounding woods. He probably lived in the area, and had grown up and played in the woods as a child: he was a long-term resident.

Medical examinations and crime scene assessments showed rape prior to death, and that death was sudden with minimal mutilation. The victims were sized up prior to the approach and the murderer knew they would not resist if he promised release after rape. He had raped before the killing started, but some life trauma had triggered the taking of the life of victim #1. Since the offender has had past problems with law enforcement, now that he had murdered, he felt he must continue to kill to avoid victims testifying against him. He did not value the life of the women he raped, since they might identify him to the police.

The profilers theorized that the assailant in all five murders was an organized, antisocial personality. He was a youthful, white male, had good intelligence, and was articulate and manipulative. He fit into the community and had lived there for many years. He lived in close proximity to all the victims. He precipitated his crimes with alcohol and/or drugs, was possibly the firstborn in his family, and was sexually competent. He probably had a girlfriend, yet had a recent problem with her before the first killing. Considering his age, he would live with a single parent and would have no car since he selected victims on foot, sometimes using their cars in the assault. He probably followed the media reports of the crime and might have been in a crowd of onlookers when the police located the bodies.

Depue read the profile, concurred with its descriptions and dispatched it to the Baltimore Homicide Detectives. Three weeks later he received a telephone call congratulating him and his Profiling and Consultation Program for a job well done. The profile led to a seventeen-year-old, white male living very close to all the victims, who lived within a one-mile radius. He was bright, yet only a marginal achiever in school, lived with his mother, and did not own a car. He was known as a macho ladies' man and a con artist among his peers. He used beer and marijuana to precipitate his offense and selected victims in an area he grew up in. He had a girlfriend he called "his fiancée," who jilted him shortly before the first murder when she went away to college. He followed the crimes in the paper and on one occasion watched police investigators from his window. He had a lengthy juvenile record, including sexual assault and rape.

This was but one of the 173 homicide requests for profiles submitted to the NCAVC in 1985 when, in June of that year, the National Center for the Analysis of Violent Crime became fully operational at the Academy. By December, there would be a total of 680 requests for either telephonic or on-site consultations, requests for personality assessment, interview techniques, investigative and prosecutive strategies, and criminal personality profiles. The requests for profiles were received for the following crimes:

- homicides, 173
- rapes, 38
- sexual assaults, 16
- child molestations, 3
- arson/bombings, 15
- robberies, 5
- kidnaps, 23
- assaults, 2
- Violent Criminal Apprehension Program (VICAP), 160
- other FBI matters, 70

Later, feedback from the requesting agencies revealed that the NCAVC teams had assisted in the identification, prosecution, and/or convictions of offenders responsible for the following crimes: 24 subjects for 52 sexual assaults; 2 subjects for 6 kidnappings; and 2 subjects for 2 equivocal deaths.

Through the expertise of its staff in crime analysis, psychology, sociology, criminology, political science, and computer science, the NCAVC is a multidisciplinary approach to a wide variety of investigative problems. It is an integral part of the Academy and many of its members are adjunct faculty with the University of Virginia.

Spawning a Nationwide System to Track Serial Killers

The educational and training activities of the Center include courses, seminars, symposia, and conferences, as well as a ten-month fellowship for police officers in criminal investigative analysis. The courses and seminars are conducted at the FBI Academy and at a variety of locations throughout North America; the fellowship, conferences, and symposia take place at the FBI Academy.

The Center's research activities include multidisciplinary studies in serial and violent crimes such as homicide, rape, sexual sadism, child abduction, arson, threats, computer crime, and counterintelligence matters, as well as hijacking, crisis management, and areas of interest relating to hostage negotiation and special weapons and tactics team operations. Joining in such research projects with the staff of the Center are faculty from major universities, members of the mental health and medical professions, and other law enforcement representatives.

The Center provides investigative support to federal, state, county, and city law enforcement agencies through its services, which include consultation on major violent crimes, profiles of unknown offenders, personality assessments, investigative strategies, interviewing techniques, search warrant affidavit assistance, prosecution strategy, and expert testimony. Investigative support is also offered through VICAP in its aim to alert law enforcement agencies that might be seeking the same offender for crimes in their jurisdictions. Administrative and logistical support is also provided to FBI field offices in crisis situations as well as for special events such as the 1990 Goodwill Games and national political conventions.

The Center also takes part in providing psychological services to FBI employees, students attending courses at the FBI Academy, and others in the law enforcement family in need of debriefing or counseling following a critical incident such as line-of-duty deaths.

In the mid-1980s, the Center was divided into three units: Behavioral Science Services, Investigative Support, and Special Operations and Research.

INTO THE MINDS OF MADMEN

The Behavioral Science Services Unit (BSSU) was one of the instructional departments of the FBI's training division. The mission of the BSSU was to develop and provide programs of training, consultation, and information in the behavioral and social sciences for the law enforcement community, that would improve their administrative and operational effectiveness. This work included conducting research and presenting a variety of courses on topics such as interpersonal violence, death investigation, applied criminal psychology, sexual exploitation of children, terrorism, hypnosis, law enforcement stress and personal problems, crime prevention, community analysis, police-community relations, and futuristics.

The unit's personnel were primarily supervisory special agents and experienced veteran police instructors with advanced degrees in the behavioral science disciplines of psychology, criminology, sociology, and political science. The BSSU conducted specialized training in the above disciplines as they pertain to law enforcement. In addition to instructors, the BSSU professional personnel included an operations research analyst and a technical information specialist.

The BSSU worked in a coordinated way with the Investigative Support Unit to provide consultation services for local police and Bureau personnel in specific areas of expertise, such as the use of hypnosis, stress awareness/management, and in other matters where a behavioral science perspective was needed.

In its research, the BSSU focused on developing new and innovative investigative approaches and techniques to the solution of violent crime by studying violent criminals, their modi operandi, their victims, and the motivation for their behavior.

The Investigative Support Unit (ISU) had primary responsibility for all violent crime case analysis and consultation. It provided administrative control over the investigative support functions of the Criminal Investigative Analysis subunit, Violent Criminal Apprehension Program (VICAP) subunit, and the Arson and Bombing Investigative Services subunit of the NCAVC.

In the Criminal Investigative Analysis subunit, profiles of unknown offenders are constructed through a detailed analysis of violent crimes and aberrant behavior. In addition, consultation is provided that may include investigative strategy, interviewing and proactive investigative techniques, search warrant information, personality assessments, and prosecution strategy. Special agent crime analysts are available for on-site, major case analysis and consultation with law enforcement officials involved with major violent crime investigations. In 1990, 742 cases were received for services, 292 of which were FBI cases.

VICAP was designed to collect, collate, and analyze the aspects of violent crimes so that through computer analysis and data processing, violent crimes can be compared, identified, and charted (see chapter 8). In addition, experienced major case specialists and crime analysts reviewed the violent crime cases submitted and were able to provide their investigative and analytical expertise to the submitting law enforcement agencies. Through this process, suspects could be identified, crimes could be linked, and widespread law enforcement agencies could combine their resources to focus on a common criminal.

The Arson and Bombing Investigative Services subunit had the primary responsibility to provide assistance in arson, bombing, terrorism, computer intrusions, and related violent crimes submitted to the NCAVC by federal, state, local, and foreign law enforcement agencies. The subunit could be called upon to provide consultation, on-site crime scene assessments, courtroom testimony, training programs, and research interviews on matters it reviewed. It maintained the Arson Information Management System (AIMS) Project, which detects temporal and geographic patterns found in serial arson and bombing incidents. The results of the AIMS program were incorporated into criminal investigative analyses.

The Special Operations and Research Unit (SOAR) provided training and research in all of the various components of crisis management and major case management within the FBI. Specifically, the unit handled all FBI training in crisis management, special weapons and tactics, observer/sniper operations, tactical air operations, crisis negotiation (hostage, barricade, and suicide), major case management, and special events management. The SOAR also advised FBI field offices in both training and operational scenarios, assisted FBI head-quarters and field offices in designing and implementing command-post/field training exercises, monitored and assessed FBI field-crisis management capability, and provided liaison with other domestic and foreign members of the crisis management community.

As reflected in the overview of the NCAVC, one of the mandates was the research and analysis of crime and crime trends. The inter-view/case study method of analysis had provided a unique insight into the dark side of the offender and offenses. The initial efforts of Robert K. Ressler, Ann W. Burgess, and John E. Douglas, reflected in their book entitled, *Sexual Homicide: Patterns and Motives* (1988), pro-vided all of the staff with an insight into the serial killer. In an effort to focus and better define who and what they were addressing, mul-tiple killers were separated into three categories:

- Serial killer: three or more separate events with a cooling-off period between homicides;
- Mass killer: four or more victims at one location within one event;
- Spree killer: killings at two or more locations with no cooling-off period between murders. The killings are all the result of a single event, and the spree can be of short or long duration.

"Research is often regarded as either a complex and arcane art form or a simple review of literature," says Dick Ault. "Consequently, it is frequently considered to be a luxury that an organization can do without." However, in the NCAVC, the Research and Development

Program was absolutely intrinsic to the analysis of violent crimes. In crime scene analysis, also known as profiling, a lot of the primary data used to profile the offender was gleaned from the research. However, much of that information was rather abstract, more useful to the Academy instructors than to those in the NCAVC engaged in profiling. Thus, the research and development component was to excite continuing research, offer management support for agreed-upon research projects, and guarantee that the results were valid, reliable, and useful.

The study that examined thirty-six convicted, incarcerated sexual killers (CPRP) was not the only research project the NCAVC conducted in the mid-1980s. For example, in 1985, a survey was taken of police attitudes toward rape, proving once and for all that police were not insensitive to the tragedy of victims of rape. Furthermore, most cops felt that rape was extremely serious and placed a high priority on identifying, arresting, and prosecuting rape suspects. This information was later incorporated into Roy Hazelwood's book on rape investigation.

In addition, the NCAVC analyzed the correlation between risk-taking and life experience stress by police officers. For years, law enforcement had wanted to see exactly what the relationship was between personal factors—divorce, marriage, change of environment, etc.—load stress, and risk taking. The result of the study: cops with greater negative life experiences, such as divorce or death in the family, took more risks, although they did not necessarily fail to achieve their goals; that is, those risks were usually successful.

Then the NCAVC took on the hitherto unresearched subject of multiple arsons. As mentioned above, Dave Icove established the initial computer-assisted system to gather, categorize, analyze, and disseminate information that was critical to the evaluation of multiple arson cases. Known as AIMS (the Arson Information Management System), the system provided computer assistance to fire and police departments in predicting and possibly preventing multiple incendiary crimes. One of the initial computer analyses of arson was based on information submitted by the Prince Georges County, Maryland, fire department. This was a case of multiple arsons committed throughout the county. That study provided Icove with pertinent information on profiles of arsonists and their motives. Armed with such data, fire investigators could, for the first time, engage in logical, motive-based investigations. The systematic approach established by this computer model assisted Prince Georges County in solving these cases.

Also, the NCAVC began studying the history of psychological services in policing and the administrative NCAVC objectives. A member of the NCAVC team began an analysis of the training programs designed to help those who might be taken and held as hostages in extremist or terrorist situations to cope more effectively with the stress of their captivity. That research emphasized hostage survival. Finally, during the late 1980s, the future itself was the focus of a study by the NCAVC. Could American law enforcement's future be predicted? The answer was yes. In fact, for the following two decades, Dr. Bill Tafoya, the FBI's futurist, worked at the Academy training law enforcement and agents alike in focusing on potential futures that affected their professions. Police Futurist International, an international organization of practitioners, found its birth in Tafoya's graduation courses for the National Academy.

As far as the NCAVC training program was concerned, it handled all education and training for the unit. This meant organizing guest speakers, the specialized training of police and FBI special agents, and managing the NCAVC Police Fellowship in criminal personality profiling. Although all the training and educational efforts were for law enforcement, the NCAVC was also eager to share its increasing knowledge and expertise with other fields in the criminal justice system such as mental health, victim advocates, and various academic fields.

In short, then, the NCAVC training commitment was achieved in four main ways: field police schools, FBI Academy courses, speaking engagements, and NCAVC police fellowships. The field police schools provided free training in violent crime investigative techniques for between one and five days at FBI sites across America. The Academy courses were three to fourteen days in length and included speakers from a variety of disciplines. In addition, the NCAVC selected and provided speakers for law enforcement and other professional organizational meetings or conferences. Since mid-1985, the NCAVC speakers have participated in over five hundred law enforcement national meetings and conferences. For carefully selected police officers, the NCAVC provided one-year fellowships in criminal personality profiling at the academy. All expenses except salary and benefits were borne by the FBI.

The FBI Academy at Quantico, Virginia is responsible for a variety of law enforcement training programs conducted at the Academy and throughout the United States. Primarily, training is offered in the following four areas: new agents, FBI in-service training, FBI National Academy (designed for administrators), and general law enforcement training. In addition, field training conducted in 1995 involved specially trained agents from headquarters and fifty-nine field offices who taught 63,888 hours of instruction to 199,326 law enforcement personnel.

8

"VICAP? Why, we're the farthest planet out there!"

"Something insidious has happened in America: crime has made victims of us all. Awareness of its dangers affects the way we think, where we live, where we go, what we buy, how we raise our children, and the quality of our lives as we age. The specter of violent crime and the knowledge that without warning any person can be attacked or crippled, robbed or killed, lurks at the fringes of consciousness. Every citizen of this country is more impoverished, less free, more fearful, and less safe because of the ever present threat of the criminal. Rather than alter a system that has proven itself incapable of dealing with crime, society has altered itself."

FINAL REPORT OF THE PRESIDENT'S TASK FORCE ON VICTIMS OF CRIME, NO. 82-24146, 1982, P. VI.

January, Los Angeles County: The body of a young female is found near Interstate 10 east of La Puente. The victim has blunt-force skull fractures and a number of mutilation knife wounds, several of which are "unique." Two days later, Los Angeles Sheriff's Office (LASO) homicide detectives forward a VICAP offense report to VICAP. This report includes coroner protocol information and the identity of the victim, a fourteen-year-old runaway from a small northern California town. All information is entered in the VICAP computer and analyzed to compare M.O. (modus operandi) and physical evidence characteristics with other reported homicides. LASO detectives are advised that the VICAP search reveals no similar pattern cases on file.

February, San Bernardino: Detectives respond to a "found body" call on the southern edge of their city. The victim is a sixteen-year-old female from Hollywood. Injuries are similar to those of the January homicide in Los Angeles County. Regardless of the proximity of the two departments and the cooperation that exists between the detectives, it is a VICAP analysis that confirms that a similar pattern does exist and both agencies are notified.

April, Marshall, Texas: Detectives of that city forward VICAP information on the mutilation and murder of a nineteen-year-old female college student whose vehicle, with a flat tire, has been located on I-20 east of Dallas. After a pattern analysis run, VICAP alerts LASO, San Bernardino, and Marshall detectives that M.O. and physical evidence elements of the three murder cases are similar. It is also apparent that the killer is traveling east on the I-10/I-20 interstate system.

VICAP, after a request received from the three police departments, prepares and transmits an information All Points Bulletin (APB) with special attention to all law enforcement agencies on or near the I-10/I-20 route. The APB requests that any department with information related in any way to the M.O. of the three murders contact the VICAP center. The following day, the police in Las Cruces, New Mexico, respond. In March in that city, a fifteen-year-old female, hitchhiking to a friend's house, escaped after being assaulted by a male subject who had identified himself as a juvenile officer "working runaway cases." A description of the suspect, description of the suspect vehicle and the M.O. of the assault are forwarded to VICAP. VICAP alerts the departments working the three murder cases. VICAP is asked to transmit an APB of the suspect and suspect vehicle description.

The VICAP center also conducts a computer run on their known offender (profile and M.O.) file using the M.O., physical evidence, and victim information elements of the murders in California and Texas, and the assault M.O. and suspect description from New Mexico. There are two possible hits. VICAP alerts the case investigators, who send for and receive mug shots from two state prisons.

One subject is positively identified by the Las Cruces victim. Arrest warrants are issued and a supplemental APB is transmitted. Two days later the suspect, a parolee from a northwestern state, is arrested after picking up a young hitchhiker in Jackson, Mississippi.

Such was the information flow of one case among hundreds in the newly established VICAP process in 1982. Local law enforcement agencies were pleased. As one officer had said, "People on the streets are quick to blame us. 'Why wasn't he caught? Why wasn't he caught?' It's not our fault. There's a gaping hole in the communication network of our police agencies. There's no national central clearing-house where information regarding the most predatory kinds of killers can be exchanged. Big business firms utilize the magic of the computer to store and cull minute details of their work. We in law enforcement must depend on word of mouth or the telephone. The media and sometimes luck help us to hook onto similar patterns of criminality in jurisdictions in other states when dealing with the often nameless serial murderer. Even the computers at the National Crime Information Center in Washington, D.C., aren't programmed to track down and identify multiple murderers."

And he was right. Ted Bundy, then on death row awaiting execution (not until 1989) in Florida's Raeford State Prison, cut a violent swath through the states of Washington, Oregon, Utah, Colorado, Florida, and probably other states, between 1974 and 1978, murdering and sexually molesting over three dozen young women. And Randall Brent Wood-field, once a high-draft pick for the Green Bay Packers—a true home-town football hero—was convicted of murder, attempted murder, rape, and sodomy in Oregon and went to trial for sixty additional similar offenses, including three for murder, in jurisdictions ranging from northern California to Washington. Then, Kenneth Bianchi, the infamous "Hillside Strangler," drove from his home in Los Angeles to Vancouver, British Columbia, killing all along the way. Gary Addison Taylor strangled women in Washington, Texas, Michigan, and Florida before he was accidentally caught. Harvey Carigan killed and mutilated females in Alaska, Michigan, Minnesota, and the entire Northwest, for that matter, leaving behind cryptic maps of the countryside, whose circled areas indicated where his corpses were buried.

There were more, of course, and no one can say how many, since the turn of the century, were also active. Obviously, this new breed of killers, these trollers and mobile murderers, were born into an increasingly mobile society. Yet, like virtually all murderers, this type of organized killer leaves a pattern of behavior behind as he moves on to kill again. It was obvious that a new type of nationwide tracking system was urgently needed.

*　　*　　*

By everyone's acknowledgement, Pierce Brooks, a retired Eugene, Oregon, chief of police and former homicide commander of the Los Angeles Police Department, is one of NCAVC's heroes. Although he never drafted a criminal profile for either the LAPD or BSU, and although he was never an FBI agent or an Academy instructor who stood before NA students and described ongoing homicide cases, Brooks nonetheless conceived and created VICAP, the Violent Criminal Apprehension Program. As its initial supervisor, Pierce fed a federal computer all the nation's unsolved homicides, and eventually other crimes, so they could be compared to other files, perhaps linking unsolved cases together or identifying unsolved murders where Behavioral Science Unit expertise might be helpful in identifying a killer, as well as planning various investigative strategies.

Pierce, who died in early 1999, attended the National Academy during the eightieth session in 1967, five years before the original FBI Academy opened in 1972 and long before "Applied Criminology" was taught. His arrival at the Academy in 1984 was strictly to facilitate setting up the VICAP program, which was entirely separate from the BSU operations.

Back in 1958, Brooks, already a ten-year veteran with the Los Angeles Police Department, had been assigned to solve two different homicides on top of a stack of other unsolved crimes scattered across his desk. Because Pierce's intuition told him that both murderers had killed previously, he decided to see if similar deaths had occurred elsewhere in the country. But resources for such research were nonexistent. No national information office or center existed to collect information on the modi operandi (M.O.s) of transient killers. There was certainly an advanced teletype system in place, but teletypes were misplaced, sometimes not even bothered with. Pierce used his common sense and began to canvass L.A. public library newspaper stacks, poring over the bound volumes of back issues, searching for any accounts of similar homicides.

"The simple use of the library newspapers to search for similar cases being worked in the late 1950s was a stroke of genius. It was, in essence, the primitive forerunner of VICAP. The short of it is that Brooks's effort spawned the idea that grew . . . into today's reality," says Roger Depue.

At any or every opportunity he could find before, during, and after national meetings and conferences throughout the 1970s and early 1980s, Pierce conferred with Justice Department officials about his ideas and concepts for some type of a violent criminal apprehension program. It would take over a decade before LEAA monies would be approved and available to fund a task force of homicide investigators, crime analysts, and other criminal justice experts from more than twenty local, state, and federal law enforcement agencies to analyze and approve VICAP.

"Coincidental with the activities of the VICAP task force," Depue recalls, "were discussions among my BSU staff regarding the development of a National Center for the Analysis of Violent Crime. We envisioned the birth of a NCAVC as the formation and extension of the existing programs already within the BSU, as well as an attempt to identify other innovative concepts being developed around the country. The BSU programs had resulted from the work in the development of criminal personality profiling and the supporting research done by members of the unit in the area of violent crime."

In 1984, Joe Harpold, a BSU staff member, joined the VICAP task force as an expert in community crime prevention, thereby merging the BSU conceptually with VICAP. Later that year, NCAVC was formally established by an interagency transfer of funds from the National Institute of Justice to the FBI.

During the early afternoon of Thursday, May 29, 1985, when Pierce Brooks stood side by side with Roger Depue, Joe Harpold, and other NCAVC and BSU colleagues and friends, to watch data from assembled crime reports enter the new VICAP computer system, he was ecstatic. His twenty-seven-year dream had come to fruition, just forty-eight hours before he headed home to his wife in Vida, Oregon, after almost a year spent at the Academy and living on the sixth floor of Jefferson Hall.

Until that afternoon, VICAP had only been a concept. Now it was online, with the decision made that the first year of operation would be considered a field test for all aspects of the program, including the use of the VICAP Crime Report Form, the computer support system, and various internal procedures. Just two days before the self-imposed deadline of June 1, 1985, VICAP officially became operational. Pierce knew his practical, down-to-earth system to identify murderers of a serial intent represented the beginnings of a new era in law enforcement. By the end of VICAP's first year, the system had not only achieved a number of its objectives but had also noted a major revision and considerable expansion.

As important as Pierce Brooks was to the creation of VICAP, Roger Depue was doubly so and in more ways than one. Says Dick Ault about Depue's role during these critical early years, "I sat as

"VICAP? Why, we're the farthest planet out there!"

Roger's 'deputy' unit chief for the whole time he was with the BSU as U/C, so I can attest to the fact that he was a prime force in causing these ideas about VICAP and NCAVC to move forward. At the same time, there were plenty of ideas from all of us about the research, the new directions, and areas of interest the BSU should take. We were never at a loss for ideas (in fact, we still are not), and Roger incorporated many of them into his actions to accomplish our goals."

In 1985, there were seventeen thousand police departments in the nation, most of whom had little or no monies to thoroughly investigate the sixty-three hundred unsolved murders that occurred annually. Now, via VICAP, more than six thousand killings over the past decade could at last be linked and even solved. Equally important, VICAP was in a prime position to assist in the investigations of attempted homicides, abductions, missing people (when violence was suspected), and the identification of corpses involving homicides.

Before Pierce and VICAP, everyone in law enforcement knew that if a particular murder was not cleared up by an arrest within the first seventy-two hours, the probability of solving the killing grew remote. Now a clearinghouse was established and centered at the Academy to isolate the facts of every unsolved murder in the country, not to actually investigate any part of the case, but to analyze it.

At long last, police investigators who had been working independently in different states or jurisdictions on similar types of cases would have access to information unavailable elsewhere. For instance, although local cops knew that similar killings were being committed in other cities and towns, they had difficulty finding out what type of personality had been singled out, what suspects were under investigation, and what similar methods of murder were employed. Pierce perceived VICAP as revolving around four main steps:

1. Enter overnight the facts of the unsolved case into the computer to simultaneously compare and contrast over one hundred

247

selected modus operandi categories with those stored in the violent crime database.

2. The next morning, provide the analyst with a computerized summary that ranked the top ten "matches" or similar cases to the new one.

3. Employ a crime pattern analysis technique known as "template pattern matching" to the new case (specifically designed and programmed for VICAP by the Bureau's Technical Services Division).

4. Produce a selected management information system report, which monitored case activities geographically.

During that first year, VICAP not only searched for homicides that were the same or similar, but also linked those in different jurisdictions. For the first time, patterns and trends were identified so that a coordinated approach, designed for early identification, location, and apprehension of serial murderers, began. Other cases were now forwarded to BSU's specialized subunits for additional analysis. The subunits included the Criminal Personality Profiling Program, psycholinguistic examinations, etc. Once established, the techniques for linking similar cases and identifying patterns and trends were directed toward other serial crimes of violence, such as rape, arson, etc., committed by highly mobile offenders.

It was during this time that a subunit called the Arson Information Management System was established. David Icove, selected to supervise the new system, applied BSU expertise to crimes of fire-setting. His computerized system also analyzed a series of arson cases in order to determine where the next arson would likely take place, as well as where the perpetrator might live or work in relation to the series of fires.

By early 1986, nearly a year after becoming operational, a number of problems with VICAP began to surface. The most obvious, from an investigative perspective, was that, unlike the National Crime Information Center (NCIC), VICAP did not allow local law enforcement agencies to assess the information being disseminated into the NCAVC files. For many, an excellent concept that originally provided for open access and good communications between agencies was encumbered with the addition of an FBI conduit of analysis and research. Accessing this information was a problem VICAP would soon address.

Another problem was that more advanced and expensive computer programs had to be installed to sufficiently read, chart, and analyze the huge amount of raw data and properly developed cases that matched. Furthermore, VICAP received fewer cases than had been anticipated—data was thus slower to accumulate. And, of course, it wasn't long before the media began criticizing VICAP for failing to catch any murderers, even though one of the reasons for this was the limited cooperation of local and state police agencies.

To accelerate assistance, both NCAVC and VICAP rapidly improved the quality and sophistication of their computer programs, reporting methods, and analytical procedures. In addition, VICAP personnel expanded their definition of a serial killer, which to that point had focused upon so-called "lust murderers" who moved about the country. But it was soon apparent that serial killers that were place-specific, those who did not become sexually involved with victims, and female serial offenders warranted recognition and appropriate inclusion in the VICAP files. Certainly, there were female lust killers. But how were they to be defined? They simply chose other methods of murder, although they, too, were known to commit mass murders and serial killings.

"During VICAP's first year," recalls Dick Ault, "Pierce Brooks, an extremely fine man, came down to our unit and tried hard to complete a VICAP questionnaire, or form, that could be used to capture the information needed to successfully feed VICAP. That original questionnaire, running . . . fifty-plus pages, was a great compendium of all the questions you ever wanted to ask about a crime scene. The problem was that nobody would take the time to sit down and answer page after page after page of questions."

The comprehensive, three-part questionnaire was officially known as the VICAP Crime Report Form and consisted of more than three hundred questions until it was revised down to 186 in March of 1986. The nine basic sections were:

1. General Administrative Information
2. Victim Information
3. Offender Information
4. Identified Offender Information
5. Vehicle Description
6. Offense M.O
7. Condition of Victim When Found
8. Cause of Death and/or Trauma
9. Forensic Evidence

The FBI's profile coordinators from each of the fifty-nine field divisions received in-depth training regarding VICAP, as well as in the use and completion of the report form. These agents were then responsible for providing the training to state and local law enforcement officers, especially homicide investigators.

The biggest job of all for the VICAP team was to continue to develop computer programs that were capable of channelling and manipulating the vast amounts of data in a useful way. This new type of case matching had never been attempted before on such a grand scale. Needless to say, the entire development process was exceedingly slow and often painfully frustrating to the VICAPers.

A second problem became evident in that first year, besides the less-than-expected number of cases submitted by law enforcement. It turned out that achieving an understanding of a case from all the information in the crime report was too difficult, because the information was so detailed that it hampered linkages among cases.

"Remember that VICAP's purpose was not to investigate cases but to analyze them. In order to do so effectively, general patterns had to be discernible, and that is better achieved by establishing the general parameters of events rather than extremely specific reconstructions," said Depue. "Crime scenes are seldom exactly replicated, but general M.O.s are. Crime analysis and criminal investigations require different levels of specificity."

Special agents, major case specialists, crime analysts from VICAP, and computer specialists from the FBI's information resource division began formulating a plan to change the nature and direction of VICAP. In 1993, legislation was acquired, with the help of Senator Orrin Hatch and through the "political" contacts of novelist Patricia Cornwall (who had a professional relationship with the Behavioral Sciences Unit) to obtain federal funding to develop a new VICAP software program. The funding was allocated through an addendum to the 1993 crime bill, and was labeled as a "ten Cities Project," in which it was envisioned ten beta test sites would operate the newly-created software and evaluate its effectiveness from an urban perspective. This new effort was based on two main themes. One was to redesign the form, decreasing the number of questions while capturing most of the previous information in a restructured and much easier format. The other theme was to develop a software product that could deliver a VICAP capability to police departments for their own use, and which could then be downloaded to the FBI's VICAP for a regional or national analysis.

One of the more fortunate twists in this complicated process had to do with the FBI's interaction with the Department of Energy. In 1994, the Critical Incident Response Group (CIRG) was established in order to bring together all the components necessary for the FBI to address major incidents from a comprehensive and balanced position.

This meant that the Investigative Support Unit (ISU, formerly BSISU) joined CIRG to support the threat assessment and negotiations aspects of whatever tactical response was required. VICAP was part of the ISU, so it became part of CIRG (see Appendix 3). The CIRG interaction with the DOE stemmed from a mutual need to coordinate activities as they related to potential threats of a nuclear, biological, or chemical nature. ISU profilers were to be used for threat assessments during major incidents, and a system was devised to coordinate their (ISU profilers') assessments with the nuclear assessors of the DOE. Through this collaborative effort, the DOE provided support to CIRG on a variety of issues, including help to upgrade the VICAP program.

A computer specialist by the name of Eric Ingersoll was employed by the DOE's government contractor at their Remote Sensing Laboratory in Las Vegas, Nevada. Eric brought unique skills to the job, and also had the ability to quickly grasp the needs of law enforcement in helping put together the new VICAP database. He also had a personality that seemed to "gel" with law enforcement personnel, and this became a major plus for what was to become the "new" VICAP program. At the same time, the FBI put together a very effective team of specialists to help redesign the VICAP form into a much more effective vehicle.

This entire effort would take three years to fully develop, and it evolved silently in the background while the old program continued to operate in the same fashion as it had in the past. The perception that VICAP wasn't working continued to evolve as well.

In December of 1995, supervisory special agent Arthur Meister, later to be known as "the man who saved VICAP," was assigned to head up the investigative support unit. Meister was a seventeen-year veteran of the FBI, and had prior homicide investigative experience with the Connecticut State Police.

Art's varied experiences and education had been excellent preparations for the job ahead of him. Born in New Haven, Connecticut, in

1945, he received his Bachelor of Science degree in public administration in 1980 from the University of New Haven. In 1992, he followed up with a graduate certificate in public management from the University of Southern California.

Before entering the FBI, Art served four years with the U.S. Air Force Police, and a decade as a state trooper with the Connecticut State Police. On entering the FBI, he was assigned to the Newark, New Jersey, division and developed a nationally significant organized crime investigation into the Colombo crime family operations in New Jersey. Art was most proud that his efforts led to the convictions of New Jersey's highest ranking member of that family, as well as a number of his associates.

In 1985, Meister was promoted to a supervisory management training program. In addition, as an adjunct instructor with the University of Virginia, he instructed mid- and upper-level management law enforcement personnel in the FBI's National Academy. In 1988, he was reassigned to FBI headquarters to be responsible for managing the Organized Crime National Strategy for San Francisco, Detroit, Los Angeles, Sacramento, and Phoenix. Meister followed that up by assuming command of the Organized Crime program in the Washington Metropolitan field office, which produced, among other cases, a major international undercover drug investigation resulting in convictions of high-ranking organized crime members in both the United States and Italy, a racketeering investigation and eventual convictions of the entire top echelon of the nation's second-largest maritime union, and the successful operation of a multi-agency Asian organized crime task force.

Art had neither profiling background nor previous involvement with the VICAP program. It was later learned that he was selected, in part, because he was "outside" the program, someone who would bring a new and different perspective to the management process. It would not be long before he began jokingly referring to VICAP as "the farthest planet out there."

In December of 1995 Meister was promoted and assumed responsibilities as unit chief of the Profiling and Behavioral Assessment Unit (PBAU). PBAU was responsible for all behavioral-based criminal investigative analysis services made available to law enforcement agencies worldwide. It wouldn't be until January of 1998 that a newly designed and restructured VICAP was established as a unit and Meister assumed command of the program.

When Meister reported for duty at CIRG he was given specific directions by the special agent in charge, Robin Montgomery. One of his assigned tasks was to "take a look at VICAP" and determine once and for all if it worked. SAC Montgomery informed him of his doubt as to its value considering what was being spent to maintain it, but wanted Meister to take a "fresh eyes" approach. He was told to "make it work or kill it!" Meister set about the task.

The ISU consisted of a major profiling program and VICAP. The unit had approximately thirty-six people assigned, of which only ten were assigned to VICAP. The ISU had a lot of issues confronting it, including an evolving responsibility in the area of weapons of mass destruction, domestic and international terrorism, and violent crime issues involving homicide and sexual assault. In spite of this extensive responsibility, Meister spent the next few months sitting with each of the VICAP analysts to learn the process. It was during this time that Meister became solidly convinced that not only did VICAP work, but it was a system that was shamefully underappreciated by all of law enforcement. Coupled with the technology developing in the background, it was something which had to be redirected in order to achieve what it was always intended to be—a national network for crime analysis and information sharing. He also realized that, for VICAP to succeed, it had to be its own entity, out from under the shadow of other unit responsibilities.

In the fall of 1997, a lot of pieces began to fall into place. The VICAP form was revised and served as the format for the new software application. Software development was nearing completion out in Las Vegas, Nevada; Kansas City, Kansas, was looking for a system which could help them better understand and deal with an escalating homicide rate. So in November of 1997, Kansas City was given the first prototype of the new VICAP software. Kansas City detective Vincent Davenport and FBI agent Dirk Tarpley, of the Kansas City division, were a two-man task force collaborating to deal with the city's crime problem. Both began entering cases into the VICAP database while conducting other investigative duties, and they soon had over four hundred cases entered. Soon after, there was a drive-by shooting death in a local suburb that had no initial suspects. However, a query of the VICAP database revealed that the deceased had been a suspect and/or witness in three other homicides, information not readily available in any other type of program. This enabled investigators to develop specific leads which led to the identification of a suspect much sooner that anticipated. The system worked. Detective Davenport and Agent Tarpley gave the system tremendous support, and it was soon adopted by the larger Kansas City across the river in Missouri.

All of this was occurring at the same time that VICAP's parent unit, the Profiling and Behavioral Assessment Unit (changed earlier from the Investigative Support Unit), was being considered for restructuring. CIRG had a new special agent in charge, Roger Allen Nisley, and he was grappling with a number of issues that affected the profiling operation. Another profiling entity had evolved out of the old Investigative Support Unit, called the Child Abduction and Serial Killer Unit. Nisley was skeptical of VICAP's effectiveness, and was preparing to divide the VICAP resources between the other units.

It was literally a "do or die" situation for VICAP. Opposing perceptions and a unique set of circumstances came together in sort of a "showdown" which would dramatically determine its future course. Despite VICAP's great intentions, its logical and necessary premise, and the efforts expended over the years to develop the concept to the point it was functioning, there were many who felt that VICAP did not work and that it would never work in an American law-enforcement setting. From a general perspective, it is easy to see why this perception existed. There was no question that, after years of developmental effort, VICAP was still struggling to become the national database for behavior-based crime analysis. This could happen to any worthy program that tries to grow up in the shadow of a more prominent program (profiling), and within a massive bureaucracy which has any number of worthy programs competing for limited resources to support it. There was also the often overwhelming challenge of introducing a very good technical application into the workday reality of fighting crime on the street in an incredibly diverse and multi-jurisdictional environment.

By the fall of 1997, VICAP had been in existence for approximately twelve years. It had an overall data base of seventeen thousand homicides. It had established a working relationship with twenty-three states, who were facilitating the VICAP process by either running a similar program or coordinating the submission of VICAP forms to the FBI program in Quantico. Some of the similar programs operated by the states were not compatible with the FBI's VICAP. The vast majority of law enforcement agencies captured violent crime data, but none of it was compatible with the other systems and most did not capture the type of data necessary to the concept of VICAP—to track serial offenders and identify similar cases through in-depth, behavior-based analysis.

VICAP was a mainframe computer program that was form driven. It was dependent upon the voluntary submission of a lengthy questionnaire, which each investigator had to fill out concerning the case they were investigating. The form would arrive at Quantico, be checked by a crime analysis for accuracy, and then the data was entered into the computer for appropriate analysis and storage. Twenty-three states formally agreed to participate in the program by signing a "Memorandum of Understanding" with the FBI to facilitate the program within their jurisdiction. Each of these states participated with varying degrees of success. By 1997, VICAP had established a fairly consistent compliance level of approximately 1,500 case submissions annually. This number represented approximately 3 to 6 percent of the homicides occurring each year. A higher percentage compliance rate usually reflected a decrease in the overall annual homicide rate in the country. It was also noticed that most of the larger cities were not participating. Many people viewed this lackluster compliance as another reason to support their perception that the program did not work.

Another statistic that seemed to haunt the program throughout its existence was the unfair overemphasis by many on the issue of actually matching cases. There were not many successes that could be flaunted by VICAP showing proven successes or cases that were linked or matched because of a VICAP intervention. Over the twelve years of operation, VICAP had documented only thirty-three matches, and many of these were actually accomplished through other investigative endeavors of the VICAP crime analyst, not by the computer. Many viewed computerized matches as the single greatest reason for the program's existence, and this contributed to a growing perception within the FBI that VICAP was a good idea but wasn't living up to expectations, even after years of effort.

In line with these dismal statistics, there seemed to be very little support for the program in terms of manpower and resource allocation. Besides, it dwelt, throughout its existence, as part of a larger entity, the Investigative Support Unit—a large investigative analysis (profiling) responsibility which overshadowed the smaller and less visible VICAP component. Throughout its existence, VICAP's manpower allocation would vary from a high of twelve people to a low of only three people trying to work a national networking program. In the meantime, the VICAP concept was copied and improved upon by the Royal Canadian Mounted Police, and by 1998 they had a national Violent Crime Linkage Analysis System (VICLAS) in place with approximately one hundred people assigned to the program. Canada only recorded approximately 660 homicide cases annually, while the United States was recording in the area of 25 thousand homicide cases for the year. And yet, VICAP continued to labor against this overwhelming tide with only ten employees, which included six crime analysts, three major case specialists (former police officers) and an FBI special agent program manager. This understaffing proved to be another issue that seemed to factor into the evolving negative view of VICAP by FBI decision makers.

9

The Art and Science of Profiling

he first information to appear in print about the Behavioral
Science Unit and its efforts to help local police in
preparing psychological profiles for unsolved criminal
cases appeared in the March 1980 issue of the *F.B.I. Law
Enforcement Bulletin.* "A Psychological Assessment of Crime: Profiling" was the introductory article in a three-part series of reports on
the use of "psychological criminal analysis as an investigative technique," coauthored by BSUers Richard L. Ault and James T. Reese.

In this first article, Ault and Reese describe how, during the
summer of 1979, a young woman in a suburban city on the East Coast
reported to the police that she had been raped. Within the past twenty-
four months, the same modus operandi had been used, but there were
no leads and no suspects. Baffled, and knowing of the BSU's growing
reputation for assisting law enforcement when called upon, the police
packaged the incident reports, victim interview transcript, and related
evidence and sent them to the FBI training division with a letter
requesting a psychological profile of a suspect. After an analysis of
material, Ault and Reese informed the police that the rapist was probably a white male, most likely in his late twenties or early thirties, and
divorced or separated. He was probably "working at marginal
employment" (a common laborer), perhaps with a high school education. Also, he had a poor self-image, lived in the immediate area of
the rapes, and was involved in crimes of voyeurism, like a Peeping
Tom. Ault and Reese also suggested that, in the recent past, the police
had stopped and talked to him for being on the neighborhood streets

in the early morning hours. Less than seventy-two hours after receiving the profile, the local police pinpointed forty suspects in the neighborhood who met the criteria. Then, armed with additional profile descriptions, they further narrowed their suspects to one! They focused their investigation on him, and the suspect was arrested within a week.

Few of the BSU's cases up to this point demonstrated how valuable psychological profiling was as an investigative technique. When Ault and Reese recounted their success, it was to acquaint the police and the public with the concepts of profiling, and with the fact that there are certain clues at a crime scene, even rope, which by their very nature do not lend themselves to being collected or examined. The two argued that, certainly, clues left at a crime scene could be of inestimable value in leading to the solution of a crime, but they were not necessarily items of physical evidence. For example, they asked, how do police investigators collect rage, hatred, fear, love, irrationality, or other intangibles? Such psychological or personality issues could be present at the crime scene, but the untrained police officer would probably miss them. "Nothing can take the place of a well-executed investigation; however, the use of psychology to assist in the assessment of a crime is an additional tool which the police officer should use in solving crimes."

In those years, the police had been carefully trained in the techniques of crime scene searches. Forensic scientists constantly provided law enforcement with the results of research, which allowed the police to upgrade their skills in gathering physical evidence. But it was becoming apparent that profiling could work in harmony with the search for physical evidence.

Behavioral scientists were beginning to develop some harmony in their initial attempts to research and catalog nonphysical items of evidence such as rage, hatred, and fear. But such attempts were oriented toward therapy rather than forensics. Nonetheless, argued Ault and

Reese, the results could be applied to teach the police how to recognize the presence of such emotions and personality characteristics at the crime scene. Once the abnormal traits were observed, local police could construct for themselves several profiles of the type of person who might exhibit such emotions and traits.

In the remainder of their pioneer article, Ault and Reese summarized the current state of profiling, an investigative tool almost ten years in the making. "The basis for profiling," the two wrote, "is nothing more than the understanding of current principles of behavioral sciences, such as psychology, sociology, criminology, and political science." To them, behavioral science was an inclusive science; the complexity of human behavior made it resistant to narrow classification. Certainly, the *Diagnostic and Statistic Manual of Mental Disorders* (DSM II), used by mental health professionals in the 1970s, was an attempt to bring abnormal behavior under a system of classification control. But the labels the DSM II offered were of little value to police professionals. The symptoms were listed strictly for the use of psychologists, to describe how each doctor might interpret and label.

To the BSUers, a symptom is the acting out of mental illness. A crime, then, particularly a bizarre crime, is as much a symptom as any other type of acting out by an individual. A crime always reflects the personality characteristics of the perpetrator "in much the same fashion as the way we keep and decorate our homes reflects something about our personality."

For Ault and Reese, and the other BSUers, the victim was gradually emerging as one of the most important aspects of the psychological profile. For example, in the case of rape, the rapist's exact conversation with the victim was of utmost importance, and since the amount of psychological evidence varies, as does the physical evidence, the profile may also vary.

Included in the information for the profile are the perpetrator's race, sex, age range, marital status, general employment, reaction to questioning by police, degree of sexual maturity, whether the individual might strike again, the possibility that he or she has committed a similar offense in the past, and possible police record.

"These profiles are not a result of magical incantations and are not always accurate," wrote Ault and Reese. "It is important that the profiler have a wide exposure to crime scenes so that he may see that these patterns may exist. It is also important that the individual attempting to profile crime scenes have some exposure to those criminals who have committed similar crimes."

To attempt a psychological evaluation of a crime scene, the BSUer asked the police to submit for analysis:

(1) Complete photographs of the crime scene, including photos of the victim, if the crime was a homicide. Especially helpful were the angles from which the police photos of the crime scene were taken, as well a general description of the immediate area;

(2) The final autopsy report and any results of the lab tests which were done on the victim;

(3) A complete incident report, including such details as date and time of offense, the site of the weapon the criminal used, the reconstruction of the sequence of events by the police, a detailed interview of any surviving victims or witnesses, and a thorough background report on the victim.

As part of the victim's background report, the BSU profiler wanted to know: the victim's former and present occupation; the former and present residence; the victim's reputation at work and in the neighborhood; his or her physical description, including dress at the time of the crime; his or her marital status, including children and close family members; the victim's educational level; the past and present financial status; information and background of the victim's family and parents, including the victim's relationship with his or her parents; the victim's medical history, both physical and mental; fears and personal habits; social habits, hobbies, and use of alcohol and drugs; a list of friends and enemies; recent changes in lifestyles and recent court actions.

Obviously, however, the primary psychological evidence the profiler is searching for is motive! "After a survey of the evidence," wrote Ault and Reese, "the profiler applies an age-old rule known as 'Occam's razor,' which originally stated, 'what can be done with fewer assumptions is done in vain with more!' This fourteenth century philosophy has, in investigative circles, generally come to mean that, given a problem with several alternative solutions, the most obvious answer is usually correct." The authors add what the BSU knew from almost day one: an aid to the application of the Ocham's razor rule is the intangible evidence that the observers gathers from the crime scene to tell them whether, for example, the crime appears to be planned or whether it is the result of an irrational thought process. "A Psychological Assessment of Crime: Profiling" concluded by advising law enforcement who wanted a psychological profile to contact a local FBI field office and indicate that it was seeking assistance from the training division's behavioral science unit.

Though professionally opening the doors of the BSU to local and state law enforcement agencies across America, Ault and Reese warned readers that profiling, although a valuable investigative tool, was not a magical formula or solution. Police officers profile virtually every day as they limit the scopes of their investigations. Such intuitive profiles are based upon the officers' experiences, insights, and knowledge of the crime investigated.

But when a crime so bizarre or horrific occurs that it is beyond the range of the local officer's experiences, there are special agents in the BSU who can provide profiles. "The FBI provides limited service in the area of profiling," wrote Ault and Reese in March, 1980, "and these limitations are based on the amount of time and manpower available to conduct such profiles. During the initial stages of the FBI's involvement in profiling, the profiles were limited to students attending the FBI National Academy. During 1979, over 100 unsolved cases were received from law enforcement officers nationwide. Due to increased instructional and research commitments, it was necessary to implement guidelines and control measures to manage and monitor effectively this investigative technique."

In their invitation, Ault and Reese insisted that the profiling technique be used exclusively where the motive was lacking and where there was enough information to suggest the presence of psychopathology at the crime scene. "Psychological analysis is not a substitute for basic investigative principles, and all logical leads must be exhausted before requesting this service. This technique is usually confined to homicides, rapes, etc., in which available evidence indicates possible mental deficiency or aberration on the part of the perpetrator. Cases will be profiled on a 'time available' basis, with the more severe cases being given priority."

MURDER, SUICIDE, OR ACCIDENT?

In early 1980, a thirty-three-year-old Indianapolis man was discovered dead in an unfinished room on the second floor of a warehouse where he was employed as a night security guard. He was in an upright position with his feet on the floor. A rope, attached to a wall behind him, passed over a beam approximately six feet above him and ended in a hangman's noose, which encircled his neck. He was nude except for a black leather belt around his waist and a pair of handcuffs that passed through the belt and secured his wrists in front. A handcuff key was found in his right hand, and his left hand held his penis. Around his left ankle was a shipping tag secured by wire, and on the tag was the notation. "77-0130 5/11/77." About the circumference of his penis was a surgical-like incision, which accommodated a washer. Beneath the victim, two cinderblocks rested on newspapers spread on the floor. Feces and semen were on the newspapers. A cigarette butt of the type smoked by the victim was located one and a half feet in front of him. Against a wall, to the rear of the victim and neatly stacked, were a pair of men's trousers, a shirt, and a pair of ankle boots. His service revolver and holster were also in the room. The large room was otherwise empty, with barren, cinderblock walls. The victim's automobile was parked outside the warehouse; its interior was in disarray and contained several empty cans, snack cartons and wrappers, and several magazines, including *Forum* and *Oui*.

The man worked as a peace officer during the day. Five days after the discovery of the body, a box containing his badge, credentials, undershorts, and uniform was found behind some boxes on the floor below the death scene.

He had lived in a one-bedroom efficiency apartment, a search of which revealed bondage magazines. Although not unkempt, the apartment was not tidy (for example, there were dirty dishes in the sink). The victim sometimes stayed with his wife of ten years, from whom he had been separated for six months. On the evening preceding his death, he had visited his wife and made arrangements to take their son (with whom he enjoyed a very close relationship) to the zoo the next day. According to his wife, he had appeared to be in normal spirits during the visit. His wife was the beneficiary of his life insurance policy. In the hours preceding his death, he had called a female acquaintance at 1:30 A.M. and again at 4:30 A.M., requesting that she visit him at the warehouse, but she had refused.

At the time of his death, he was experiencing financial difficulties, was working a second job, and was said to have been occupationally dissatisfied. His coworkers described him as having changed from a relatively outgoing individual to one who seemed depressed and overworked (he worked an excessive amount of overtime to obtain additional salary). On at least two occasions during the week preceding his death, he had made suicidal statements, such as "I ought to put a .38 in my mouth" and "I can understand why someone would kill themselves."

His wife said that approximately two years previously he had begun practicing sexual bondage at home and had requested that she tie him up and whip him and that she allow him to reciprocate. She said that she had declined to participate.

Such a sexual fatality is a death that occurs as a result of or in association with sexual activity. Sexual fatalities span a broad range, including deaths from causes during intercourse or masturbation, lust murder, and autoerotic asphyxial death. Since the inception of autoerotic fatality study in 1978, the Behavioral Science Unit received 160 such cases through 1985. Of these deaths, 150 were quickly determined to have occurred accidentally. The remaining ten were cases involving a second party or cases in which the manner of death remained equivocal after thorough investigation and analysis, even by such a BSUer as Roy Hazelwood and outside consultants Dr. Park Dietz, associate professor of behavioral medicine and psychiatry at the University of Virginia School of Medicine, and Ann Burgess, professor at the Boston University School of Nursing.

In the above case of the police officer, Roger Depue, the BSU chief, received a large package of official investigative reports, death scene photographs, and autopsy reports, and promptly handed them over to Hazelwood. In addition to reviewing the case reports, Hazelwood spoke with the officer's wife and family members, the investigative officers, the medical examiner, and the victim's neighbors. The questions that arose were whether the individual committed suicide or died accidentally, whether his wife or another person had been present, and, if another person was present, whether the death was intended. Hazelwood's questions involved complex issues of fact, behavior, and intent. Some questions, of course, would not be answered. He could not render an opinion on how the police officer died without detailed information about both the scene and the victim's history. Hazelwood's reconstruction of the death scenario was as follows:

"In this case, the death scene had many features commonly found in autoerotic fatalities: secluded location, incomplete suspension, bondage, the use of a hangman's noose, nudity, and the presence of ejaculate. When further investigation uncovered the victim's history, however, the manner of death became uncertain because indicators of suicide were also present. The victim had experienced some of the stressors and exhibited some of the behaviors commonly found among persons with suicidal intent. He was experiencing marital, financial, and occupational problems; his coworkers described him as being overworked and depressed; he had been rejected by his female acquaintance on two occasions on the very morning of his death; his possessions had been neatly placed at the scene; and he had made two suicidal statements in the week preceding his death. These are highly suggestive that the victim intended to end his life. We believe, however, that the victim did not intend to die on this occasion but died accidentally during autoerotic activity. This opinion was derived through several considerations.

"The victim's interest and involvement in sexual bondage and sadomasochistic activities are well documented by his wife's verification of his interest in bondage and flagellation for at least two years before his death. Bondage materials were found in his apartment, and at the time of his death he was handcuffed and held the key in his right hand. Handcuffs are a common bondage device, and the key serves as a self-release mechanism. The washer fixed around his penis is a masochistic feature. At the time of death, he was totally nude except for the belt and was holding his penis in his left hand. While nudity is consistent with autoerotic fatalities, it is most unusual in suicide. The black leather belt suggests a leather fetish symbolic bondage.

"Had the victim intended to take his life by hanging, it would not have been necessary to fashion so exotic a ligature as a hangman's noose; a simple loop would have sufficed. Having previously stated, 'I ought to put a .38 in my mouth,' he might have used his .38 revolver, which was found in the room where he died. It is probable that he kept the weapon in close proximity in the event someone entered the building. Had he intended to die by hanging, he would have had no need for this weapon. He had affixed a tag to his ankle. While it may be argued that the numerals "0130" represent the time (in military hours) of the first call to his friend, there are thirteen wraps in a hangman's noose and the middle digits in the notation are also 13. In our opinion, the tag was a prop used by the victim in his ritualistic fantasy. In our opinion, if the victim had intended to die, he would not have hidden his uniform and identification but would have placed them where they could readily be found.

"Typically, a person with suicidal intent makes plans for death, but not plans for the future. In this instance, the victim visited his son on the evening preceding his death and arranged to take him to the zoo the following day. The victim's automobile and residence were extremely cluttered and contained sexual materials and bondage paraphernalia. It is unlikely that an individual would intend for such materials to be found.

"Despite his separation, he had made no changes in the beneficiary of his life insurance policy. Considering the close father-son relationship, it seems likely that if he had planned to die, he would have taken steps to ensure that his preadolescent son would be financially secure.

"Our reconstruction of the death scenario is that the victim was acting out an execution fantasy when he accidentally died (such a fantasy is not uncommon and is documented in several cases in our study). This is evidenced by the hangman's noose, the secured wrists, the "body tag" on the ankle, and the cigarette butt immediately in front of him, representing the last smoke."

*   *   *

Later that same year, Depue handed Hazelwood another sexual fatality case. "Is this Cleveland case a murder?" he asked.

A twenty-two-year-old, single woman was discovered dead by her sister, who had been staying with the victim temporarily. The sister had been away for two days and returned on a Sunday evening at 9:00 P.M. to discover a note on the front door requesting that she be as quiet as possible because a man was sleeping on the kitchen floor. She went directly to her bedroom and did not discover the victim until the following morning.

The deceased was found in an arched position with an electrical cord wrapped around her ankles that passed over a door knob and was attached to her neck via a slipknot. Her abdomen, thighs, and forearms rested on the floor, and her feet were pulled back toward her head. The right side of her head was against the door's edge, and her hair was entangled in the slipknot. She was clothed only in a blouse that she normally wore for sleeping. Commercial lubrication cream was found in the victim's vagina, and a battery-operated vibrator was found four feet from her body. The only trauma exhibited was a half-inch contusion above and behind her right ear. The scene was not disturbed, and there was no sign of a struggle. On her bed were a series of drafted letters she had written in response to an advertisement seeking a possible sexual liaison.

The autopsy revealed no evidence of recent intercourse, and no alcohol or other drugs were detected in the body. The cause of death was determined to be asphyxia resulting from laryngeal compression.

The victim had been in excellent physical condition, had made plans for a canoe trip on the day following her death, and had recently been in good spirits. She was sexually active but was reportedly disappointed in her sexual relationships because she had difficulty attaining orgasm. She used contraceptive cream and a diaphragm to prevent pregnancy, and these items were located in her car. Although her sister found the note at 9:00 P.M. Sunday, a neighbor reported seeing the note early that morning.

Again, after consulting with Dietz and Burgess, Hazelwood typed out a memorandum answering Depue's question:

"The victim's position illustrates features found in a number of autoerotic asphyxias, including interconnection of the neck with the limbs, and the arching and binding of the body. Her state of undress and the presence of lubrication cream and a battery-operated vibrator indicate sexual activity.

"A critical element in the resolution of this case was the fact that examination of the slipknot (self-rescue mechanism) revealed that the victim's hair was entangled in it and would have precluded its release. This observation, coupled with the contusion above the right ear and the fact that her head was adjacent to the door's edge, suggests that the victim attempted to disengage the ligature by pulling the slipknot. Not being able to do so, she thrashed about, striking her head on the edge of the door, thereby causing the contusion. The autopsy surgeon reported that the contusion would have been insufficient to render her unconscious and that it is not likely that the victim could have been forced into such a position without being unconscious or leaving evidence of a defensive struggle. The question of the note on the door was never resolved. Its presence since early Sunday morning suggests that a male visitor had been there on Saturday evening. The victim's draft letters to a male, whom she had not yet met, further suggest that she was alone at the time of her death, as it is unlikely that she would have had such letters on her bed had she been entertaining a male friend there."

Although the Cleveland homicide detectives believed the death to be accidental, and were considering closing the case, Hazelwood added a postscript to his memorandum:

"The possibility remains that in this case murder occurred during the course of sexual activity. Remember that asphyxia, while a frequent mechanism in sexual murders, is far more often accomplished in murders through manual or ligature strangulation or through suffocation with an external object, such as a pillow, than through the use of gag materials."[1]

By the summer of 1986, the NCAVC's Criminal Profiling and

Consultation Program was receiving more than six hundred requests annually for profiling assistance. Depue and his staff believed that once VICAP became fully operational, the number of profiling requests would nearly double each year.

The BSUers were profiling more than unsolved homicides; they were profiling rapists, arsonists, extortionists, and various other violent and nonviolent offenders, including spies, traitors, and terrorists. The key to their success was the BSU's criminal profile coordinators, who were trained by the BSU and located in each of the FBI's fifty-nine field offices. These specially selected and trained agents were responsible for screening cases and suggesting the initial investigative procedures. Although the field coordinators had no authority to provide profilers to requesting law enforcement agencies, they were in a prime position to prepare preliminary draft profiles, which were then reviewed by the BSU profilers at the Academy before being dispatched back to the requesting agency.

Of course, not every unsolved violent crime was capable of being profiled. The criminal profile coordinator had the responsibility of judging whether the case could indeed be profiled. Even if the coordinator felt the crime was unsuitable for profiling, he could nonetheless forward it to the BSU for other analyses and help, such as interview and interrogation techniques, suggestions for establishing probable cause for search warrants, etc. Establishing probable cause for search warrants was one of the results of the NCAVC's violent offender research findings. The other contributions were offered testimony as a witness for the prosecution, or as an expert.

AUTOMATED CRIME PROFILING

During October and November of 1983, BSU staff developed a profile of a man who was probably responsible for a series of fires at religious homes and churches that summer in an exclusive New England neighborhood. Dr. David Icove was asked to look at these cases with his new computer program. The profile was constructed at the formal written request of the community's police department, which soon discovered that the BSU's profile not only accurately portrayed the suspect in surprising detail but also determined his exact residence based upon a series of intricate computer calculations using new artificial intelligence technology. It was no surprise to BSUers when the suspect confessed to the arsons soon after being detained.

"This pioneering use of artificial intelligence technology in crime analysis and criminal personality profiling provided the groundwork for the present automation efforts at NCAVC," wrote Dave Icove, the senior systems analyst in the Behavioral Science Investigative Support Unit. "In an active project at the NCAVC, experts in criminal personality profiling were taking advantage of the existing technology of artificial intelligence, or AI, as it is known to its users, to capture the elusive decision-making rules associated with the profiling of serial violent criminals."

Designed and implemented during the conceptualization and establishment of the NCAVC computer systems, the Violent Crime Systems Analysis Model traces the philosophical activities involved with the detection, prediction, and prevention of violent crime (see fig. 9.1).

"The model is divided into reactive and proactive investigative strategies. Reactive strategies include crime scene investigative support during immediate response to incidents, while proactive strategies explore effective anti-crime programs to both deter and apprehend offenders," wrote Icove at the time.

In short, the model stresses the reporting of violent crimes to the NCAVC for crime pattern analysis and classification; that critical information usually emanated from written media reports, crime scene processing, VICAP crime reports, or violent crime research findings. Crime pattern analysis could determine if any case trends were

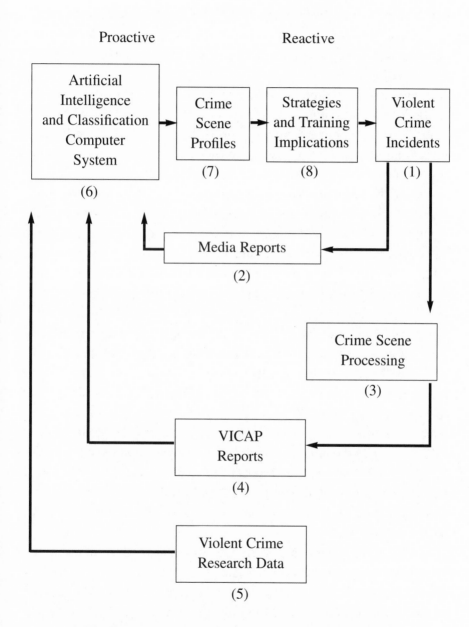

Fig. 9.1. The Violent Crime System Analysis Model

detected in the profiled incident that had existed in the past. In addition, it could predict, as well as check for, the possible identification of prior known and unknown criminal offenders based on their past methods of operation.

Icove wrote, "Crime pattern recognition analysis can also classify incidents into naturally occurring groups, such as the type of crime, motive, or temporal conditions. Furthermore, pattern analysis can reveal multidimensional trends and profiles in the crime data which in the past have gone undetected."

Then, based upon past profiling successes in solving violent crimes, sound, effective strategies were documented and categorized for future operations and training use. By carefully employing historical data, actual probabilities of success could be assigned to the suggestions of specific, proven prevention strategies.

In an article entitled, "Automated Crime Profiling," that he prepared for the Ressler-Burgess-Douglas text, *Sexual Homicide: Patterns and Motives* (1988), Icove wrote, "The use of effective crime prevention strategies will minimize the risk of future violent crime incidents. Many strategies include operational, personnel, and physical security programs. However, once an incident occurs, the effective case management of the investigation must be carried out. The violent crime investigator at the scene summarizes the incident and submits a VICAP report. The feedback loop is then completed with an inquiry into the model of the encoded case data. Several computer systems serving NCAVC in support of VICAP, profiling and consultation, and research programs are located at both Quantico and Headquarters in Washington, D.C."

When a new case was entered, the system almost simultaneously compared and contrasted some one hundred previously selected modus operandi (M.O.) categories for that case with all other cases stored in the database. Once the processing was completed, usually overnight, a printed report was available to the individual handling the case. Known as "template pattern matching," this crime pattern analysis technique had been especially programmed for VICAP by the FBI's technical services division. In addition, the system was capable of producing selected management information system reports, which monitored case activities geographically in the belief it could trace the routes of serial violent criminals across the country.

The new insights and experiences gleaned from the VICAP and AIMS computer technologies helped NCAVCers refine the comprehensive AI, knowledge-based expert system, which tracked and predicted violent crimes. These knowledge-based expert systems had been successful in applying knowledge to solve problems that ordinarily required human intelligence.

According to Icove, the "knowledge engineer" transforms prior experiences of the crime profiler and the results of violent crime research into a knowledge base. By using artificial-intelligence computer software, the knowledge base is transformed into rules for making decisions, or an "inference engine." The NCAVC investigators input new cases and receive consultation via a user interface (see fig. 9.2).

By 1988, the expert-based computer system allowed the NCAVC to, among other things (1) discard worthless profiling and identification techniques; (2) file and retrieve information of similar cases, criminal profiles, and research studies; (3) train novices to think like an experienced profiler; (4) store information in an active form as a knowledge base rather than as a passive listing of facts and figures; (5) receive advice and consultation from the expert system on new and existing cases, based on prior knowledge captured by the system. There was little question that AI applications demonstrated great potential for solving complicated crime profiling and assessment problems.

The three other areas that artificial intelligence technology began exploring in the mid-1980s were social network analysis, the behavioral analysis of extortion letters, and computer-assisted linguistic analysis technique. Social network analysis was a behavioral science

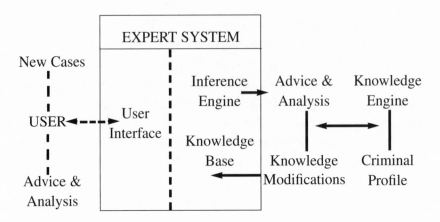

Fig. 9.2. A Schematic Diagram of the NCAVC's Artificial Intelligence, Knowledge-Based Expert System.

exploration of the interactive patterns between human beings. Such an approach could identify strategies an individual or group might employ. In addition, it could determine the hierarchical structure of criminal groups like motorcycle gangs, organized crime mobs and cartels, and domestic extremist groups. For the first time, the FBI was capable of manipulating data and computing the probable hierarchies and interactions of complex organizations through the AI procedures designed and developed by staff.

Another viable application of artificial intelligence technology to real-world law enforcement problems was the behavioral analysis of threatening oral and written communications in extortion, bombings, and other extremist incidents. By 1988, the NCAVC was actively researching and experimenting with computer-assisted linguistic analysis techniques to evaluate the contents of these threats in an effort to determine the authorship profile and assess the validity of the threat.

PROBLEMS PROFILING THE UNABOMBER

The UNABOM Task Force (UTF) was created in late June of 1993, following bombs that were sent to Dr. Charles Epstein in Tiburon, California, and to Dr. David Gelernter in New Haven, Connecticut. A letter was also sent at that time to the *New York Times* that claimed responsibility for the two bombs and identified the bomber as FC, an individual referred to by the FBI as the Unabomber. The Unabomber had been responsible for twelve previous bombings, the last of which had occurred in February 1987 in Salt Lake City, Utah. Newly appointed Attorney General Janet Reno, with the concurrence of the United States Postal Inspection Service and the United States Department of the Treasury, established the UNABOM Task Force. She designated the FBI as the lead agency to head the task force. FBI director Louis B. Freeh appointed the chief inspector of the FBI, George B. Clow III, to serve as the inspector-in-charge of the task force. Inspector Clow established the UTF at the headquarters of the San Francisco division of the FBI. The UTF became operational on Monday, July 12, 1993.

Under Inspector Clow's direction, the newly formed UTF initiated several major investigative projects. One of those projects was the "Victimology Project," whose purpose was to conduct an exhaustive analysis of the intended victims of UNABOM devices in an effort to determine if there was some link or "common thread" among the victims. Inspector Clow delegated the responsibility for conducting the project to William C. Megary, the ASAC of the Baltimore division. ASAC Megary assembled a team of experienced investigators, including special agents Mary Ellen O'Toole and William L. Tafoya. SA O'Toole was a certified FBI profiler. She was one of a very few profilers assigned outside of the BSU who were allowed to independently develop offender profiles. SA Tafoya's field of expertise was in computers and the future of policing. He had previously been assigned to the

277

FBI Academy. Other UTF members of the Victimology team were experienced investigators from the Postal Inspection Service and the Bureau of Alcohol, Tobacco and Firearms. Additionally, Dr. David Icove and Joseph J. Chisholm of the Arson and Bombing Investigative Services subunit of CIRG were assigned to assist the Victimology team.

Under the direction of SA Tafoya, the Victimology team designed a comprehensive "victimology protocol" questionnaire. This questionnaire was sent to each of the known intended victims of a UNABOM device. The victims were requested to fill out the lengthy questionnaire and return it to the UTF. In conjunction with this questionnaire, SA Tafoya designed a multidimensional computer program that was capable of storing and sorting substantial quantities of data across a broad matrix. Information obtained from the questionnaires was entered into this program and analyzed by members of the team. The victims were also requested to travel to San Francisco to be interviewed by the team. If the victim was unable to travel to San Francisco, members of the team went to the victim's location and conducted the interview there.

In mid-August of 1993, the Victimology team was ready to begin interviewing victims of UNABOM attacks. For the next several months, comprehensive, in-depth interviews of the victims were conducted. Each of these detailed interviews was conducted over a two-day period and covered a broad range of subject matter. In total, eleven individuals were interviewed. Some were not intended victims, but random victims for whom the team felt a compelling argument could be made that they might have been the intended target of the UNABOM device. The information derived from these interviews was reviewed and analyzed by the team and entered into the computer for further analysis. Following each interview, voluminous amounts of additional information, including but not limited to each victim's associations, acquaintances, education, affiliations, associates, and friends, were obtained by other investigative techniques. Particular emphasis was given to educational affiliations and associations, in view of the fact that many of the UNABOM devices were placed on university campuses or sent to university professors. All of the information gathered by these other investigative techniques was also entered into the computer for analysis.

Despite this comprehensive, massive investigative effort, detailed analysis failed to establish any commonalities among the victims of UNABOM attacks. In early August 1993, ASAC Megary requested that SAs O'Toole and Tafoya provide the UTF with an updated behavioral assessment of the UNABOM suspect. The last behavioral profile had been done by in September of 1986, and the O'Toole-Tafoya profile would be the fourth official profile done in this seventeen-year series of bombings.

The first UNABOM profile had been done following the bomb that was sent to the Lake Forrest, Illinois, residence of Percy Wood on June 10, 1980. Wood was the president of United Airlines at the time. This was the fourth bomb in this series of bombings. Previous bombs had been placed at the Chicago Circle campus of the University of Illinois, in the Technological Institute of Northwestern University in Evanston, Illinois, and in a mail pod contained in the cargo hold of American Airlines flight 444 bound from Chicago's O'Hare Airport to Washington, D.C.'s, National Airport. This initial profile had been done by SAs John Douglas and Russell E. Vorpagel of the BSU.

The second official profile was done by Douglas and Dr. David Icove in July 1985 following bombs 5 through 9, which were:

- placed in the hallway of the business classroom building on the campus of the University of Utah, Salt Lake City, on 10/8/81;
- mailed to a professor at Vanderbilt University, Nashville, Tennessee, on 5/5/82;
- placed in a coffee room in Corey Hall on the campus of the University of California, Berkeley, on 7/2/82;

- mailed to the fabrication division of Boeing Aircraft, Auburn, Washington, on 5/8/85; and
- placed in a computer terminal laboratory in Corey Hall on the campus of the University of California, Berkeley, on 5/15/85.

The third official profile was done by Icove on September 16, 1986, after bomb 10, which was mailed to a professor at the University of Michigan, Ann Arbor, on November 15, 1985, and after bomb 11, which had been placed behind the Rentech Computer Company on Howe Avenue in Sacramento, California, on December 11, 1985. Bomb 11 had resulted in the death of Rentech owner Hugh Scrutton, the first of the Unabomber's homicides.

On August 5, 1993, O'Toole and Tafoya advised ASAC Megary that they believed the suspect was likely a white male between the ages of forty-three and fifty-three years old. They made no observation about the suspect's education or residence, but did observe that they felt the suspect's employment record was "varied" but would reflect research and/or teaching positions, or occupations where interaction in such an environment was regular or routine. They also advised that they believed the suspect to be a highly intelligent, deliberate, patient, imaginative, technically competent individual who had high self-esteem but low self-concept. They also said they believed that the suspect lacked interpersonal interaction skills and was a loner who was likely to be unmarried. Additionally, they believed that the UNABOM suspect was an avid reader of current affairs and technical publications. O'Toole and Tafoya did not comment on the suspect's criminal history or lack thereof, nor did they speculate on the suspect's physical description or appearance. They did, however, say that they believed the suspect's motivation was revenge and that the UNABOM suspect wanted recognition and credit for his "work."

In November 1993, SA O'Toole elaborated the August profile. This additional information concerned only her beliefs about the

UNABOM suspect's personality characteristics, interpersonal/social relationships, interests/avocation, and motivation.

With regard to personality characteristics, O'Toole believed that the UNABOM suspect was seen by people who live or work with him as a fairly opinionated person. O'Toole believed that he had a pessimistic outlook on life and at times might appear moody or brooding. She also believed that the suspect possessed a macabre, at times tasteless, and inappropriate sense of humor. She believed that some people might describe the suspect as distrustful, even somewhat paranoid at times, and although he might be seen as critical and defensive, he was probably viewed as normal and definitely in touch with reality.

Speaking of the suspect's interpersonal/social relationships, O'Toole went on to say that she believed that while the UNABOM suspect might have people in his life that he referred to as "friends," he was much more of a loner, preferring solitary activity and spending time alone. She believed he was secretive about certain aspects of his life, which he discussed with few, if any, people. There was possibly a "significant other" in the UNABOM suspect's life, and this person, because of his or her relationship to the suspect, knew or strongly suspected that this friend, family member, or coworker was responsible for the series of crimes. The "significant other" would recognize many, if not most, of the characteristics described previously by O'Toole. The "significant other" was very likely aware of the suspect's preference to spend time alone, especially in areas of his residence or work environment, which he (the suspect) had declared "off limits" to anyone else. He/she (the significant other) would be aware of unexplained absences by the suspect and knew not to ask questions regarding them.

With regard to the suspect's interests and avocation, O'Toole believed that the suspect read a great deal in a variety of areas, including science and technology, history, psychology, the social sciences, and law enforcement, and that his reading materials would include professional journals, newspapers, and books.

O'Toole believed that the motivation for these crimes had evolved and changed, to some extent, over the years as the suspect got older and "matured."

During the fall of 1993, O'Toole and Tafoya became convinced that a particular individual was, in fact, the Unabomber. From that time forward they seemed to spend the majority of their time attempting to convince the other members of the UTF that this particular individual was indeed responsible. However, evidence indicated that that person could not possibly have committed the crimes, even though that person comfortably fit their profile. However, they continued to focus their attention on that individual.

The rest of the UTF continued with several other major investigative projects for the next several months while the Victimology team continued to amass voluminous amounts of information concerning the various victims, their associations, associates, education, and employment records.

By March of 1994, the UTF began to deteriorate administratively. Inspector Clow had been transferred to another position and his successor, ASAC Bruce Gebhart, returned to his former job in Newark, New Jersey. The administration of the UTF fell to the San Francisco division of the FBI, SAC James Freeman. In April 1994, he named SSA Terry T. Turchie as the administrator in charge of the daily management of the UTF. In November 1994, FBI headquarters approved a plan whereby the UTF was completely assimilated into the San Francisco division of the FBI, as SFFBI Squad 18.

The investigation continued on numerous fronts during this time. SSA Turchie made several requests of the BSU and of O'Toole and Tafoya for specific types of behavioral information regarding this case; for example, a behavioral assessment of the book, *Ice Brothers* (this is the book in which the bomb to UAL president Percy Wood had been secreted), a new profile based upon a study of serial bombers, not on serial arsonists and murderers as in the past, and a request that the BSU conduct a comprehensive survey of all sites of UNABOM devices in an effort to learn something that might have been overlooked. O'Toole and Tafoya failed to provide the behavioral assessment of *Ice Brothers* and the BSU failed to conduct a study of known serial bombers (such as the Alphabet Bomber, the Mad Bomber, and the VanPac Bomber). Although Joe Chisholm of the BSU was assigned to conduct a site survey of all of the UNABOM sites and provide the UTF with a report of his findings, no such report was forthcoming. This necessitated Turchie to assign these matters to others. He selected Kathleen Puckett from the behavioral assessment program of the foreign counterintelligence program of the San Francisco division to provide the assessment of *Ice Brothers*. Turchie assigned various members of the UTF to travel to Chicago, Evanston, and Elgin, Illinois; Salt Lake City and Provo, Utah; Auburn, Washington; Nashville, Tennessee; Ann Arbor, Michigan; and Sacramento, California, to conduct site surveys and neighborhood investigations, and to photograph and videotape the appropriate crime scenes and neighborhoods for future reference and investigation. Later, ATF-BSU representative Chisholm provided the UTF with an oral report and eventually a written summary of his work, as well as with photographs and videos he had taken during a summer-long trip to the crime scenes. An in-depth study of serial bombers was never completed and subsequent profiles provided to the UTF by the BSU continued to be based primarily on studies of serial arsonists and serial murders.

The investigation continued on several fronts: event reinvestigation, forensic reinvestigation, computer analysis, behavioral analysis, and suspect evaluations. These proactive investigative techniques, as well as a comprehensive program of public information, an Internet Web site, and a 1-800 telephone line kept the various members of the UTF extremely busy.

On December 10, 1994, a bomb received through the mail detonated at the North Caldwell, New Jersey, home of New York advertising executive, Thomas Mosser, killing Mr. Mosser.

In early January 1995, FBI director Louis B. Freeh visited with investigators of the UTF in San Francisco. Director Freeh asked what he could do to help investigators solve this seventeen-year bombing spree. The fact that the UTF found it necessary to go outside of the criminal division of the FBI to find a behavioral profiler to assist in the daily investigative efforts of the UTF was cited to Director Freeh as a problem.

In late January 1995, Turchie and SAs Neil Oltman and Donald Max Noel traveled to Washington, D.C., to make a presentation to FBI headquarters personnel, Department of Justice officials, and United States Postal Inspection Service headquarters personnel. Problems inhibiting the investigation were pointed out to the group. Among those problems was the ineffectiveness of the BSU in providing the UTF with a satisfactory work product in a timely fashion.

As a result, later in the spring of 1995, SSA James Fitzgerald was named as the BSU member assigned to the UTF. In July, Fitzgerald went to San Francisco, where he remained until after the capture of Theodore J. Kaczynski. Fitzgerald and Puckett provided valuable daily assistance to the UTF management team and investigators with regard to behavioral issues.

On April 24, 1995, a bomb in a package was delivered through the mail to the California Forestry Association's headquarters in Sacramento, California. CFA president Gilbert Murray opened the package, and the resulting explosion killed him. At the same time, the Unabomber also mailed four letters. One of these went to the *New York Times*. In it, the Unabomber claimed responsibility for the previous bombs and explained how he was now capable of making more deadly bombs. He said that he would desist from further acts of terrorism if the *Times* agreed to publish a thirty-thousand-word manifesto. Another letter was sent to David Gelernter, the victim of bomb 14. The Unabomber taunted Gelernter for having opened the package containing the bomb. The remaining two letters were sent to 1993

Nobel Prize–winning geneticists, Dr. Richard Roberts and Dr. Phillip Sharp. In each of these letters, the Unabomber advised the geneticists that it would be beneficial to their health if they stopped their genetics research.

On June 27, 1995, the *San Francisco Chronicle* received a letter from the Unabomber in which he stated that the "Terrorist Group FC" was planning to blow up an airliner out of Los Angeles International Airport during the "next six days." This threat severely impacted nationwide air travel over the Fourth of July weekend.

On June 28, 1995, the *New York Times* received a letter from the Unabomber in which he said that the threat he had made to bring down an airliner out of Los Angeles had been a "prank." Enclosed with the letter was a sixty-seven-page manuscript, commonly referred to as the "UNABOM Manifesto." The Unabomber also sent copies of the manuscript to a University of California, Berkeley, professor, Dr. Tom Tyler. Each of the manuscripts was accompanied by a letter. *Scientific American* magazine also received a letter.

Never before in the nearly seventeen years of this investigation had so much written material been available for behavioral analysis. Behavioral analysis subsequent to the first four bombs (Douglas/Vorpagel Profile) had described the suspect as a male, approximately eighteen to twenty-two years of age; a college student with some undergraduate education in physics or engineering; with a residence in an environment that was most likely upper-middle or lower-high class (Kaczynski was living a very spartan existence in an isolated, rural area near Lincoln, Montana, at that time). The Unabomber was characterized in this initial profile as "anger-motivated."

The second behavioral assessment of the UNABOM suspect (Douglas/Vorpagel 7/85) described him as a white male, approximately twenty-eight to thirty-five years of age, with at least a high school education and probably some college or technical school. The profile said that the suspect might live or work within walking distance of the crime scenes (Kaczynski, who was unemployed, had received his Ph.D. in mathematics from the University of Michigan and a Bachelor of Science degree from Harvard years earlier and had been living in Lincoln since the early 1970s). The profile also suggested that the suspect was most likely to be employed as a technician or researcher, possibly at a university, and was anger-motivated.

The third official UNABOM suspect profile (Icove, 1986) described the suspect as a male in his late thirties or forties, with two or four years of undergraduate education, and possibly a B.S. The profile stated that the suspect might live in an apartment rather than a house, and that he changed jobs frequently, but had a technical employment background. It also said that the suspect was likely to be excessively clean and neat (Kaczynski was extremely dirty and his clothing was literally falling apart at the time he was arrested. Interviews with Lincoln residents established the fact that this was the way Kaczynski normally appeared, and had for years).

A fifth behavioral analysis was done in May 1995 by SSA James Wright. This assessment updated the July 1985 profile and a profile that had been written by Wright and published in *Police Chief* magazine in October 1991. This profile characterized the suspect as a white male, forty to fifty years of age, with a high school education and some college. It noted that the suspect had more than a passing knowledge of the postgraduate education process and requirements, and that the suspect had probably attended trade school. It went on to suggest that the suspect would be employed in an area that would not require public contact and communication. The profile said that the suspect's job would not be menial, but would require technical knowledge and craftsmanship. It suggested that the suspect could be a technician or a researcher who had spent time on college campuses. Once again, the profile said that the suspect was anger- or revenge-motivated.

Following the receipt of the UNABOM Manifesto and the numerous letters sent to various individuals in June of 1995, the

CIRG/ISU prepared and provided the UTF with an extensive behavioral assessment of the UNABOM suspect in November of 1995. This assessment characterized the suspect as a white male between forty and fifty-five years of age who was comfortable in the environs of higher education and the postgraduate process, and who had possibly attempted, but failed, to achieve a postgraduate or even an undergraduate degree. It noted that the suspect possibly attended trade school. It said that the suspect either lived, worked, attended school, or made extensive visits to the Chicago area (I believe that we had already sufficiently established that possibility through traditional investigative techniques). The profile also said that the suspect was possibly involved in a trade or craft which would utilize a better-than-average knowledge of wood- and metalwork and, once again, that the suspect's motivation was anger or revenge.

Over the years, the UNABOM suspect's various profiles remained remarkably consistent. A white male, forty to fifty-five years of age who failed to achieve a postgraduate degree; who lived, worked, attended school, or made extensive visits to the Chicago area; who possibly attended trade school; and who was anger- or revenge-motivated.

In their analysis of the Manifesto, SSA Wright and SA Chisholm advised the UTF that it appeared that the UNABOM suspect was highly likely to have communicated the thoughts, ideas, and concepts contained in the Manifesto to associates, family, and coworkers. This is a belief that was held by the entire UTF, and the very reason that the reward, publicity campaign, and 1-800 number had been established in the fall of 1993 and maintained throughout the years of the UTF investigation. Looking for the person or persons that would recognize the UNABOM suspect and be willing to come forward to the UTF was an important part of the overall investigative strategy of the UTF from the beginning.

INTO THE MINDS OF MADMEN

THE USS *IOWA* DEBACLE

The events of April 19, 1989, created an extraordinary challenge for the Behavioral Science Unit. Some three hundred miles northeast of Puerto Rico, near Vieques Island, USS *Iowa* was undergoing routine gunnery training involving nine 16" guns, each sixty-eight feet long, weighing 120 tons, and capable of firing 2,700-pound explosive projectiles twenty-two miles. Housed in the two forward turrets and the 2' No. 3 turret, the giant rifles could fire independently every thirty seconds in a series of complex steps that required a 500-page Bureau of Ordnance manual to describe. They were placed on triple-gunned firing platforms featuring better protection, not only for the crew in the gun room, but also for those sailors handling the powder four decks below in the multitiered turret.

Turret No. 1 fired four rounds of reduced-charge projectiles from the center and right guns before there was a misfire in the left. Then, with Gunner's Mate Clayton Michael Hartwig serving as gun captain that day, it was turret No. 2's turn. Ordered to load, the crew rammed D881 projectiles and five bag-charges into the left and right guns, then slammed the breeches shut.

A few weeks earlier, USS *Iowa*'s Captain Fred Moosally and his staff picked the personnel for the usual gunnery exercises, although shift changes were expected. Since No. 2's turret crew was short one sailor, the person assigned to be cradle operator was shifted to powder hoist operator while Petty Officer Eric Lawrence, who was designated gun captain for his initial shoot, was moved to the hoist position. GMGZ Hartwig, who was certainly a qualified gun captain, was designated Lawrence's replacement. Sailor Kendall Truitt was stationed below in the magazine.

Since April of 1952, when the *Iowa* launched her monster-sized shells at military targets along the North Korean coast, the standard loading operations had remained the same: from the lower magazine, a small elevator lifts large silk bags of gunpowder to the crew, who in turn load the bags onto a cradle, which is then pushed into the gun. That morning, the process was duplicated as it had been hundreds of times. Hartwig ordered his crew to place two lead foils between the first two bags, to serve as a decoppering agent as well as to help keep the gun clean. The rammer fed the powder bags into the gun, shoving them against the projectile. The breech was then closed. Through several wars and countless engagements spanning more than four decades, not a single sailor inside a 16" gun turret on any U.S. Naval craft had ever been killed due to a misfiring.[2]

Then, just as the gun was about to be fired at 9:54 A.M., Petty Officer Eric Lawrence shouted over the communication network: "Hold up just a minute. We've got a problem here." Less than thirty seconds later, a horrendous blast rocked the battleship, instantly decimating all forty-seven sailors working inside turret No. 2. Deep below in the magazine, Truitt and John Mullaney were slammed against the magazine wall. The 1,450 remaining crewmembers looked at each other in shock and astonishment.

Later, as BSUer Roy Hazelwood put it, "Clay Hartwig was stationed near the gun breech, the perfect spot to do mischief." Forensic investigation would show that Hartwig was bending forward, peering upward through the open breech when 660 pounds of gunpowder packed in the silk bags exploded back down the barrel at him. Accelerating to nearly twice the speed of sound at a temperature of 3,000 degrees Fahrenheit, the blast hit Hartwig's face in about one-twelfth of a second. Needless to say, he and the other forty-six helpless crewmembers were killed without feeling a thing.

Was the explosion a tragic mishap? To this day no one can say for certain, although Roy Hazelwood, Dick Ault, and the majority of the current and retired Behavioral Science Unit staff have their theories.

The Pentagon placed Rear Admiral Richard D. Milligan, a former battleship captain, in charge of investigating the unprecedented explosion. He, along with top naval investigators, focused on the technical aspects of the explosion—how the tragic explosion could happen after almost a half a century of impeccable safety records. But a few weeks after the explosion, a letter from an Ohio woman, Kathlene Kubicina, Hartwig's twenty-four-year-old sister, was received by the Navy Department, inquiring whether her parents qualified for part of a $100,000 insurance policy Hartwig had taken out on Kendall Truitt.

Since Kubicina's letter arrived just as naval technical experts were beginning to suspect the fatal detonation was no accident, the Naval Investigative Service was called. NIS investigators went to work. They scoured the country for anyone connected to Hartwig or Truitt. Meanwhile, Commander Tom Mountz telephoned Dick Ault, whom he had met when Ault, whose specialty was spies and espionage cases, was interviewing some thirty traitors as part a top-secret government research project.[3] Would the BSU engage in an equivocal death analysis on the *Iowa* explosion? Dick, in his relaxed, smiling manner, answered, "Sure, we can do that." A former Marine, Ault would naturally help out the Navy.

After consulting with unit chief Roger Depue and Hazelwood, whom he had worked with on many analyses before, it was agreed that Dick and Roy would comprise the team that would respond to the Navy's need for assistance. "Of course we were going to help out," Roy recalled recently. "But at the time, even before we got started, we understood what was probably going to happen if our verdict flew against the popular view that the explosion was nothing more than an unfortunate accident. Either we would make the Navy unhappy, or the politicians and the media, to say nothing of Hartwig's family, would attack us and the BSU. We were going to get hammered one way or another."

The two profilers did not take part in any field investigation nor did they interview witnesses. However, from the information Mountz provided it was obvious the explosion was no accident. The Navy was equally confident that no accident had occurred. But the Navy requested the BSU to determine one of three options: Had Gunner's Mate Clayton

Hartwig committed a suicide, a homicide, or a suicide-homicide? And, for what reason? Psychological and personality profiles were needed of Hartwig and Truitt. In the weeks that followed, Hazelwood and Ault received more than three hundred investigative dossiers, along with all the photographic records and forensic evidence collected to date. They worked on their analyses independent of each other.

Where Hazelwood had recently been pioneering research into equivocal death (that is, deducing from all available evidence whether unexplained deaths were due to accidents, murders, suicides, or murder-suicides), Ault, who had already spent some fourteen years in the BSU, was now in charge of the NCAVC research program, including a project on suicide. Although the *Iowa* incident was of sudden national concern, the two quietly considered the case as any other equivocal death: 1) Was the explosion a murder by Truitt in order to collect the $100,000 insurance? 2) Since Hartwig and Truitt were rumored by some of the crew to be homosexual—some swear they saw the two kissing—did Hartwig want revenge via a murder-suicide when Truitt, who always insisted neither were gay, married a heterosexual? 3) Or, was the detonation caused by Hartwig's suicide due to depression and other psychological issues?

In the final BSU report to the Naval Investigative Service dated June 16, 1989, Ault and Hazelwood concluded in part that Hartwig was a "troubled young man with low self-esteem who coveted the power and authority he felt he did not possess. He had been emotionally devastated by real and perceived rejections of significant others and was facing a multitude of stressors, from a young woman's sexual demands to his unavoidable exposure as a sham. The combination of stressors in Hartwig's life virtually assured some type of reaction. In this case, it was suicide." Ault and Hazelwood were unequivocal in their joint conclusion.

On September 7, 1989, Admiral Milligan called a press conference to announce, "A wrongful intentional act caused the explosion in Turret Two and that Gunner's Mate Clayton M. Hartwig most probably committed the act. We have an FBI profile by FBI psychologists with the opinion he took his own life and hoped it would look like an accident."

Needless to say, the expected reaction was almost instantaneous: Hartwig's sister, Kathy Kubicina, and family, along with Kendall Truitt, demanded an immediate congressional investigation. Hazelwood recalls, "The allegations touched a chord both in the press and on Capitol Hill, and in retrospect it is simple to see why. In the aftermath of Vietnam, Watergate, and the Reagan Administration's secret sale of U.S. arms to Iran to finance the Nicaraguan Contras, when significant numbers of people still doubted that Lee Harvey Oswald or James Earl Ray acted alone, it was not difficult to believe the U.S. Navy was capable of conspiracy, too."[4]

Within a few days, the *New York Times* blasted the Navy's conclusion as "unproven, probably unprovable, that one dead crewmember is the culprit." Syndicated columnist Lars-Erik Nelson wrote that Hazelwood and Ault's analysis was little more than "quack evidence." In New York's *Newsday*, Lester Bernstein accused the Navy of "scapegoating Hartwig as a consequence of the service's hidebound commitment to its four half-century-old battleships." A few days after its first editorial, the *New York Times* followed with another, declaring in part, "The Navy must be scolded for its decision to smear a crewman's memory on flimsy evidence and for relying on a libelous psychological profile of Mr. Hartwig." With all this uproar, both the U.S. House and Senate announced their own investigation of the tragedy. Although even then the FBI was used to being severely admonished in the presses of America, Capitol Hill was usually safe ground for the Bureau, especially for the BSU. Only a handful of years before, Roger Depue and the staff of the BSU had been praised before a House committee for their exemplary work in identifying and apprehending aberrant-type criminals. Furthermore, Congress had appropriated $4 million to organize, establish, and fund VICAP. But on the cold, rainy morning of December 2, 1989, as Ault, Hazelwood, and Assistant

The Art and Science of Profiling

Director Anthony Daniels, then in charge of the FBI Academy, sat down before a congressional subcommittee, they were greeted with less than kindly glances. Seated before a microphone, Hazelwood slowly read into the record a thirteen-page summary laying out the eight main factors, in addition to the buttressing evidence, as to why he and Ault had arrived at their conclusion of suicide:

1. "Hartwig was a loner who believed that four of his six known friends had rejected him and the fifth, a female, was applying pressure on him for an intimate relationship he was not capable of."

2. "He was dissatisfied with life and his fantasies went far beyond the realities of his true life." Such a statement was based upon numerous facts, from his subscription to "Soldier of Fortune" to false exaggerations about impending Naval security assignments.

3. "He had good reasons for not returning from the cruise." If he killed himself, he'd be free of the lies he had told others about himself; of the pending sexual demands; and of the onboard insults. Above all, he'd be free of the constant feeling of inferiority and rejection.

4. "He had a revenge motive, disliking his shipmates, the ship itself, and the various disciplines he had received while on board."

5. "Hartwig had a history of immature reactions to changes in his life and interpersonal relationships. He was known to carry grudges against those he felt wronged him."

6. "He was experiencing a number of stressors at one time: besides his other problems, he was broke, his car needed repairs, and his telephone had been turned off."

7. "Hartwig had suicide ideation—he talked about it; was discovered in his room playing with a knife; and in his last letter to the woman he knew closed with 'Love always and forever, Clayton,' instead of the usual 'Clay.' Then he added, 'I'm sorry I didn't take you home to meet my mother.' To another woman, he wrote, 'I could become one of those little white headstones in Arlington National Cemetery any day!'"

8. "Finally," read Hazelwood, "Hartwig possessed the knowledge, ability, and opportunity to ignite the powder in the same fashion that occurred on the USS *Iowa*."

At the conclusion of his presentation, Indiana democrat Frank McCloskey wondered if BSU agents were any better at making psychological evaluations than teachers or insurance agents. He asked, "Is it unusual for someone working around explosives to believe he or she might die in an explosion?"

"No, sir," answered Hazelwood. "But it is unusual for them say 'I want to die' in the line of duty, not 'I may die,' not 'I'm in danger of dying,' but 'I want to die in the line of duty' to two different people. That is unusual, yes sir."

Hazelwood made it clear that a BSU profile or analysis "can be used, discarded or discounted, it is our opinion, simply our opinion, that Petty Officer Clay Hartwig deliberately blew up Turret Two."

The final subcommittee report excoriated Ault and Hazelwood's analysis for "doubtful professionalism" and declared "the false air of certainty generated by the FBI analysis was probably the single major factor inducing the Navy to single out Clayton Hartwig as the likely guilty party."

Adding to the controversy was the fact that the House committee had also asked the American Psychological Association to form an ad hoc committee to review both the NIS evidence and the Ault-Hazelwood conclusions. Of the fourteen panel members, three felt Hartwig was probably guiltless. Several simply said they were dubious, while the remainder were generally supportive. Next, Ault and Hazelwood had to face the Senate Armed Services Committee, where, as Hazelwood put it, "the reception was only marginally more civil." The questioning was severe, although the two BSUers remained certain they were correct in their analysis. After the hearings, FBI Director William Sessions and Associate Director John Otto telephoned both Ault and Hazelwood thanking them for jobs well done.

Subsequent retests of the forensic material by both the Sandia National Laboratory in New Mexico and the Naval Sea System Command (NAVSEA) offered no new hard evidence whether the explosion was of suicidal nature or an accident. Yet an unexplained substance was recovered from the gun's barrel—a material consistent with a chemical detonator used to ignite powder. Nonetheless, the discovery was insufficient to prove Hartwig's involvement.

The report by the Investigations Subcommittee of the House Armed Services was entitled "U.S.S. *Iowa* Tragedy: An Investigative Failure" and released to the public. The *New York Times* praised the report for its "clear, dry prose" and blasted the FBI equivocal-death analysis as "a sci-fi psychological profile of the gunner-suspect based upon the Navy's supply of biased evidence." Lars-Erik Nelson added, "Deep within the FBI there exists a unit of people who—without ever talking to you or anyone who knows you—are prepared to go into court and testify that you are a homicidal maniac" and hoped that "any defense lawyer, any lawyer, any judge, any jury would laugh this kind of quack evidence out of court."

Despite the lack of new hard evidence, Admiral Frank B. Kelso, Chief of Naval Operations, announced at a Washington news conference on October 18, 1991, that the Navy had changed its mind. After spending $25 million in an unsuccessful search for conclusive evidence, Kelso told reporters, "There is no certain answer to what caused the tragedy. Accordingly, the opinion that the explosion resulted from a wrongful intentional act is disapproved. An exact cause cannot be determined." The Admiral then apologized to the Hartwig family. "We're sorry Clayton Hartwig was accused of this."

Then, within a week of Kelso's news conference and public apology, the Naval Sea System Command (NAVSEA) issued its own final report, reasserting that the Navy had been right all along! In part, it read, "The review of the original investigation has not produced any information, data, or analysis that supports any material change to the conclusions of the original report . . . in the absence of a plausible accidental cause and having found material consistent with a chemical device, the NAVSEA team concludes that an intentional act must be considered as a cause of the accident."

To this day, Roy Hazelwood and Dick Ault stand by their analysis: the tragedy, they insist, is explained in the terms of a murder-suicide by Clayton Hartwig.

NOTES

1. An excellent fictional account of a murder camouflaged as an auto-erotic fatality and subsequently altered to appear like a suicide is *An Unsuitable Job For A Woman*, by P. D. James, a novelist with forensic science experience. Although published in 1972, it is considered by BSUers to be one of the three best such murder mysteries employing that theme.

2. For a superb summary of the standard operating procedures of an *Iowa*-class battleship, as well as the events leading up to the explosion, see H. Paul Jeffers, *Who Killed Precious? How FBI Special Agents Combine High Technology and Psychology to Identify Violent Criminals* (New York: Pharos Books, 1991).

3. Neither the project nor its results have been declassified to this day.

4. Stephen G. Michaud with Roy Hazelwood, *The Evil That Men Do: FBI Profiler Roy Hazelwood's Journey into the Minds of Sexual Predators* (New York: St. Martin's Press, 1998), chap. 15, "We Changed the Rules."

10 "Helping Hands"

During the late 1970s and early 1980s, there were a series of events that thrust the Behavioral Science Unit in a new direction. These events challenged the resolve, human understanding, and fortitude of the FBI, and the Behavioral Science Unit was tasked to address these challenges. The first event involved a police shooting in Austin, Texas, which highlighted the need for understanding the crises that police officers are confronted with. The second series of events were Police Psychological Services conferences held at the FBI academy to examine what support was available for law enforcement officers during times of crisis. The third event was the unfortunate, first shooting death of a female agent, Special Agent Robin Ahrens in October of 1985. The fourth event was a Miami shoot-out, where special agents Ben Grogan and Jerry Dove were killed. That shooting incident resulted in law enforcement examining and adopting automatic weapons instead of revolvers.

THE POLICE STRESS–PERSONAL PROBLEMS COURSE

In June 1974, John Mindermann, a tall, strapping, former police officer from San Francisco, reported as a newly assigned staff member to the Behavioral Science Unit at the FBI academy. Jack Pfaff, the unit chief, assigned him to conduct research and develop a course of instruction in the area of the noncriminal role of the police. This broad field was titled "Crisis Intervention" and included interpersonal disputes of every variety, with emphasis placed on domestic violence.

Domestics were the most common calls and were fraught with unpredictability and danger. Officers were often killed or hurt handling these potentially eruptive service requests. Drawing on work done outside psychology with the Richmond, California, police department, Mindermann developed a model which addressed officer safety while "diffusing/calming," "securing information," "interviewing," and engaging a dispute resolution strategy picked from a variety of options which included arrest, referral, and mediation.

Mediation skills were taught in abundance. Class members were involved in role-playing skits or scenarios wherein mediation and other skills essential to successful dispute resolution could be evaluated, analyzed, criticized, and learned. Mindermann and his partner, Dick Harper, analyzed the survey of FBI data on officers killed from the LEOKA (Law Enforcement Officers Killed and Assaulted) manual. This data pointed out that one out of four or five officers were killed with their own handguns after being disarmed or dropping their weapons during a scuffle. Significant attention was paid to this deadly trend in each class and to the fact that there is a gun involved in every run or every call a police officer attends: "officers themselves bring a loaded, high-caliber pistol into every situation they handle." Shortly after the course began, there was further recognition of this issue when Kansas City, Missouri, police department firearms instructors began their own course on "weapons retention."

In September of 1974, Harper and Mindermann began teaching a three-day field school in crisis intervention with the first stop in Toledo, Ohio. During the ensuing two or three years, the two probably taught fifty or more of these schools throughout the United States for officers representing every type of law enforcement agency. The course remained in demand into the late 1970s, even when the BSU attempted to phase it out. Because of the immersion with officers and the topics of crisis, Mindermann began talking during breaks and lunch about a topical area which was of special interest to him, police stress and personal problems. Officers would open up and discuss their particular problems, and regardless of their agency's size, location, or structure, the stressors and problems were identical.

In October 1975, a crisis-intervention school at the University of Texas in Austin offered Harper and Mindermann an unusual opportunity. The two BSUers were requested on a "hurry-up" basis, because an officer in Austin had shot and killed a father in his home while attempting to quell a dispute between him and his sixteen-year-old son. Because the officer involved in the shooting, as well as the police department, had been bombarded with community criticism, challenges, and press inquiries about their tactics, much of the local press coverage was directed to the training session. Attending officers were emotionally hurt and confused by the barrage of negative community comments directed towards them.

Toward the end of the course, a reporter specifically asked Mindermann about issues in policing. John responded by asking, "What about the crisis the police themselves are experiencing?" He went on to identify several stresses associated with police and their work as well as stressful family events and problems emanating from them. He referred to the unknown number of victim officers as "time-bombs" and criticized police executives for ignoring those problems. The interview was published in the *Austin-American Statesman* and it served as a loose blueprint for future FBI "helping hands" efforts.

The area of police stress and personal problems had been and still remains a "blind eye" or "swept under the rug" topic. Guardians are not supposed to have emotional problems. Men and women attracted to policing become involved in a work lifestyle defined and driven by external clues. Introspection is avoided because one only has to respond to the next radio call or assigned case. Rules and regulations comfortably guide an officer's life. The work environment and culture become a restricted room that stifles individual thought and contemplation. With a culture and organization so rigidly defined, deviance is seen as a threat. Failing or being flawed should never flow from the work environment. The subculture carefully selects those actions or incidents to which it acknowledges identification. Scandal, corruption, and individual acts connote legal or moral difficulties and are seen as an aberration or the act of a maverick officer. The "rotten apple in the barrel" theory is offered as an explanation. Whenever an officer is injured or killed in the line of duty, there is much vocalization and chest-beating about the police family and its unity.

John Mindermann first rubbed up against the dark side of policing during his eight and a half years as a working officer in San Francisco, whose police department was born in the California Gold Rush of 1849. This experience as an accepted peer in a culture provided him with an intimate view of a wide variety of police personnel and organizational problems. It was a robust department which clung to a police style that supported socially sanctioned gambling, prostitution, and other forms of vice. During his tenure as an officer in that department, he emerged untouched from a long period of contact with organized bribery and corruption. Pockets of those illegalities remained during the years of his employment. This extra departmental challenge came in addition to his routine police work. In the long run, it provided John with extremely valuable lessons and insights.

Later, being able to talk with police officers as peers rather than merely as an FBI instructor gave him an edge with officers on their home turf during the crisis intervention field schools. Mindermann was convinced there was a need for a formal course in such a topical area.

After discussing the potential with unit chief Jack Pfaff in mid-1976, John wrote a historic, formal memo to the Bureau in which he proposed that the academy host a one-week conference in the area of police stress and personal problems. Fifty administrators from representative departments would be invited. Lectures on defined topics would be presented by psychologists currently employed by police agencies throughout the nation. The conference was authorized and held at Quantico in mid-January of 1977. Howard Teten and Mindermann coauthored a six-page article titled "Police Personal Problems: Practical Considerations for Administrators." The article was published in the January 1977 edition of the *Law Enforcement Bulletin*. This was the beginning of the recognition of police problems.

The conference consisted of three and a half days of presentations by established police stress experts. The lecturers of significance were John Stratton of the Los Angeles Sheriff's Department; John Berberich of the Seattle Police Department; Illana Hadar, Susan Saxe, and Martin Reiser of the Los Angeles Police Department; Mike Roberts of the San Jose Police Department; Joe Barry of the Boston Police Department; and Ed Donovan and Joe Ravino of the Boston Police Department's Peer Counseling Program. In addition, Inspector Richard Caretti of the Detroit Police Department presented data assembled from a survey conducted by the Detroit Police Department. This was the first comprehensive examination of the existing knowledge, application, and relevance of helping programs for police agencies.

The conference had two general objectives. The first was to raise awareness of the topical areas among police administrators. The second was to bring together experts who would share knowledge which could be incorporated into a new Behavioral Science Unit course for the National Academy and police field schools. This was the first effort by the FBI to recognize that police do have personal problems and that there are specific organizational and individual stressors in law enforcement.

From the conference, John Mindermann developed the original "Police Stress-Personal Problems" course. He also completed supplemental research both before and after the conference. Planning and organizing the conference was the easy part. Much more challenging for John was presenting the material to the police students in a nonthreatening manner. Material and illustrative examples could never directly refer to classroom students unless they themselves brought up the topics for discussion. The course, through feedback and class dialogue, enabled officers to become introspective in a nonjudgmental atmosphere. Mindermann used a casual but structured approach in which he never identified the source behind a specific problem, although he identified potential embarrassing incidents. Humor, a "high risk-high gain technique," was often used as a distracter and diffusing tool. John defined the concept of stress medically and tied it to policing, organizational, and family stressors, while highlighting the interaction between police work and the police family. He applied stress facts and theory by basically analyzing actual stressful events involving police officers. From such exercises, class members themselves proposed preventative and handling strategies. They examined the impact of stress in extreme situations where, for example, an officer had lost a significant partner, job, etc., or where the partner was severely injured or killed.

Isolated specialty areas were of particular interest. One was the "John Wayne Syndrome," a hyper-macho cluster of attitudes and actions which police officers embraced between the fourth and seventh years of their career. Emerging language, attitudes, and actions of the affected officers could often be hilarious in their overt manifestations, but had devastating consequences in their personal lives. Handling traumatized victims over a long period of time, as well as the direct experience of "post-shooting trauma" or "survivors' guilt," were examined. Mindermann required each officer in attendance to write a paper about an actual stressful event, identifying the various stressors. Then the student was asked to propose the most positive manner for handling the conflict or issue. Preventative strategies were then listed and identified.

John continued to develop and teach this course until headquarters transferred him back to the field in February of 1981. Jim Reese was assigned his block of instruction. Jim shared some concern about teaching the material since he had not been a law enforcement officer before coming into the FBI. Mindermann assured him that all he had to do with cops was consistently be "dead bang completely honest." That was the one guideline that John provided for the future focus of stress in law enforcement.

During the early 1980s, the Police Psychological Services, or Psychological Services for Law Enforcement Units, surfaced as a key force among state, local, and federal law enforcement agencies. Part of the identity for that group of professionals was provided by the FBI. During the early eighties, the Behavioral Science Unit hosted the National Symposium on Police Psychological Services, the World Conference on Police Psychology, and a Critical Incident Conference. These conferences were all designed to improve and maintain mental health services to all the nation's law enforcement officers. They also provided a forum for police psychologists to share their insights, skills, and techniques in dealing with the particular challenging issues that confront law enforcement on a national basis.

Since the turn of the century, when Louis Terman first tested police candidates for selection by using a modified version of the Stanford-Binet test, mental health professionals have been involved in various aspects of law enforcement. Over the years, their interest and research has resulted in increased knowledge of law enforcement personnel organizations and function. Many mental health professionals are specializing in police psychology today, researching virtually every aspect of this unique and stressful occupation.

THE BSU AND POLICE PSYCHOLOGY

Post-shooting trauma is an issue in law enforcement that has been recognized, understood, and treated only during the past fifteen to twenty years. The first recognized full police psychologist dates back to 1968, when Dr. Marty Reiser was hired by the Los Angeles Police Department. Reiser and his cohorts developed an understanding of stress and applied it to law enforcement professionals. They recognized that the serious nature of the effects, problems, and general aftermath of an extreme stressor, such as shooting, had a direct impact on the officers involved. From their insights and experiences, the psychologists were able to provide new information about the causes, symptoms, and effects of the reaction to the exercise of deadly force.

Two significant events provided a natural framework for developing a systematic review of the importance of research and literature searches pertaining to post-traumatic stress. On September 17, 1984, a dedicated group of professionals came together for the first time at the FBI Academy in Virginia for the National Symposium on Police Psychological Services. Throughout the week, the 150 professionals discussed provisions that addressed and maintained mental health services for the national law enforcement officers. The conference was cosponsored by Reese and Harvey A. Goldstein, Director Psychological Services, Prince George County Police Department, Upper Marlboro, Maryland. A call for papers before the symposium laid the academic and professional foundation for progress. The proceedings of that effort was titled "Psychological Services for Law Enforcement" and published in the *Law Enforcement Bulletin* in 1986.

A second conference, expanding professional research efforts, focused upon post–critical incident trauma. In August 1989, fifty mental health professionals, employee assistance providers, chaplains, and law enforcement officers met at the academy for a Critical Incident Conference. The week-long conference allowed each individual to share thoughts, research ideas, and techniques for dealing with critical incidents in law enforcement. The resulting publication, "Critical Incidents in Policing," a product of their knowledge and their dedication to assist law enforcement, was edited by James T. Reese, James Horn, and Chris Dunning, and appeared in the *Law Enforcement Bulletin*.

"Helping Hands"

In the early 1980s, police psychologists around the country were aware of the reactions of police officers involved in shooting incidents. Mike Roberts, police psychologist for the San Jose Police Department, offered insights into the post-shooting reaction. His position was that post-shooting trauma is a transient situational disorder that can be easily alleviated if dealt with at the time. Roberts identified frequent reactions and concerns that police officers experience during and after a shooting. A few of the reactions and concerns that he identified included sensory distortions, flashbacks, fear of insanity, crying, and general sorrow over depriving the person of life.

Meanwhile, Massad Ayoob, in his article "The Killing Experience," described the experience of an officer involved in a shooting as a mystical situation. He found that one of the things that most affects the officer involved in the shooting incident is the administrative inquiry after the shooting. Ayoob pointed out that often the incident is compounded or exacerbated when the officer's gun is removed. Specifically, he focused on the fact that a gun is part of the identity of the officer. In a second article published in 1982, he stated that most officers that are involved in shootings will have some type of reaction, including nightmares, sleepless nights, social withdrawal, and avoidance. Ayoob coined the term "Mark of Cain Complex" which he defined as a feeling that everyone is watching the particular officer and concerned about not only his or her behavior, but also the reactions of the officer after a critical incident.

Actually, prior to these initial groundbreaking articles, Martin Symonds, an associate professor of psychiatry at New York University, and newly appointed psychological services expert for the New York City Police Department, made a presentation at John Jay College in 1978. At that conference, he discussed a traumatic syndrome which follows physical injury to officers. Symonds specifically detailed reaction stages and some of the feelings that the officer goes through in a post-shooting incident. A number of other police psychologists,

305

including Martin VanMaanen, Cohen, Lippert, and Saper, Jim Shaw, and Edward Donovan, as well as Carson and Ken Matula, identified and wrote anecdotal articles and conducted limited anecdotal research in the area of post-shooting trauma.

In June of 1983, the director of the FBI, William H. Webster, commissioned a pilot study to examine post-shooting trauma and its ramifications and effects on special agents of the FBI, since they were involved in the exercise of deadly force. This specific pilot study actually evolved from questions and concerns expressed by John J. Schreiber, section chief, Personal and Property Crimes Program, in his memorandum to "Buck" Revell on May 4, 1983.

Meanwhile, the husband and wife team of David and Carol Soskis brought a new emphasis to the issues they dealt with initially in the Behavioral Science Unit and ultimately throughout the Bureau. Dr. David Soskis was a prominent Philadelphia psychiatrist and Carol was an attorney with an expertise in client confidentiality. She also had a background in psychiatric social work. For more than ten years they had been the "helping hands" of the FBI. In fact, the Soskises were the first consultants hired by the Bureau, specifically by the Behavioral Science Unit. Not only were they psychological consultants, but they also had a chance to interact at all levels of the organization. They gained confidence by working with and through human tragedies, including those of family members of FBI employees, who experienced suicide, issues of depression, and also other areas classified as critical incidents. They both had a very unique insight into the FBI. In fact, several top officials at headquarters even suggested that David had a better knowledge of the FBI than the employees themselves.

The confidence that Soskis established by working with assistant directors and other high Bureau managers allowed him to ensure that the psychological health of the FBI was being addressed. On the post-shooting trauma project, the Soskises were contacted regarding the question, "Do agents of the FBI suffer the same types of post-shooting trauma that the anecdotal literature has indicated that police officers suffer from?" David's initial reaction was "No." His rationale was that those agents who are making "split-second decisions" during arrests on the street are well trained. "They are highly educated," said Soskis, "and the situations in which they are involved are well planned and addressed."

Another participant in the initiative was John Henry Campbell. John came to the Behavioral Science Unit in the early 1980s after some nine years of street experience as a "real agent" in St. Louis, Detroit, and Lansing, where he pursued his Ph.D. at Michigan State University. John was involved as a generalist in the Behavioral Science Unit and had an opportunity to expand or conduct research specifically focused on deadly force. This was a natural blend into post-shooting trauma. Campbell and John Hall, a premier legal instructor at the academy, actually offered a series of National Academy seminars entitled, "Deadly Force and Post-Shooting Trauma." Hall later became the Bureau's expert in both the use of deadly force and the legal aspects of deadly force. In addition, he has written prolifically on the issue of the use of deadly force while working diligently on the Bureau's deadly force policy.

Campbell disagreed with Soskis regarding the question, "Do agents of the FBI suffer from post-shooting trauma?" John's answer was an absolute "Yes. Agents are human beings and we have the same human frailties as well as the same psychological reactions that confront those law enforcement officers when they are required to exercise deadly force."

Based on the challenge and questions presented by section chief John Schreiber, a conference was convened at the Academy on June 20, 1983. The focus was on postshooting trauma and its effects on agents involved in the exercise of deadly force. In attendance were John J. Schreiber; David Soskis, the Bureau psychiatric consultant; Larry J. Monroe, unit chief Firearms Training Unit; Robert Schaefer and Campbell, supervisor special agents, Behavioral Science Unit. Soskis stated that he was requested by Executive Assistant Director John E. Otto to conduct a research and interview project to determine if Bureau agents have problems, physical or psychological, resulting from the use of deadly force. Soskis indicated that the project's goal was to make appropriate recommendations to establish a Bureau policy which would neutralize the effects of post-shooting trauma. He further indicated that the project would be completed through a minimal number of interviews and requested assistance from the Behavioral Science Unit in completing this project.

On June 29, 1983, approval was granted by Assistant Director James D. McKenzie to conduct the interviews during a conference to be scheduled at the FBI Academy. The scope of that conference would be to elicit, from special agents of the FBI who had recently been involved in shooting incidents, their physical and psychological reactions attributable to the use of deadly force. On July 14 and 15, 1983, fourteen special agents convened at the academy with Dr. Soskis and Supervisor Special Agent Campbell. Those fourteen agents had been involved in a total of seventeen shooting incidents. The continued goal of the project was to determine if the agents suffered from post-shooting trauma and if so, make appropriate recommendations with the cooperation of the conference attendees to minimize the negative aspects of the trauma.

The conference format included an address by Assistant Director McKenzie; an introduction to the conference's goals and objectives; the completion of a formal questionnaire; personal interviews; and a conference group discussion. This discussion opened the door. Follow-up interviews with the spouses of several of the agents attending the conference were conducted by Carol Soskis. From the formal questionnaires answered at the conference, the interviews, and the analysis of the research conducted by Soskis and Campbell, a formulation of positive recommendations was instituted. The recommendations included intervention both at the shooting scene, during the first week, long-term issues, prevention, and training. An extensive report was published by the Bureau not only detailing the results of the conference, but also presenting a specific series of recommendations to address post-shooting trauma. One result of this meeting was that Supervisory Special Agent Campbell's focus and interpretation of post–critical incident trauma was supported by the concept of transient situational disturbance. This meant that if the acute stress reaction was addressed immediately it could reduce the probability or possibility of long-term stress reaction or chronic stress. Also interesting to note is that of seventeen incidents, fifteen supported evidence of reexperiencing trauma, classifying the experience as post-traumatic stress disorder. Other frequently supported statements were that repressed thoughts or memories about the shooting kept reappearing in the agents' minds. Not only were the agents sleeping more poorly, but also there was considerable guilt and hyper-alertness, or startle reaction, after the incident. Of course, there was a whole series of additional reactions. One was the automatic response that came into play during the incident where deadly force was involved. This automatic response was appropriately based on training and conditioning responses in the use of firearms.

This was the first FBI organizational insight into the issues of human frailty which specifically focused on incidents involving employment that may impact an individual's psyche. A whole range of factors that assisted these agents in coping with the aftermath of the shooting incident were identified. There were other factors that directly affected and compounded the trauma that they were going through as well as the majority of those from the Bureau and local law enforcement agencies who surrounded the investigations.

As mentioned, one of the goals of the project was to determine what, if any, post-shooting trauma reactions special agents of the FBI might encounter and suffer from, and then make recommendations to alleviate or minimize the effects. The data collected included the responses of the fourteen special agents who attended the conference and interviews by the authors with a similar number of agents involved in shooting incidents over several years. From such a diversity of knowledge and experiences, a series of conclusions and recommendations evolved, thanks to the conference participants, who were able to achieve consensus. All of the recommendations are part of the FBI's official policy today.

Such was the basis for the FBI's Post-shooting Program. It ultimately evolved into a post–critical incident seminar and became a model for all of federal law enforcement. The good work that was conducted afterward by Bob Schaefer and Jim Horn and supported by Jim Reese contributed to the evolution of a model program for dealing with post–critical incident trauma beyond just the post-shooting issues, including all human tragedies that befall employees of the FBI. Later, the program evolved into a federal model encompassing employees of all the federal agencies. This model program has been shared with law enforcement agencies all over the world. The recommendations and approaches have served as the foundation for law enforcement initiatives in addressing post-shooting trauma.

A series of seminars continued to explore and expand on the Bureau's knowledge of post-shooting trauma and those seminars were directly coordinated by Supervisory Special Agent Campbell. John had the opportunity on numerous occasions to provide the results of these series of conferences directly to Mr. Otto, who was the executive assistant director of the FBI.

During the summer of 1984, Campbell, who was interested in new and interesting challenges, volunteered for several supervisory positions in the Midwest. Because of the fine work he did on the project, he was rewarded by being sent to Butte, Montana, which at that time was the field office responsible for Idaho and Montana. In the Bureau generally, if you screw up, commit a sin, are unfortunate in a judgement, or make a huge mistake, you are sent to Butte. In Campbell's case, he volunteered to be assigned to Montana. He was selected by the FBI Career Board for the supervisory special agent position in Butte and was dispatched in the fall of 1984. Friends and colleagues were convinced he was exiled there for some transgression against the FBI because of Hoover's prior labeling of Butte as a disciplinary office. It may be of interest to note that often when agents were sent to Montana, they were never heard from again, not because they disappeared, but because of their good life in "the big sky country." If an individual is interested in quality of experiences, hunting, fishing and family life, Butte and its surrounding counties are extraordinarily popular. Therefore, nobody at FBI Headquarters ever heard from those employees again, because they were well satisfied with their assignments in Montana and Idaho. Another aspect of the good life there is that the work in Montana and Idaho was generally reactive. Agents would respond to bank robberies and crimes on Indian reservations. There were no real problems or issues in Montana or Idaho confronting the agents or employees. As far as the work was concerned, it was at times mundane, but never overwhelming. Six months after Campbell arrived, things began to change dramatically.

THE TIE MAN

Robert B. Schaefer joined the Behavioral Science Unit during the summer of 1982 and jumped in with both feet to study, teach, and conduct research in the area of police stress. Born, raised, and educated in New York City, Bob attended Queens College and Fordham University before enlisting for two years of active duty in the U.S. Navy. He chose to become an air traffic controller, hoping to avoid sea duty; however, he spent two years at sea on USS *Wasp*, the last aircraft carrier in the fleet with a wooden flight deck.

Schaefer's tour was not without incident: he witnessed a fixed-wing aircraft land on top of two helicopters during night operations on a Mediterranean cruise. He also managed to ride out a hurricane in the north Atlantic during the winter. Before discharge, he took the written examination to become a New York State Trooper. Bob joined the state police during 1963 and served in numerous capacities throughout New York State. While a state trooper, he volunteered to serve on the Thruway detail at the New York City line, in order to complete his bachelor's degree at Queens College. He then completed all of the coursework, but not his thesis for a Master of Public Administration at John Jay College of Criminal Justice. Bob applied for and was accepted as a special agent of the Federal Bureau of Investigation in 1971. He brought a wealth of experience and maturity in the area of dealing with tragedies, especially after policing numerous multiple fatalities and even a homicide, while assigned to the New York State Thruway detail.

Bob served in the Jacksonville field office, the Pensacola resident agency, and the Philadelphia field office before being assigned to the FBI Academy. His road to the academy was not easy. Bob had been an alternate instructor while serving as a state trooper and, once accepted into the FBI became a very active field police instructor teaching stress management courses. He had always dreamed of becoming an instructor at the FBI Academy, although he realized this required a minimum of a master's degree. Bob needed only to write his master's thesis, but had to put that on the back burner when an FBI agent attending John Jay College wrote a paper that was critical of Director J. Edgar Hoover. The paper became public and all FBI agents were required to drop out of John Jay College. Several years passed before Bob wrote a personal memorandum to Mr. Hoover requesting permission to complete his master's studies at John Jay. Permission was granted and Bob received his MPA during 1976.

But all along, Schaefer was intent on getting to Quantico. He formally applied for a position, only to be abruptly turned down by the special agent in charge of the Philadelphia division, who was locked in a battle with FBI headquarters for additional manpower. He dismissed Bob from his office by stating, "It makes me think that you are underassigned if you can sit around and think about going to the training division." Bob was crushed at the time and feared that his dream would never be fulfilled. He was transferred from his position as the night supervisor of the Philadelphia division to the fugitive squad, which was perceived as a dumping ground for agents not in the SAC's favor. Bob was on limited duty at the time for a shattered ankle that required a year in a nonwalking cast, which was not conducive to fugitive work. During mid-1982, after additional manpower had been assigned to Philadelphia, he was asked to volunteer for a special assignment which involved teaching the new Performance Appraisal System to managers and supervisors across the country. The assignment was to last at least one year. At the end of that year, Bob was asked if he wanted to remain with the Management Science Unit, or transfer to another unit. He immediately requested the Behavioral Science Unit, which put him into the middle of a new chapter that was about to unfold for the BSU.

Schaefer was initially assigned to work as a backup for Jim Reese in the Stress Management Program. Bob was enthusiastic about this new assignment and started attending profiling in-services in hope of becoming a backup for that program, too. Soon he began to work with Campbell, coteaching the use of deadly force and post-shooting trauma across the country. The question that was posed to Bob and John, and embarrassed them at every such seminar, was, "What type of a program does the FBI have to help FBI agents deal with post-shooting trauma?" It was devastating to answer that the FBI didn't have any such program. Yet the two were instructing other departments how they should handle such incidents.

Campbell, meanwhile, was searching for a doctoral dissertation topic. Deciding that his work in the area of post-shooting trauma was just what he wanted to pursue, he developed a questionnaire that was thereafter distributed to all victims of recent FBI shooting incidents. Schaefer worked closely with Campbell on the project and a seminar of sorts was organized. The participants of recent shooting incidents were brought back to the academy for a two-and-a-half-day debriefing. The goal was to determine what, if anything, caused trauma for FBI agents after involvement in a shooting incident. The scope from day one continued to expand as spouses were included in the initial debriefings for input and their unique perspectives. But just as things began to develop, Campbell was transferred to Butte as a field supervisor. Bob was to be in the hot seat from that point on, and he wasn't quite sure if that was a reward or punishment for Campbell. Schaefer was then selected to continue the development of the FBI's Critical Incident Program, as it became known. He worked very closely with Otto and Soskis, the two individuals who he says, "made this program a reality."

The Critical Incident Program became an obsession with Schaefer. In addition to spending untold hours developing a comprehensive, two-and-one-half-day seminar that was to be attended by all agents involved in shooting incidents, he reviewed all shooting incident reports and chose attendees for each seminar. There was a great deal of paranoia and resistance to the program, since many agents considered themselves to be "macho" and beyond the need for help. One major finding and perception recognized in this program was that most agents honestly believed that the only one that could help them, or that they could confide in, after a shooting incident was another FBI agent who had experienced a similar tragedy. That finding was the start of the Peer Support Program.

Schaefer began to feel stressed as he dealt directly with John Otto, the number two man in the Bureau, especially since John was affectionately referred to as the "Incredible Hulk." Otto would call him directly concerning the program without notifying the front office (the assistant director of the training division) at the academy. Bob, who was not permitted to call Otto directly without the front office knowing about it, found himself in an awkward situation. Otto volunteered to personally appear at each and every Critical Incident Seminar for the concluding hours and address any problems identified. Bob would meet Otto at the front office and brief him on the issues before the two appeared before the class. Bob was very careful to make sure that all issues, whether sensitive or not, were brought to Otto's attention prior to his appearance, so that he could prepare himself for responses. Stress continued to mount as Bob took copious notes during Otto's appearances for preparation the next day of an appropriate memo to him at headquarters not only addressing that problem, but also providing possible solutions. Bob would then drive into Washington, D.C., and verbally present the identified issues to all of the division heads (assistant directors). He recalls that Otto's secretary, Darlene Fitzsimmons, was both a pleasure to deal with as well as a strong support. "Darlene saved me from the wrath of the Incredible Hulk on many occasions. She knew Mr. Otto like a book and never steered me wrong," Bob chuckles.

Otto's appearances at the Academy continued to become especially awkward, since the attendees at post–critical incident seminars held nothing back. Here was Bob trying to tell the number two man in the FBI diplomatically, on their way from the front office to the classroom, that the FBI was doing it all wrong. Bob smiled, "They're going to tell you the FBI lacks sensitivity. Things need to be fine-tuned to make conditions better for agents, support personnel, and their families."

Schaefer found that the shooting inquiry following an incident and the administrative handling thereafter were more stressful than the event itself. Medical payments and worker's compensation claims were found to be abominable. Bob was astounded to find that Otto took most of these issues in stride and made the personnel, even if from other agencies, responsible for the agents who were wronged.

Bob began to believe the program was in place and finally beginning to work for the good of the agents and their support personnel. "What a reward to see this all fall into place and gain momentum." Bob even recalled being called out half-naked from his annual physical examination at FBI headquarters to discuss radio problems at a shooting incident with the assistant director of technical services.

Schaefer was tasked with explaining to all the agents the impact of critical incidents. What resulted was a pamphlet, which took approximately two years to publish, and was entitled, "Shooting Incidents: Issues and Explanations for FBI Agents and Managers." The explanation was followed by a videotape and slide presentations. Bob additionally began teaching this topic to all supervisors' in-services, at training sessions for new inspectors' aides, and to all new FBI agents. Fortunately, Schaefer continued to treat the matter as a challenge, and his unique ability to deal with and manipulate the bureaucratic system flourished. It's interesting to note that in Bob's writings at that time, he was advised by FBIHQ that the then-director did not care for the use of the word "feel." It was suggested that "feel" be replaced with "believe." "Wow," laughed Bob, "Can you say, I believe hungry and convey the same message?"

The Post–Critical Incident Program was now in place and ready for its first test. That came rather unexpectedly when Schaefer was sent to a shooting incident in Phoenix, on a moment's notice, to render psychological support to those involved. In October of 1985, Robin Ahrens was killed in Phoenix, Arizona. Robin was a special agent with the FBI and her death was a double tragedy. She was shot and killed in an arrest situation by other agents accidentally. The arrest was of a violent subject and Robin responded when shots were fired. Unfortunately, she was thought to be an accomplice, fired upon by two other agents, and tragically killed. This was a Bureau nightmare.

Schaefer was told that he would personally respond to the Phoenix shooting. He was both sad and anxious. As he thought about his response while flying to Phoenix, Bob began to feel butterflies in his stomach. He didn't have many details about the shooting incident, but he didn't feel very good about what he had heard. He became apprehensive about responding to a negative shooting incident, especially since it was the "first response." There were so many things that he didn't know. The future of the Critical Incident/Peer Support Program could very well depend upon Bob's performance in the aftermath of this incident. So by the time he arrived in Phoenix, he was uptight and stressed out. He not only perceived this to be one hell of a trial run, but also was beginning to doubt himself and his abilities. Schaefer was afraid that this would be more than he was equipped to handle. He recalled, "I was scared because I didn't want to fail such an important program."

The first thing that Schaefer did was to seek out Dave Soskis for moral support. He found the psychologist walking around the resort complex. When Bob first saw Dave, he thought to himself, "What have I gotten myself into?" This was the point where Schaefer became really nervous and apprehensive. There was the famed specialist walking around the resort in plaid shorts with high black socks and business shoes. Dave's quirk was something Bob promised himself he would never do. How scary it was to see his mentor doing it.

Dave greeted Bob and advised him that he might as well jump in with both feet and take Robin Ahren's mother and brother to breakfast in the morning. Bob agreed, but at the same time was reaching out to Dave to see if he was going to be there for guidance. Schaefer wasn't certain he had the confidence to take on such a responsibility. Dave said that he would stop and see everyone in the morning, but it would be Bob's job to stay with family members to offer support and answer their questions.

Bob met Ahren's family for breakfast after a very anxious and sleepless night. He used just about every bit of strength and energy he had during this first meeting, hoping and praying that he would do and say the right things. Looking back, it was the longest and most tense breakfast Bob ever attended. Although it started out calmly enough, questions soon came at him from both barrels, "Why did the FBI let this happen?" "How could the FBI have done this to Robin?" It was back and forth with a great deal of the anger and grief directed at Bob since he was "the representative of the FBI." Psychologically unprepared for the onslaught, Bob couldn't understand why he was being attacked when he was there to help. Although he had been living in a dream world, it didn't take long for him to face the reality of the situation. This was a situation the Academy and its sterile environment could not have prepared him for. Bob knew he had to experience and learn to deal with it. Dave Soskis arrived at the right time and supported Bob as he struggled to do his best for the family.

This response was especially tough for Bob because he knew Robin Ahrens personally. Robin had been temporarily assigned to the Behavioral Science Unit while recovering from a physical injury sustained during new agents training. She learned soon enough Bob's reputation as the "Tie Man." She made sure that she commented on his selection of ties when they met to discuss her progress and plans for the future. Bob's opinion was that Robin was a fine person and had a great career ahead of her.

The focus shifted next to those who had been involved in or present at the shooting incident. Schaefer began to feel more uneasy during this phase because he thought back to his arrival in the Phoenix division. Bob arrived on the same flight as many of the inspector's aides, who were tasked to investigate the shooting incident. He sensed he was being perceived as part of that team by the Phoenix agents and staff. It didn't matter initially what Bob said, because he was considered to be a headquarters agent since he was "arriving" with the "enemy." To add more apprehension and stress to the situation, the special agent in charge wanted to throw Bob out of his division. His position was that he and the agents involved in the shooting didn't need any help. He had been a Marine and never needed any help when he was in battle, so why should his agents? Frankly, Bob considered the SAC's attitude and behavior to be macho, offensive, and repulsive. Schaefer and Soskis, along with John Campbell, who had been called in from the Butte division, remained in the Phoenix division and worked with the employees. It wasn't easy.

The three could feel distrust from the other agents, both those who were involved in the arrest and shooting and also those who were not there. It made them want to pack up and head back home. None of the three had anticipated any type of opposition, especially on the part of a SAC. Although it seemed hopeless, Schaefer, Soskis, and Campbell started their debriefings. Gradually, some of the initial opposition began to dissipate. But the three soon ran into another stumbling block. How far could the trio go during the debriefings of the shooters when they were asked what was going to happen? It was so difficult for them to accept that they would just have to wait for the outcome of the inspection team's report. Bob felt that the shooters needed support more than anyone else at the scene, but it made everyone feel inadequate not to be able to give them what they needed. The investigation would ultimately decide their fate, but that would be months later. The judgment of the shooters was the big question, and the ultimate result was that both were fired. In fact, none of the three believed they could have given them what they wanted at that time. "I would be lying if I didn't say that I feared being in the middle of a civil law suit after having debriefed both of the shooters," Bob later recalled. He became very concerned that the Critical Incident/Peer Support Program could be totally destroyed by a challenge of confidentiality in court. Federal court rulings could destroy all of their work in seconds. Bob had given the promise of confidentiality during debriefings and vowed to abide by that. As he looked back, Schaefer conducted so many debriefings, it would be extremely difficult, if not impossible, for him to have accurately reconstructed any one of the accountings. It would not have been intentional on his part.

Bob put so much of his strength and effort into trying to make the individual being debriefed feel better that his mind was constantly focusing on the step ahead rather than on the details of the incident.

As the three finished their debriefings and started working with the remainder of the agents and support population, Bob began to doubt himself and the worth of this program. He felt that they had made some headway, but he saw the program crumbling right before his eyes. It was discouraging and disheartening, especially since so much work had gone into the effort to make things better for anyone experiencing a tragedy within the FBI.

Overall, Schaefer was mentally and physically exhausted. He sensed the program was destined to failure. Totally frustrated, he reflected upon the trio's response on the flight back to Washington, D.C., Bob flashed back to the many tragedies that he had witnessed as a state trooper. In one instance, he had attempted to keep a young woman alive until the ambulance arrived, telling the doctor at the scene that he could not save the woman even if she was in the operating room at a hospital. In another instance, Schaefer wrapped gauze around the head of a teenager who hit a bridge abutment in excess of 100 miles per hour. A nurse who arrived at the scene yelled at him incessantly for letting the gauze touch the boys brain as it was sliding out of his head. It was a "special type of helplessness," just as when Bob dealt with Ahren's family, the SAC trying to throw him out of his division, the agent population not trusting them, and the shooters wanting assurances from them that nothing would happen to them. It is difficult to explain unless you experience it yourself. Bob felt that if this program survived he surely would never experience anything like this again. How wrong he was!

Bob Schaefer felt much more confident when he responded to a Miami shooting incident. The team had survived the initial response in Phoenix, as negative as it was, and they were beginning to receive some positive vibes concerning the Post–Critical Incident Program.

This was a great morale booster. But with the initial reports on the loss of life and injuries, it sparked a new type of stress and apprehension on John Campbell's part.

Bob tried to implement all of those lessons learned in Phoenix as he distanced himself from the inspection team and took a low-key approach to the fact that this was very different and more positive than the Phoenix experience. The caregivers felt good about that and it helped to build the trio's confidence in what they were doing. Things progressed well as they visited wounded agents and their families in the hospital and later at their homes. But all of a sudden Bob's confidence was challenged again! With Dr. Soskis out of the country, a mental health professional was sent in his place to oversee the workings of the program, as well as render his own psychological support to all Miami division personnel. This same individual had completed a "fitness for duty" evaluation in Miami several months prior to the shooting. Unfortunately no mental health professional could wear both hats as "helper" and "enforcer" and expect anyone to trust him or her. Once again, Otto responded quickly to Bob's request to have this mental health professional immediately replaced, based on the estimation by Schaefer and Campbell—who was again called in from the Butte division—that this psychologist was causing harm.

Schaefer and Campbell did their thing just as they had planned while setting up the program back at the Academy. Bob remembers being plagued by constant feelings of inadequacy as he debriefed those who had been involved in this incident. Up to this point, between his years in the state police and as an FBI agent, he had a great deal of experience. He could easily fill a book with stories, experiences, tragedies, and traumas that he had witnessed or been involved in. Somehow, as a helper in Miami, Bob perceived that those involved in the shooting looked at him and the other helpers, at times, as if they didn't need them. This was an unusual shooting involving some very talented, brave, and dedicated agents. Bob perceived that they were searching for those same traits in the "helpers." They were dealing with them as if they were total unknowns. They did not have the benefit of knowing anything about the caregivers' experience and background, and frankly, there was not enough time to get into such discussions. They had to work extra hard to overcome those perceptions and gain acceptance and momentum without stepping on anyone's toes. The bottom line was that it slowed the process of acceptance.

Schaefer felt personally privileged and honored to have assisted with the aftermath of the Miami shooting. He and Campbell felt a sense of accomplishment that the program was much more readily accepted in Miami. This incident introduced them to many new aspects of the still young program, such as visitations with wounded agents in the hospital, and working with spouses, children, and teenagers. This added a total new dimension to the program. Bob's flight home from Miami was much more pleasant than the flight from Phoenix. He believed that the Critical Incident Program was going to be given a chance to survive. Although Schaefer felt enthusiastic, he experienced that same sense of total physical and mental exhaustion after spending several weeks in Miami. When he arrived back in the safety of his office at the Academy, Bob remembered thinking that he would never experience the likes of Phoenix again in his career, and here he was some six months later right back in the thick of things!

It seemed only minutes before he was notified that SA James McAllister had been killed while rappelling from a helicopter at Quantico. Headquarters was preparing a demonstration for Attorney General Edward Meese when the accident occurred. Bob had a difficult time moving. He began to wonder when all of these tragedies were going to end or at least slow down. He felt numb and sat in disbelief. His first reaction was, "Oh no, not again, and so soon." Bob was relieved when Jim Reese went to Potomac Hospital to be with Jim's wife, who was an agent assigned to the Washington field office. AG Meese and Otto also visited the hospital.

"Helping Hands"

Bob remembers continuing to feel numb, almost mentally exhausted, throughout the entire incident. Reese and Bob addressed headquarters later that day, answering questions concerning the incident, including what and how they should expect to feel after experiencing such a tragedy. At the time, Schaefer didn't feel at his best or comfortable dealing with this special, macho group of elite agents. Normally he didn't feel this way. He was thankful that Jim was at his side assisting him. Looking back, Bob is convinced he did not have an ounce of strength left to assist anyone else so soon after Phoenix and Miami.

Otto saw Bob after the HQ briefings. He commented that Bob looked tired and ordered him to take a much-needed rest, since Bob had cancelled a planned vacation in order to respond to Miami. He left for two weeks the next morning.

Bob returned to the Academy fully rested and refreshed. But he always had it in the back of his mind that at any moment a telephone call would dispatch him to another tragedy. He began feeling as if he needed some breathing room and some time away from being a full-time helper. Bob started volunteering to return to the field as a field supervisor. His wish was granted in 1987, when he was transferred to the Norfolk division. Over the next eight years at Norfolk, Schaefer continued to work part-time with the Critical Incident/Peer Support Program and personally responded to tragedies that occurred within that area.

In 1998, Schaefer made a tough decision regarding a relocation to the Richmond area in order to be closer to his children. Bob continues in his role as a full-time caregiver, dedicating twenty-four hours a day, seven days a week, to his wife of thirty-six years. Though in retirement, Schaefer feels as if he is back to square one as he looks at his career in law enforcement. As a full-time caregiver for his wife, he is facing the same burnout and overload that he faced several times before. However, over the years, he has learned some valuable lessons that he is now implementing. Bob is actively willing to debrief himself through family and special friends as he continues to seek relief in the form of respite care from his church and the local community. Bob realizes that he cannot carry this burden alone. He is also keeping in touch with the law enforcement community, which helps by providing statewide, mandatory training in the area of Alzheimer's disease.

Schaefer recalled a few cherished incidents from his memory bank since his tour with the Behavioral Science Unit. Most of these stories demonstrate that BSUers are as human as everyone else. Known affectionately throughout the law enforcement community as "The Tie Man" because of the bizarre neckties that he wore, Bob considered the nickname a rapport builder with his students. It was not uncommon for him to leave his office and return to find his entire desk covered with the loudest and most bizarre ties ever created. Thus started his collection of over one thousand ties, donated to him over the years by National Academy students who scoured their closets and attics for unused neckties on trips home from the Academy.

THE NEXT IN LINE

Jim Horn, another deeply committed BSUer, was sworn into the FBI on December 14, 1970, along with forty-nine other agents, including John Douglas. Little did anyone realize at that time that John's inclusion in this class would have a major impact on Jim's career thirteen years later, when the BSU was authorized to build the psychological profiling program by bringing in four agents from the field to be trained as profilers.

Horn had attended all of the BSU in-services as the Denver division representative and had been designated by the Denver SAC, Bill Gavin, as the behavioral science coordinator for the division. Trained as a police instructor, Jim had attended in-services for advanced criminology, hypnosis coordinators, stress management instructors, and profile coordinators, and had even submitted some local unsolved murder cases to the BSU for profiling. When John Douglas called Horn in the spring of 1983 and asked him to transfer to the BSU as one of the four new profilers, he was touched. Because he felt his previous experiences prepared him for the challenge, Jim actually believed it was his destiny to devote the rest of his career to the BSU. Because behavioral science in law enforcement was still being resisted in varying degrees by agents and local police officers, a transfer to the Academy was a welcome change and a chance to be surrounded by others who not only spoke the same language, but also understood the contributions the behavioral sciences offered.

As mentioned in previous chapters, the assembled talent in the BSU during the 1970s was most impressive, from the top to the raw new arrivals. Jim admired no one more than the BSU chief Roger Depue. He was the consummate leader, handling everyone with dignity. In fact, he was so self-secure that he would support any agent's effort to develop a program, though it might mean the program being recognized worldwide as state of the art and the agent becoming famous as the duty expert for that program. Many FBI managers would never allow subordinates to become more well known, or accredited, than themselves. But Roger seemed to revel in the idea that all the subprograms in the BSU would rise to the highest level of prominence. In psychologist Abraham Maslow's terms, he wanted everyone in his unit to self-actualize.

John Douglas was the supervisor for the four new profilers and they marveled at his abilities. They sensed they could learn a great deal just by listening to John discuss cases with officers over the phone. Some of his abilities seemed to be instinctive or innate. It was obvious a structured training program was needed which would immerse the new profilers in the work and facilitate their absorption of the knowledge they needed to be effective profilers. When John was stricken with encephalitis while working on the Green River serial murder case in Washington State, Roy Hazelwood stepped in immediately to take over the training of the new profilers. Although Roy may not have been the profiler that John was, he was outstanding in his ability to organize and conduct an effective training program for them.

As an example of John's innate ability, when Jim arrived at the Academy, he had just attended his twentieth high-school reunion. When the class picture arrived with the seventy-five classmates pictured who attended the reunion, Jim pointed out to his colleagues that one of his classmates had shockingly turned out to be a pedophile who had twice been to prison for molesting boys. With John sitting in the corner doing paper work and seemingly inattentive to them, two of the profiling interns tried to spot the pedophile by simply guessing which one in the picture he was. Their two guesses were humorous and it would be insulting to the highly successful people they fingered. They had only asked two questions of Jim: (1) Is he down and out? and (2) Is he a little overweight?

The answers were: (1) No, he is the happy-go-lucky type, just like he was in school, and (2) His weight is similar to everyone else's in the picture. Since everyone in the picture was happy and smiling, Jim felt like he had given them zero clues in fingering the culprit. After colleagues, too, had failed miserably, John looked up from the corner and said, "Let me try it." He walked over, took the picture, silently studied it for two to three minutes and then put his finger directly on the pedophile's nose. Jim knew then and there that John had the abilities that were beyond his own and were probably not teachable.

When Jim arrived at the BSU in June 1983, he had been teaching stress management to police for six years. Dr. Soskis, the Bureau's psychiatrist, told the staff that working the most heinous violent crimes in the country, as they were, was toxic, and one should not do it for too many years continuously. John Douglas and Bob Ressler had warned them two years before at in-service training sessions that profiling changes those who work in it, and that their families had told them they were different now than before they immersed themselves in man's inhumanity to man. Jim recognized the stress the profilers were under from the concentrated exposure to the graphic vulgarity of brutal murders, and recommended that they all sit down together each Friday and talk about their work as well as anything else that bothered them. Unfortunately, the BSU, with all its incredibly talented people, was not yet ready for what Jim thought was obviously needed to debrief themselves as a means of stress management and preventive maintenance.

One of Campbell's criticisms of the BSU and its programs was that, as intense as the work was, the pace was almost obsessive-compulsive. The moderation of that pace was never discussed in the eleven years that he was in the BSU. Although the pace produced great results, Jim couldn't help but wonder what price each of them paid. The price was high in Jim's case between 1984 and 1986: working a full load in the BSU; adding a second son who was born in 1984; and going to night school in D.C. at George Washington University to finish his master of forensic science degree. Without a doubt, it was the hardest two years of his life. Although he had been encouraged to continue working on his Ph.D., Jim felt that since the previous two years had affected his health considerably, he wouldn't give education any more thought. Horn observed the other BSU staffers engaged in graduate work, writing their dissertations, and knew from observation, the staffers' own words, and from Roger Depue, that their efforts were almost killing them. As a former Marine infantry officer who completed two tours in Vietnam, Jim knew how far people can push themselves. In war, of course, that is certainly necessary. But the pace in the BSU never seemed rational to him or John Campbell.

Horn's other major concern was the work environment that the staff wound up in when the BSU moved to the subbasement of the dining room building of the FBI Academy. This was an area that had been prepared only as a relocation site in case of WWIII or some other grave national emergency. The DEA had been offered the location for their office space and flatly rejected it as unfit. Since the contiguous space provided enough room to house all the BSU personnel together, it was renovated to create small offices.

The problem was one of serious fresh air and ventilation. The space was never designed to be used as offices, especially for dozens of people. The whole time the BSU staff were located there, the personnel suffered an inordinate amount of respiratory and sinus problems. Jim once told Assistant Director Tony Daniels that the BSU staff were so dedicated to their important work that they might not mind dying from hard work, but no one wanted to die because of an unhealthy work space. The profilers and adjunct staff met, discussed, and even had the air debris analyzed. But there was no significant relief while Jim was there through 1994. Dick Ault and Horn had offices across the hall from each other and were both diagnosed with asthma in 1992. Analyzed by the FBI lab, the dust was found to include rat hairs and a few unidentified elements. Horn, Campbell, and Ault, among others, didn't believe then, and still don't, that the FBI lab was unable to identify exactly what the so-called unidentified elements were.

While the work space left much to be desired, the academy was an unbelievable opportunity for all. The BSUers worked with the highest caliber people, were exposed to law enforcement people and experts from all over the world, and got to travel the country and free world spreading the word of their work and learning.

In 1985, Horn was assigned to the teaching side of the BSU and teamed with Jim Reese in his course, "Stress Management in Law Enforcement" or SMILE. At the time, Reese was working on his doctorate and when he started working on his dissertation, Horn took over the course from him for about two years. When he returned, they team-taught it.

Horn always felt that we do not wind up in places by accident, and in 1987 the real reason he was at the academy was realized. In 1983, during his first summer at Quantico, John Campbell had obtained permission from the director to study the effects of shooting incidents on agents. Horn had been teaching post-shooting trauma to police for several years, had spent time at the Wounded Knee and Pine Ridge specials, in addition to John's combat experience in Vietnam, and knew firsthand that the impact of such incidents could be devastating to the participants. Jack Coler, who was killed execution-style by Leonard Peltier at Pine Ridge on June 26, 1975, was a fellow Denver SWAT-team member who was in the wrong place at the wrong time, since he and fellow agents were on rotating assignments from Denver. When the Post–Critical Incident Seminars (PCIS) began, to Jim's utter disbelief, the Bureau's psychiatrist said Bureau agents were not affected by shooting incidents like the police. Agents were different. It only took the PCISs and their protocols to prove him wrong. This was just one of the examples of a mistake by a mental health professional that has made Jim take their opinions with a grain of salt.

Robert Schaefer inherited the PCISs in 1984 from John Campbell when John transferred to Butte to be a field supervisor. Bob was particularly skilled at the bureaucratic paperwork necessary to establish and advance the Critical Incident Program (CIP). Without the proper paper work, any program in a bureaucracy, especially the FBI, is doomed, and Bob did a superlative job in establishing CIP on paper. Jim supported Bob in the CIP and when Bob accepted a field supervisor's position in Norfolk in 1987, Jim was asked by John Otto to run the program. John asked Jim if he was up to the job. Jim responded, "John, you wouldn't believe the meaning this job gives to my life. I think the good Lord has been preparing me for this job for forty-two years." Jim had grown up in an alcoholic family, been hit by a car at fourteen while riding his motor scooter, had a ruptured appendix at nineteen, and somehow survived Vietnam. He knew he would be able to use his experiences at the training facility and he was right. Jim ran the CIP from 1987 to 1994 and used every single lesson learned from trauma in his life at one time or another to help support and validate other people.

Jim had written a policy for handling shooting for the Denver division in 1981 and his boss, Bill Gavin, was savvy to the needs of traumatized law enforcement officers and their families. He employed Jim as a peer counselor and sent him to respond to FBI and police shootings as well as domestic crises, such as FBI family automobile deaths. When Jim inherited the CIP, he knew the Bureau needed to help the staff deal with their shootings and other traumas. The efforts were predictably effective. But as a one-man army responding around the country, Jim was biting off more than one person could possibly chew. As Horn expected, Roger Depue supported his efforts, always finding ways to pay for his unplanned travel expenses. But not all of his colleagues supported his productive efforts from on-site responses, because not all were as psychologically secure as Depue. Ever-present jealousy kept Jim from getting unanimous support. "But that's human nature and I ignored it for what it was," said Jim years later.

The major personal lesson Jim learned from his on-site responses was that this work should *never* be done alone. He was physically, mentally, and emotionally exhausted by some of his efforts. The solutions were obvious. The first was to train a cadre of peers across the country to respond in their region as peer supporters. The first Advanced Peer Support In-Service was run for two weeks in 1989. With forty more trained in 1990, the BSU had eighty trained peers to help employees and their families deal with the traumas of life. Thus, for the first time, his load was shared.

In several of his on-site responses, the local police chaplains volunteered to help. Jim started seeking chaplains out on each site and always found them willing to assist in any way possible. After eighty years, it was time for the FBI to diversify its support base. Each PCIS collected and presented a list of issues and concerns for the Bureau leaders to consider for policy considerations. In fact, the whole CIP had been based on the suggestions of the PCIS participants. On April 7, 1989, the PCIS team met at FBI headquarters with director William

Sessions and recommended that the FBI establish a chaplains program. Sessions response was, "As a matter of fact, my father was a minister and I think it's a pretty good idea." Jim soon found the director did not rule with an iron fist or receive the full compliance of all his subordinates. Although a memo to establish an FBI Chaplains Program went through channels and was approved, all efforts to announce the program and recruit the first class of chaplains for training at the FBI Academy were smothered by upper-middle management at the Academy. Jim's communication to all field offices introducing the program and directing each office to select a local chaplain to serve as the field division chaplain languished in the front office at Quantico. The initial official memo to establish the FBI Chaplains Program had also been rat-holed somewhere, but Jeff Higginbotham, a Quantico agent who worked in the director's office, and former assistant director of the training division, made a call to Quantico about the whereabouts and status of the chaplains program memo. The memo was found and soon made its rounds through the necessary channels at headquarters. But the training scheduled for August 1990 never occurred because the communication was never sent out to the field offices. A new date was set for the inaugural FBI chaplains in-service for January 1991, but again Jim could not get the communication out of the front office. He was baffled. Because Jim knew the front office to be staffed by good people, it was obvious they had planned to scuttle the chaplains program all along despite official approval and authorization for the program.

Schaefer told Horn that he had gotten some of the necessary paperwork completed and approved by the back-door method. So Jim decided to fight fire with fire. He concluded that unless he found another way to broadcast the program and recruit volunteers to be chaplains, the program would never be born. Jim received valuable counsel and guidance from David DeRevere, executive director of the International Conference of Police Chaplains. Horn had planned all along to use the ICPC newsletter to help spread the word to chaplains about the new FBI program. He hoped to guide them in how to volunteer to be a FBI chaplain in each office once the official FBI communication went out to all the fields. Jim, seeing no other way to get the program initiated, decided to put the cart before the horse, knowing it would not be well received by some of the field office bosses. He announced the program in the ICPC newsletter and instructed any interested volunteers to contact their local field office. Some of the FBI SACs were understandably irate. They had only a few weeks to select a volunteer chaplain for their division and submit the name for the upcoming training session. It was not the best way to initiate such a program, but it worked, and in January 1991, Horn and his team trained fifty-five charter FBI chaplains. Two months later, an FBI chaplain saved the life of an agent who had suddenly become suicidal. Jim felt the program was now paid for in full and all the other good results would be icing on the cake.

A second in-service brought the number of FBI chaplains to over one hundred. To this day, what Jim appreciates the most was being able to establish a program which gave a new impetus to chaplaincy programs across the country. One of the special privileges and responsibilities of being assigned to the FBI Academy is that the programs there are models for all of law enforcement. "If the FBI has a chaplaincy program, or CIP peer support program, then why don't we?" Many agencies were starting to use the "separation of church and state" argument to justify not having a chaplains program, or severely reducing it. By establishing an FBI chaplains program under the strict guidelines of the FBI's Legal Counsel division, led by Joe Davis, separation of church and state became a moot point, and the tide against chaplains programs were turned. ICPC has since experienced rapid growth and development, still under the outstanding leadership of David DeRevere.

Several years of trauma is a lot of trauma, even when you're only responding to it. In September 1994, Jim had the opportunity to transfer back to his home state of Oklahoma, which seemed like a good way to transition away from all the trauma. After all, nothing ever happens in Oklahoma. Seven months later the bomb went off in Oklahoma City, creating traumas that few participants knew existed. Friends and colleagues questioned why Jim was leaving Virginia for Oklahoma. After the bombing, many called or sent Jim notes saying they now knew why he had transferred to Oklahoma: "That's where you are supposed to be!" Jim reflected, "We don't wind up where we are by accident, do we?"

NOT THE END BUT THE BEGINNING

In 1988, John Campbell returned from his assignment at FBI headquarters to become the unit chief of the Behavioral Science Unit. Meanwhile, during the next several years, John completed his Ph.D. dissertation, "A Comparative Analysis of the Effect of Post-Shooting Trauma on Special Agents of the Federal Bureau of Investigation." The purpose of the study was to evaluate the Post–Critical Incident Program of the FBI. Did the decade-long program provide the necessary resources for agents?

The mission of the FBI continued to require special agents to make split-second decisions whether to shoot or not to shoot. When an agent did shoot and kill, or was shot, the incident had an effect on the agent for the rest of his or her life. That effect, whether psychological, physical, or emotional, is defined as post-traumatic stress. John's Ph.D. study was essentially an evaluation of the FBI intervention program to address post-shooting trauma. The analysis compared the responses of two different groups, the first a group of special agents who had been involved in shootings between 1973 and 1983.

The second respondents were obtained through the use of a formal protocol or questionnaire completed after 1984. The initial group of agents did not have the benefit of the FBI's Post–Critical Incident Program and the second group were agents involved in serious shooting incidents who attended post–critical incident seminars and completed the questionnaire form during 1986 to 1989. Those agents received the benefits, organization, and individual attention of the program.

The findings of this study supported the value of the Post–Critical Incident Program. It identified not only positive and healthy adjustment trends, but also the significant reduction of negative behavioral patterns of adjustment after a shooting incident. The program reflected an organizational commitment to the special agents who have been put to the ultimate test. That program had evolved into a model for all of law enforcement. The value and success of the Post–Critical Incident Program as measured in this study was exemplary. It also became more than just a program for those employees that were involved in shooting incidents. It became a program for all of the employees of the Federal Bureau of Investigation who were suffering from critical incidents, tragedies, deaths, assaults, homicides, suicides, as well as shooting incidents.

These were some general recommendations that came from Dr. Campbell's study into post-shooting trauma. The first one revolved around a holistic approach to dealing with critical incident trauma. From a holistic point of view, only part of the traumatized family is provided this healing process. Documented throughout this research was the awareness and need of assistance for the spouse and other family members. If this was to be a systematic approach, a very important trait of that employee was not being provided assistance. Those individuals identified as a support group for agents involved, the families, also needed attention, care, nurturing, and an opportunity to participate in the healing process of the post–critical incident seminars. There were prohibitions that limited travel by the whole family or the family members who were also suffering from post–critical incident trauma, and it was felt that there would be a need to devise a way to provide the whole family with support. Members of the Behavioral Science Unit testified before Congress in legislation hearings chaired by Congresswoman Patricia Schroeder focusing on problems and issues confronting the police family. Concern of Police Survivors (COPS) recognized the extraordinary need to address the whole family as suffering from the event of a critical incident tragedy.

A second general recommendation that developed from the study surrounded the awareness that there is a second injury beyond the participant in the critical incident. The second injury could be defined as vicarious traumatization. Essentially, vicarious traumatization is a transfer of the trauma experienced by the victim to the caregiver. This was keenly obvious from the limited work performed by special agents of the Behavioral Science Unit as they dealt with the trauma and critical incidents throughout the agency. The impact on Jim Horn and Bob Schaefer, as well as John Campbell was measurable. Jim Horn was aware that the caregivers also needed a chance to debrief or face a burnout point in the long-term process. This study recognized that there was a need for a healthy evaluation through discussion, debriefing, and resolution of traumatic issues. The heightened sensitivity and enhanced empathy of all caregivers opened the individuals up to the traumatic experience. This vicarious impact could also be observed in health problems of the caregivers and also some of the health problems of the profilers who deal with tragedies and violence on a daily basis. John Douglas, the premier profiler, went through a near-death incident. Stress, violence, and tragedies have an impact on all of us. Exposure threatens everyone's well-being.

A third general observation was that there was a need for a formalized debriefing process following critical incidents experienced by the FBI. During the time of this study, when an employee of the FBI was involved in a shooting incident or accident, the determination to send out a peer support team was left to the discretion of the senior manager of that field office. Many times that senior manager was also affected by the trauma involving the individuals for whom he or she was directly responsible. The manager's decision could be clouded by those events that personally affected him or her at the time of the tragedy. By formally defining the role and responsibility of a post–critical incident team, the debriefing process and the need for the debriefing process could be measured, articulated, and supported.

Another very significant recommendation that grew from this study, as well as from the twentieth post–critical incident seminar held in April of 1989, was the need to establish an FBI chaplaincy program. The chaplaincy program, approved in 1991, has provided support and assistance during several shooting incidents, as well as numerous life tragedies of the employees of the FBI. The intervention by the chaplains in real life tragedies are too numerous to recount, but the resounding call for spiritual and practical support was exemplified by more than half of the agents who were involved in shooting incidents responding affirmatively to the statement "I was helped by my religious beliefs and/or practices." The success of the Bureau's initial steps in providing that helping hand was very directly attributable to the outstanding efforts provided by members of the Behavioral Science Unit, including John Mindermann, Jim Reese, John Campbell, Bob Schaefer, and Jim Horn. The FBI's Post–Critical Incident Program became recognized throughout the organization as being there in times of tragedy. It became a credit to those individuals who were supporting the program as program managers. It also became a focal point for the employees of the FBI to demand more services from their Employee Assistance Program. This became one of the significant challenges that confronted John Campbell when he replaced Roger Depue in 1988 as the unit chief of the Behavioral Science Unit. However, the perseverance, dedication, and caring demonstrated by the managers of the Post–Critical Incident Program provided the foundation for its success.

JAMES REESE

Jim Reese had graduated from Arkansas State University in 1968 with a bachelor's degree in social science. He went to Arkansas State for several reasons. His brother Ronald (who would later retire after twenty-seven years as an FBI agent) was there ahead of him and it was inexpensive. Their dad was a house painter in Miami, Florida, and due to his limited income, Ronald and Jim worked at odd jobs while going to school. The Reserve Officer Training Corps (ROTC) also paid $50 a month and it turned out to be just one more source of income for Jim.

Jim's first set of orders following his graduation and subsequent commission as an officer in the army made it clear that he would be spending a year in Vietnam. He arrived in Vietnam in April of 1969 and was immediately dispatched to IV Corps (Four Corps) which was, for the most part, the Mekong Delta. Upon bailing out of a Delta model "huey" helicopter in Ving Binh province, Jim was met by his sergeant. His greeting to Jim was, "Welcome aboard, Lieutenant Reese. The lieutenant you're replacing hit a mine. Follow me." Jim was scared. He led Jim back to the sandbagged compound that he would call home for the next three hundred sixty-one days. Little did Jim know that this would be the first in a long line of stress-related encounters that would shape his professional career and life.

More than one hundred ambushes and dozens of helicopter assaults later, Jim left the Republic of South Vietnam, glad to be alive. He had earned the United States Bronze Star, the National Defense Medal, the Republic of South Vietnam Campaign Medal, the United States Vietnam Campaign Medal as well as the Republic of South Vietnam Distinguished Service Cross. Upon his return Jim was determined to never work again for anyone who told him what to do, what to wear, or how to act. That thought didn't last long. America and J. Edgar Hoover needed FBI agents.

While assigned to Fort Gordon, Georgia, Jim applied to be an FBI agent. His older (and only) brother Ron had applied and been accepted and he encouraged him to apply. Jim drove from Fort Gordon to the FBI's field office in Savannah, Georgia, where he applied and was interviewed, fingerprinted, etc. All seemed to go well. Jim received an honorable discharge from the Army in November of 1970 and entered FBI training in Washington, D.C., in April of 1971. His life, as he was to know it for the next two decades and a half, had just begun. At the time, he had no idea where his future would take him. He was never sure what he wanted to be when he grew up, but he was pretty sure it wasn't this.

Following sixteen weeks of training Jim was assigned as a "first office" agent in the Albany, New York, field office, and after a few months, was transferred to the Syracuse, New York, resident agency. His few months in Albany would prove to be the only time in his Bureau career that he would spend working in a large field office around a lot of other agents. He was destined to work in small resident agencies prior to his Academy experience.

Jim met his wife, Sandra Patton of Falls Church, in August of 1971, while learning to be an agent in Washington, D.C. She lived in northern Virginia. After his transfer to Syracuse, New York, he returned to marry her in March of 1972. Interestingly, J. Edgar Hoover demanded to be informed when his agents were married, divorced, etc. Therefore, out of necessity, Jim drove through ice and snow from Syracuse to Albany in January of 1972 to tell the SAC in person of his impending marriage on March 7. A few weeks following their marriage, Jim was summoned to Albany by SAC Todd Jacobson and summarily chastised for not telling the SAC that he had gotten married. Although Jim knew he had told him just a few months prior, he had learned that being an SAC did not necessarily mean that you were endowed with wisdom or excessive attention to details. Also, during the Hoover years, there was no right and wrong when it came to superiors. What the boss said was gospel. He took his lumps, whether deserved or not, and got on with his life. Jim drove back to Syracuse without any scars or marks. Just a little dazed and confused regarding the unwarranted "time in the woodshed."

Jim worked general criminal matters while in Syracuse. During that first year, he received his first letter of commendation from the director due to his investigative efforts and the subsequent conviction of a bank robber. In August of 1972, he was transferred to the Springfield, Massachusetts, resident agency in the Boston division, where his daughter Jamie was born in 1977, and where he would stay until his transfer to the FBI Academy in January of 1978.

As early as 1974, Jim knew that he wanted to be a faculty member at the FBI Academy; he wanted to have a voice in training this nation's law enforcement elite and to learn the skills of a profiler and make a difference in the world. He had been training law enforcement officers in New England since his assignment to the Springfield, Massachusetts, resident agency in August of 1973. The training consisted of defensive tactics, crime scene searches, crime scene preservation, evidence collection, and other topics. He taught in Springfield, Chicopee, Holyoke, Amherst, Northhampton, Westfield, and other neighboring Massachusetts cities. For whatever reason, his critiques were consistently good. Getting good critiques didn't bolster his ego. It was already strong or he could never have stood in front of all of those experienced police officers and taught them. In fact, he learned early on that without a strong ego, the FBI Academy isn't a place you'll likely survive. The positive critiques did, however, give him some confidence to "try his wings" at the national level of training.

Springfield, Massachusetts, had become home to the Reese family. He worked for a senior agent named Walter Brady, perhaps the most colorful and interesting agent Jim ever met during his career. Jim applied and was accepted to the Master of Science program at American International College. In 1976, after going to classes nights and weekends while carrying a caseload of as many as one hundred cases at any one time, Jim graduated with a master's degree in criminal justice studies. His emphasis was on the law and social control of deviance. It was a long road for Sandy and Jim, but he knew that to be considered for the FBI Academy, an advanced degree was a necessity.

The same year, he applied to be a counselor for the FBI National Academy. This would require that he travel to Quantico, Virginia, and live at the Academy for eleven weeks, during which time he would help support fifty of the 250 police officers from around the world who were attending the National Academy. Seven months after Jamie was born, in September of 1977, Jim got his wish. He was assigned as a counselor to the 111th session of the FBINA (September to December).

During November 1977, while a counselor at the FBINA, Jim was offered a faculty position by Bob Martz in the Management Science Unit. The same day, Jack Pfaff, the unit chief of BSU, offered him a position in the Behavioral Science Unit. After careful consideration, Jim made the best move of his career; he accepted Mr. Pfaff's offer. Jim was to learn later that much of his acceptance was based upon his academic credentials, reputation as a police instructor, and (according to Bob Ressler) his time in the military and Vietnam.

Upon entry into the Behavioral Science Unit, Jim was paired with a man who was to be his friend and colleague for the next seventeen years, Dick Ault, who was a supervisory special agent in the unit. He had been there for several years prior to Jim's arrival and could have said no to the offer to mentor Jim. Jim is glad he didn't, because he was to learn a lot from Dick. He would not only mentor Jim in the unit, he would be one of the men who encouraged Jim to continue his education.

Dick and Roger Depue were enrolled in the doctoral program at American University (AU). Jim was interested in the program and had discussed it with Dick on several occasions. Jim didn't know where he would find the time, but he knew he wanted to continue learning. On a rainy day in the spring of 1980, Dick drove Jim to AU and personally introduced him to Dr. Bernard Hodinko, his dissertation chairman.

Dick's as well as Roger's endorsement of Jim as a likely candidate for the doctoral program helped a great deal towards his eventual admission.

Depue, a fellow instructor in the BSU, also encouraged his education. Jim entered the Ph.D. program in the summer of 1980. When his father passed away on December 5, 1980, Jim had to immediately leave for Miami. Roger unselfishly kept him current in class and helped him get through that semester. Dick and Roger were always there for him. Without their encouragement and the support of his family, Jim might not be Dr. Reese today.

Teaching in the Behavioral Science Unit was fun. There were days when he couldn't believe he was actually getting paid to do this. It was inspirational, almost recreational. On the operational side, BSU members were all trying their hand at profiling, learning from those who had experience in profiling and adding their opinions to their expertise. They had a great deal of respect for each other's opinions. They celebrated the profiles they got right and reviewed the misses so that they could improve their skills.

Jim was one of the profilers pictured in *Psychology Today*'s, "The Mindhunters." He had his successes and failures. His first attempt at profiling came from the South. A young lady had been found strangled and left nude. Jim's profile included the fact that whoever committed this crime would not show remorse or guilt when apprehended. To his dismay, the subject was apprehended and hung himself in his cell that night. Chalk one up to experience! Fortunately, Jim had plenty of successes, not the least of which was a serial rapist in Maryland. Police had been searching for this individual for more than two years. The police reports, area maps, interviews, etc., were brought to the FBI Academy by a detective. Jim's profile in that case led to the arrest of the rapist within a matter of a few weeks. A miss now and then didn't bother Jim. In fact, he never trusted a profiler who claimed to be batting .1000.

Aside from profiling, Jim became interested in a course that John Mindermann, Larry Monroe, and Roger Depue were teaching, "Contemporary Police Problems." Jim was teaching socio-psychological aspects of community behavior and advanced criminology. He also attended the Law Enforcement Hypnosis Institute, taught by the country's first ever, full-time police psychologist, Dr. Martin Reiser of the Los Angeles Police Department. He then became a deputy in the FBI's hypnosis program.

Jim's first "road schools" were with Bob Ressler in Atlanta, John Douglas in Boise, Idaho, Dick Ault in Oklahoma City, and Howard Teten in Little Rock, Arkansas, and Lincoln, Nebraska. During the school in Lincoln, Howard informed Jim on the morning of the third day that he had slept through a tornado the night before. He got a kick out of the fact that Jim either didn't hear the tornado warnings or chose to ignore them. Howard was a fine gentlemen to travel and teach with.

Howard had a way of making his audience "get into the subject with him," and then he would release them to think on their own with new knowledge and energy. Teaching beside him was intimidating at times to say the least. On one occasion when Jim was teaching with him, Howard simply gave Jim his notes and slides during one of the instructional breaks and told Jim to "take it." Jim recalled teaching the class while watching Bud Teten's head as he sat in the back of the room. Thank God his head was moving up and down most of the time.

Jim admitted that profiling, looking at crime after crime, became burdensome. He did not relish the thought of looking at dead and disfigured bodies for the rest of his career. After all, he had almost twenty years left before he could retire. Jim had seen enough of that stuff firsthand in Vietnam. Now it was being fed to him in pictures from law enforcement officers who were trying to solve crimes. Teaching, on the other hand, was exciting. Although he was one of the original "Mind Hunters," it was never really "his thing." On the other hand, teaching profiling skills, as well as exploring ways to deal with the stress profiling created, and law enforcement stress in general, excited Jim immeasurably.

During 1979, Jim was assigned to teach at a homicide/profiling school near Newport News, Virginia. He was staying at Fort Monroe with his wife and daughter, who had come along for the sake of being with him. After teaching all day and retiring in their room for the night, the phone rang about 11:00 P.M. It was the deputy chief of the Newport News Police Department, a man who had been a student in his class that day. He reported that the body of a young woman had been found in a motel room in Newport News. She had been shot in the stomach with a high-powered rifle. The body was handcuffed (apparently post mortem) and the door to the motel room was barricaded from the inside. She was a manager in housekeeping and apparently surprised the murderer when she entered the room. The murderer had escaped through a rear bathroom window and fled into the woods behind the motel (see chapter 1).

Jim was taken to the scene and asked to do a profile, or assessment of the subject. Jim was not a weathered veteran at this profiling stuff but he had done many of them. He had been teaching the deputy chief that day about homicides and people who kept diaries and the like. The subject had left a diary and a sea bag full of clothes at the motel room. The diaries provided psycholinguistic clues (taught by Dr. Murray Miron) concerning the identity of the subject.

Because Jim was about to cause an entire police department to engage in a tactical course of action, he called another member of the unit to obtain a confirmation, rejection, or alteration of his findings. He called John Douglas, who was able to provide more information based on what Jim told him of the case.

They decided that it was not a good idea to go into the woods at night. The subject either was or had been a Marine and probably mentally ill. While not qualified to diagnose, they believed him to be a paranoid schizophrenic based upon the writings found in the diaries in his sea bag. They had learned however, not to label people with mental health terms. Therefore, the profiles simply described the individuals and their expected behavior.

Jim suggested the police wait for the first light of the morning to enter the woods. He emphasized that they should continue during the night to call him out with bullhorns but that he would not surrender. He did not. A suggestion was made to use helicopters to "light up" the area. Jim recommended that they not do that due to his paranoia and delusional thinking about Vietnam.

The profile worked, and perhaps some officers are alive today because of it. The director of the FBI gave Jim a letter of commendation for his efforts. Jim thanked John Douglas more than once for his confirmation of his opinions and his additional information.

In the same year, and not long after the Newport News case, Special Agent Anthony Rider and Jim traveled to Jacksonville, Florida, to teach an advanced criminology school. During the week they were there, Tony arranged for them to interview Arthur Frederick Goode III. Goode was a child killer who was incarcerated at Raeford State Prison in Starkville, Florida, awaiting execution.

They interviewed him for six hours about his homosexual, homicidal behaviors with his victims. Ken Lanning was and is the expert in this area. They were merely trying to establish motives, etc. While Jim didn't expect to see any remorse, what he did see surprised him. A cold, calculated response to even the most sensitive questions regarding the murders. Upon leaving the cell, Goode reinforced what they knew about psychopathic behavior. In an effort to assert his ego and recapture control at the last minute, he asked them, "Do you have any little boys at home?"

Goode was executed in Florida's electric chair, "Sparky," without showing remorse, guilt, or pity for any of his victims or their parents. Interviews like this taught them more than any textbook could have ever taught them. Jim thanked Bob Ressler for initiating the unit's interest in interviewing incarcerated criminals. Bob was doing it long before everyone else agreed that it should be done.

Following that interview of Goode, and upon attempting to leave the prison that night, Tony and Jim had to pass through two very high containment wire fences. The guards had taken their guns upon their initial entry so they were unarmed. As soon as they were locked in between the two fence gates, they were caught in a volley of live rifle fire from a guard in a tower.

They learned later that, during their exit from the prison, three "lifers" used smoke bombs for distraction and mattresses for protection from the barbed wire to climb over the fences. They were running for freedom just twenty yards from where Jim and Tony were trying to exit. They immediately retrieved their guns and spent the rest of the night helping the deputies and police look for the escapees. Tony and Jim agreed later that they were quite concerned while lying on their stomachs with bullets whizzing over our heads. Jim remembers stating to someone, "We would have gotten down lower to the ground but we had buttons on our shirts!"

By 1981 Jim had moved away from applied criminology and began taking an interest in John Mindermann's work. His class incorporated the concepts of stress in law enforcement. John had been a cop and brought a great deal of credibility to the classroom. When it was learned that John would become a supervisor in the San Francisco office of the FBI, his class was "up for grabs." Jim made a bid and was given a chance to teach stress. Jim then developed a course with Mindermann's course as the foundation. Jim named it S.M.I.L.E. (Stress Management in Law Enforcement). The SMILE course is still a three-hour undergraduate course at the University of Virginia and is still being taught at the FBI National Academy. He would encourage it as a requirement.

In 1982 another event gave his career in stress management more credibility. Jim applied to be selected as the FBI's exchange faculty member at the Police Staff College, Bramshill, Hampshire, England. With the overwhelming endorsement and eloquent support of Roger Depue, then the unit chief, Jim was selected to go to Bramshill.

Bob Shaefer unselfishly took on the task of teaching the stress class single-handed so Jim could go to England. He was a gifted instructor and because of his skills and popularity, Jim wondered if he would ever be able to snatch the course back from him.

Upon his return it was business as usual, trying to teach, travel, parent, and finish his Ph.D. by 1987. Jim earned a Doctor of Philosophy degree in counseling and human development. With these credentials and his experience, Jim was able to provide expert testimony on law enforcement stress to the United States Congress as well as address the President Bush Council on Integrity and Efficiency. These were proud moments for Jim and he was proud to be a FBI agent and a member of the Behavioral Science Unit.

All the support Jim gained and the experiences he had allowed his confidence to grow, his energy to swell, and his desire to learn seemed unbridled. Jim asked to conduct an international conference on psychological services in law enforcement. He was given permission for that and four others within the next seven years. They accounted for five books, the "bibles" of law enforcement psychology. These works, edited by Jim and others, contain the work of some of the best police officers, police psychologists, mental health professionals, chaplains, and employee assistance providers of the time. They are something Jim was able to leave behind to assist those who would follow.

Replacing an Icon

In 1988, Roger Depue became eligible for retirement from the FBI. Folks reaching retirement age and eligibility had a saying in the Bureau, that one gained entry into the KMA (kiss my ass) club. It was also expressed by saying that one had become "bullet proof," meaning that the Bureau could not hurt you much anymore, because if you didn't like the way things were going you could put in your retirement papers and leave it all behind.

Roger's career in the Bureau had been very rewarding and he felt no pressure to leave it. In 1985, they had established the National Center for the Analysis of Violent Crime (NCAVC) and things were finally going as they had hoped for so many years. The Behavioral Science Unit (BSU) had split into two units; the BSIRU and the BSISU. Roger served as the administrator of the NCAVC and the chief of the BSIRU, and Alan "Smokey" Burgess became the deputy administrator of the NCAVC and unit chief of the BSISU. Smokey had had no previous experience in FBI behavioral sciences but was a competent administrator of a fine staff of persons who did have the requisite knowledge.

It was at this time Roger began to think about the private sector. They had just created an applied forensic behavioral science resource for the public sector, the criminal justice community. It was a place for investigators, prosecuting attorneys, judges, and corrections officials to go for assistance with perplexing crimes and baffling criminal behaviors. NCAVC was a national clearinghouse for the unusual, bizarre, serial, and particularly violent crimes, a place which studied these more rare crimes and behaviors and professed to understand them in order to assist authorities to analyze and explain them, identify perpetrators, locate and apprehend them, successfully prosecute the cases, and convict and incarcerate the offenders. The Violent Criminal Apprehension Program (VICAP) was a subunit supervised by Pierce Brooks, which had the task of feeding into the computer all unsolved homicides (and eventually other violent crimes) so that they could be compared with other crimes on file for the purpose of linking unsolved cases together, and to identify unsolved cases where BSU expertise might be helpful in identifying a culprit and planning various investigative strategies. There was also a subunit called Arson Information Management System headed by Dr. David Icove, which applied BSU expertise to crimes of fire-setting as well as housing Icove's computerized system to analyze a series of arson cases in order to determine where the next arson would likely take place, and where the perpetrator might live or work in relation to the series of fires.

Roger observed that there was nothing like NCAVC in the private sector. In the world of corporate security, private investigation, civil law, etc., there was no forensic behavioral science resource. They had to do what the public criminal justice community had to do prior to the NCAVC, turn to mental health professionals, who often had little or no experience as criminal investigators. Most mental health professionals do not examine in great detail the crimes which a perpetrator has committed. The BSU had learned that the best insights into a criminal's personality came from his actual crime scenes. The crime scene represented his most important project, his most revealing behavior, his most serious effort to turn his fantasy into reality. To fail to look at his actual crime scene is to deny his expression of personality.

Roger reasoned that if he had played a role in the FBI in establishing the NCAVC, then why could he not establish a national forensic behavioral science resource for the private sector? He called a meeting to discuss the idea with two of his associates: Conrad V.

Hassel, former (retired) chief of the FBI Special Operations and Research Unit, and Bertram Brown, M.D., former director of the National Institute of Mental Health (1970–1978). They each responded to the idea with enthusiasm. The Academy Group, Inc. (AGI) was born in 1989.

There was a disproportionate number of former Marines in the BSU over the years. Roger recalls Jim Siano, Al Whitaker, Howard Teten, Larry Monroe, Con Hassel, Tom Strentz, Dick Ault, Jim Horn, Joe Conley, John Campbell, Smokey Burgess, and himself. Marines have great *esprit de corps* and allegiance to their outfit. Roger believes that's one reason the unit stuck together so well during tough times when management never knew if an assault team might be directed to take over the head shed.

Based on Depue's decision to retire and form the Academy Group, John Campbell was selected as the unit chief of the Behavioral Science Unit in the summer of 1989. John took an unusual route to that assignment. He was previously in the Behavioral Science Unit from 1980 to 1984 and then transferred out to Butte, Montana. In the FBI, if an individual is assigned to the Butte division, it is generally a disciplinary transfer. In John's case, he went out as a supervisor. He was told when he arrived in Butte that there was little work, but it was a great place for hunting and fishing. What exploded in the Butte division over the next six months turned out to be the first look in this country at the Aryan Nation violence. That particular investigation went on for approximately two years, with multiple convictions achieved in the Seattle division.

John was summoned back to FBI headquarters and again his paths crossed with John Otto, the deputy director of the FBI at that time. Otto was responsible for the Executive Career Board, which essentially made the selections for all of the managerial positions in the FBI. Directly under John Otto was a position entitled the Executive Secretary of the Career Board. One of John Campbell's friends was serving in this assignment in 1986 and 1987, and convinced John to opt for it. He was transferred back to Washington, D.C., and worked directly for Mr. Otto for more than two years. Depue and John Otto retired during that same time frame. John approached Otto with a request to be transferred laterally to the unit chief of the Behavioral Science Unit as a career development transfer. This was an unusual request, because generally the individuals who worked and were assigned as the executive secretary of the Career Board were then transferred back out to the field as assistant special agent in charge. Otto considered Campbell's request and, ultimately, the career board approved the transfer.

Campbell recognized that there were significant challenges and opportunities confronting him as unit chief. His peers would now be his subordinates and in fact, Dick Ault, who had trained John, was the acting unit chief and demonstrated a remarkable talent for getting things done. Ault remained one of John's closest allies and associates and contributed significantly over the next several years to the accomplishments of the BSU and the NCAVC. The position of the Behavioral Science unit chief also carried with it a collateral title of administrator of the NCAVC. The senior unit chief at that time was Smokey Burgess, so he was the administrator and Campbell was the deputy administrator of the NCAVC.

One of the challenges that confronted Campbell was that there was a prevailing attitude of "I'm doing my own thing," or "I versus we." Some of that had to do with individual expertise rather than what was necessary, appropriate, and needed by the Behavioral Science Unit. It evolved to what was necessary and appropriate for the individuals and that was one of the areas that John was required to address. In fact, it became readily apparent that the style Campbell used was a "we versus I" way of dealing with issues, problems, challenges, and training responsibilities. All of the agents were thus required to provide a block of training for the new agents, including some of the experts like Roy Hazelwood. Roy had for numerous years been exempt from training the new agents, but once he had that opportunity he commented on how much he enjoyed working with the new agents.

Some of the other challenges that loomed as John took over the Behavioral Science Unit was a confrontation with the FBI's Employee Assistance Program (EAP). There was a deep dissatisfaction organizationally as to the quality of service being provided by the EAP and many of the coordinators and persons involved in providing services throughout the FBI, particularly in the field offices, felt that they weren't being provided necessary training nor support to effectively perform as representatives of the EAP. They had previously approached Roger Depue and a series of meetings was held at Quantico with representatives from the EAP, the BSU, the training division, administrative services division, and personnel as to the best possible recourse for providing services to those in need throughout the FBI.

This was one huge issue that Campbell was thrown into. He developed an understanding and appreciation for what an effective Employee Assistance Program was to provide. That development came through numerous contacts with representatives of employee assistance programs, not only within the federal structure but within the private sector, including IBM, Anheuser-Busch, and a number of other major corporations. A series of very strong recommendations were completed by the training division that suggested that the FBI consolidate the Employee Assistance Program and the Psychological Services Program and that the new entity be transferred to the training division, because training was a main objective of the Employee Assistance Program. The training division, particularly the Behavioral Science Unit, was equipped to provide all the necessary training both at the Academy and in the field. Experienced instructors were presently on board with professional expertise and knowledge to address training for management personnel and employee assistance counselors.

The second reason for the recommendation included research. The training division was internationally known for the quality of its research staff in the Behavioral Science Unit, who were well aquainted with all the facets of professional research. Evaluation was a requirement for continued excellence in training. Other assets provided by the training division included organizational structure and manpower. The training division, particularly the Behavioral Science Unit, was staffed with counselors with international reputations as well as credibility among FBI employees. Another asset was the operational experience of the training division, particularly in running critical incidents, peer support, and stress awareness programs. They were perceived by employees of the FBI as contributing to the general health and welfare of the employees. Another aspect that was recognized—it was, in fact, the hallmark of the Behavioral Science Unit—was innovation. The Behavioral Science Unit maintained a position at the cutting edge of law enforcement, training, and program implementation.

The recommendations put together by Campbell and his staff lit a fire. They were sent up to Floyd Clark, who was then the deputy director of the FBI, and created a tremendous turmoil at FBI headquarters, resulting in several very contentious meetings with the personnel division. Those meetings evolved to the point of a joint recommendation to the director of the FBI to upgrade the EAP to provide sufficient staff and resources to make that program the best program in the federal government and to elevate that program in status and visibility for employees of the FBI. From that struggle and from very difficult times came significant support for employees of the FBI, and that was a win for everybody.

There were several other issues that were initially required to be addressed by the unit chief of the BSU. One was the revitalizing of the exchanges with institutions of excellence. John initiated a faculty exchange between Michigan State University and the NCAVC. The interaction between the institutions over several previous years had revealed the possibility of mutual benefits to be derived from the faculty exchanges, resulting in the sharing of research and expertise. Both organizations possessed unique skills to support their respective missions. They had to go to resources and personnel to conduct research, training, and instruction in a broad field of criminal justice. The pilot exchange took place in March of 1990 and Supervisory Special Agent Robert Ressler from the NCAVC was the first participant. John strategically used that to keep Bob aboard for another six months. Bob was a graduate of the Michigan State undergraduate program, and by offering him the opportunity, John secured a commitment from Bob to stay with the Behavioral Science Unit at least six more months after he completed the exchange.

Very strong support and participation in this faculty exchange was received from Dr. Robert Trojanowicz, an expert in community policing. He contributed significantly to numerous conferences held at the training division and served as an ex-official advisor to both Roger Depue and John Campbell. Dr. David Carter was another member of the staff of Michigan State and the first Michigan State representative to participate in the exchange. A member of the Behavioral Science Unit who participated was Campbell himself, who used that exchange period to complete his Ph.D. dissertation.

"Doing your own thing" was a pervasive attitude with some of the members of the NCAVC and eventually evolved to a more separate approach toward criminal profiling. The training and research was primarily the responsibility of the Behavioral Science Unit; Criminal Investigative Analysis, VICAP, and the Arson and Bombing Investigative Services became the Investigative Support Unit. Needless to say, several members of the Behavioral Science Unit were not only experts at Quantico, but national and international experts in their particular fields. That included Ken Lanning, Roy Hazelwood, Bob Ressler, Al Brantley, and a number of other members of the staff. Brantley was the first instructor in the Behavioral Science Unit to take over a class and get the highest possible evaluations. He also conducted research and developed a course on gangs. He completed other research in the area of dangerousness and his background as a correctional counselor provided him with tremendous insight into the criminal mind.

During his tenure as unit chief Campbell had to deal with diverse personalities. One of the members of the unit, Tom Strentz, (who retired before Campbell took over) was halfway around the world in Australia or New Zealand when he decided that he was going to retire and send in his badge and credentials. Another personality who required understanding and the ability to motivate was Bill Tafoya, who was on assignment to the Congressional Clearinghouse of the Future, a think tank for Congress. A number of other members of the Behavioral Science Unit who performed in an outstanding manner were Joe Conley, a national expert in terrorism; Joe Harpold, a crime prevention and community policing specialist; Roy Hazelwood, internationally known for his work, research, and training in sexual assaults; Jim Horn, who coordinated the Bureau's Critical Incident/Peer Support Program as well as the FBI chaplain's program; Ken Lanning, internationally known for his work on the sexual exploitation of children; Jim Reese, whose course "Stress Management In Law Enforcement" (SMILE) was overwhelmingly recognized as one of the top courses at the training division; Bob Ressler, with research and training in serial murder; and Ed Sulzbach, the best known, best liked agent in the state of Virginia for his work as training coordinator in the Richmond division. Art Westveer was also in the unit, an experienced homicide investigator who also taught death investigation. The unit chief's secretary was Bernadette Cloniger. There were a number of other significant employees within the unit, including Cindy Lent, a technical information specialist who coordinated much of the research and writing within the unit, as well as the intern program. There were several training technicians, including Connie Dodd and Beth Griffin.

Replacing an Icon

It was an extraordinary unit and an extraordinary time. In the 1990 annual report for the NCAVC, Campbell stated that in the nineties, crimes were going to be more complex and "the law enforcement profession is more complex and more dangerous than ever before. . . . The violence and turbulent years are upon us. That turbulence has directly impacted the entire Criminal Justice system. The courts are choked with violent cases. Overcrowded prisons have become the norm. Crime and violence have become media events. Violence coupled with fear breeds more violence."

Efforts to address violent crimes by the FBI were characterized by innovation, adaptation, and commitment of resources. In response to President George Bush's comprehensive program to combat the escalation of violent crime, FBI director William S. Sessions established crimes of violence as a national priority. In the FBI, this elevation mandates expanded resources to meet the challenges of violence in our society.

Dr. Sessions's initiative continued to support the efforts of the NCAVC. With the inclusion of the Special Operations and Research Unit in the NCAVC, it was strengthened with another training, research, and operational area.

"Challenges to address violent crime were taken very seriously by members of the NCAVC, the SOARS Unit, the Investigative Support Unit, and the Behavioral Science Unit. Much of the research, much of the consultation, much of the training was focused specifically on the issues of violence," said Campbell. Solutions were exemplified by the center's research activities, including multidisciplinary studies on serial and violent crimes such as homicide, rape, sexual sadism, child abduction, arson, threats, computer crime, and counterespionage matters as well as highjacking, crisis management, and areas related to hostage negotiation and special weapons and tactics operation.

One of the initiatives taken by Campbell and the Behavioral Science Unit was in establishing an internship program. Cindy Lent supervised and coordinated it with a number of the universities, initially in Virginia. The FBI has had a long-standing intern program, referred to as the "Honors Intern," which selects talented students from all over the country to participate in different units throughout FBI headquarters. Those positions are paid positions. Campbell, in coordination with Cindy Lent, prepared a memorandum explaining the value and need for a year-round intern program which provided talented students with an opportunity to participate with world experts in the Behavioral Science Unit. This initial coordination was with the University of Virginia, Radford University, and Mary Washington University, and has since expanded to major participants from all over the country.

During the late 1980s and 1990, the NCAVC supported the Police Fellowship Program. It also offered a fellowship in criminal investigative analysis to selected police investigators. The fellowship was approximately ten months long and training was provided at no cost to the individual agency other than salary and benefits. The first three months of the fellowship were devoted to intensive training and academic programs designed to prepare the attendees for the second, practical phase of the fellowship. The second phase of the program involved having the officers analyze and consult on ongoing, unsolved crimes of violence. The fellowship was discontinued after 1990 because of financial reasons, the challenge of finding space, and the tremendous challenges that were confronting the NCAVC for human resources to work on cases and conduct research.

During this time, the NCAVC was conducting research into violent crime from a law enforcement perspective, attempting to gain insight into criminal thought processes, motivations, and behavior. The research was needed to learn how violent criminals committed their crimes repeatedly, successfully evading detection, apprehension, and incarceration. The research involved examining the crimes associated with particular criminals as well as developing history and background. Special agents and staff of the BSIRU, SOARS, and the BSISU conducted extensive interviews of incarcerated criminals using research protocols. The insights gained through this research were refined into innovative investigative techniques and applied to case-work to increase law enforcement effectiveness against violent criminals. The research activities of the NCAVC during the period of 1989 to 1992 included aircraft highjacking, arson and bombing, artificial intelligence, chemical, biological, and emergency response teams, child abduction/molesters, computer crime, infant abduction, homicide by poisoning, crime classification manual, crisis negotiation assessment scales, less-than-lethal weapon research projects, mechanical breaching research, murders of abducted children, nuclear emergency search teams, observer/sniper research project, serial rape, sexual assault against the aging, sexual sadism, geography of rape, computer crime, and community policing.

Ken Lanning took over a floundering research project focused on serial child molestation and abduction. He worked directly with the National Center for Missing and Exploited Children and the University of Pennsylvania and produced a series of exemplary, case-in-point publications focusing on child abduction and child molestation. This project had been headed for failure before Ken took it over and managed the money, while producing high-quality results. This was an example of the quality of research being conducted by the NCAVC at that time.

Throughout this period, numerous members of the faculty and staff of the National Center and the individual units were participating in faculty development programs. Many completed master's degrees and Campbell completed his Ph.D. Members of the different units, during 1989–1992, were called upon to provide expert witness testimony on an increasingly frequent basis. In previous years, testimony was primarily offered during the sentencing phase of proceedings, but NCAVC experts began to be asked to testify during the trial phase as well. The agents who testified as expert witnesses included Roy Hazelwood, John Douglas, Ken Lanning, Bob Ressler, and John Campbell (on deadly force).

In 1990, *Silence of the Lambs* was completed at the FBI Academy by Orion Pictures. The media attention surrounding it created a significant interest in issues of violence and the Behavioral Science Unit. Bob Ressler, John Douglas, and John Campbell had an opportunity to review the film script and had made extensive and numerous recommendations, specifically to make it more realistic and less offensive to law enforcement. The producers disregarded all of the recommendations except for one: In the script, the unit chief's last name was Campbell. Douglas, Ressler, and Campbell persuaded the producers to change the name, but none of the other changes were made.

In 1990, Smokey Burgess retired from the FBI. Burgess was responsible for the Behavioral Science Investigative Support Unit and was replaced by John Douglas, an extraordinary profiler who was responsible for many of the initiatives in criminal investigative analysis. Douglas attempted to professionalize the case files and the file review process, and better organize the many research projects. He was responsible for the Criminal Investigative Analysis subunit, the Violent Crime Apprehension Program, and the Arson and Bombing Investigation subunit. He was undoubtedly the very best criminal profiler in the NCAVC, but his management style, at times, created tensions and interactions between the units that were unnecessary or counterproductive. Those tensions surrounded who was handling different cases, particularly with the expertise of Roy Hazelwood and Ken Lanning as well as Al Brantley, who had transferred from the Investigative Support unit. Many of these individuals carried cases of extraordinary value and consequence. One of those particular cases had to do with USS *Iowa* (see chapter 10). Hazelwood and Ault were criticized for their conclusions by members of the NCAVC though they had done their job appropriately and with the professionalism that they always demonstrated.

Replacing an Icon

When the units were split and criminal profiling was moved out of the Behavioral Science Unit, it was the beginning of the end of an era. Members of the NCAVC and, in particular, the Investigative Support unit, were always contending with managerial decisions of the training division. Many times those decisions focused on the fact that the training division was just that: for training and not for operations. A continued challenge to many of the units was why they were conducting operational consultations or providing services other than training. This also affected initiatives in the Behavioral Science Unit, particularly those programs evolving around critical incidents. Whether there was a death, shooting incident, a suicide, or a tragedy, members of the Behavioral Science Unit accompanied Peer Support. Those coordinators in many of the field offices were individuals who had gone through the two-week, peer support in-service, had personally been involved in critical incidents, and were there with members of the Behavioral Science Unit to provide a "helping hand."

The whole operational entity of the NCAVC was continually challenged by managers within the training division as well as FBI headquarters. There was no question of the quality of the service or of the experts involved, but at the same time, the challenges came from the different divisions, in part because the training division, the NCAVC, and BSU were receiving attention that was somehow perceived as diminishing the reputations of these other divisions. In other words, they were jealous, but that attention was well deserved. Many of the members of the staff had established national and international reputations. Their publications and research set a standard for all of law enforcement.

One of the first initiatives that John Campbell undertook when he became unit chief was to establish several consulting contracts. Contracts had already been in existence with Dr. and Mrs. Soskis and Campbell also initiated a contract with Dr. Park Elliot Dietz. Dr. Dietz was an internationally recognized forensic psychiatrist who had followed the steps of American misfits and monsters for twenty-five years. He founded the Threat Assessment Group in 1987 and had worked with many members of the Behavioral Science Unit. His specialty focused on forensic psychiatry and psychology, criminology, behavioral science techniques, and criminal investigation with regard to violent criminal or mentally disordered behavior by employees, former employees, and the public. Another contract that John set up was with Roger Depue and AGI. The third group of contracts included contracts with Dr. James Luke, forensic pathologist, and Dr. Ann Burgess, who assisted John Douglas and Bob Ressler as well as numerous members of the Behavioral Science Unit in their writing and publishing careers. Another significant contributor, as far as writing and research, was Janet Warren of the University of Virginia.

Any time there was anything to do with violence, violent behavior, or violence perpetrated by individuals, the FBI was asked to tackle it. The media was, at times, challenging. Dealing with the media became a full-time occupation for many of the staff of the Behavioral Science Unit and the NCAVC. It was said that some of the staff, when they opened a refrigerator and the light came on, would give a news commentary. At the same time, the media attention was taking the heat and absorbing the tension of much of the general public. The Bureau was able to operate without significant criticism. This was the explanation by many of the top officials as to why they allowed the media to interject themselves so continually and constantly into the work of the Behavioral Science Unit and the National Center for the Analysis of Violent Crime.

Attracting even more media attention were the significant number of publications being completed by members of the NCAVC, particularly those in the Behavioral Science Unit. Ken Lanning had numerous publications on satanism, child molestation, and child sex rings. Dick Ault presented papers on hypnosis. Park Dietz, Roy Hazelwood, and Janet Warren conducted research on sexual sadism and published articles in law enforcement and referee journals. Roy Hazelwood focused on classifying geographic patterns of serial rape. Tafoya wrote *Future Research Implications for Criminal Investigators*. Jim Reese worked with a number of editors and completed publications on critical incidents in law enforcement. Ann Burgess coordinated work with Ken Lanning and others, looking at child molesters who abduct. The publications were numerous, and the exciting research resulted in knowledge for law enforcement, investigators, and prosecutors who were seeking ways to deal with serial offenders, critical incidents, and issues of violence and victims. It was a "golden age" for the Behavioral Science Unit. Not only was the NCAVC recognized, but the members of the units received attention from law enforcement on a national and international basis. It also was a good time for securing grants, conducting research, publishing, and working on case consultation.

In July of 1992, Campbell was offered a promotion to assistant special agent in charge in the Omaha division. It was a very difficult decision to make. The assignment as unit chief in the Behavioral Science Unit was extraordinarily rewarding, educating, and challenging. However, Omaha was attractive to John because his oldest son, Sean, had decided on a career in meteorology and he was pursuing his undergraduate degree at Creighton University in Omaha. It was with some mixed feelings that John accepted the promotion and left the Behavioral Science Unit, though it wasn't his last opportunity to work with and be part of the training division.

12 Rider's Reign

he BSU has been subterranean since its inception, except for a short period in the 1980s when the unit was moved to the main floor of the Forensic Science Building at the FBI Academy. The unit was located in the basement of the Academy's library, later to be known as the Learning Resource Center. The space was cold, stark, and barren in appearance. Tony came to the unit in mid-1978 after a special assignment at FBI headquarters under the executive assistant to the director. Generally, BSU instructors shared cubicles that afforded no privacy and were less than optimal for serious research or quiet thinking. Tony went to the upper floors of the library to do his writing or to have one-on-one discussions with National Academy students. There was always loud talk among colleagues and interruptions by students and visitors in the BSU, but that was the nature of the unit. It seemed to promote uncommon camaraderie, and produced a sense of exclusivity among its inhabitants. There was always excitement in sharing ideas, cases, and investigative experiences. Bantering was commonplace and drew the BSU closer together. Everyone had a fervor for expressing their own points of view, as well as thinking in creative ways. One could not be thin-skinned and survive the often blunt and critical discourse that went on. The BSU was building bodies of knowledge in special areas and welcomed critical discussion and challenge. In short, members of the BSU had fun and were unruly.

Tony was certified by the University of Virginia to teach many National Academy courses. As the instructor for applied criminology, he wrote two study guides for the course. One was quite extensive and focused on a review of criminological theory. The second was even longer and was a comprehensive overview of the dynamics of human behavior and how mental illness, emotional instability, and personality defects may be expressed in crime. Tony used these study guides to supplement his NA course instruction. He also taught a new agents block in behavioral science. Several BSU instructors alternated in teaching new agents.

Tony's favorite colleague and self-selected mentor was Russ Vorpagel. He was extraordinary in his knowledge and skill in profiling psychopathology in crime scenes. Russ also had a distorted sense of humor, was a nonconformist, and continually played jokes on his NA students in the classroom; for example, pretending to commit suicide in front of his students. Tony was assigned to the same cubical in the BSU and Russ graciously shared his experiences and tutored Tony as a fledgling member of the unit.

THE FIRESETTER: A PSYCHOLOGICAL PROFILE

On December 12, 1979, Vice President Walter F. Mondale announced a new administration program to combat arson in the United States. The goals of this program were to coordinate federal anti-arson efforts, improve data collection and research, upgrade arson laboratory capabilities, eliminate economic incentives for arson, and provide training for arson investigators. During December 17–20 of 1979, the FBI Academy hosted a National Symposium on economic arson, sponsored by the FBI and the Law Enforcement Assistance Administration (LEAA), which was attended by over 170 persons. Four of the five seminars held during this symposium included topics on economic arson intelligence, advanced techniques in economic arson, investigative problems of fire scene investigation, and analytical investigative methods. Tony Rider conducted the fifth seminar, which was on the psychodynamics of arson for profit. This had been no easy task to research and to prepare, especially with the time constraints Tony had to operate under.

BSU instructors, who were devoting attention to profiling at that time, were focusing primarily on homicide, rape, and sexual assault cases. No one had focused on arson. Sometime during the middle of 1979, John Velier, an FBI instructor assigned to a different unit at the Academy, approached the BSU and solicited unit participation in an upcoming, interagency symposium on arson. Tony decided to take on the challenge because the unit did not have a body of knowledge on the subject and arson had become a national investigative priority. He believed there needed to be research available that would aid fire and law enforcement investigators in understanding the psychological aspects of firesetting. Larry Monroe, now BSU unit chief, sanctioned the project. However, there was no lessening of any of Tony's other duties. He taught National Academy courses and new agent classes, and also participated in field police training while attempting to research this new area. BSU instructors generally carried multiple responsibilities and conducted research and profiling on the side to acquire more depth of knowledge and experience regarding psychopathology in violent crime.

This was not a formal or sophisticated research project, and no funding was allocated to support it. Basically, Tony had about six months to conduct a literature review of existing scholarly research and publications on arsonists, synthesize the materials, and develop useful information that would assist arson investigators in identifying suspected arsonists, understanding their motivations and associated behaviors, and interviewing arsonists. Most of his research was initially conducted between class assignments, at night, and on weekends because of his other required duties. This proved to be awkward, consuming, and difficult to sustain along with all his other work. Nevertheless, Tony was able to synthesis a considerable volume of existing literature on the subject, identify and construct a number of firesetting profiles, and begin to draft a handout paper for possible presentation to symposium attendees. As the symposium date neared, he realized he would be unable to finalize any paper in time to meet the deadline. Consequently, Tony redirected his attention to the development of a presentation.

The third Rider daughter was expected immediately after this symposium, so things were busy at home, too, preparing for the new arrival. However, early on Sunday morning, December 16, 1979, just one day before the National Symposium was to commence, Tony's wife, Ruth, experienced a medical emergency. Her water broke and the umbilical cord became prolapsed, cutting off the baby's oxygen supply. Fairfax County paramedics were frantically summoned to their home, but were unable to completely rectify the problem. They immediately transported Ruth to Fairfax Hospital, where the baby was delivered by emergency caesarean. It was a time of immense distress for the family. They had to hastily leave their two oldest daughters, Kim and Heather, ages seven and five, with a neighbor. All the girls knew, as their parents left the house in a rush, was that Mommy was in pain and the baby was in jeopardy.

Within minutes of her delivery, Kristin's oxygen level soared. Over the next day or two, she experienced a number of closely monitored convulsions and seizures. The doctors were concerned about potential brain damage and physical impairment. However, on Saturday of that week, Ruth and Kristin were released from the hospital in good health. The prognosis for Kristin was excellent. She did not appear to have permanent damage of any kind.

Tony spent most of that week at the hospital with Ruth and Kristin; however, by Wednesday Kristin had improved so significantly that he was able to participate in the national symposium. He still doesn't know how he managed to put together a presentation and actually deliver it in three days. Though Tony had had little sleep, the doctor's prognosis of Kristin's health just seemed to energize him. As an aside, Kristin later became an honor student in school and is now entering her junior year in college. The doctors at Fairfax Hospital called Kristin their miracle baby.

Following the symposium, Tony decided to continue his research into arson and write a comprehensive work on firesetting and the personalities of arsonists. This undertaking took another year and resulted in a 193-page document, entitled *The Firesetter: A Psychological Profile*, which became a resource document for fire and criminal investigators in the United States and many foreign countries. Eventually, the *FBI Law Enforcement Bulletin* published a series of three articles during June, July, and August 1980, from this major body of work, also entitled "The Firesetter: A Psychological Profile."

In early 1980, Tony was requested by the Michigan state police to assist in a 1979 unsolved homicide of a young girl in Clare County, Michigan. Tony provided a profile based on the information furnished. By letter, dated November 12, 1980, Lieutenant Jerry Hyland, commanding officer of the Michigan state police, commended Tony for the profile. He stated in his letter: "This profile was very near a perfect overlay of a former boyfriend of the deceased. This subject had been talked with several times and had passed two polygraph tests. A reinvestigation of this suspect was made and another interview was conducted in Norfolk, Virginia, as the subject was in the U.S. Navy. A signed confession was obtained and the subject was convicted of Manslaughter. It is felt by myself and the investigators, that Special Agent Rider should be commended for his fine work. . . . The profile played an important part in the successful conclusion of the case."

In March 1980, Tony was selected for temporary intradivisional detail to the training division's Performance Appraisal/Merit Pay Task Force, which was established to assist the then-personnel division in developing policy and a training program for its new performance appraisal system. The Civil Service Reform Act of 1978 mandated all federal agencies to develop procedures to monitor performance appraisal systems. The Bureau was behind in the design, training, and implementation of its system, and was attempting to expedite the process to meet the statutory deadline. BSU chief Roger Depue authorized Tony's detail until the end of the year. For a while, Tony tried to profile cases and conduct other BSU business while engaged in this project, but found himself exhausted and frustrated, unable to devote appropriate time to either. He even continued to do research on firesetting and wrote articles for publication during the first three months of being assigned to the task force. It was an extremely difficult time. Finally, by the end of December 1980, he had completed his role in the project.

Before leaving the task force, Tony decided to seek reassignment to the Performance Appraisal Unit at FBIHQ. This was an opportunity for him to develop managerial skills and to seek administrative advancement. Although he would dearly miss the BSU, Tony hoped to return some time in the future. His transfer was approved and he reported to the personnel division on January 2, 1981.

In the meantime, the Division of Continuing Education, University of Virginia, established an award honoring research conducted by staff members of the FBI National Academy at Quantico. The award, named the Jefferson Award, was created by Adelle Robertson, then dean of the division, to promote the generation of knowledge related to criminal justice education.

On October 15, 1981, Tony became the first recipient of the Jefferson Award, in recognition of his research and writing on the personality of arsonists. The BSU has received a number of such awards over the years. To date, of the sixteen Jefferson Awards presented, eleven have been presented to members of the Behavioral Science Unit. Roy Hazelwood, Bob Ressler, and John Douglas have each been honored twice. The Jefferson Award signifies a high level of creativity and significant and relevant research. At the FBI Academy it is considered the most prestigious recognition.

SELECTED AS UNIT CHIEF

In the summer of 1992, after almost twenty-one years in the Bureau and eight years of supervising violent crime investigations and the Special Operations Group in the San Diego division, Tony was ready for change. Though the work had been exhilarating and professionally satisfying, the pace had been physically exhausting, and the work unending, as well as often administratively frustrating because of resource constraints and administration. Most of his squad cases demanded immediate attention due to their character and the caseload became overwhelming many times. Consequently, the squad was often on the street all hours of the day and night, seven days a week, investigating a multiplicity of sensitive cases, including kidnappings, extortions, bank robberies, crimes on government reservations (military bases in the territory), and assault of federal officers, often border patrol agents at the port of entry at San Ysidro.

Though Tony had left the BSU in 1981 for managerial and promotional opportunities, he lost neither interest in its work nor his desire to return to the Unit for assignment before retirement. However, Tony's family loved San Diego and had vowed never to leave California. But when Tony heard that John Campbell had been promoted and a vacancy existed for the BSU chief's position, he instantly applied. This was like a dream come true. The timing was perfect: Heather, their middle daughter, was graduating from high school and getting ready to begin college at Cal State Northridge, and their oldest daughter, Kim, was completing her sophomore year at Cal State Fullerton. If he were selected for the position, Kim and Heather would stay in California and finish their college education. The transition for

Kristin, their youngest, who was finishing the sixth grade, would be at an optimal time. The opportunity to work again in the BSU and help foster its entry into the twenty-first century overshadowed any concerns that Tony might have had about moving back to the East Coast or going back into a work environment that he had left almost eleven years earlier. Within a month or so, he got a phone call advising him that he had been selected by the Career Board and approved as the new unit chief of the BSU. His reporting date was early September 1992. What he didn't know was that the next five and a half years would be the most grueling and testing period of his tenure in the FBI.

While waiting for the Career Board decision and giving thought to this possible new assignment, Tony began to realize that he would probably be faced with some very difficult programmatic and staffing challenges in the future. Many of the instructors in the BSU had been there fifteen years or more, were eligible to retire, or would be eligible for retirement within the next few years. Such losses, he knew, would dramatically impact the unit's operations and training mandate, its level of expertise, and, of course, its reputation in the law enforcement community. Tony was also aware that budget constraints existed, some proposed staffing positions were not approved or budgeted, and the unit remained two levels underground at the FBI Academy, which was a sore point among unit members. He assumed that once in the unit chief's slot, he would be able to find reasonable solutions to these issues, but one of his greatest challenges was unforeseen: the case of Earl Pitts.

THE SPY IN THE CELLAR

Earl E. Pitts was the second FBI agent ever convicted of treason. It was inconceivable that Pitts would betray his country, but he did. Pitts had been working FCI (Foreign Counterintelligence) in the FBI's New

York field office for only a short period of time when he contacted the KGB and initiated his treasonous acts.

Pitts grew up in a farming community in Urbana, Missouri. He was considered a perfectionist and an intelligent individual. His high-school classmates were surprised and shocked when he went into the FBI, because he really wasn't an aggressive type of individual. He attended Central Missouri State on an ROTC scholarship and considered becoming a journalist. Those who recall him at Central Missouri described him as ambitious and disciplined. Before attending law school at the University of Missouri, Kansas City, he served in the U.S. Army and attained the rank of captain. He was in the military police in Korea. He then completed law school at the University of Missouri and sought employment with the Federal Bureau of Investigation.

In his explanation of his crimes, Earl stated, "I never experienced anything like it before or since. I had an overwhelming need to lash out and strike out. I realized at the time that the way to hurt the FBI was to screw around with its secrets." Pitts sold his access to the KGB. That access included records and information from the FBI's flagship New York office. Included in that information were an administrative list of Soviet personnel within the United States, secret memos about potentially vulnerable assets, and anything else that he could lay his hands on. The KGB have divided what motivates spies into four areas: money, ideology, sex, and ego. In Pitts's case it was more than just the money that motivated him, though he received approximately $124,000 from the Soviet Union from 1987 to 1992, and allegedly there was $100,000 more being held in Russia for him.

According to Pitts, what motivated him was getting even with the FBI for sending him to New York. Ultimately, after a period of two years in New York, Pitts grasped at an opportunity to leave New York and transfer to FBI headquarters to the records management division, which is considered a dull and boring job. By that time, Pitts's interaction with the KGB had become dormant. As it turned out, Pitts's handler, after the break-up of the Soviet Union, wanted to obtain a green card and stay in the United States. He contacted the FBI and indicated that he had an FBI agent in his pocket. That was the basis for the False Flag operation. To prevent Pitts from accepting a transfer to Denver with the downsizing of FBI headquarters, an opportunity to work in the prestigious Behavioral Science Unit at the FBI Academy was dangled in front of him, and the temptation was too great. This provided the FBI with the opportunity to maintain a close surveillance on the activity of Earl Pitts.

He was selected for the position and reported to the unit in January 1995, following secret briefings of selected training division executives, including BSU chief Rider, by Washington field office Foreign Counterintelligence (FCI) officials and agents investigating Pitts. Those executives who were briefed pledged to maintain secrecy of the operation and to support the Washington field office in its False Flag investigation. No one at the Academy or in the BSU was to be apprised of the operation unless approved by the case agent.

Shortly after his assignment to the BSU in January of 1995, Pitts was recontacted by his Russian handler and advised that he was now an employee with the successor of the KGB, the SVRR, and he wanted to continue to work with Earl. In this contact, which was made at Earl's residence, Pitts was provided with $15,000 as an incentive to continue to work with this Russian agency. There was not a significant amount of secret information at the FBI Academy and Earl grabbed whatever was available, including lists of employees, background information, files of employees, and also some equipment that could have been damaging in the future. In fact, Pitts was handed off to another undercover agent of the FBI. During one particular incident, Earl admitted that he happened to look straight up at the ceiling and the holes did not look right. He removed the tile and discovered a lens with a fiber-optic cable, technically advanced surveillance equipment.

That, however, did not deter Pitts's activities. During April and May of 1996, he made frequent visits to a drop, providing information which he thought was going to the Russians. It included information used for recruitment purposes, videotapes from the Counterintelligence Training Program, and assessments of FBI special agents, including one agent's medical condition.

Rider's assignment in this matter was to help administratively oversee Earl and to provide appropriate feedback on his behavior and conduct in the workplace. Tony tried to provide a work environment that would allow an effective FCI investigation. Initially, it was projected that the investigation might last six months. Tony thought he would be able support such an operation for six months while also continuing to run his unit in a manner that would not inadvertently reveal the covert operation. He was not certain if he would be able to handle Earl for more than six months without Earl detecting something unusual.

Because Earl had a law degree as well as a master's in criminal justice, Tony assigned him a number of legal research projects pertaining to behavioral issues during his first six months or more of assignment to the BSU. These were legitimate projects and he worked on them in earnest. Although these matters were intended to draw upon his legal expertise, they were also meant to keep him out of the National Academy (NA) and also from teaching the new agents. Eventually, however, Tony had no alternative but to assign him a NA course to teach. Rider was unable to exclude Earl from the classroom without raising questions among his colleagues, because every BSU instructor was expected to teach. But it was a conflict for Rider because he really did not want Earl's presence in the NA to later taint their instructional reputation. Rider expected Pitts's eventual arrest would be a bombshell for the unit, the Academy, the NA, the FBI, and the law enforcement community in general. He made certain, however, that Earl did not teach new agent classes. It was imperative that his involvement in the FBI training programs be minimized to avoid contamination of the institution when the operation was finally announced. Everyone involved in the operation supported this position.

As Rider watched Pitts and interacted with him over months, Pitts seemed to become increasingly emotionally flat. He also appeared psychologically fragile and detached. His demeanor was generally aloof and gave the impression that he was moderately depressed, unhappy, or stressed about something. One might also conclude that Pitts was often mentally preoccupied. Generally, Pitts's behavior and responsiveness seemed controlled and stoic. He had a sense of humor, though seldom expressed, that was dry and restrained. He did not smile much. Pitts had a look of vulnerability, but was not as weak psychodynamically as he appeared. It was Rider's assessment that he masked his stress and anxiety through self-restraint and isolation of affect. Earl seemed to be able, fairly efficiently, to compartmentalize his emotions. Rider was amazed at times at his level of functioning, especially when he knew Pitts should have been under overwhelming stress. It was obvious to Rider that he was in denial and on a self-destructive path. As time passed, Rider thought Pitts was like a runaway train that could only be stopped if derailed by arrest.

Pitts seemed to possess a subtle arrogance and sense of personal superiority that was not really obvious to the casual acquaintance. This arrogance and egocentricity was not obvious in his behavior, but was disguised in his verbal expression. For instance, on one particular occasion, Earl expressed criticism of spies who did stupid things to get caught. It was Rider's impression that Pitts thought himself clever and cunning, and invincible. Although Pitts prided himself on knowing about the personalities and characteristics of spies and criminals, he did not seem to have the capacity to accept his own criminality or to recognize his vulnerability.

Nevertheless, Rider found Pitts to be of above-average intelligence, extremely analytical in processing information, and independent in thinking. He had an extraordinary memory and was very knowledgeable of law and legal precepts. However, he seemed rather slow and calculating in his decision-making, and was cautious in drawing conclusions. He seemed to want to ensure that he would not make a mistake or bring criticism on himself, or more precisely, his intellect. Such thinking was paradoxical to his risk-taking in committing espionage.

Pitts was not easily influenced by others. He seemed to be suspicious of others' motivations, but did not demonstrate hypersensitivity to ideas or attitudes of others that might have been incongruent with his own. Though he did not hesitate to express his point of view, he often appeared indifferent to the fervor of the unit and more entertained by his own secret thoughts. Although he appeared to be a good listener, he had difficulty connecting personally with others. For the most part, he was a loner. Rider had a sense that Pitts monitored everyone, especially him, like an electronic scanner, looking for evidence that his deep, dark secret was known. When Rider engaged him in conversation, no matter how innocuous, he sat motionless with his eyes fixed on Rider's face, as if searching for evidence of manipulation or deception. He seemed to watch Rider's every move and appeared to mentally dissect his statements. Every day, Rider carefully monitored his own behavior to ensure that he neither treated Pitts in a special way nor revealed his disdain for him. Tony was constantly role-playing to ensure that Earl felt comfortable and safe in the BSU environment, and at the same time endeavored not to be seen as manipulative. The BSU was undergoing significant change during this period, so there was no shortage of issues or managerial dynamics to divert attention away from Pitts.

Rider never saw Pitts get angry or lose control at work. He was not excitable and generally demonstrated, at least outwardly, low-level anxiety, even when under severe stress. It was obvious that Earl internalized his stress and used every defense mechanism he could muster to maintain an appearance of normalcy. When the isolation and quiet of his office was interrupted unexpectedly, he did not react with indignation, but rather seemed to evidence restrained annoyance. The door to his office was often shut, which was unusual for unit members. Other BSU instructors welcomed visitors as a general rule and enjoyed interaction. Conversely, Pitts tended to be reclusive and avoided social interaction much of the time.

No one in the Bureau was aware of Pitts's espionage until briefed by Assistant Director Joe Wolfinger the morning of his arrest. Rider had no advance notice of Pitts's arrest. Rider arrived at the Academy the morning of December 18, 1996, shortly after Pitts got there. Rider watched him hurriedly walk toward the BSU building. When Rider got to the BSU, Pitts had his office door shut, but Tony heard him opening and closing file-cabinet drawers in his room. Rider went on to his office and immediately heard Pitts shut his office door as he left. He thought to himself, "it is going down." Within minutes, he received a phone call from Assistant Director Wolfinger, asking Rider to meet him at a certain location in the Academy. Rider knew Pitts was about to be arrested. After meeting with Assistant Director Wolfinger and others, he was informed that Pitts was being interviewed. After a period of waiting, Rider and others entered a room where Pitts was seated and witnessed his arrest. Earl looked dejected and totally defeated when told he was under arrest. It was a very sad experience to witness a fellow agent being arrested. But on the other hand, Tony had pride that the FBI was cleaning its own house. Pitts had betrayed the FBI and the American people. He had violated their trust and brought shame on himself and his family. He gave up everything out of greed and selfishness. Tony had no pity for him, just disgust.

Earl Pitts's betrayal, not only of the FBI, but of his friends in the Behavioral Science Unit and the U.S. government, was reflected in his behavior. Dick Ault, the FBI Behavioral Science coordinator of "Project Slammer," which was an extended government agency study of traitors designed to help predict those individuals that might be susceptible to committing acts of treason, stated it clearly, "What you see in these people is a way to alleviate psychological pain and discomfort, because betraying your country is often the end-game of years of suppressed anger as in the case of Earl Pitts. This is a guy who betrayed every friendship and oath that he ever took. It is a result of deep personality flaws. He had no understanding that he would ever be caught." Dick Ault did a thorough assessment of Pitts during the complete investigation and suggested that he would not be cooperative, which was the case, unless the information, investigation, and prosecution could "crush him." This was a sorry time for all of those associated with the FBI Academy, the Behavioral Science Unit, and the FBI.

Pitts later entered a plea of guilty and was sentenced to twenty-seven years in federal prison. Rider and other members of the BSU attended his sentencing in Federal District Court in Alexandria, Virginia. Although they sat directly behind him in the courtroom, Pitts never once looked at them or acknowledged their presence.

THE REAL CHALLENGE: REENGINEERING THE BSU

During the time that Tony Rider served as unit chief, many of the nationally and internationally renowned experts started to retire from the FBI. That included Roy Hazelwood, Dick Ault, Jim Reese, and Joe Conley, who was the behavioral science expert in the area of terrorism. Several other employees, including Jim Horn, requested transfer and reassignment from the Behavioral Science Unit. Jim was transferred down to Oklahoma City. Al Brantley, who was one of the premier instructors, was reassigned to the Critical Incident Response Group to continue to work on profiling; and Ken Lanning, the Bureau's expert on child abduction, sexual exploitation, and pedophiles, requested transfer to CIRG to work in the Child Abduction and Serial Killer Unit in that division. The significant loss of experience and talent also opened the door for Tony Rider to select the future leaders and experts in the Behavioral Science Unit. The individuals that were recruited included Dr. Anthony Pinizzotto, a forensic psychologist and former professor at Georgetown University; Ed Davis, a retired officer of the Metropolitan Police Department; Dr. John Jarvis, a researcher and crime analyst; John Lanata, who developed expertise in gang investigations; Donald Sheehan, who also developed into an expert in psychological testing and undercover operation; Sharon Smith, who became an expert in psycholinguistics; George Deshazor, who developed an expertise in criminal psychology; Terri Arthur, who developed an expertise in school violence and juvenile justice; and Carl Jensen, who expanded the terrorism and future crimes focus of the Behavioral Science Unit.

During his first year as BSU unit chief, Rider initiated liaison with the Bureau's Employee Assistance Program (EAP) and recommended the transfer of the BSU's Critical Incident and Peer Counseling Program and Chaplains Program to the EAP as collateral programs. These programs required almost full-time attention of SSA Horn, which limited his participation in other BSU responsibilities; for example, the NA, field school training, and research. Although these programs were heralded as immense successes, they flourished almost exclusively because of the untiring devotion of Horn. In Rider's view, the work was more than one person could reasonably or continually bear. Moreover, the BSU did not receive specific operational funding to support the Critical Incident and Peer Counseling Program. Monies expended by the BSU to support the program, except for funds received from FBIHQ, were deducted from allocations designated for BSU field training. These fiscal-year allocations, which were meant to cover all training travel of unit instructors, were too minimal and restrictive to be used for other purposes. Although the Critical Incident and Peer

Counseling Program was exceptional and widely championed by Bureau personnel and executives, it really needed to be incorporated into the EAP, which was created to meet similar needs within the Bureau. The program was eventually transferred, though it took a year or more to effect. It was a difficult decision for Rider, and certainly one that was interpreted by some unit members as an effort on his part to dismantle the unit. In Rider's opinion, the move was necessary to eliminate possible duplication of services in the FBI, to ensure continuing funding and cost effectiveness of the program, and to consolidate resources and responsiveness to critical incidents in the Bureau. Reassignment of the program also allowed for more allocated funding to be used on BSU field training travel.

RETIREMENT AND REPLACEMENT

During his very tumultuous time as unit chief, Tony Rider met with many challenges. The most significant was the Earl Pitts investigation, but from a managerial point of view, the loss of programs and expertise was equally challenging. That loss and instability created an atmosphere of change that led to Rider's decision to retire from the FBI.

At first the thought of retiring was almost unthinkable. The Bureau had been a significant part of Rider's life and identity for almost twenty-seven years. He had affection for the organization in spite of its dependency on regimens and rules, and top-down management, which certainly had influenced Tony's management style no matter how hard he fought the urge. He admired Bureau people and their commitment to excellence, as well as their unrelenting tenacity regardless of circumstances. But in 1998, he knew it was time to go. He had taken the BSU through hard and reluctant days of change, restaffed it with bright and talented agents and professional experts, and saw through to completion the unit's role in the investigation of Earl Pitts. The unit now needed new leadership to move it forward.

Tony had wanted to retire earlier, but certain personal and professional circumstances inhibited it. A year earlier, he had given retirement serious consideration, but the Earl Pitts case was just being wrapped up and the unit was still undergoing transition and healing. Tony wanted to see matters settled down before departing. Retirement was inviting for two primary reasons. One was that he was experiencing serious physical pain and needed surgery. In August 1997, Tony herniated a disc in his lower lumbar spine while running near home. He finally scheduled a laminectomy, but during the interim period he was in constant excruciating pain and had difficulty sitting at his desk and even walking. He also suffered unusually sensitive pain in his left heel, but had dismissed it as associated with his herniated disc. It was not until after his back surgery that he learned he had plantar fasciitis. His days of running were essentially over. He had relied on running daily for fitness, as well as a means to cope with stress. He had been running five or six miles a day for years and would sorely miss this routine. Also, about this time frame, Rider's dad, a widower, was diagnosed with a heart problem. He underwent triple-bypass heart surgery just a week before Tony's scheduled laminectomy. Although his surgery went well, he developed blood clots and various other medical complications, which eventually resulted in the amputation of his right leg above the knee. Because of his own illness, Tony was unable to be with him right away, though he promised he would come as quickly as possible. Retirement was now inevitable. Rider went on sick leave to recuperate following his surgery and retired on January 2, 1998.

STEVE BAND: THE NEW UNIT CHIEF OF THE BSU

Supervisory Special Agent Stephen R. Band had formerly been the manager of the Bureau's Undercover Safeguard Program, which was responsible for conducting psychological assessments of Bureau undercover operatives. This program was assimilated with the BSU in 1996, and then subsequently divested from the BSU and established as a separate unit. While Band served in the BSU, Rider recommended him for a tour of duty in the inspection division, which allowed Steve to seek eventual promotional consideration. After he completed his inspection division assignment, he was designated as unit chief of the Undercover Safeguard Unit. Though Band did not go back to BSU at that time, he nevertheless remained a strong ally and supporter of the BSU and its work.

When Tony announced his retirement, a number of Bureau supervisory special agents, including Dr. Steve Band, applied for the position vacancy. Band was eventually selected as the new chief of the BSU, where he currently serves.

13 The Present and the Future

The location of the Behavioral Science Unit at the FBI Academy hasn't changed since 1985, when it was sentenced to the "national cellar," the subbasement of building 9. The working atmosphere and the lack of sunlight have not changed. However, there have been significant changes since the institution of the NCAVC and the evolution of the Behavioral Science Unit. Bob Ressler is no longer a member of the Behavioral Science Unit. He has retired and is doing consulting, autobiographies, and other books about his experiences in the BSU.

John Douglas also consults, publishes books, and has recently authored a fiction novel regarding criminal profiling in the FBI.

The criminal profiling program is no longer in the Behavioral Science Unit or in the training division. After Waco and Ruby Ridge, based on some directives from Attorney General Janet Reno, the behavioral branch that supported the operations in those two major events was transferred to CIRG, the Critical Incident Response Group. CIRG has reconfigured itself on several occasions since its creation. Initially, there were two separate profiling units: one was a general profiling unit and the second one was a child abductor/serial killer unit. Those units have been reunited and there is a central focus and direction within CIRG that channels all cases being profiled, as well as other resources for law enforcement in addressing violent crime. The new entity has reclaimed the title of the National Center for Analysis of Violent Crime.

Bob Schaefer has retired and relocated to Richmond, Virginia, and is doing consulting and presentations, particularly in the area of stress management in dealing with Alzheimer's. Jim Horn has retired to Oklahoma and is currently consulting and conducting training and focusing his energies and attention on helping others.

Cindy Lent no longer coordinates research and edits writing of the Behavioral Science Unit, nor does she coordinate the internship program for BSU. However, she is performing her magic and great work for CIRG.

The Critical Incident Program, Peer Support, and the Chaplains Program are no longer part of the training division. These programs were transferred to the FBI's Employee Assistance Program, which is coordinated from all over the FBI. These programs provide credibility and additional resources and illustrate the evolution of the good programs that developed initially in the Behavioral Science Unit and have since been reassigned but still have great credibility within the FBI.

All of the operational entities of the Behavioral Science Unit have since been transferred to other divisions, particularly the personnel division, which received the recognized support programs of the Behavioral Science Unit, and also the Critical Incident Response Group, which received the criminal investigative analysis functions of the training division.

Roy Hazelwood has retired and joined the Academy Group and does extensive training throughout the world, using his research at Quantico and the Behavioral Science Unit as the basis of his training. Roy's work on autoerotic fatalities and rape has been published in two textbooks that are landmark publications and remain resources for law enforcement.

Ken Lanning, the FBI and law enforcement expert on child abuse and pedophiles, served in CIRG and continued to provide his expert attention in the investigations regarding child abduction and child molestation as well as the profiling of those unique cases. Ken's "three-legged stool" analogy remains very appropriate: research, interviews of offenders, and delivering the information developed through the interviews and research to law enforcement audiences, particularly the FBI National Academy. Ken retired and continues to work as a consultant.

The terrorist expert, Joe Conley, retired and continues to do consulting work. Al Brantley, Bill Hagmaier, Judd Ray, Jim Carter, Swanson Carter, Blaine McIlvaine, Larry Ankrom, Steve Etter, Ron Walker, Winston Norman, Dr. Dave Icove, Dr. Roger Davis, Jim Wright, Bernadette Cloniger, Don Sheehan, and many others are off meeting other challenges and successes.

Ed Sulzbach, who inspired Patricia Cornwell's FBI profiler, has retired to southern Virginia, where he does consulting work, training, teaching and research, runs a police academy, and continues sharing his unique focus with law enforcement around the world.

In 1989, Roger Depue created the Academy Group, which is essentially a private service entity. The Academy Group provides similar services as the Behavioral Science Unit to law enforcement in the public and private sectors, including information on investigations, training, and the behavioral sciences. Since the creation of the Academy Group, a number of very talented people have joined him, including several retirees from the Behavioral Science Unit. They are extremely successful.

Many of the other very talented instructors, researchers, and profilers have retired or transferred from the Behavioral Science Unit. Jim Reese, the Bureau's "expert" in stress management and undoubtedly the best stand-up speaker in the history of the FBI, continues to do his thing very successfully. He shares stress management with Fortune 500 companies and travels all over the world, being recognized as a very gifted presenter and motivational speaker. Dick Ault has retired, taking his expertise and the real backbone of the Behavioral Science Unit with him. He was that backbone for so many years, providing services not only to law enforcement, but also to his colleagues, developing and mentoring many of the staff of the Behavioral Science Unit as they grew in knowledge and expertise. Dick joined Roger Depue at the Academy Group and serves as director.

What remains of the Behavioral Science Unit? Actually, it is very healthy and currently reflects a tremendous amount of talent and potential. BSU members continue to focus their talent, energy, and expertise on issues that confront law enforcement on a daily basis. An example is the outstanding work of Tony Pinizzotto and Ed Davis. These gentlemen are in the process of completing a trilogy focused on officer shooting. The first part was completed in 1992 and entitled *Killed in the Line of Duty*. The second part, completed in 1995, was *In the Line of Fire*. The third part—underway at this time—focuses on the survivability of law enforcement, the theme that was key to all of their publications. It started because they were looking at issues that surfaced in the annual reports of the Uniform Crime Reporting Section publication entitled "Law Enforcement Officers Killed and Assaulted." That publication, completed on an annual basis, merely touched the surface of the tragedies that confronted law enforcement officers. It reflected that, in an average year, seventy-five to eighty officers were killed feloniously and another seventy-five to eighty were killed accidentally in the line of duty.

Beyond brief descriptions of the encounters, there were many questions to be answered. The initial research, conducted by Pinizzoto, Davis, and Jim Miller of the Uniform Crime Reporting section, answered some of the questions about why fatal interactions happen. The study researched and analyzed fifty-plus cases of officers killed in the line of duty. It included an analysis of the types of personalities that could kill police officers, and interviews with the killers in these respective cases to develop a further understanding of the issues surrounding officers' deaths in the line of duty. However, the initial research and the publication of *Killed in the Line of Duty* left a number of questions unanswered.

A second study was commissioned, whose focus was understanding, from the law enforcement perspective, the issues of survival. Another set of cases presenting a national demographic picture was completed, and in this case, there were both interviews with people who had shot police officers and interviews of police officers that survived. Many of the answers to the questions that arose in the first study were answered by those officers. Yet there were still a number of questions. Why the fatal interaction or why that challenge? Why did some of the officers survive and some didn't? Who were those officers that potentially jeopardized their lives by placing themselves in positions that required some use of deadly force? Pinizzoto and Davis's research and continued focus on this very important issue in law enforcement will again provide the Behavioral Science Unit with another, very important embodiment of that three-legged stool. The research, the interviews, and the knowledge that comes from them is being shared on a national and international basis through symposia, conferences, and seminars put on by the Behavioral Science Unit and presented by Davis, Pinizzotto, and others.

The legacy of the Behavioral Science Unit, which involves creativity, research initiatives, and the sponsorship of major conferences, continues to operate. In recent years, the Behavioral Science Unit has sponsored major conferences attended by mental health experts, police psychological services, and law enforcement officers from around the world. Those conferences included domestic violence by police officers, suicide of police officers, issues of school violence (which had national and international participation), and future issues in law enforcement. These types of major seminars continue to place the BSU and its individual members in the national limelight. The expertise of these new members continues to grow. Like their predecessors, they develop national reputations through their research. Through their interaction with the FBI National Academy Program, and through presentations and contributions, they have become the third wave of behavioral scientists.

It is worth noting the current members of the Behavioral Science

Unit and recognizing their areas of expertise, research, and instruction. The following is a short glimpse of the current and future talent being developed through the tremendously entrepreneurial atmosphere of the Behavioral Science Unit. That atmosphere was initially fostered by Roger Depue, enhanced by John Campbell, and is currently being groomed by Dr. Steve Band. Band is a uniquely qualified individual whose background includes counseling, psychology, a Ph.D. from Fordham University, and postdoctorate work at the Indiana University of Medicine. He has a variety of experience within the FBI, including assignments as a "real" agent. He was a special agent in the Indiana field office and served in the New York field office as well as the training division. He was the unit chief of the Undercover Safeguard Unit from 1994 to 1998 and took over the Behavioral Science Unit in February of 1998.

All members of the unit are very strong academically and possess advanced degrees such as Ph.D.'s. John Jarvis, for example, is a Ph.D. from the University of Virginia. He has been involved in numerous investigative activities as well as several crime analysis projects. Jarvis's background includes research analyst and forecaster for the Virginia Department of Corrections. He currently teaches at the National Academy and publishes prolifically. His most recent publications include *Challenges of Computer Crimes*, *Incidence of Family Violence*, and issues pertaining to hate crimes. He also contributed to the publication of *Killed in the Line of Duty* during his time in the Uniform Crime Reporting section.

Another current member of the unit is Sharon S. Smith. She is currently working on her Ph.D. in psychology at Georgetown University. She served more than twenty years as a special agent in the FBI and has a variety of experience. Her master's degree in education was from the University of Maryland and emphasized psycholinguistics. She is the behavioral science coordinator for the National Center for the Analysis of Violent Crime and she has published numerous articles, including her recent "Using Brain Fingerprinting to Detect Knowledge Despite Efforts to Conceal: A Multifaceted Electroencephalographic Response Analysis Approach." She has served in the training division and has taught new agents at the National Academy and possesses extraordinary skills and ability.

Art Westveer completed his master's degree at John Hopkins University. He was employed by the Baltimore Police Department and had a distinguished career. He served as assistant director in their training division and was also responsible for investigations surrounding crimes against persons. Art currently teaches a number of courses for the FBI National Academy and has been a member of the Behavioral Science Unit since October of 1986.

Dr. Anthony Pinizzotto is currently an instructor and researcher in the BSU. He holds a Ph.D. in psychology from Georgetown University. His doctorate dealt with criminal personality assessment and crime scene investigation. He served for fifteen years in law enforcement and has been employed with the FBI since 1987. During his first assignments in the FBI, he was a coordinator of research projects for the Uniform Crime Reporting section and received the distinguished Jefferson Award for his work on *Killed in the Line of Duty* and *In the Line of Fire*. Dr. Pinizotto is internationally known for his research, writing, and presentations and has contributed significantly to the current reputation of the Behavioral Science Unit. His partner in crime is Edward F. Davis. Davis completed his Master of Science degree in justice from American University and has served in law enforcement for more than thirty-seven years. He was a member of the Metropolitan Police Department, Washington, D.C. His last assignment was as a lieutenant commanding a district investigative section responsible for all general crime investigation. He joined the FBI in 1984 and worked in the Uniform Crime Reporting section and on the task force focused on hate crimes. He has conducted in-depth studies into circumstances surrounding felonious killing and serious assault of police officers, and has consulted with law enforcement throughout the United States, Canada, and England on topics of law enforcement safety, management of death, deadly force, hate-related crimes and hate groups, and interviewing and interrogation methods.

Another current member of the Behavioral Science Unit is Supervisory Special Agent Carl Jensen, who joined the FBI in 1984 after completing a tour with the Navy. He is a graduate of the U.S. Naval Academy. He served as a field agent in Atlanta, Georgia; Monterey, California; and Youngstown, Ohio. He also served in the FBI laboratory as a drug subunit program coordinator for Racketeering Records Analysis. In June of 1997, SSA Jensen reported to the Behavioral Science Unit. He currently instructs at the National Academy, conducts research, and provides consultation. He is coordinating a futures course for the FBI National Academy and is completing his doctorate at the University of Maryland. Jensen has written a number of articles for forensic science publications and the *Law Enforcement Bulletin*. Add into that mix John Lanata, Terry Royster, Harry Kern, and an outstanding support staff. And Joe Harpold remains a backbone of BSU.

RUMINATIONS ON BEING IN THE BEHAVIORAL SCIENCE UNIT

On a snowy December 20, 1984, Joe Harpold reported to the BSU at the FBI Academy. He had been an agent for ten years and four months, all in the Cleveland, Ohio, office. Anne Harpold, a renowned singer-songwriter and his spouse for eighteen years, and their two lovely children, Leslie and Stephen, were in temporary quarters with him at the Springfield, Virginia, Hilton Hotel. It was Stephen's twelfth birthday and Joe was hoping to report into the unit and take care of some of the paperwork. Upon arrival, he was told that there would not be any work done that day because it was the day of the unit's annual

Christmas party at the Officer's Club, located main side at the Marine Corps base, Quantico.

Roger Depue was the unit chief of BSU at this time. After settling into the unit, Harpold was assigned to work in the VICAP program under the temporary leadership of Pierce Brooks, the retired Los Angeles detective of *The Onion Field* fame. Pierce, under contract, had brought some people with him. Harpold was the only FBI agent initially assigned to VICAP.

Harpold's position was as a violent crime analyst, but more importantly, Roger Depue envisioned that Harpold should become the violent crime prevention specialist for NCAVC. Depue called Harpold into his office within a few days of his arrival. He told him that he wanted him to take a look at everything that was going on in the unit from a crime prevention perspective and initiate whatever actions he deemed appropriate to reduce violence in our society. Roger especially wanted Joe to look at the new research findings in the serial murderer and serial rapists research projects that were underway to see what might be done with this new body of knowledge. These were big tasks and Harpold wasn't sure that his previous training or experience were sufficient to accomplish them.

As a former police officer and field agent, Harpold had been involved in the investigation of violent crimes and a research project on rape that had led to the development of a Metropolitan Organization to Counter Sexual Assault (MOCSA). This was long before he had received any training in the topics of crime prevention or community relations. This project, however, did give him special skills in aggregate crime analysis because he had to analyze over six hundred rape investigations. After he had been in the FBI for about three years, he received specialized training in police community relations and crime resistance (the FBI's version of crime prevention).

Bob Ressler, Dick Ault, John Douglas, Ken Lanning, and Roy Hazelwood were Harpold's mentors in the BSU, and they helped him overcome his anxieties and feelings of inferiority by giving him ideas about how he could develop meaningful approaches to violent crime, based on their own research findings. In early 1985, Roy Hazelwood was in the process of writing his second book, this one on the subject of rape investigations. Roy invited Harpold to write a chapter on crime prevention. After Joe wrote this chapter, they mutually decided that it would be better to write an article for the FBI's *Law Enforcement Bulletin*, which Roy wrote with Joe's input. The article, "Rape: The Dangers of Providing Confrontational Advice," was Harpold's first exposure to the field of writing. It was very painful, but thanks to Hazelwood doing most of the writing, the article finally got published.

By the summer of 1985, the concept of NCAVC was approved and, at about the same time, the Drug Enforcement Agency came to the Academy with their faculty from the Federal Law Enforcement Training Center in Glynco, Georgia. In order to accommodate their needs, the BSIRU and the BSISU had to be relocated. The only space large enough to accommodate that many people was a federal relocation site situated in the subbasement of the cafeteria building at the Academy. This was a bomb shelter that had been designed to house the key elements of the federal government. After that plan changed, the space became available for use, and construction began on what became affectionately known as the "National Cellar for the Analysis of Violent Crime."

The move to the new space actually occurred in the late summer of 1985. Just prior to the move, Harpold had sought Depue's permission to move from VICAP to the BSIRU, the instruction side of the house. Joe wanted to teach in the National Academy because he had enjoyed teaching as a police instructor when he was a field agent, and he had revised his previous course on crime resistance to crime prevention. He asked to teach this course even though he did not have the requisite master's degree. Depue told him that he could teach the course and that he would serve as the instructor of record with the University of Virginia until he finished his master's.

The Present and the Future

In the early fall of 1985, Hazelwood came to Joe and asked him if he had any thoughts on a citizen organization they might work with to disseminate some of the preliminary findings from the Serial Rapists Research Project to women who were the potential victims of such predators. From working with national and international crime prevention and victim service organizations, Harpold had learned of the volunteer work of the General Federation of Women's Clubs (GFWC). In some parts of rural America, these volunteer women were the crime prevention officers for the sheriffs and small town chiefs of police. They arranged a meeting at Quantico with the president of the GFWC, which resulted in a two-year joint project with them, the GFWC/FBI New Sexual Assault Awareness/Victim Assistance Program. It involved a joint training program at the FBI Academy with GFWC public affairs or crime prevention chairs and the NCAVC coordinators from each of the fifty-nine FBI field offices. One agent and one GFWC representative from each state worked together as a team to make presentations and help with or start victim services programs. The results of this program were, they believed, fewer victims of rape, and victims who had not received treatment were treated. It was the first time that the Bureau had ever worked a program with such a large citizen organization and it was a huge success from a public-relations perspective. The GFWC has ten million members world-wide and over 10,000 clubs in the United States.

The information was out to a lot of citizens in this country concerning what the BSU had learned from these predators. They shared an insight into the victim through the eyes of the offender so that potential victims might be better able to avoid being confronted by such violent assailants. They shared information concerning how victims are selected and assessed by the offender, and the general behavior of the different types of rapists. They spent a great deal of time discussing how to avoid situations that could lead to rape and how to create a plan based on an understanding of one's own personality. Many members of the GFWC were very appreciative of the efforts to make them harder targets.

Another area of accomplishment was Harpold's association with the American Association of Retired Persons, Criminal Justice Services (AARP-CJS). While still a field agent in 1976, he was invited to attend an in-service training program at the FBI Academy which was cosponsored by the AARP-CJS and was designed to address preventing the victimization of the elderly. Leaders in crime prevention from around the country came to this in-service and Harpold was present during a discussion that resulted in the ultimate formation of the International Society of Crime Prevention Practitioners (ISCPP).

It was quite logical that Joe should then want to be the one to hold the first ISCPP conference sponsored by the newly formed NCAVC in June, 1986. This conference was cosponsored by AARP-CJS and the International Association of Chiefs of Police. The subject was "Violent Crime against The Elderly."

The concept of the TRIAD program grew out of this conference. TRIAD stands for the three organizations of IACP, NSA, and AARP working together to address the criminal victimization of the elderly. Depue and Harpold were on separate committees of IACP and they worked through these committees to create an awareness of the need to prevent and address the violent victimization of the elderly. The following year, 1988, Joe cohosted the first TRIAD conference at the FBI Academy. A total of almost two hundred chiefs, sheriffs, and AARP executives came from around the country. This conference was a very proud moment in Harpold's career because in many parts of the country, chiefs and sheriffs did not speak, much less work together.

Another crowning moment in Joe's time in the BSU came in 1991, when John Campbell, his unit chief, asked him to help run a symposium. Campbell wanted to recommend that the director personally host a symposium on violent crime. His vision was to address violent crime through community partnerships. Hence, Harpold's next major effort came to be entitled, "The Director's Symposium on Addressing Violent Crime through Community Involvement." The concept was for the Director, William S. Sessions, to invite selected SACs to the FBI Academy. The SACs were to be trained as teams, then go back to their respective jurisdictions and implement tailored initiatives to fight violence.

The Bureau was awakening to the idea of community policing, and one way for the FBI to support local initiatives was to have SACs help executives target the more serious crimes in their areas, especially violent crimes.

These symposia were historic because the FBI had never had community leaders en mass at the FBI Academy before. They resulted in a great bond between law enforcement executives and community leaders. In fact, immediately after the first one, a kidnapping was solved by one of the community leaders telephoning the SAC with the kidnapper's name and location. This was the direct result of the bonding that had occurred between these two men at the symposia. There were other successes as well. Several of the SACs held mini-symposia when they returned home. These conferences were very successful and teamed people up at the local level in much the same way that they had been teamed up at the Academy for the Director's Symposium. If we haven't learned anything else, we have learned that there is power in numbers and that, according to the famous English statesman, Edmund Burke, "All it takes for the triumph of evil is for a few good people to do nothing."

As one can see, the talent, expertise, and direction of the Behavioral Science Unit are clearly reclaiming the "limelight." Unit members uphold the mission of the unit, which is to develop and provide relevant programs of training, research, and consultation in behavioral and social sciences for the law enforcement community that will improve administrative and operational efficiency. The BSU staff are primarily special agents and experienced veteran police officers with advanced degrees in behavioral science, psychology, criminology, and sociology.

Professional personnel in the Behavioral Science Unit includes forensic psychologists, research analysts, two management assistants, three training technicians, a technical information specialist, and a secretary. There are currently nineteen BSU members, with several vacancies. The unit conducts specialized and applied training in specific teaching disciplines as they pertain to law enforcement for new agents. They conduct FBI in-services and symposia for the National Academy program and international police officers, field police schools in criminal-justice-related organizations, and conferences.

The current initiatives of the Behavioral Science Unit, the expertise and the quality of staff, foretell a significant and bright future for the Behavioral Sciences Unit. However, one cannot help but think that the "three-legged stool" described by Ken Lanning has parts that are missed by the Behavioral Science Unit and the National Center for the Analysis of Violent Crime. The need to work, play, learn, research, laugh, and even cry together was the basis for the success of the Behavioral Science Unit in the 1980s. Until that ability to conduct research, provide consultative services, educate, and train are brought back together under that "three-legged stool" concept, there will be something missing.

Appendix - Historical Evolution:
The Behavioral Science Unit Today

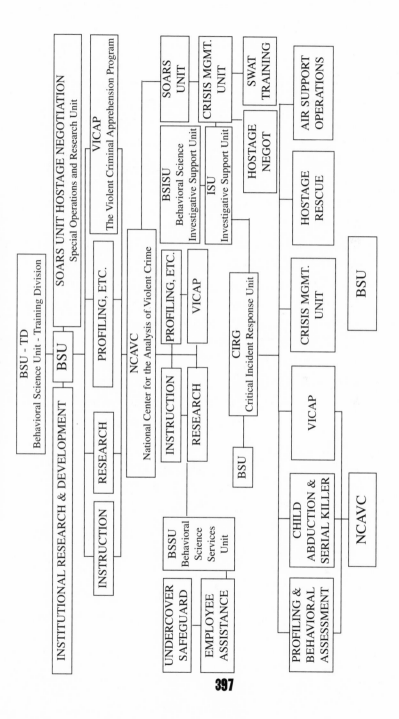

BSU - TD
Behavioral Science Unit - Training Division

INSTITUTIONAL RESEARCH & DEVELOPMENT

BSU

SOARS UNIT HOSTAGE NEGOTIATION
Special Operations and Research Unit

VICAP
The Violent Criminal Apprehension Program

INSTRUCTION

RESEARCH

PROFILING, ETC.

NCAVC
National Center for the Analysis of Violent Crime

SOARS UNIT

CRISIS MGMT. UNIT

SWAT TRAINING

BSISU
Behavioral Science
Investigative Support Unit

ISU
Investigative Support Unit

INSTRUCTION

RESEARCH

PROFILING, ETC.

VICAP

HOSTAGE NEGOT

AIR SUPPORT OPERATIONS

BSU

CIRG
Critical Incident Response Unit

HOSTAGE RESCUE

BSSU
Behavioral Science Services Unit

UNDERCOVER SAFEGUARD

EMPLOYEE ASSISTANCE

CRISIS MGMT. UNIT

BSU

CHILD ABDUCTION & SERIAL KILLER

VICAP

PROFILING & BEHAVIORAL ASSESSMENT

NCAVC

Selective
Bibliography

The following, highly selective bibliography is but a fraction of the more than five hundred articles and books published on criminal profiling and related subjects. To present a complete and comprehensive list would require an additional dozen or so pages. What follows, then, are the writings of only those who served in the BSU.

Ault, Richard L., Jr. "FBI Guidelines for Use of Hypnosis." *International Journal of Clinical and Experimental Hypnosis* 27 (October 1979): 449–51.

———. "Hypnosis: The FBI's Team Approach." *FBI Law Enforcement Bulletin* 49 (January 1980): 5–8.

———. "NCAVC's Research and Development Program." *FBI Law Enforcement Bulletin* 55, no. 12 (1986): 6–8.

Ault, Richard L., Jr., Roy Hazelwood, and R. Reboussin. "The Epistemological Status of Equivocal Death Analysis." *American Psychologist* 49 (1994): 72–73.

Ault, Richard L., Jr., and James T. Reese. "A Psychological Assessment of Crime: Profiling." *FBI Law Enforcement Bulletin* 49 (March 1980): 22–25. Reprinted in *Campus Law Enforcement Journal* 13 (November–December 1983): 28–31; and as part of U.S. Senate Committee on the Judiciary. *Serial Murders: Hearing before the Subcommittee on Juvenile Justice.* 98th Cong., 1st sess. July 12, 1983. Washington, D.C.: U.S. Goverment Printing Office, pp. 58–61.

Band, Stephen R., and Joseph Harpold. "School Violence: Lessons Learned." *FBI Law Enforcement Bulletin* (September 1999): 9–18.

SELECTIVE BIBLIOGRAPHY

Band, Stephen R., and D. Sheehan. "Managing Undercover Stress: The Supervisor's Role." *FBI Law Enforcement Bulletin* (February 1999): 1–6.

Boyd, Robert M. "Buried Body Cases." *FBI Law Enforcement Bulletin* 48 (February 1979): 1–7.

Brooks, Pierce R. "Investigative Methodology: Homicide, Rape, and Related Crimes of Violence." *FBI Law Enforcement Bulletin* 54 (December 1985): 14–21.

Bull-Ray. "Police Psychology: The World Conference." *Policing* 2, no. 1 (1986): 56–67.

Burgess, Alan, J. Douglas, and R. Ressler. *Crime Classification Manual*. San Fransisco: Jossey-Bass, Inc., 1992.

———. *Sexual Homicide: Patterns and Motives*. New York: Lexington Books, 1988.

Burgess, Alan, and Roy Hazelwood, eds. *Practical Aspects of Rape Investigation: A Multidisciplinary Approach*. 2d ed. New York: CRC Press, 1995.

Chilton, Roland, and John Jarvis. "Using the National Incident Based Reporting System (NIBRS) to Test Estimates of Arrestee and Offender Characteristics." *Journal of Quantitative Criminology* (June 1999): 207–24.

Depue, Roger L. "Community Analysis Worksheet, Appendix B." In *A Manual for Establishment and Operation of a Foot Patrol Program*, by Robert C. Trojanowicz and Paul R. Smyth. East Lansing, Mich.: Michigan State University, School of Criminal Justice, 1984, pp. 38–47.

———. "High Risk Lifestyle: The Police Family." *FBI Law Enforcement Bulletin* 50 (August 1981): 7–13. Reprinted in *Constabulary Gazette: The Ulter Police Magazine* 49 (February 1982): 8–12; *Police Association Victoria* (Australia) 48 (March 1982): 59–69; *Criminal Investigator* (spring 1983): 65–68.

———. "Prepared Statement of Roger L. Depue." U.S. Senate Committee on the Judiciary. *Serial Murders, Hearing before the Subcommittee on Juvenile Justice*. 98th Cong., 1st sess. July 12, 1983. Washington, D.C.: U.S. Government Printing Office, pp. 46–54.

———. "Turning Inward: The Police Officer Counselor." *FBI Law Enforcement Bulletin* 48 (February 1979): 8–12.

Selective Bibliography

Dietz, Parker Elliot, "Sex Offender Profiling by the FBI: A Preliminary Conceptual Model." In *Clinical Criminology: The Assessment and Treatment of Criminal Behavior*, edited by M. H. Ben-Aron, S. J. Hucker, and C. D. Webster. Toronto: M & M Graphics Ltd., 1985, pp. 207–19.

Dietz, Parker Elliot, and James T. Reese. "The Perils of Police Psychology: Ten Strategies for Minimizing Role Conflicts When Providing Mental Health Services and Consultation to Law Enforcement Agencies." *Behavioral Sciences and the Law* 4 (1986): 385–400.

Douglas, John E., and Alan E. Burgess. "Criminal Profiling: A Viable Investigative Tool against Violent Crime," *FBI Law Enforcement Bulletin* (December 1986): 9.

Douglas, John E., Ann W. Burgess, Alan G. Burgess, and Robert K. Ressler. *Crime Classification Manual: A Standard System for Investigating and Classifying Violent Crimes.* New York: Lexington Books, 1992. Reprint, San Francisco: Jossey-Bass, 1997.

Douglas, John E., Ann W. Burgess, and Robert K. Ressler. "Rape and Rape-Murder: One Offender and Twelve Victims." *American Journal of Psychiatry* 140 (January 1983): 36–40.

Douglas, John E., and Roy Hazelwood. "The Lust Murderer." *FBI Law Enforcement Bulletin* 49 (April 1980): 18–22. Reprinted in *Australian Federal Police Journal* 1 (July 1980): 57–69; and *Royal Canadian Mounted Police Gazette* 42 (1980): 10–14.

Douglas, John E., and Murray S. Miron. "Threat Analysis: The Psycholinguistic Approach." *FBI Law Enforcement Bulletin* 48 (September 1979): 5–9.

Douglas, John E., and C. M. Munn. "The Detection of Staging and Personation at the Crime Scene." In *Crime Classification Manual*, edited by John Douglas et al. New York: Lexington Books, 1992.

———. "Modus Operandi and the Signature Aspects of Violent Crime." In *Crime Classification Manual*, edited by John Douglas et al. New York: Lexington Books, 1992.

———. "Violent Crime Scene Analysis: Modus Operandi, Signature, and Staging." *FBI Law Enforcement Bulletin* 61, no. 2 (1992): 1–10.

Douglas, John, and Mark Olshaker. *Mindhunter: Inside the FBI's Elite Serial Crime Unit.* New York: Simon and Schuster, 1995.

SELECTIVE BIBLIOGRAPHY

———. *Obsession: The FBI's Legendary Profiler Probes the Psyches of Killers, Rapists, and Stalkers and Their Victims and Tells How to Fight Back*. New York: Scribner, 1998.

Douglas, John E., Robert K. Ressler, Ann W. Burgess, and C. R. Hartman. "Criminal Profiling from Crime Scene Analysis." *Behavioral Sciences and the Law* 4 (1986): 401–21.

Douglas, John E., Robert K. Ressler, N. A. Groth, and Ann W. Burgess. "Offender Profiles: A Multidisciplinary Approach." *FBI Law Enforcement Bulletin* 49 (September 1980): 16–20. Reprinted in U.S. Senate Committee on the Judiciary. *Serial Murders, Hearing before the Subcommittee on Juvenile Justice*. 98th Cong., 1st sess. July 12, 1983. Washington, D.C.: U.S. Government Printing Office. pp. 62–66.

Douglas, John E., and Anthony O. Rider. "FBI Psychological Profile Instrumental in Identifying Arson Suspect." *Arson Resource Exchange Bulletin* (February 1980): 21–23.

Harpold, Joseph A. "Community Policing: The Medical Model." *National Academy Associate* (October 1999): 4–6.

———. "Crime Prevention: The Changing Role of the Beat Officer." *Police Chief* (December 1998): 83–84.

———. "Triad: A Must Aspect of Community Policing." *Sheriff* (January–February 1997): 30–31.

Hassel, Conrad V. "Criminal Law v. Criminology: A Question of Responsibility." *FBI Law Enforcement Bulletin* 44 (October 1975): 11–15.

———. "The Hostage Situation: Exploring the Motivation and Cause." *Police Chief* 42 (September 1975): 55–58.

———. "Interactions of Law Enforcement and Behavioral Science Personnel." In *Victims of Terrorism*, edited by Frank M. Ochberg and David A. Soskis. Boulder, Colo.: Westview Press, 1982.

———. "The Political Assassin." *Journal of Police Science and Administration* 2 (December 1974): 399–403.

———. "Terror: The Crime of the Privileged: An Examination and Prognosis." *Terrorism: An International Journal* 1 (1977): 1–16.

Hazelwood, Roy. "The Behavior-Oriented Interview of Rape Victims: The Key to Profiling." *FBI Law Enforcement Bulletin* 52 (September 1983): 8–15.

Selective Bibliography

————. "Equivocal Deaths: A Case Study." *American Society of Criminology* (November 11, 1983).

————. "The NCAVC Training Program: A Commitment to Law Enforcement." *FBI Law Enforcement Bulletin* (December 1986): 23.

————. "Sexual Deviations Dangerous to the Self." In *Psychiatric Nursing in the Hospital and the Community*, by Ann Wolbert Burgess. 3d ed. Englewood Cliffs, N.J.: Prentice-Hall, 1981, pp. 316–18.

————, et al. "The Criminal Sexual Sadist." *FBI Law Enforcement Bulletin* (February 1992): 12–19.

Hazelwood, Roy, and Ann W. Burgess. "Autoerotic Asphyxial Deaths and Social Network Response." *American Journal of Orthopsychiatry* 53 (January 1983): 166–70.

————. "An Introduction to the Serial Rapist: Research by the FBI." *FBI Law Enforcement Bulletom* (September 1987): 16.

Hazelwood, Roy, Ann W. Burgess, and Parker Elliot Dietz. "The Investigation of Autoerotic Fatalities." *Journal of Police Science and Administration* 9 (December 1981): 404–11.

————. "Sexual Fatalities: Behavioral Reconstruction in Equivocal Cases." *Journal of Forensic Sciences* 27 (October 1982): 763–73.

Hazelwood, Roy, Ann W. Burgess, and A. N. Groth. "Death during Dangerous Autoerotic Practices." *Social Science Medicine Journal* 15E (1981): 129–33.

Hazelwood, Roy, Parker Elliot Dietz, and Ann W. Burgess. *Autoerotic Fatalities*. Boston: D.C. Heath, 1983.

Hazelwood, Roy, R. Reboussin, and J. Warren. "The Dynamics of Serial Rape." Paper presented at the annual meeting of the American Society of Criminology. Chicago, November 1988.

————. "Serial rape: Correlates of Increased Aggression and the Relationship of Offender Pleasure to Victim Resistance." *Journal of Interpersonal Violence* 4 (1989): 65–78.

Hazelwood, Roy, and J. Warren. "The Criminal Behavior of the Serial Rapist." *FBI Law Enforcement Bulletin* (February, 1990): 11–16.

————. "The Serial Rapist: His Characteristics and Victims (Part I)." *FBI Law Enforcement Bulletin* (January 1989): 11–17.

SELECTIVE BIBLIOGRAPHY

———. "The Serial Rapist: His Characteristics and Victims (Part II)." *FBI Law Enforcement Bulletin* (February 1989): 18–25.

Howlett, J. B., K. A. Hanfland, and Robert K. Ressler. "The Violent Criminal Apprehension Program—VICAP: A Progress Report." *FBI Law Enforcement Bulletin* (December 1986): 14.

Icove, David J. "Automated Crime Profiling." *FBI Law Enforcement Bulletin* (December 1986): 27.

———, et al. "Incendiary Fire Analysis and Investigation." In *Open Fire Service Learning Program*, edited by David J. Icove. Lexington, Mass.: Ginn Publishing, 1984.

Icove, David J., and J. L. Bryan. "Recent Advances in Computer-Assisted Arson Investigation." *Fire Journal* (National Fire Protection Association) 71, no. 1 (January 1977).

Icove, David J., and H. L. Crisman. "Application of Pattern Recognition to Arson Investigation." *Fire Technology* (National Fire Protection Association) (February 1975); "Arson, the Prevention Chain," National Clearinghouse for Criminal Justice Systems, U.S. Department of Justice, May 1980.

Icove, David J., and J. H. Estepp. "Motive-Based Offender Profiles of Arson and Fire-Related Crimes." *FBI Law Enforcement Bulletin* (April 1987): 17.

Icove, David J., and M. Osama Soliman. "Computer-Assisted Arson Information Management." *International Fire Chief* 49 (December 1983): 28–31.

Icove, David J., V. B. Wherry, and J. D. Schroeder. *Combating Arson-For-Profit: Advanced Techniques for Investigators*. Columbus, Ohio: Battelle Press, 1980.

Jensen, Carl J., III, and Yvonne Hsieh. "Law Enforcement and the Millennialist Vision." *FBI Law Enforcement Bulletin* (September 1999): 1–6.

Jung, C. G. *Jung on Evil*. Edited by Murray Stein. Princeton, N.J.: Princeton University Press, 1995.

Knight, R. A., J. I. Warren, R. Reboussin, and B. Soley. "Predicting Rapist Type from Crime-Scene Variables." *Criminal Justice and Behavior* 25 (1997): 46–80.

Selective Bibliography

Lanata, John C. "Gangs: Ten Points of Interest" *LEO* (*Law Enforcement Online*), 1998. Available by e-mailing the author, jlanata@FBIAcademy.edu.

————. "Identifying and Interviewing Gang Members." *Law Enforcement Technology* (October 1998): 86–90.

Lanning, Kenneth V. "Collectors." In *Child Pornography and Sex Rings*, by Ann Wolbert Burgess. Lexington, Mass.: Lexington Books, 1984, pp. 83–92.

————. "Overview of Autoerotic Activity." *FBI Law Enforcement Bulletin* (February 1982).

Lanning, Kenneth V., and Ann Wolbert Burgess. "Child Pornography and Sex Rings." *FBI Law Enforcement Bulletin* 53 (January 1984): 10–16.

Lanning, Kenneth V., Carol Hartman, and Ann Wolbert Burgess. "Typology of Collectors." In *Child Pornography and Sex Rings*, by Ann Wolbert Burgess. Lexington, Mass.: Lexington Books, 1984, pp. 83–92.

Mindermann, John W., and Howard D. Teten. "Police Personal Problems: Practical Considerations for Administrators." *FBI Law Enforcement Bulletin* 46 (January 1977): 8–15.

Monroe, Lawrence J. "Affirmative Action and Quotas." In *The Police Yearbook*. Gaithersburg, Maryland: International Association of Chiefs of Police, 1980, pp. 56–59.

————. "An Analysis of Affirmative Action and Its Impact on Training." In *The Police Yearbook*. Gaithersburg, Maryland: International Association of Chiefs of Police, 1976, pp. 73–76.

O'Conner, James A. "Bramshill: An American's Perception." *Police Chief* 43 (August 1976): 66–68, 90.

————. "Evaluation: Sheriff's Concern-Trainer's Challenge." *National Sheriff* 32 (December 1980–January 1981): 11–15, 25.

————. "Explosive Words and Phrases." *FBI Law Enforcement Bulletin* 39 (January 1970): 7–11.

————. "The Supervisor and Morale." *FBI Law Enforcement Bulletin* 39 (November 1970): 13–15, 30.

O'Conner, James A., and John W. Pfaff Jr. "Methods of Presenting Supervisory Training." *FBI Law Enforcement Bulletin* 40 (January 1971): 7–10, 26–27. Reprinted as "Training Methods for the Supervisor." *Supervisory Management* 16 (June 1971): 28–32.

SELECTIVE BIBLIOGRAPHY

Pinizzotto, Anthony J. "Deviant Social Groups." *Law & Order* (October 1996): 70–80.

———. "Forensic Psychology: Criminal Personality Profiling." *Journal of Police Science and Administration* 12 (1984): 32–40.

Pinizzotto, Anthony J., and Edward F. Davis. "Interviewing Methods: A Specialized Approach Is Needed When Investigating Police Deaths." *Law & Order* (November 1996): 68–72.

———. "Offenders' Perceptual Shorthand: What Messages Are Law Enforcement Officers Sending to Offenders?" *FBI Law Enforcement Bulletin* (June 1999): 1–4.

Pinizzotto, Anthony J., Edward F. Davis, and Charles E. Miller. "In the Line of Fire: Learning from Assaults on Law Enforcement Officers." *FBI Law Enforcement Bulletin* (February 1998): 15–23.

Pinizzotto, Anthony J., and George DeShazor. "Interviewing Erratic Subjects." *FBI Law Enforcement Bulletin* (November 1997): 1–5.

Pinizzotto, Anthony J., and M. J. Finkel. "Criminal Personality Profiling: An Outcome and Process Study." *Law and Human Behavior* 14 (1990): 215–33.

Reboussin, R. "Development of a Rule-Based Expert System for Profiling Murderers." Paper presented at the annual meeting of the Academy of Criminal Justice Sciences. St. Louis, Missouri, March 1987.

———. *An Evaluation of Domestic Violence Projects Funded by the Wisconsin Council on Criminal Justice*. Madison: Wisconsin Council on Criminal Justice, 1981.

———. "An Expert System for Profiling Murderers." In *Computers in Criminal Justice*, edited by F. Schmalleger. Bristol, Ind.: Wyndham Hall Press, 1990, pp. 237–44.

———. "Expert Systems and Their Future in Law Enforcement." Address to SEARCH Group, Inc., Conference on New Technologies in Criminal Justice. Denver, Colorado, August 1991.

———. "Expert Systems for Law Enforcement." Address to First International Conference on Community Policing. Sao Paolo, Brazil, December 1991.

———. "Expert Systems in Law Enforcement." Governor's Conference on Victim Services and Public Safety. Anaheim, California, May 1990.

Selective Bibliography

———. "The Potential Utility of Expert Systems to State Statistical Analysis Centers." Paper presented at the annual meeting of the Criminal Justice Statistics Association. San Francisco, California, September 1987.

———. *Sexual assault in Wisconsin, 1984.* Madison: Wisconsin Council on Criminal Justice, 1985.

———. "Using Expert Systems to Identify Violent Offenders." Paper presented at the annual meeting of the American Society of Criminology. Reno, Nevada, November 1989.

Reboussin, R., and J. Cameron. "Expert Systems for Law Enforcement." *FBI Law Enforcement Bulletin* (August 1989): 12–16.

Reboussin, R., R. Gilmour, and B. Tolstedt. "Non-verbal Concommitants of Machiavellianism." Paper presented at the annual conference of the Social Psychology Section, British Esychological Society. York, England, September 1975.

Reboussin, R., and J. Goldstein. "Achievement Motivation in Navaho and White Students." *American Anthropologist* 68 (1966): 740–45. Reprinted in *Native Americans Today*, edited by H. Bahr, B. Chadwick, and R. Day. New York: Harper and Row, 1972.

Reboussin, R., and C. J. Schwimer. "Grant Writing: A Mystery Solved" *FBI Law Enforcement Bulletin* (September 1997): 18–24.

Reboussin, R., and William L. Tafoya. "The Development of Artificial Intelligence Expert Systems in Law Enforcement." In *Computers in Criminal Justice*, edited by F. Schmalleger. Bristol, Ind.: Wyndham Hall Press, 1990, pp. 245–55.

Reboussin, R., J. Warren, and Roy Hazelwood. "Classifying Geographical Patterns of Serial Rape." Paper presented at the annual meeting of the Classification Society of North America. East Lansing, Michigan, June 1992.

———. "Geographic Distribution of Serial Rapes: A Taxonomy." Paper presented at the annual meeting of the Academy of Criminal Justice Sciences. Pittsburgh, Pennsylvania, March 1992.

———. "Mapless Mapping and the Windshield Wiper Effect in the Spatial Distribution of Serial Rapes." Paper presented at the second annual meeting of the Homicide Research Working Group, Quantico, Virginia. Published with the proceedings of that conference, *Questions and*

SELECTIVE BIBLIOGRAPHY

Answers in Lethal and Non-Lethal Violence: 1993. National Institute of Justice, 1994.

————. Mapless Mapping in Analyzing the Spatial Distribution of Serial Rapes." Paper presented at the Workshop on Crime Analysis through Computer Mapping. Chicago, Illinois. Published with the proceedings of that conference, *Workshop on Crime Analysis through Computer Mapping Proceedings: 1993*. Illinois Criminal Justice Information Authority, 1994. Reprinted in *Crime Analysis through Computer Mapping*, edited by C. R. Block, M. Dabdoub, and S. Fregley. Washington, D.C.: Police Executive Research Forum, 1995, pp. 69–74.

————. "Rapist Correlates of the Spatial Distribution of Serial Rapes." Paper presented at the annual meeting of the Academy of Criminal Justice Sciences. Boston, Massachusetts, March 1995.

————. "The Spatial Distribution of Serial Crimes." Paper presented at the annual meeting of the American Society of Criminology. San Francisco, California, November 1991. Revised and presented at the annual meeting of the American Society of Criminology. Phoenix, Arizona, October 1993; and at the annual meeting of the Academy of Criminal Justice Sciences. Las Vegas, Nevada, March 1996.

Reboussin, R., J. Warren, Roy Hazelwood, and J. Wright. "Prediction of Rapist Type and Violence in Serial Rape from Offender and Victim Statements." Paper presented at the annual meeting of the Academy of Criminal Justice Sciences. Denver, Colorado, March 1990.

————. "Prediction of Rapist Violence and Type from Offender and Victim Rape Accounts Using Verbal and Physical Behavioral Scales." Paper presented at the annual meeting of the American Society of Criminology. Reno, Nevada, November 1989.

Reboussin, R., J. Warren, and J. P. Jarvis. "Mapping Block-Level Census Data onto Maps of Rapist Hunting Patterns." Paper presented at the annual meeting of the American Society of Criminology. San Diego, California, November 1997.

Reese, James T. "Bureaucratic Burnout: A Challenge to Managers." *Management Quarterly* 3 (January 1982): 1–7.

————. "Family Therapy in Law Enforcement: A New Approach to an Old

Problem." *FBI Law Enforcement Bulletin* 51 (September 1982): 7–11. Reprinted in *Sheriff and Police Reporter* (October–December 1982): 4–8; and *Victoria Police Association Journal* 48 (November 1982): 55–61.

———. "Life in the High-Speed Lane: Managing Police Burnout." *Police Chief* 49 (June 1982): 49–53. Reprinted in *Managing Marginal Performance*, edited by Hillary M. Robinette. Quantico, Virginia: U.S. Federal Bureau of Investigation, 1983, pp. 21–24.

———. "Minority Stress: The Police Executive." *Police Chief* 50 (March 1983): 27–39.

———. "Motivations of Criminal Informants." *FBI Law Enforcement Bulletin* 49 (May 1980): 23–27. Reprinted in *Police Association* (Victoria, Australia) 47 (August 1980): 31–35.

———. "Obsessive Compulsive Behavior: The Nuisance Offender." *FBI Law Enforcement Bulletin* 48 (August 1979): 6–12. Reprinted in *Journal of the American Polygraph Association* 8 (September 1979): 258–70.

———. "A Prescription for Burn-Out." *FBI National Academy Associates Newsletter* (summer 1981).

Reese, James T., and D. K. Bright. "Stress Management: A Proactive Approach." *National Sheriff* 34 (June/July 1982): 6–10.

Ressler, Robert K., "Army Hostage Negotiations: An Insight into AR 190-52." *Detective* (summer 1979): 6–13.

———. "Hostage Marries Abductor." *Veritas* 22 (March/April 1980): 20–24, 36.

———, et al. "Offender Profiles: A Multidisciplinary Approach." *FBI Law Enforcement Bulletin* (September 1980).

———, et al. "Rape and Rape-Murder: One Offender and Twelve Victims." *American Journal of Psychiatry* 140, no. 1 (January 1983).

———. *Sexual Homicide: Patterns and Motives*. New York: Lexington Books, 1988.

Ressler, Robert K., and Ann W. Burgess. "Crime Scene and Profile Characteristics of Organized and Disorganized Murderers." *FBI Law Enforcement Bulletin* (August 1985): 18.

———. "The Split Reality of Murder." *FBI Law Enforcement Bulletin* (August 1985): 7.

SELECTIVE BIBLIOGRAPHY

————. "Violent Crime: The Men Who Murdered." *FBI Law Enforcement Bulletin* (August 1985): 2.

Ressler, Robert K., John E. Douglas, and Ann W. Burgess. "Sex-Related Murder and Crime Scene Investigation." Paper presented at International Society for Research on Aggression. Boston Regional Meeting, August 21, 1981.

Ressler, Robert K., John E. Douglas, R. B. D'Agostino, and Ann W. Burgess. "Serial Murder: A New Phenomenon of Homicide." Paper presented at the 10th triennial meeting of the International Association of Forensic Sciences. Oxford, England, September 18–25, 1984.

Ressler, Robert K., John E. Douglas, A. N. Groth, and Ann W. Burgess. "Offender Profiles: A Multidisciplinary Approach." *FBI Law Enforcement Bulletin* (September 1980): 16.

Ressler, Robert K., and T. Swachtman. *I Have Lived in the Monster: A Report from the Abyss*. New York: St. Martin's Press, 1997.

————. *Whoever Fights Monsters: My Twenty Years Hunting Serial Killers*. New York: St. Martin's Press, 1992. Revised and repinted as *Whoever Fights Monsters*. New York: St. Martin's Press, 1994.

Rider, Anthony O., "The Firesetter: A Psychological Profile (Part 1)," *FBI Law Enforcement Bulletin* 49 (June 1980): 7–13. Part 2 in *FBI Law Enforcement Bulletin* 49 (July 1980): 7–17. Part 3 in *FBI Law Enforcement Bulletin* 49 (August 1980): 5–11.

————. "A Projected Psychological Profile of the Professional Profile of the Professional Torch." *Arson Resource Exchange Bulletin* (January 1981): 20–21.

Royster, Terri. "Programs to Combat Juvenile Crime." September 1998. *LEO* (*Law Enforcement Online*) available by e-mailing the author, troyster@FBIAcademy.edu.

Schaefer, Robert B. "The Stress of Police Promotion." *FBI Law Enforcement Bulletin* 52 (May 1983): 2–6. Reprinted in *Arkansas Municipal Association Journal 1983–1984, Arkansas Municipal Police Association Annual* (1984): 259–60, 473.

Sheehan, Donald C. "Stress Management in the Federal Bureau of Investigation: Principles for Program Development." *International Journal of Emergency Mental Health* 1, no. 1 (April 1999): 39–42.

Selective Bibliography

Strentz, Thomas. "Inadequate Personality as a Hostage Taker." *Journal of Police Science and Administration* 11 (September 1983): 363–68.

———. "Preparing the Person with High Potential for Victimization as a Hostage." In *Violence in the Medical Core Setting*, edited by James T. Turner. Rockville, Md: Aspen Publications, 1984, pp. 183–209.

———. "Proxemics and the Interview." *Police Chief* 44 (September 1977): 74–76.

———. "The Sociopath: A Criminal Enigma." *Journal of Police Science and Administration* 6 (June 1978): 135–40. Reprinted in *Psychiatric Nursing in the Hospital and the Community*, by Ann Wolbert Burgess. 3d ed. Englewood Cliffs, N.J.: Prentice Hall, 1981, pp. 310–11.

———. "The Stockholm Syndrome: Law Enforcement Policy and Ego Defenses of the Hostage." *FBI Law Enforcement Bulletin* 48 (April 1979): 2–12. Reprinted as "Law Enforcement Policy and Ego Defenses of the Hostage." *Forensic Psychology and Psychiatry. Annals of the New York Academy of Sciences* 347 (June 1980): 137–50; and in *Victims of Terrorisms*, edited by Frank M. Ochberg and David A. Soskis. Boulder, Colo.: Westview Press, 1982, pp. 149–63.

———. "Terrorist Organization Profile." In *Behavioral and Quantitative Perspectives on Terrrorism*, edited by Yonah Alexander and John M. Gleason. New York: Pergamon Press, 1981, pp. 86–104.

———. "A Terrorist Psychological Profile: Past and Present." *FBI Law Enforcement Bulletin* (April 1988): 13.

———. "Transactional Analysis and the Police: Or 'Why Aren't You Out Catching Crooks?'" *Police Chief* 42 (October 1975): 248–50.

Tafoya, William L. "Corruption in the Criminal Justice System," *Agenda (IACP)* 1 (January 1975): 3–13.

———. "The Grand Jury." In *Principles and Procedures of the Justice System*, edited by Harry W. More. New York: John Wiley and Sons, 1975, pp. 273–95.

———. "The Grand Jury and the Watergate Case." *Administration of Justice Journal* 1 (fall 1973): 29–32.

———. "Lateral Entry: A Management Perspective." *Police Chief* 41 (April 1974): 60–62.

SELECTIVE BIBLIOGRAPHY

———. "Needs Assessment: Key to Organizational Change." *Journal of Police Science and Administration* 11 (September 1983): 303–10.

———. "Police Risk Reduction." *Agenda (IACP)* 1 (May 1975): 3–11.

———. "Project Intercept: The Los Angeles Experience." *Journal of Criminal Justice* 2 (spring 1974): 55–60.

———. "Project Intercept: Precursor to the Criminal Justice Team." *Journal of California Law Enforcement* 8 (January 1974): 147–52.

———. "Review of: Policing by Objectives." *California Peace Officer* 1 (March–April 1980): 39.

———. "Special Weapons and Tactics." *Police Chief* 42 (July 1975): 70–74.

———. "SWAT (Special Weapons and Tactics): Part I." *Police Weapons Center Bulletin (IACP)* 75 (February 1975): 4–5. Part 2 in *Police Weapons Center Bulletin (IACP)* 75 (March 1975): 4–5.

Tafoya, William L., and Peter C. Unsinger. "Overview of Police Services." *Introduction to the Administration of Justice*, edited by Robert E. Blanchard. New York: John Wiley & Sons, 1975, pp. 197–227.

Teten, Howard D. *Applied Criminology for Law Enforcement.* Washington, D.C.: United States Government Printing Office, 1975.

———. "Class and Delinquency: An Action Approach." *Georgia Journal of Corrections* 1 (April 1972): 44–53.

———. "Hypnosis: The Ultimate Lie Detector?" *International Security Review* (July 1980): 82–83, 85.

U.S. Senate Committee on the Judiciary. *Serial Murders: Hearing before the Subcommittee on Juvenile Justice.* 98th Cong., 1st sess., July 12, 1983.

Van Zandt, Clintor R. "The Real Silence of the Lambs: The National Center for the Analysis of Violent Crime (NCAVC)." *Police Chief* 61, no. 4 (April 1994): 45–46.

Vorpagel, Russell E. "Painting Psychological Profiles: Charlatanism, Coincidence, Charisma, Chance, or a New Science?" *Police Chief* 49 (January 1982): 156–59.

Warren, J., Roy Hazelwood, and R. Reboussin. "Serial Rape: The Offender and His Rape Career." In *A Research Manual.* Vol. 3 of *Rape and Sexual Assault*, edited by Ann W. Burgess. New York: Garland, 1991, pp. 275–311.

Selective Bibliography

Warren, J. I., R. Reboussin, Roy Hazelwood, A. J. Cummings, N. A. Gibbs, and S. Trumbetta. "Crime Scene and Distance Correlates of Serial Rape." *Journal of Quantitative Criminology* 14 (1998): 35–59.

Warren, J. I., R. Reboussin, Roy Hazelwood, N.A. Gibbs, S. L. Trumbetta, and A. Cummings. "Crime Scene Analysis and the Escalation of Violence in Serial Rape." *Forensic Science International* 100, no. 1–2 (1999): 37–56.

Warren, J. I. , R. Reboussin, Roy Hazelwood, and J. Wright. "Prediction of Rape Type and Violence from Verbal, Physical, and Sexual Scales." *Journal of Interpersonal Violence* 6 (1991): 55–67.

Westveer, Arthur E., Anthony J. Pinizzotto, and John H. Trestrial III. "Homicidal Poisoning in the United States: An Analysis of the Uniform Crime Reports from 1980 through 1989." *American Journal of Forensic Medicine and Pathology* (December 1996): 283–88.

Index

INDEX

Ault, Richard L., Jr., "Dick," 41,
120–22, 124, 129, 162, 328
criticisms of, 358
former Marine, 134, 349
one of "the nine," 139, 177–79
and other agents, 173, 246–47,
249–50, 340–41, 391
profiling, 117, 259–64
"Project Slammer," 376–77
publications, 360
research on violent offenders, 212,
236
retirement, 377, 385–86
as teacher, 123, 183, 342
unit chief, 350
USS *Iowa*, 289–96
Austin, George C., 34, 36
Austin-American Statesman, 299
Autoerotic Fatalities (Hazelwood,
Deitz, and Burgess), 177
autoerotic fatality, 266–68, 270
vs. murder, 296 n. 1
automated crime profiling, 271–76
"Automated Crime Profiling" (Icove),
274
Ayoob, Massad, 305

Baltimore, Maryland, killings, 229–
32
Baltimore Police Department, 389
Band, Stephen R., 381, 388
Barker, "Ma," 53
Barrow, Clyde, 53
Barry, Joe, 301

Bates, Alfred, 53
Baxter, Wynne E., 46
Beaver, Rufus R., 80
behavioral analysis of threatening
communication, 275, 276
Behavioral Science Instruction and
Research Unit, 226, 227
Behavioral Science Investigative
Support Unit, 357
and artificial intelligence, 272
formation of, 226, 227, 347
John Douglas, 184
relocation of offices, 392
See also Investigative Support
Unit
Behavioral Science Services Unit,
234, 347, 357
Bell Curve, The (Herrnstein and
Murray), 49, 77 n. 9
Berberich, John, 301
Berkowitz, David, "Son of Sam," 30,
32 n. 2, 36, 71–72, 183, 206–207
Bernstein, Lester, 292
Bianchi, Kenneth, "Hillside Stran-
gler," 206, 243–44
Big Manual of FBI, 90
biker gang killings, 132–33
Billik, Herman, 75
body types and criminals, 49
Boeing Aircraft, 280
Boltz, Francis, "Frank," 118, 119, 149
bomb explosions, 73
Bond, Thomas, 45–46
bondage, 267

INDEX

420

Index

INDEX

Index

INDEX

INDEX

INDEX

INDEX

profiling, 95–96, 165–66, 190, 208, 221

psycholinguistic analysis, 77 n. 15

Susan Jaeger disappearance, 102–106

as teacher, 83, 123, 124, 166, 183, 342

teamed with Mullaney, 160–61

threat assessment, 161

Threat Assessment Group, 360

"three legged stool," 123, 384–85, 396

Tie Man. *See* Schaefer, Robert B.

Tolson, Clyde Anderson, 81, 85, 107 n. 4

Toole, Ottis, 191

Tracey, Spencer, 142

traitors, 370–77

trauma counseling, 161

treason, 370–77

TRIAD program, 394

Trojanowicz, Robert, 353

Truitt, Kendall, 288, 289, 290, 291, 292

Tulley, Ed, 110

Turchie, Terry T., 282–83

Tyler, Tom, 285

Unabomber, 277–87

UNABOM Manifesto, 285

UNABOM Task Force, 277–87

undercover agents, 127–28, 157, 161, 381

Undercover Management Unit, 127

Undercover Safeguard Program, 381, 388

Uniform Crime Reporting section, 386, 389

United Airlines, 279, 282

United Nations, 148

University of California, Berkeley, and Unabomber, 279, 285

University of Houston Law Center, 184

University of Illinois and Unabomber, 279

University of Pennsylvania, 184, 357

University of Utah and Unabomber, 279

University of Virginia, 266, 360, 363

adjunct faculty, 183–84, 232, 253

FBI affiliation with, 97, 99, 168, 345, 356

Jefferson Award, 368

Unsuitable Job For A Woman, An (James), 296 n. 1

"Urban Police Problems" course, 99

USATREX International, 168

USS *Iowa*, 288–96, 358

USS *Wasp*, 311

U.S. Task Force on Violent Crime, 222

UTF. *See* UNABOM Task Force

Vampire Killer, 23–26, 217

Vanderbilt University and Unabomber, 279

VanMaanen, Martin, 306

436

INDEX